FOR DUMMIES™
BESTSELLING BOOK SERIES

P9-DCI-072

Cheat Sheet

Where to Get Information about Franchise Opportunities

Directories are the best places to begin your search because they provide the most information on the opportunities available in a capsule format.

✔ **The Franchise Opportunities Guide:** Published semiannually by the International Franchise Association. $15. www.franchise.org or 800-543-1038 or 202-628-8000.

✔ **The Executives Guide to Franchise Opportunities, Food Service Guide to Franchise Opportunities** and **The Guide to Multiple-Unit Franchise Opportunities:** Published by *Franchise Update* magazine. www.Franchise-Update.com or 408-997-7796.

✔ **Bond's Franchise Guide:** Published annually by Robert Bond. $29.95. www.worldfranchising.com or 800-841-0873.

✔ **The Franchise Annual:** Published annually by Info Press. $39.95. www.infonews.com/franchise or 716-754-4669.

✔ **The Franchise Handbook:** Published quarterly by *Enterprise* magazine. $22.95. www.franchise1.com or 414-272-9977.

✔ **International Herald Tribune International Franchise Guide:** Published annually by Source Book Publications. $34.95. www.franchiseintl.com or 510-839-5471.

Several magazines and newspapers regularly publish franchising-related sections that contain articles and advertisements on franchising.

✔ *Franchise Update* **magazine:** A must-read by the professionals in franchising. Contains well-written articles about business issues and franchise management. www.franchise-update.com or 408-997-7796.

✔ *Franchise World* **magazine:** The official publication of the International Franchise Association covers the latest developments in the franchising industry. www.franchise.org or 202-628-8000.

✔ *Entrepreneur* **magazine:** Targeted to small businesses is the Entrepreneur 500 edition, published in January, which ranks franchise companies on a variety of criteria. www.entrepreneurmag.com or 800-274-6229.

✔ *Franchise Times* **magazine:** This publication focuses on the franchise industry and has well-written articles on trends in franchising. www.franchisetimes.com or 651-631-4995.

Trade shows and expositions give you the opportunity to meet franchisors face to face. The International Franchise Exposition is the largest show in the world of franchisors seeking new franchisees. Contact the International Franchise Association, the sponsor, at www.franchise.org or 202-628-8000, or contact MFV Expositions, the producer, at www.betheboss.com or 201-226-1130.

Franchising For Dummies®

Cheat Sheet

What to Do Before You Decide to Become a Franchisee

✔ Decide whether to start your own independent business or to become a franchisee — there's a big difference.

✔ Do your own research; do not use a franchise broker.

✔ Learn as much as you can about the opportunities available.

✔ Select the right industry or industries for you.

✔ Investigate the opportunities in each industry you select.

Dave's Ten Nuggets of Experience Gained in the Franchise Business

1. Be truthful about everything.

2. Create a mission statement for your company and make sure that all your employees know it and practice it.

3. Remember that *profit* is not a dirty word.

4. Take care of your business, and your business will take care of you.

5. Stay focused on the important things.

6. Surround yourself with the best possible people. Learn to delegate, and don't give responsibility without also giving authority.

7. Don't be afraid to prune out the dead wood in your business.

8. Have convictions and stand by them.

9. Treat your people with respect; you can't get it unless you give it.

10. Give something back.

Hungry Minds™

For Dummies: Bestselling Book Series for Beginners

Praise for Franchising For Dummies

"I have had the privilege of working with Michael Seid for many years in support of franchising at the International Franchise Association. Dave Thomas and Michael Seid have penned a must read for anyone interested in the fundamentals of franchising. Franchisees and franchisors alike owe a debt of gratitude to Michael and Dave for this fine work."

> — James H. Amos, Jr., President and CEO,
> Mail Boxes, Etc.

"*Franchising For Dummies* offers invaluable information for prospective franchisees in their search for the best franchise opportunity that suits them. Franchisees will benefit from the guidance Michael and Dave provide in operating their business and working with their franchisor and other franchisees."

> — Regina Gardner, Franchisee, UNIGLOBE Travel

"Dave and Michael have written the ultimate franchise primer. Don't go into franchising without it!"

> — Lawrence "Doc" Cohen, Franchisee,
> Great American Cookie Company

"If you want to understand the world of franchising, *Franchising For Dummies* is a must read!"

> — Richard Rennick, CEO, American Leak Detection

"Dave Thomas and Michael Seid really separate the wheat from the chaff in their entertaining and educational tome on franchising. I only wish that I had this book 18 years ago when I embarked upon a franchising career at Moto Photo. We could have avoided the dozens (maybe hundreds or even thousands) of mistakes we made in our formative years. This book is a roadmap for success for both the franchisee and the franchisor."

> — Michael Adler, Chairman & CEO, Moto Photo

"It's all right here in *Franchising For Dummies*. If there are things that Dave Thomas and Michael Seid don't know about franchising, they aren't worth printing. Two great entrepreneurial minds have created one fantastic book."

> — Don DeBolt, President,
> International Franchise Association

TM

References for the Rest of Us!®

BESTSELLING BOOK SERIES

Do you find that traditional reference books are overloaded with technical details and advice you'll never use? Do you postpone important life decisions because you just don't want to deal with them? Then our *For Dummies*® business and general reference book series is for you.

For Dummies business and general reference books are written for those frustrated and hard-working souls who know they aren't dumb, but find that the myriad of personal and business issues and the accompanying horror stories make them feel helpless. *For Dummies* books use a lighthearted approach, a down-to-earth style, and even cartoons and humorous icons to dispel fears and build confidence. Lighthearted but not lightweight, these books are perfect survival guides to solve your everyday personal and business problems.

> *"More than a publishing phenomenon, 'Dummies' is a sign of the times."*
>
> — *The New York Times*

> *"A world of detailed and authoritative information is packed into them..."*
>
> — *U.S. News and World Report*

> *"...you won't go wrong buying them."*
>
> — *Walter Mossberg, Wall Street Journal, on For Dummies books*

Already, millions of satisfied readers agree. They have made For Dummies the #1 introductory level computer book series and a best-selling business book series. They have written asking for more. So, if you're looking for the best and easiest way to learn about business and other general reference topics, look to *For Dummies* to give you a helping hand.

Hungry Minds™

1/01

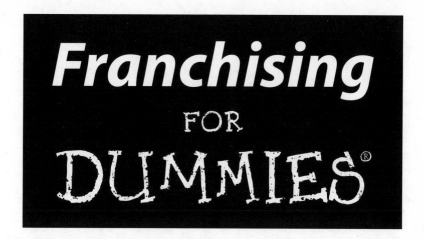

Franchising
FOR
DUMMIES®

by Dave Thomas
and Michael Seid

Hungry Minds™

Best-Selling Books • Digital Downloads • e-Books • Answer Networks • e-Newsletters • Branded Web Sites • e-Learning

New York, NY ◆ Cleveland, OH ◆ Indianapolis, IN

Franchising For Dummies®

Published by
Hungry Minds, Inc.
909 Third Avenue
New York, NY 10022
www.hungryminds.com
www.dummies.com

Library of Congress Catalog Card No.: 99-66332

ISBN: 0-7645-5160-4

Printed in the United States of America

10 9 8 7 6 5 4 3

1O/SR/QV/QS/IN

Distributed in the United States by Hungry Minds, Inc.

Distributed by CDG Books Canada Inc. for Canada; by Transworld Publishers Limited in the United Kingdom; by IDG Norge Books for Norway; by IDG Sweden Books for Sweden; by IDG Books Australia Publishing Corporation Pty. Ltd. for Australia and New Zealand; by TransQuest Publishers Pte Ltd. for Singapore, Malaysia, Thailand, Indonesia, and Hong Kong; by Gotop Information Inc. for Taiwan; by ICG Muse, Inc. for Japan; by Intersoft for South Africa; by Eyrolles for France; by International Thomson Publishing for Germany, Austria and Switzerland; by Distribuidora Cuspide for Argentina; by LR International for Brazil; by Galileo Libros for Chile; by Ediciones ZETA S.C.R. Ltda. for Peru; by WS Computer Publishing Corporation, Inc., for the Philippines; by Contemporanea de Ediciones for Venezuela; by Express Computer Distributors for the Caribbean and West Indies; by Micronesia Media Distributor, Inc. for Micronesia; by Chips Computadoras S.A. de C.V. for Mexico; by Editorial Norma de Panama S.A. for Panama; by American Bookshops for Finland.

For general information on Hungry Minds' products and services please contact our Customer Care Department within the U.S. at 800-762-2974, outside the U.S. at 317-572-3993 or fax 317-572-4002.

For sales inquiries and reseller information, including discounts, premium and bulk quantity sales, and foreign-language translations, please contact our Customer Care Department at 800-434-3422, fax 317-572-4002, or write to Hungry Minds, Inc., Attn: Customer Care Department, 10475 Crosspoint Boulevard, Indianapolis, IN 46256.

For information on licensing foreign or domestic rights, please contact our Sub-Rights Customer Care Department at 212-884-5000.

For information on using Hungry Minds' products and services in the classroom or for ordering examination copies, please contact our Educational Sales Department at 800-434-2086 or fax 317-572-4005.

Please contact our Public Relations Department at 212-884-5163 for press review copies or 212-884-5000 for author interviews and other publicity information or fax 212-884-5400.

For authorization to photocopy items for corporate, personal, or educational use, please contact Copyright Clearance Center, 222 Rosewood Drive, Danvers, MA 01923, or fax 978-750-4470.

Hungry Minds™ is a trademark of Hungry Minds, Inc.

About the Authors

Dave Thomas, Founder and Senior Chairman, Wendy's International

Dave Thomas (Fort Lauderdale, FL) began his lifelong career in the restaurant industry at the age of 12, working the counter at the Regas Restaurant in Knoxville, TN. There, he fell in love with the restaurant business and learned that you could be anything you want to be if you worked hard and had a burning desire to succeed.

Dave was a franchisee of KFC until 1968 when at the age of 35 the restaurants were sold back to KFC and Dave became a millionaire. In 1969, Dave opened the first Wendy's Old Fashioned Hamburgers restaurant in downtown Columbus, Ohio. By 1973, Dave began franchising Wendy's, and today, there are more than 5,600 Wendy's restaurants around the globe. In 1995 Wendy's merged with Tim Hortons, the second largest quick service restaurant chain in Canada. Tim Hortons features coffee and fresh baked goods and today has over 1,800 locations.

In 1989, Dave agreed to appear in a few Wendy's commercials. Ten years and more than 700 commercials later, Dave admits he never says his lines correctly in one take and practice doesn't necessarily make perfect. He is one of the nation's most recognizable television spokesmen. If dropping out of high school was Dave's biggest mistake, it led to one of his greatest accomplishments. In 1993, 45 years after leaving school, Dave earned his GED certificate and received his high school diploma from Coconut Creek High School in Ft. Lauderdale. He was voted Most Likely to Succeed by the graduating class, and attended the prom with his wife Lorraine, where they were named Prom King and Queen.

Dave believes in giving back to the community. He is a long-time supporter of a variety of children's charities, but the cause closest to his heart is adoption. As an adopted child, Dave knows the importance of a permanent home and family. Dave has been invited to speak before Congress and has participated in several adoption celebrations at the White House. In 1992, Dave established the Dave Thomas Foundation for Adoption, donating speakers' fees and profits from sales of his books to adoption causes. He's accomplished a great deal, but he considers his family — Lorraine (his wife of 45 years), five children and 15 grandchildren — his greatest accomplishment. For more information about Dave Thomas and Wendy's, visit the Web site at www.wendys.com.

Michael H. Seid, Managing Director, Michael H. Seid & Associates

Michael Seid (West Hartford, CT) is founder and Managing Director of Michael H. Seid & Associates (MSA) a consulting firm specializing in franchising and other methods of distribution. At the age of six, Michael began to work in his family's business, Ruth and Daves in Brooklyn, NY, and traces his success as a businessperson to the lessons taught to him by his parents. It is from working with his family that he learned the lifelong meaning of quality, consistency, entrepreneurship, ethics, fair play and respect for the customer.

During his over twenty years in franchising, Michael has been a Senior Operations and Financial Executive or Consultant for companies within the franchise, retail, restaurant and service industries. He has also been a franchisee. Michael is the Past Chairman of the International Franchise Association's Council of Franchise Suppliers and is a former member of IFA's Board of Directors and Executive Committee. Michael is a CFE (Certified Franchise Executive) and a very non-practicing CPA.

At MSA, Michael consults with companies on the appropriateness of franchising and in the development of new franchise systems. MSA assists established franchisors and other companies in the development of strategies for domestic and international expansion, marketing and e-commerce programs, franchise relationships, litigation support, operating manuals, training programs, and strategic internal reengineering. MSA's clients range from large multinational Fortune 10 companies to two guys working out of their garage.

Michael is a noted author of numerous articles on franchising, an often-quoted expert in the field and is a frequent lecturer on the subject of franchising. Michael is married to his wife of 25 years, Susan, and has two children, Rachel and Andrew. For more information on the services offered by MSA, including speaking or consulting services, call 860-523-8309. Michael's email address is michaelhseid@msn.com and MSA's Web site is at http://michaelhseid.com.

Dedication

From Dave:

This book is dedicated to my family — the most important thing in my life. I consider my family my greatest success and I'm proud to be their husband, father, and grandfather.

This book is also dedicated to those franchisors whose innovations, hard work, and integrity have created unique opportunities for others to achieve their dream of being successful business owners. And to the thousands of franchisees whose ambitions, commitment and passion to succeed make the business world so exciting. I salute their efforts and wish them continued success.

Editor's Note: Dave Thomas will donate all of his proceeds from the sale of this book to the Dave Thomas Foundation for Adoption, which generates awareness for the thousands of children waiting for a permanent home and loving family of their own.

From Michael:

This book is dedicated to my parents — Ruth and David Seid. It is from them that I began my business education at the age of six and from where I learned the lessons of hard work, integrity and compassion. Their wisdom has been part of every aspect of my life and I am forever in their debt for their continued guidance, support, and love.

This book is also dedicated to my wife Susan and our children Rachel and Andrew. They are the greatest joy in my life. Watching Rachel and Andrew exceed every expectation we as parents have had for them since birth and maturing into responsible and committed young adults has been an immeasurable source of pride.

Finally to the franchisor and franchisees that drive this innovative engine of small business growth and from whom I have learned my craft. Franchising has grown and prospered because of your efforts and I wish you continued prosperity.

Authors' Acknowledgments

From Dave:

This book wouldn't exist if it weren't for the assistance, enthusiasm and persistence of many people on the Wendy's and Hungry Minds teams.

First, special thanks to Michael Seid, writer and consultant extraordinaire. Michael played a key role in making this book a reality. He took my words and thoughts and together with his own, created a wonderful resource for those interested in franchising.

I want to also acknowledge Denny Lynch, Wendy's VP of Communications and our internal editor. He read every word in this book twice, three times, four times — I'm sure he lost count. A 20-year veteran at Wendy's, he's helped to edit every one of my books. Thanks, Doctor!

Thanks, too, to Steve Wirt and Mark Inzetta, two important players on the Wendy's team, and our friends at Vorys, Sater, Seymour & Pease, who helped us mind our "P's and Q's" regarding franchise law.

I don't want to leave out a very important group of people: Wendy's and Tim Hortons franchisees, both current and those who started with us decades ago. I learned a lot from our early business partners. They show me how the franchise concept I developed really could work. Their commitment to Wendy's and their support, along with that of our current franchisees, means a great deal to me.

I think Wendy's and Tim Hortons franchisees are the best in the restaurant industry and I know we wouldn't be as successful if it wasn't for their hard work and dedication to franchising.

From Michael:

I realized as we wrote this book why Dave is an immensely important person in the field of franchising and, even more so, as a human being. I am forever in his debt for teaching me, after more than 20 years in franchising, why great franchise systems operate the way they do and how to be a better franchise executive. I am also forever in his debt for sharing his personal beliefs on what is important — the immense satisfaction of caring about other people. He is truly a great gentleman and someone to emulate. I am privileged to have had the opportunity of collaborating with him on *Franchising For Dummies* and, more so, to be able to call him a mentor and a friend.

There are some other folks who were instrumental to *Franchising For Dummies.* Certainly, my family for putting up with the long hours, the interruptions in our lives, and the lack of attention I gave them as we crunched through the book. I am inspired by my talented partner Kay Marie Ainsley. Her wisdom on the totality of the subject of franchising, especially when it came to marketing, strategy, and international expansion, were critical. To Joyce Mazero (Jenkens & Gilchrist), Rupert Barkoff (Kilpatrick & Cody), Arthur Cantor (Wiley, Rein & Fielding), and Phil Zeidman (Piper Marbury Rudnick & Wolfe), the experts on the law who reviewed parts of the manuscript, made suggestions for changes, focused us on the important issues, and provided balance in the legal debate between franchisors and franchisees, I want to offer my particular thanks. You are truly some of the finest legal minds in franchising today and I am grateful for your support and your assistance. I would not be a good consultant if I did not thank my clients for putting up with me during the process. Their encouragement, their adjusting their schedules at the last minute to accommodate my schedule, and — most important for any consultant — their always paying their bills on time, made the job easier. Finally, to our editors at Hungry Minds and especially Pam Sourelis. *Franchising For Dummies* would not have been possible without Pam's patience, her clarity of language, and her understanding of what you, the reader, need to know. If you enjoy reading *Franchising For Dummies,* Pam is responsible for that.

As you begin exploring franchising, it's important to remember that — when done right — there's simply no better way to spend your life in business than being a franchisee in a great system or being a franchisor who has a system full of great franchisees.

Publisher's Acknowledgments

We're proud of this book; please send us your comments through our Online Registration Form located at www.dummies.com.

Some of the people who helped bring this book to market include the following:

Acquisitions, Editorial, and Media Development

Project Editor: Jeanne Criswell

Acquisitions Editor: Mark Butler

Copy Editors: Susan Diane Smith, Donna Frederick, Tina Sims

Acquisitions Coordinator: Lisa Roule

Permissions Editor: Carmen Krikorian

Editorial Manager: Pam Mourouzis

Media Development Manager: Heather Heath Dismore

Editorial Assistant: Carol Strickland

Production

Project Coordinator: Kristy Nash

Layout and Graphics: Amy Adrian, Natalie Hollifield, Tracy K. Oliver, Jill Piscitelli, Jacque Schneider, Janet Seib, Kendra Span, Brian Torwelle

Proofreaders: John Greenough, Susan Moritz, Marianne Santy, Jeannie Smith

Indexer: Mary Mortensen

Special Help: Amanda Foxworth

Hungry Minds Consumer Reference Group

Business: Kathleen A. Welton, Vice President and Publisher; Kevin Thornton, Acquisitions Manager

Cooking/Gardening: Jennifer Feldman, Associate Vice President and Publisher

Education/Reference: Diane Graves Steele, Vice President and Publisher

Lifestyles/Pets: Kathleen Nebenhaus, Vice President and Publisher; Tracy Boggier, Managing Editor

Travel: Michael Spring, Vice President and Publisher; Suzanne Jannetta, Editorial Director; Brice Gosnell, Publishing Director

Hungry Minds Consumer Editorial Services: Kathleen Nebenhaus, Vice President and Publisher; Kristin A. Cocks, Editorial Director; Cindy Kitchel, Editorial Director

Hungry Minds Consumer Production: Debbie Stailey, Production Director

Contents at a Glance

Cartoons at a Glance

By Rich Tennant

page 7

page 101

page 147

page 331

page 211

page 273

Fax: 978-546-7747
E-mail: richtennant@the5thwave.com
World Wide Web: www.the5thwave.com

Table of Contents

Introduction

●●

*Y*ou may be reading this book for any of a number of reasons:

- You work for someone else and have dreamed about getting into business for yourself, being your own boss, and charting your own destiny.

- You are nearing retirement because 30 years have passed since you met your first boss or because you've been downsized, rightsized, or outsourced.

- You're looking over the fence and seeing that the grass is greener on the other side — the grass grown by the folks who own their own businesses.

- You're the head of a sophisticated investor group or management company and you want to improve the return on investment that the "bricks and mortar" opportunities in your portfolio have been achieving for your investors.

- You have a terrific product or service business that's burning up your local market, and everyone — starting with your mother, your Great-Aunt Rose, and your Uncle Harry — thinks that now is a perfect time for you to spread your wings and start a new national franchise program.

- You're already a franchisor, maybe even experienced in a few countries, and you want to challenge some of the assumptions under which you've been operating. Maybe you want to look at new or fresh techniques and score yourself against the best practices in franchising. Maybe you're having difficulty with your franchisees and you want to understand what they're thinking so that you can improve your relationships and your system's performance. That information may be all you need to take your business to the next level — whatever that level may be.

Whatever your reason for reading this book, we hope that *Franchising For Dummies* meets your needs.

Franchising For Dummies is perfect for both novices and experts. Prospective franchisees can find out what to look for in a great franchisor; existing franchisees can take a peek at what great franchisors are providing their franchisees. Business owners can find out how to determine whether franchising is the right growth strategy for their company, and experienced franchisors can pick up new tricks on how to improve their franchise systems.

About This Book

Your authors have been fortunate to work in franchising. Dave started out as one of the early franchisees of Kentucky Fried Chicken. Later, he founded and built Wendy's into one of the giants in franchising and became a leader in the operation of quick service restaurants. Michael was a franchisee and a franchisor before he became a consultant. He founded and is the managing director of one of the leading management consulting firms specializing in franchising. We wrote *Franchising For Dummies* because we wanted to return to franchising just a few of the blessings that franchising has bestowed upon us.

Many people think that they understand something about franchising because they shop in franchised locations nearly every day. But over the years, myths have developed about franchising, its rate of success, and its ease of entry, as well as about how franchise systems should be managed and grown.

When we started writing *Franchising For Dummies,* our goal was to help prospective franchisees make the right decision on whether to become franchisees. We wanted to give useful information and advice in a non-threatening, maybe even fun, easy-to-use format. As we progressed, we expanded our goals and decided also to provide information to help businesspeople determine whether franchising is a good expansion strategy for their companies, and if it is, how to design, develop, and manage their new franchise systems. In addition, we also tailored the book to help experienced franchisors improve their current operations.

How to Use This Book

You can use this book in three ways:

- ✔ If you want to find out about a specific area in franchising, such as how to get information about a particular franchisor or how to recruit, hire, and fire staff, you can go directly to those sections and get the information you need quickly.

- ✔ If you want a crash course on franchising, read the book from cover to cover. Franchising isn't as simple as it appears on the surface; reading the whole book will give you a good starting point in your understanding, and we hope will enable you to make the right choices — for you.

- ✔ If you're experienced in franchising, this book may challenge some of your assumptions, make you angry, provide you with some new insight, or enable you to rest easy at night knowing that someone agrees with what you're doing.

Franchising For Dummies is like a road map. In a simple, straightforward, and hopefully entertaining way, we have tried to provide you with guideposts, options, and our opinions. We hope that *Franchising For Dummies* gives you a jumping-off point as you make your franchise decisions.

A Stateside Viewpoint

Much about *Franchising For Dummies* is written from the viewpoint of franchising as practiced in the United States. Although franchising began in early China, was a method of government control throughout the Middle Ages, and can even be credited with the exploration of the New World, modern business format franchising is primarily a product of U.S. engineering. Although it has grown substantially from its first uses commercially in England and in the United States — and has prospered through the advances made by non-U.S. franchisors and franchisees — the bulk of world experience still rests with the success and failures of franchising in the United States.

Whether you are located in the United States or anywhere else in the world where franchising has taken root, we think that the basics of what makes franchising such a success are universal.

How This Book Is Organized

Franchising For Dummies is organized into six parts, each covering a major aspect of franchising. The chapters in each part cover specific information in detail. You can read each chapter independently, which is useful if you have other things to do today. In each chapter, we note other areas of the book that explore in greater detail some of the information you see.

You can also sit back and read this book from cover to cover. We hope that you do, because it's designed to give you information in a logical progression. Here's a summary of what you can find in each part.

Part I: Just the Facts: Franchising Basics

Part I gives you an overview of franchising and insight into the relationship between franchisors and franchisees. It tells you about the types of opportunities available within franchising and can help you determine whether you are cut out to be a franchisee. It also provides you with sources of information about franchise opportunities and a process for making your franchise decision.

Finding the money to become a franchisee is also important, so we help you determine how much you can afford to invest and where you can get the money. For prospective franchisees, this section is important because it helps you decide whether to become a franchisee and how to choose which franchise may be right for you.

Part II: The Start-Up: Establishing Your Franchise

Before you sign on the dotted line, you'd better understand what you're signing! Part II explains the Uniform Franchise Offering Circular, the disclosure document provided to franchisees in the United States. It also talks about how to evaluate a franchise agreement, what you can negotiate with a franchisor, and how to find pros who can help you through the process. Although franchising is a method of business expansion, a significant body of law also surrounds it. Part II helps you navigate the legal process of investing in a franchise, so even if you're not one of the pros, you can look like you are.

Part III: A Well-Oiled Machine: Operating Your Franchise

Every franchise system has a different personality. By that, we mean that they offer different services to their franchisees and provide them with different types and levels of support. Even the way that you, the franchisor, and the other franchisees work together will differ. Part III walks you through some of the most important elements of the franchise relationship and the types of support you are likely to receive. These include training and other support services; assistance in finding and developing your location; how and where you get your inventory and supplies; marketing to your customers; merchandising your location; and hiring, firing, and training your employees. Part III also gives you a glimpse of how you can interact with your franchisor and fellow franchisees. This part begins your process of understanding the difference between a great franchisor and those that might not be ready for prime time.

Part IV: Times Change: Deciding What to Do Next

Part IV talks about the life cycle. The first three parts of the book give you information on selecting the right franchise. Now it's time to talk about your growth options: investing in additional opportunities with the same franchise system and even investing in opportunities that other franchisors may have available. Many franchisees find that owning one franchise just isn't enough. Part IV explains the opportunities and some of the pitfalls of multi-unit ownership. Part IV also addresses a reality of business: At some point, the relationship is likely to end. We discuss how to prepare for this end and what to do when it happens.

Part V: But I Want to Be a Franchisor!

Ever wonder where big franchisors come from? They come from companies that have chosen to expand by offering franchises to other people. Part V examines what it takes to become a franchisor; whether your business has what it takes; how to develop a franchise system; how to set fees; and, most important, what *not* to do. This part also looks at how franchisors expand, both domestically and internationally; what it takes to support a growing franchise system; and some of the mistakes you can avoid.

Part VI: The Part of Tens

In a few short chapters, we give you insight into what Dave has learned in franchising, what we consider to be the ten keys to franchise success, and ten questions to ask before you buy a franchise.

Icons Used in This Book

To help you along as you read *Franchising For Dummies,* we include useful icons to alert you to important matters.

These items, though not essential to your basic understanding of the subject, help you become an advanced student. After you become familiar with the basics, it makes sense to glance at the technical stuff to get your advanced degree.

The Tip icon flags important information about the topic being discussed.

This icon is a friendly reminder of information discussed elsewhere in the book or of facts that we think you'll want to remember.

Watch out! This icon alerts you to common mistakes that people make in franchising, and dangers to avoid.

If you skip the Dave Says sections, you'll miss out on the opportunity to learn from the master. This information gives you insight into what makes Dave one of the leading franchisors in the world today and why Wendy's is regarded as the franchise system to emulate.

The information following the Michael Says icon emphasizes and further explains issues that are particularly near and dear to Michael's heart.

Where to Go from Here

You've embarked on a journey. Neither of us can be with you in person as you make this journey, but we try to be your trusted guides throughout this book.

To make the journey, you have to read this book. If you're new to franchising, start at the beginning and read it all the way through to the end. Flag those sections that you think are the most important to you, or that you may not have understood fully. Then go back and read them again; with a broader knowledge of franchising, they may start to make better sense to you. If you're experienced in franchising, skim the book and focus on the subjects that interest you most or on which you need additional guidance. Either way, *Franchising For Dummies* contains a wealth of information and practical advice. Simply turn the pages and begin.

Part I
Just the Facts: Franchising Basics

The 5th Wave   By Rich Tennant

"Ahhh, Mr. Dorfman. Already I can tell you're just the sort of person we're looking for to own a McFee Detective Agency franchise."

In this part . . .

Are you ready to become a franchisee? Before you make that decision, you need to understand a bit about what franchising is all about. In this part, we give you an overview of franchising and the types of opportunities that are available. We also explain how to select a franchise that's right for you and where to find the money.

Before you invest in any franchise, you are asked to sign a franchise agreement. In this part, we also discuss the disclosure document that you receive from the franchisor, give you some guidance on what's in it, and tell you how to evaluate a franchise agreement. We also give you some tips on negotiating with your franchisor.

Chapter 1

Understanding How Franchising Works

In This Chapter

▶ What is a franchise?

▶ What are the roles of the franchisor and the franchisee?

▶ What are franchise wannabes, and why should you avoid them?

▶ Does the franchise agreement grant ownership and a guarantee of profitability?

*F*ranchising has a long history stretching back to ancient China, but we won't bore you with it (even though some of it is pretty interesting). Instead, we're going to jump right into the thick of things so that you can talk the talk of franchising with the best of them.

What Is a Franchise?

Franchising is a system for expanding a business and distributing goods and services — and an opportunity to operate a business under a recognized brand name. For example, Wendy's doesn't franchise hamburgers, and Midas doesn't franchise car mufflers; they franchise business systems that deliver hamburgers and mufflers to customers with consistency — of the products, the services, and the customer experience.

A franchise occurs when a business (the *franchisor*) licenses its trade name (the *brand,* such as Wendy's or Midas) and its operating methods (its system of doing business) to a person or group (the *franchisee*) who agrees to operate according to the terms of a contract (the *franchise agreement*). The franchisor provides the franchisee with support and, in some cases, exercises some control over the way the franchisee operates under the brand.

In exchange, the franchisee usually pays the franchisor an initial fee (called a *franchise fee*) and a continuing fee (known as a *royalty*) for the use of the trade name and operating methods.

Method of distribution or industry?

We use the term *industry* when we discuss franchising. Purists may remind us that franchising is really a method of distribution used by a variety of industries. They're right. But continually describing franchising as a method of distribution is cumbersome, and so we beg forgiveness for this slight literary allowance.

Internationally, franchising has become one of the United States' major exports. In emerging economies, franchising acts as a stabilizing force, creating jobs, satisfying consumer demand, and fueling development of resources, such as agriculture, manufacturing, and education. More important, franchising creates opportunities for business ownership and personal wealth — both part of the foundation for the growth of democracies.

Consumers everywhere love the consistency that comes from shopping in a franchised business. From the cleanliness of the rooms at a Hilton Hotel to the one-hour film development available at Moto Photo, people know what they will get when they purchase under a franchisor's brand. The number of industries bringing goods and services to customers through franchising is growing, limited only by the imagination of the businesspeople who are beginning to understand the potential of this ancient method of distribution.

For years, the International Franchise Association (IFA) kept statistics on the growth and success of franchising. However, many of the studies that the statistics were based on, including those claiming that franchisees have a success rate of 95 percent while nonfranchised startups have a failure rate of 85 percent in their first five years in business, turned out to be inaccurate, or at least misleading. IFA no longer publishes those statistics.

So what is the truth? Overall, in three studies conducted by the IFA from 1993 to 1996, the median turnover rate (the change in ownership [transfer] or closure) was

- ✔ Between 8 percent and 11 percent including transfers to new owners
- ✔ Between 4 percent and 6 percent without transfers to new owners

In the most recent study that examined the turnover rates from 1995 to 1996, the results were a median turnover rate of

- ✔ 10.8 percent with transfers to new owners
- ✔ 6.3 percent without transfers to new owners

The studies also show that turnover rates vary widely among industry categories, with a low of 6 percent and a high of 14 percent. Franchisors with one year or less in business have the highest turnover rate.

But even a simple turnover study can measure only which locations have survived. It can't measure whether the franchisees were satisfied with their decision to become franchisees or were making any money.

In September and October 1997, the Gallup Organization conducted a market research study for the IFA's Education Foundation that examined franchise owners' attitudes and opinions toward their franchise experience. Gallup interviewed 1,001 franchise owners across the continental United States, 78 percent of whom owned just one unit. (According to Gallup, at the 95-percent level of confidence, the maximum expected error range for a sample of 1,001 respondents is + or − 3.1 percent.) The major findings of that study showed the following:

✔ More than nine of ten franchise owners said that they considered their franchise to be somewhat or very successful.

✔ Nine of ten respondents' expectations were exceeded (18 percent), mostly met (48 percent), or somewhat met (24 percent).

The high ratings, however, did not come without hard work. Nearly six of ten said that they had worked more hours as the owner of the franchise than they had in other businesses they'd owned or operated or on other jobs they'd held.

Making money also seemed to have an effect on their satisfaction. On average, respondents reported their *annual gross income* (the amount of money remaining after expenses are paid but before paying taxes) as franchise owners was $91,630.

The most telling information from the study is that two of three respondents felt that they would not have been as successful if they had tried to open the same business on their own. Nearly two-thirds said that they would buy or invest in the same franchise again if they had the opportunity.

Although industry studies and statistics are somewhat useful, the only statistic that is truly useful in examining a franchise opportunity is how well the franchisees in that system are doing. It's sort of like the looking at the stock market. Do you really care whether the market went up if your stock lost six points?

Two Types of Franchises

Two types of franchises exist: *product distribution franchises* and *business format franchises.*

Because most franchisees buy a business format franchise, this is the type of franchise we focus on in this book — but we think you should know something about the other type as well.

Product distribution franchises

Coca-Cola, Goodyear Tires, Ford Motor Company, and John Deere distributors are all product distribution franchises. In a product distribution franchise, the franchisee typically sells products that are manufactured by their franchisor. The industries where you most often find product distribution franchising are soft drinks, automobiles and trucks, mobile homes, automobile accessories, and gasoline. The products sold by a product distribution franchisee usually require some preparation by the franchisee before they are sold — such as you find with Coca-Cola — or some additional servicing after the sale, such as you find at a Ford dealer. But the major difference in product distribution franchising is that the franchisor licenses its trademark and logo to its franchisees but typically does not provide them with an entire system for running their business. Providing a business system is the hallmark of business format franchising. Although product distribution franchises represent the largest percentage of total retail sales coming from all franchises, most franchises available today are business format opportunities.

Product distribution franchises look a lot like what are called *supplier-dealer relationships* — and they are. The difference is in the degree of the relationship. In a product distribution franchise, the franchisee may handle the franchisor's products on an exclusive or semi-exclusive basis, as opposed to a supplier-dealer who may handle several products — even competing ones. With the growth in auto dealerships that sell multiple brands, this distinction is getting just a bit clouded. The franchisee in a product distribution franchise, though, is closely associated with the company's brand name and receives more services from its franchisor than a dealer from its supplier would. Supplier-dealer relationships are often found in business opportunities relationships (we discuss this later in the chapter).

Business format franchises

Wendy's, Maaco, Uniglobe, and GNC are all business format franchises. Even DuPont has a business format franchise: Its franchisees sell and service commercial carpet and flooring.

In product distribution franchising — which we discuss earlier in the chapter — the most important part is the product that the franchisor manufactures. The business format franchisee also gets to use the parent company's trade name and logo, but more importantly, it gets the complete system for delivering the product or service and for doing business. It's this system that produces consistency — and consistency is a franchise's foundation for success. The business structure offers a detailed plan that explains how to do almost everything from the ground up. A franchisee is trained to manage the construction of the building, order the right equipment, and even hang the signs.

The Confidential Operating and Procedures Manuals (the how-to guide of every great franchise) give information on how to market and advertise; open the front door; recruit, hire, train, and dress the staff; and greet customers. To ensure quality, the franchisor provides information in the manuals on how and where to order inventory, how to prepare products, and how to present them to customers. The franchisor even includes procedures for taking out the garbage, turning out the lights, and closing up at night. All of this is a system. And in a good system, the franchisor prepares and then supports the franchisee.

Franchise systems do not prescribe identical levels of controls and consistency, but most systems do have standards that ensure minimum levels of operations. This means that whether it's owned by a franchisor or a franchisee, every location, no matter where it is in the world, looks the same and feels the same, and in restaurants, the food tastes the same. In other words, with some minor variations, your experience at every location should be the same. Every well-managed franchise system strives to achieve a high degree of consistency.

Conversion franchising

Although not truly a third type of franchising, *conversion franchising* is a modification of the standard franchise relationships. In conversion franchising, an independent operator in the same business as the franchisor adopts the franchisor's service or trademarks and its system. In many cases, the new franchisee, who is likely an experienced operator, is reluctant to make all the changes or conversions required to make it identical to all other locations in the system, and the franchisor may not be able to require those changes. However the franchisee adopts the system's service or trademarks, advertising programs, buying relationships, training, and the critical customer service standards. Examples of industries that have used conversion franchising extensively are real estate brokers, florists, and the trades (home remodeling, plumbing, electricians, and so on).

The Roles and Goals of Franchisors and Franchisees

A good franchisor gives its new franchisees the system and training they need to run their business without having to figure out everything on their own. The franchisor has already made most, if not all, of the mistakes. Franchisees get the benefit of the franchisor's experience, so they can take a shortcut through the minefields that startup businesses usually face. The franchisee purchases the right to use the franchisor's expertise, brand name, experience, methods, and initial and ongoing support.

Businesses don't usually fail because their products or services **are of** low quality. Some of the best hamburgers in the world are made at small, independent coffee shops and diners. Businesses usually fail because the owners are not prepared or are absentee owners; they make mistakes from which they can't recover. Great franchisors have already made the mistakes — and have survived. Their survival is the basis for the road map they provide, and that map is part of what franchisees pay for when they buy a franchise.

You have to remember, though, that the franchisor isn't providing all this assistance out of the kindness of its heart. The franchisor wants the whole system to grow, prosper, and turn profits. So the goal of a great franchisor is to provide a great system. If it does, the franchisees make money, stay in business, expand, and pay fees. And the franchisor's brand value grows as more people shop at its branded outlets and more people want to become franchisees.

Who is a franchisor?

A *franchisor* is the owner of a franchising company — the entity that grants the franchisee the right to operate under its trade and service marks. Franchisors come in all sizes and levels of experience:

- ✔ Often, the owners are large public or private companies with their founders (such as Dave Thomas) still at the helm.

- ✔ Sometimes, the franchisors are former franchisees who bought the companies from the founders (as Tom McDonnell did in 1996 with U-Save Auto Rental).

- ✔ Sometimes, the franchisors are huge conglomerates (such as Tricon, the spinoff from Pepsi, which owns Pizza Hut, Taco Bell, and KFC).

- ✔ Sometimes, the franchisors are international companies (such as Uniglobe Travel).

Franchisors can be companies founded by individuals with a great deal of experience or founded by individuals with little or no experience and just concluding an arrangement with the company's first franchisee.

Franchise systems are built on the relationships that the franchisor establishes with its franchisees. It's important to understand that, just as every franchise system is not the same, the relationship between franchisor and franchisee in every system is not the same. And this relationship may change as business conditions change. What follows are a few of the terms franchisees use to describe their relationship with their franchisor.

Partner

In a certain sense, although not a legal one, a franchisor and franchisee are partners. After all, they're in this business arrangement together. Each partner has a role, and each partner depends on the performance of the other. But are they equal partners? No.

Gary Charlwood, Chairman and CEO of Uniglobe Travel, expresses the arrangement best. He considers his franchisees partners but says that "In a partnership, there is always a senior partner. In this case, that's the franchisor."

Both partners have their roles in the relationship; the success of the relationship rests on their interdependence. Only one, though, can make the system-wide decisions, and that is the senior partner — the franchisor. As part of this "partnership," the franchisor provides the system, and the franchisee supplies the capital and the labor. In great systems, the partners discuss individual issues both one-on-one and communally, through franchise advisory councils.

Don't read too much into a franchisor's use of the word *partner*. Legally speaking, you aren't. That doesn't mean that you can't have a good working relationship with your franchisor. It only means that a franchisor has a responsibility to look out for *its* — not necessarily *your* — best interest. Of course, over time, a franchisor can't succeed without successful franchisees, so your interests do coincide to some degree.

Parent

Just like parents, franchisors provide the early guidance necessary for healthy growth. Franchisors provide franchisees with a safety net in the form of training and nurturing during the franchisee's early days in the system. Like parents, they offer a support mechanism that franchisees can turn to for help when they're off track. Franchisors provide a set of training wheels to keep new franchisees balanced until they can pedal on their own. And like real parents, they are a continuing source of advice, ideas, and wisdom as franchisees mature.

But franchisors aren't parents, and franchisees aren't children. Children don't get to choose their parents; franchisees *do* get to choose their franchisors. And unless parents today are a lot different from ours, they don't make their children sign a lengthy agreement at birth, spelling out the obligations each party has to the other. Franchising is a business relationship.

Dictator

Ask some franchisees to describe their franchisor, and they may use a word such as *dictator* or *tyrant.* Why? A lot of reasons exist.

Some franchisees find the franchise relationship too constricting. They see themselves as entrepreneurs — someone who starts a business and can make all the decisions about how the business should operate. After all, don't they own their own businesses? Entrepreneurs have a lot more flexibility than franchisees. In a franchise situation, the franchisor owns the concept and the name; the franchisor determines how the franchisee's business deals with consumers. For true entrepreneurs, the restrictions of a franchise can be overwhelming — like a dictatorship. So if you see yourself as an entrepreneur, start your own business. You probably won't be happy as a franchisee.

Every order of Biggie fries should be the same. Every hotel room at Marriott Courtyards should have a coffeepot, a couch, and telephones that hook up to a modem. That's consistency. To ensure that consistency, a franchisor has to make decisions about how the business operates globally. Franchisees may think that they have the next great idea, and often they do, but it's up to the franchisor to look at those great ideas and make systemwide decisions. Sometimes, the answer is no. But if the only reason a franchisor says no is that the franchisor didn't come up with the ideas, they're not only dictators, they're poor businesspeople. If the franchisor lets the franchisee try every idea, they're not good parents, either; good parents protect their children from making unnecessary mistakes.

In most cases, however, franchisors aren't being dictatorial when they say no, and they're not being bad parents, either. They are usually looking at the big picture and acting as the senior partner.

It's becoming more fashionable for franchisors and franchisees to share some of the decision making — but in limited circumstances. According to Rupert Barkoff, Partner, Kilpatrick Stockton, LLP, Atlanta, Georgia, "Holiday Inn, for example, is contractually committed to submit certain proposed changes in its system to its franchisee association before they are implemented and the franchisees of Sylvan Learning Center have a veto right over marketing programs."

Most great franchise systems that work as a "partnership" have a Franchisee Advisory Council (FAC) in place to assist the franchisor in evolving and improving the system. Often, one of the FAC's functions is to review ideas for new products and services, whether the ideas come from the franchisor or a franchisee. FACs also work with franchisors to review system advertising and

Watch out for franchise wannabes

What's a franchise wannabe? It's a *business opportunity (biz-op)* that looks an awful lot like either a business format franchise or a product distribution franchise. It masquerades at many franchise and business opportunity trade shows. The most common types are rack jobbers, supplier-dealer distributorships, and vending machine routes.

Although every franchise is a license, not every license is a franchise. The difference is in the definition of *franchise* that the Federal Trade Commission established. This definition requires the following elements to be in place before a license is classified as a franchise:

✔ The franchisee needs to distribute products or services that are identified or associated with the franchisor's trade or service marks.

✔ The franchisee is required to meet the franchisor's quality standards when using the marks; the franchisor has significant control over the business or provides significant assistance to the franchisee.

✔ The franchisee pays $500 or more to the franchisor.

Business opportunities have several advantages over franchising, the principal one being that business opportunities offer far more independence and flexibility. Business opportunities usually cost less to start up than franchises and don't require you to pay continuing royalties.

The biggest drawback of a business opportunity is that you seldom receive any significant help in setting up the business, in training, or in marketing, and you don't get much in the way of ongoing support, either.

Franchisors like to say that in a franchise you are in business *for* yourself but not *by* yourself. In a business opportunity, or biz-op, you're not only in business *for* yourself, but you're also usually in business *by* yourself. For most people looking for the support that comes from a franchise system, our advice is to stay clear of biz-ops and buy a real franchise.

cooperative buying arrangements, and make other changes to improve the system for the benefit of both partners. When you're looking at franchisors, look for systems that have an active and participatory relationship with their FAC.

The Franchising Agreement

You need to understand the following distinction: When you buy a franchise, you don't *own* the business. You own the *rights to do business using the franchisor's trademark, brand name, product or service, and operating methods.* What you typically own are the physical assets, the land, and the building and equipment, but not the brand or systems. In many systems, in fact, the franchisor may even have the right to buy the assets you do own if the relationship ends. Doesn't sound like much of a deal? Here's what you *do* get when you join a good franchise system:

- A proven and successful way of doing business
- A nationally known brand name
- A complete training program with advanced training and updates
- Research and development into new products and services
- Professionally designed local, regional, and national advertising and marketing programs
- A chance to own more than one franchise
- A shortcut around the common mistakes of startup businesses
- Your fellow franchisees as a network of peer advisors
- Thorough and ongoing field and headquarters support
- Oftentimes, a protected market or territory

Franchisors often give their franchisees an area around their location in which no other company-owned or franchisee-owned location is allowed to operate. This is called a *protected market* or *territory*. Protected territories may be defined

- As a radius or area around the franchisee's location
- As a number of households or businesses in an area
- As a number of people that live in an area
- By zip codes
- By boundaries using highways and streets
- By any method that defines the area in which no other same-branded location may be established

If the territory is too large, the total market won't contain enough locations to achieve brand recognition. If it's too small, or other locations are too close, there may not be enough customers to support the business. The goal in a good franchise system is to establish the right number of units in the right locations to ensure that consumers see the brand frequently. We call that *brand penetration*. When there are too many units close by and that proximity negatively affects unit sales, we call that *encroachment*.

Are Franchises Always Profitable?

If you buy a franchise, you get rich — or at least financially secure. Right? We hate to burst your bubble, but that's a myth. Not all franchises are successful. Not all are profitable, and many fail. But based on the most recent industry studies, including the survey conducted by the Gallup Organization for the IFA's Education Foundation, most franchisees are satisfied with their decision. A logical assumption has to be that most are profitable — unless you can imagine a businessperson being satisfied with losing money.

Owning a franchise — like owning any small business — is hard work. Even though you get proven systems and training when you hook up with a solid franchisor, no one guarantees your success. Often, the variable in this equation is you. Business ownership is not a passive investment. It requires long hours and dedication. Even with the best franchise system and the most popular brand name, the franchisee is often the key ingredient to making the business successful.

Even with hard work, if you make the wrong choice and buy a franchise that you end up hating, chances are good that you won't be successful — or very happy.

Have we discouraged you? Scared you? Confused you? Don't worry. Franchising, when done right and entered into with eyes open, can be a profitable, highly enjoyable way to spend your future.

Remember, what makes a hamburger great isn't the sizzle or the smell — it's the taste. The same goes for great franchises. The brochure may be hot and the salesperson persuasive, but you're not buying the sizzle — you're investing in the steak.

Chapter 2

Exploring Franchise Opportunities: There's More to Franchising Than Restaurants

*T*he number of available franchise opportunities is growing all the time and is limited only by the imagination and skills of the franchisors that create them. More than 80 industries use franchising to get their products and services — and their brands — to market. Your task, as you begin your exploration, is to cast a wide net into the pool of franchise opportunities and begin to see what interests you. While running a restaurant is one of the most popular types of franchising, it's not the only — or necessarily the best — way for everyone. (Although you could have a hard time convincing Dave of that!)

What's Out There

As you begin your exploration of franchising, you'll immediately begin to see the wide variety of opportunities: e-commerce companies, companies that deal in the health industry, hotels, car washes, haircut shops, travel agencies, one-hour photo processing, lawn care, leak detection, laundromats, and dry cleaners. There are even environmentally focused "dry cleaning" opportunities that do not use *perc* — the solvent used by traditional dry cleaners — but use CO_2 instead. (The franchise is called Hangers Cleaners by Micell Technologies of Raleigh, North Carolina.) Some of these concepts, like those involving e-commerce, didn't even exist five years ago. Restaurants make up only approximately a third of the available opportunities.

What's popular

While many people look at restaurants and food-related franchises first (probably because of the number of opportunities available in those segments), non-restaurant opportunities deserve a look, too. Don't be surprised if many of them actually do better financially than some of the better-known restaurant concepts.

Ron Harrison, past chairman of the International Franchise Association, points out that "Nearly half of the franchise companies out there have initial investment levels below $100,000." So franchising offers opportunities that fit your needs, no matter how small your pocketbook is.

As a personal investment strategy, you may want to consider starting multiple locations (we'll explain how later in the chapter) with a less expensive franchise rather than owning just one location of a concept that requires a larger investment. Some investors find that by spreading their risks over more than one location, they improve their odds for success.

In a special edition published at the International Franchise Association's annual convention in San Diego in February 2000, *USA Today* reported that the ten most popular franchise opportunities can be found in the following industries:

- ✔ Fast food
- ✔ Retail
- ✔ Service
- ✔ Automotive
- ✔ Restaurants
- ✔ Maintenance
- ✔ Building and construction
- ✔ Retail — food
- ✔ Business services
- ✔ Lodging

In fact, the list of industries that have been successfully franchised is much longer, so don't limit your search to those on *USA Today*'s list.

If you simply must have a franchise in one of the popular industries, consider a newer or smaller franchise system, which may be more flexible than the larger, more established ones. You may also find it advantageous to go down the less worn path and look closely at opportunities in less popular industries. Keep in mind, though, that the smaller systems, while possibly more flexible in working with you, may not have all of the benefits and services of the larger, better established franchisors.

Franchising's industries

When you begin to look in the source guides (see Chapter 4 for a discussion of where to look for lists of available franchises), you will notice that each guide categorizes franchise opportunities into different industries. You can find a list of industries that offer franchises on the International Franchise Association's Web page at www.franchise.org.

Are the industry classifications used by the different source guides standard in franchising? Source guides do not use a universally adopted classification system. You may think that companies in a category are similar, but that's not always true. Take "Food — Pizza," for example.

Now, some of the pizza franchisors provide a system where pizza is delivered to the customer's house; others don't. Some have only eat-in facilities. Some do both. Some do neither — you can only pick up your pie. They all are pizza franchises and may show up in some source guides under the same category. But the feature of delivery or non-delivery makes them significantly different types of franchise opportunities. The investment varies widely, the types and number of employees you need vary, the types of real estate vary, and the amount of money you can earn also certainly varies. Although franchise opportunities may be listed in the same category, they are truly different opportunities.

Now take "Hair Salons & Services." Some franchises are geared to cutting only men's hair. Others focus on women. Some provide perms and other chemical services; others don't. Manicures here, maybe not there. Some franchises specialize in children's haircuts. Another, Sport Clips, a haircutting franchise based in Georgetown, Texas, is based on a sports theme and has TV screens tuned to sporting events at each haircutting station. Their locations are designed to look like locker rooms; big screen TVs entertain clients while they wait. Where other haircutting shops sell shampoo and conditioner, Sport Clips also sells baseball hats, logo trashcans, and other sports-related merchandise. All hair salons work on hair, but the opportunities may be radically different from company to company.

One of the wonderful things about franchising is its variety of opportunities.

What's the Big Deal about Brand?

Brand is the franchise system's most valuable asset. Consumers decide what and whether to buy at a particular location based on what they know, or think that they know, about the brand. Unless they have a relationship with the local franchisee, they probably don't give any thought to who owns the business. In their minds, they're shopping at a branch of a chain.

In the consumer's mind, brand equals the company's reputation — the experience they expect to get. Franchisors spend a lot of time, energy, and money developing their brands so that consumers know what to expect before they even come in the door. A good brand communicates a message to the customer. When you see an advertisement for a Wendy's hamburger, you immediately associate it with your experience of ordering and eating a Wendy's hamburger. You may think of a "Cheddar Lovers Bacon Cheeseburger," or maybe a baked potato or the freshness of the product. Maybe you think that the line moves just a bit faster, that the service is better, or the staff is friendlier. You may remember seeing Dave in that last commercial or think back to Clara Peller and her sidekicks Mildred Lane and Elizabeth Shaw in the "Where's the Beef?" ads. ("Where's the Beef?" registered the highest consumer awareness levels in the advertising industry's history. It stole the show at the 1984 Clio Awards, winning three of the industry's highest honors, and was voted the most popular commercial in America in 1984.) The experience of visiting a Wendy's, supported by the message in its advertising, communicates to the public just what Wendy's is. You can visualize and almost taste the experience.

The same can be said for other companies, such as Midas. When you see an ad for the brake services that Midas offers, you can almost feel your car stopping safely at the light. That's the power of a brand.

Brand recognition is part of what a franchisee hopes to get when purchasing a franchise. A good brand is immediately familiar in consumers' minds. With a well-known brand, you don't have to build brand awareness in your market. The franchisor and the other franchisees have taken care of that for you. This is one of the major advantages of investing in a larger, well-established franchise system. Smaller systems with limited brand recognition can't deliver that until you help them grow.

Ongoing advertising and marketing programs help ensure that the brand remains strong and growing. And if the franchise system is successful in making the brand mean something positive to the consumer, that success means possible increased sales for you.

Brands are not born fully grown. Almost every start-up franchisor begins with some local brand recognition (it may be only a neighborhood) and has to grow that brand to achieve regional or national status.

A company can provide the best dry-cleaning in town, have a system for one-hour service, be loved by their customers, and yet only be known locally. For start-up franchisors with limited brand recognition outside of their home market, this is an issue. Franchisees in markets where the franchisor's brand has little or no consumer recognition use advertising and promotions provided by the franchisor to build brand recognition in their market. Those franchisees that must build brand recognition need to spend more on advertising and promotion, and may require a different message than franchisees who enter a market in which the franchisor's brand is well known.

What Types of Franchise Arrangements Are Available?

Because so many kinds of franchising opportunities exist, franchising is an ideal way for individuals, investor groups, and business entities to become business owners. The number of franchisors, the variety of types of industries represented in franchising, and the range of investments available create opportunities for the smallest single-unit mom-and-pop operator to the large multimillion-dollar investor group looking to add a franchise investment to its portfolio.

A *franchisee* is the person or entity granted the right to operate the business. The *franchise* is the business that the franchisee is granted the right to operate.

Single-unit or direct-unit franchises

A *single-unit* or *direct-unit franchise* is just what it says it is. A franchisee obtains the rights from a franchise system to operate one franchise. This is the simplest form of franchise relationship.

Most franchise systems have grown over the years — one franchise at a time. It's the classic and still the most common type of relationship in franchising. As people looked for a way to get to their dream of independence through business ownership, franchising became their vehicle.

But single-unit or direct-unit franchising is not the only way, and we want you to know something about the other arrangements.

Multi-unit franchises

Many franchisees own several locations. Multi-unit franchises take many forms.

Multiple single-unit operators

More and more often, as the classic single-unit operators prosper, they acquire another franchise from the same franchisor. They know their franchisor, have established a relationship with the franchise system, and can predict what they can earn from investing in additional units. Because they already know how to operate the business, the initial training they took when they opened their first location may not be necessary, and some of the key employees they have in their first location may be perfect to become managers in their second and third locations. It's a terrific way to grow, because their knowledge of the business and the franchise system makes their risk lower than when they made their initial franchise decision.

Except for the added burden (or, possibly, *joy*) of operating additional locations, the franchise relationship between the franchisor and franchisee is substantially the same. The franchisee simply has multiple single-unit agreements. If there's a significant difference, it's in the leverage that multi-unit ownership may have. With more units and more invested, a multi-unit franchisee stands out more on the franchisor's radar than maybe a single-unit operator would.

Franchisors periodically update their franchise agreements. The franchisor may modify some of the fees, require some additional equipment or investment in new technology, change some of the obligations between the parties, or make some other changes. Franchisees who over time acquire multiple single-unit agreements will likely find variations between their original contract with the franchisor for the first unit and the new franchise agreement for later units. Additionally, many franchise agreements provide for what is called a *cross-default*. This provision allows the franchisor to consider a violation of one of the agreements to be a violation of all of the agreements. As with all franchise agreements, you should have a franchise attorney review the documents. (We discuss how to select advisors in Chapter 6.)

Area development

An *area development agreement* is a relationship that grants a franchisee the right to open more than one location. It differs from a multiple single-unit relationship primarily because the franchisee agrees up front to open a specific number of locations during a defined period of time and within a specified area.

For example, say you want to open ten haircutting shops in your town. You can go to the franchisor and buy one franchise at a time, as we discussed earlier, but you risk having to share the market with other franchisees from the system or risk that the franchisor will have sold all the available franchises for your market before you're ready to purchase them.

Instead, you enter into an area development agreement. This means you agree to open and operate the ten units over a defined period — say, five years — and the franchisor grants you exclusive rights for the development of locations in your area.

Make sure that your development agreement gives you market exclusivity. In some franchise systems, a development agreement may not.

Typically, you pay the franchisor a fee for the development rights and sign an area development agreement obligating you to open the ten locations during the five years. The opening dates are usually specified, so you may have to have one open on January 1, the next on July 1, and so on.

When it comes to applying the fee you pay for the development rights, nothing is typical; it varies from company to company. As you identify each location, you will usually sign a single-unit franchise agreement. What you pay and how the franchisor applies the fee will vary, depending on the agreement:

✔ You may pay a full, initial franchise fee for the new location.

✔ The initial franchise fee for the new location may be a reduced fee from the franchisor's standard fee.

✔ A portion of the fee you paid for the development rights may be credited to the initial franchise fee you owe for each location.

✔ Each franchise system is different. As with every contract you sign, you need to review the agreements with your lawyer. (See Chapter 6 for information on how to select your advisors.)

Why are there two agreements — an area development agreement and a franchise agreement? Simply put, the area development agreement gives you the right to enter into those single-unit agreements and obligates the franchisor to allow you to complete your development schedule. The unit franchise agreement gives you the right to operate each location as a franchise of the system. The agreements serve two different purposes.

Keep in mind, though, if you fail to meet the development schedule, the franchisor typically has the right to cancel the development agreement and keep the area development fee. So make sure that the market you select can handle the number of locations you have committed to opening and that you have the financial backing to live up to the agreement if the first store gets off to a slower start than anticipated.

Master franchises

A *master franchise relationship* is similar to an area development agreement, with one significant variation.

The master franchisee, in addition to having the right and obligation to open and operate a number of locations in a defined area, also has the right and sometimes the obligation to offer and sell franchises to other people looking to become franchisees of the system. You become sort of a franchisor to those people who buy franchises through your master franchise.

We use the same example that we used in the "Area development" section earlier, with one important variation: You don't want to own and operate all of the haircutting locations.

As a master franchisee, you will probably be required to own and operate at least one or two locations yourself. After they have been opened, you can then sell the rights to open additional locations to other franchisees — often called "sub-franchisees" — that want to open and operate hair salons in your market.

When you sign the master franchise agreement, you pay a fee — the *master franchise fee*. As you sell franchises to your sub-franchisees, they pay a franchise fee, which you typically share with your franchisor. They also typically pay a royalty, which you also share with the franchisor. The percentage of each that you share with the franchisor varies widely depending on the system and the type of master relationship you enter into.

There are several variations of the master franchise relationship:

✔ The sub-franchisee may execute a franchise agreement directly with the franchisor or with you as the master franchisee.

✔ The franchisor may have the right to approve the new sub-franchisee, or you may hold that right.

✔ The sub-franchisee may receive training and continuing support from the franchisor, the master franchisee, or a combination of both.

✔ The sub-franchisee may pay fees directly to you, to the franchisor, or to a combination of both.

Every master franchise relationship may have variations from others, and again, you should enlist the help of a qualified franchise attorney.

Of all of the types of relationships in franchising, the master franchise or sub-franchise relationship is the most complex for all the parties: the franchisor, the master franchisee, and the sub-franchisee.

Master franchising is less popular in the United States today than it was in years past; however, it is still the most prevalent method used by U.S. franchisors entering other countries. Internationally, though, the trend is shifting to area development relationships for U.S.-based franchisors.

In Chapter 1, we introduce you to a form of franchise relationship called a *conversion franchise*. This is a variation of a typical franchise relationship where an independent operator, in the same business as the franchise system, converts the operation substantially to the franchise system.

Other variations of the "standard" franchise fall into a broad category usually referred to as *nontraditional locations*.

Nontraditional locations

Nontraditional locations can include airports, train stations, hospitals, college campuses, sports stadiums, ballparks, food courts, gas stations, portable kiosks in parks — you get the idea. In franchising, these are often referred to as *mass gathering locations.*

The strength of mass gathering locations is that the operations benefit from customers drawn to the location by something other than the product you are offering, such as the baseball game at the stadium or to college students between classes.

If you visit a convenience store when you purchase gasoline, you are also visiting a nontraditional location. Gas stations operated, for example, by Texaco, Shell, and ExxonMobil often share space with quick service restaurants (QSRs). Some may even have a small branch of a service franchise, such as Mail Boxes Etc. In fact, you can now find Mail Boxes Etc. at airports and hotels.

The traffic from customers buying gas helps the franchise sell more product and services, while the traffic generated by the franchise helps sell more gas.

Single- or multi-unit operators can operate from nontraditional locations. The franchisees can be either the dealer who operates the gas station or another person or entity that simply is renting space from the dealer. Sometimes, the operator may even be the franchisor.

Dual branding

Another type of nontraditional relationship is called *dual branding,* or *co-branding.* You see these businesses all over. Dual branding occurs when two or more franchises with different concepts set up shop next to one another or within the same location, offering customers a one-stop shopping experience. Tricon, the owner of KFC, Pizza Hut, and Taco Bell, often places two or three of its brands in one location. So does Wendy's, which shares locations with its sister brand, Tim Hortons, the Canadian coffee and fresh baked goods chain.

There are nearly 150 co-branded Wendy's and Tim Hortons locations in the United States and Canada. Franchisees can save around 25 percent on the development cost when the two concepts are operated from a co-branded location.

A dual branding location uses labor and real estate more efficiently because it expands a location's *daypart.* In the restaurant industry, breakfast, lunch, and dinner are called dayparts. For example, donut chains usually are busiest during the breakfast daypart and slow down during the lunch and dinner dayparts. Other concepts are slow during the breakfast daypart but are busier during the lunch or dinner dayparts. By dual branding a location, the operator hopes to capture traffic to the location that is generated by the other product offering and use the location more fully.

Mass gathering and dual branding are the latest and fastest-growing trends in franchising.

Retrofranchising

The growth in the use of retrofranchising and re-franchising is increasing. (*Retrofranchising* refers to locations that were company owned and may never have been franchised; *refranchising* refers to locations that once were franchised but were acquired and operated by the franchisor.)

Franchisors have many reasons for wanting to sell these locations:

- Operating company-owned locations may no longer fit the company's strategic plan.

- The company may still want to operate company-owned locations, but wants to consolidate the number of markets in which it directly operates. It uses the capital from the sale of owned locations in some markets for the development of new locations in other markets. In essence, it is adjusting its "inventory" of stores to better suit the company's strategy.

- To facilitate the growth of franchising in a market, the company may offer the sale of company-owned locations to franchisees to stimulate their development of additional units in the market.

- The company may have financial difficulties and need the capital from the sale.

- In some situations, franchisees are better at operating locations than the franchisor. This may be due to the distance from headquarters to the local operations, the skills of management and other personnel, or other reasons. In those situations, franchisors may sell locations simply because they believe the locations work better under the control of a franchisee than under the franchisor's own personnel. You should be on the lookout for retrofranchising and re-franchising opportunities.

There are many advantages to acquiring an existing location:

- The time it will take to get the business up and running will be shorter because you don't have to find the location or work through constructing and equipping the business.

- Bank financing may be easier because the business is already up and running.

- ✔ The franchisor may be willing to help you finance the location and also cut you a good deal on the purchase price. Franchisors are, after all, "motivated sellers."

- ✔ You're buying a business that is currently operating, has existing customers, and has an established cash flow.

- ✔ You know what the performance of the operation is and can base your investment and operating decisions on facts rather than projections.

- ✔ The location may have trained staff and management.

Refranchising can be confused with churning. *Churning* occurs when a franchisor takes back a location from a franchisee, resells it, takes it back again, resells it again, and so on. This scenario often occurs when the original franchisee can't make a go of the location, the location is not economically viable, or the location can't operate to company standards and is terminated. If a non-franchisor owned the location, it would probably be a candidate for closure. However, some franchisors take back the poorly performing location and, to protect themselves from having to disclose a failure in their disclosure document or to make additional income or recoup their investment, simply sell the business to another franchisee.

These "opportunities" need to be examined carefully. Don't assume that you're a smarter or better operator than the last guy. Also, a company that has a high percentage of churning may offer little chance for success and so may not be a sound franchising investment — even for franchisees not buying these recycled locations. Always ask how many owners have run the operation before you sign on the dotted line. Thankfully, not many franchisors churn their locations, but you still have to be alert to the possibility.

Diversity in Franchising

While you won't encounter a special type of franchise arrangement for members of minorities or women looking to invest in a franchise, many franchise systems have developed opportunities designed to increase the diversity of their franchisee ownership and management.

In most franchise systems, women and members of minorities are under-represented. One of the exceptions is Jani-King, a Dallas-based franchisor where over 80 percent of the franchisees are members of minority groups. Many minority franchisees were excluded from franchising in the past, primarily, among other causes, because of limited equity in homes that most new franchisees use to finance their first franchise purchase. Women, who traditionally were also under-represented in the general workforce, were not considered prime targets for franchisors. But the rapidly expanding minority middle class and the increase in the numbers of Hispanics, Asians, other immigrants, and women, both entering the workforce and achieving management positions, have changed the economic climate and the potential pool of franchisees.

Franchisors are also finding that during the strong economy we have had during the past few years, people who may be candidates for franchise ownership are electing to remain employees. The increase in the pool of minority franchisees comes at a time when many franchisors are actively seeking new candidates for franchisee ownership.

Franchisors recognize the social implication of this historic fact of underrepresentation. They also realize that improving diversity is important to their brand and to their bottom line. And with the aid of local, state, and federal programs designed to level the playing field for minority investments, as well as lenders who are targeting franchise systems, the diversity of franchise ownership is increasing rapidly.

Franchisors are not talking about "redlining," or targeting minority franchisees to particular markets. However, many minority franchisees are electing to open locations in underserved inner-city and urban areas (the *emerging markets*) where franchise brands are underrepresented. Others, in growing number, are investing in opportunities in markets that are more traditional (that is, the suburbs) to franchising.

Some franchisors are offering special arrangements to minority franchisees to stimulate growth in the emerging markets. In addition to reducing some of their fees, some franchisors are adjusting their net worth and liquidity requirements for new franchisees. Others are providing increased levels of support and are developing retail marketing programs tailored to these neighborhoods.

Why are these emerging markets so attractive to franchisors?

- ✔ **Opportunity:** Many franchisors avoided inner-city and urban locations — the emerging markets — simply because opportunities in their more traditional markets were readily available and the opportunities in the emerging markets did not appear as strong. Now that many of the traditional markets have been fully developed, these franchisors are looking for new opportunities. The emerging markets provide them with a ready customer base that knows their brand and is ready and willing to buy.

- ✔ **Strategic location:** Many of these locations are strategically located near downtown, mainstream markets. This makes them perfect locations for establishing businesses that can service customers in those areas, because the location of the franchisee to the customer is less important than in other types of businesses. This includes franchisors in industries such as printing, janitorial services, personnel agencies, maintenance and repair, delivery, and others that do not require a local market demand.

- ✔ **Real estate availability:** Often, large tracts of real estate exist within these markets that franchisees can assemble and develop at a lower cost than in suburban markets.

- ✔ **Labor:** Because of a higher-than-average rate of unemployment in these areas, labor is plentiful and often at a lower cost than in areas where job opportunities are more abundant. Also, training programs run by government and not-for-profit organizations train a significant portion of this labor pool in the skills that small businesses require.

- ✔ **Government programs:** Government programs, including tax credits, tax-free bonds, depreciation advantages, and other assistance, make operating in these markets economically advantageous.

- ✔ **Local demand:** Although *per-capita spending* (the amount of money each person spends) may often be lower, these markets are usually high-density areas — a lot of people in a small area. In fact, spending in some emerging markets actually exceeds per capita spending in suburban markets for certain products and services. Therefore, the combined demand for goods and services in these markets often exceeds that of suburban markets.

- ✔ **Lack of existing merchants:** Although the demand for products and services is high, quality suppliers are often in short supply. The absence of quality retail, services, and restaurants in some areas forces residents to travel great distances to get what they need. Locally based and owned businesses have the opportunity to secure these customers as their own.

Except for the quick service restaurant segment of franchising (fast food), franchising is underrepresented in the emerging markets of the United States. In a study conducted by MSA (Michael's consulting firm), the opportunity for franchising in the emerging markets was measured by testing for consumer leakage in several markets in New York City. *Leakage* is the amount spent by consumers outside the market in which they live.

What the study determined was that for certain restaurant, retail, and service franchisors, the opportunities in the emerging markets are potentially stronger than in their more traditional, suburban markets.

It's important to recognize, though, that not every franchisor does equally well in the emerging markets — any more than every franchisor does equally well in all the suburban markets. Ethnic background, consumer preferences, economic conditions, quality local competitors, the quality of franchisees and their operations, and community support, among other factors, all are part of the success equation.

In addition to QSRs such as Wendy's, AFC (Church's and Popeye's), Blimpie, and Tricon (KFC, Taco Bell, and Pizza Hut), which already have strong representation in the emerging markets, many other franchisors such as Athletes

Foot, Ben & Jerry's, IHOP, 800 Flowers, Triple Check Income Tax Service, Mail Boxes Etc., Marriott, and Sterling Optical have focused on these opportunities and a more diverse franchisee representation.

Sterling Optical, a New York–based optical franchise, recently opened its first location in Harlem. Working with the Local Initiative Support Corporation, Bankers Trust Co., a local community development corporation (Abyssinian Development Corporation), a local investment group, local entrepreneurs and other community leaders, Sterling's first inner-city franchise opened in Harlem. The Sterling location was an ideal fit for Harlem's "fashion forward" consumer, where the availability of both high- and mid-priced merchandise contributed to the venture's success. According to Jerry Darnell, Sterling's executive vice president and the person responsible for developing Sterling's diversity program, "The location was an immediate success. We are committed to opening locations in other inner-city areas in New York, as well as in other cities. If we've learned anything, it's that our product and system works in the market, and the opportunity for us and our franchisees is outstanding."

To increase diversity in franchising, the International Franchise Association has begun a "Franchise Trade Delegation Program" to educate potential minority franchisees in cities around the United States on franchising and the opportunities of franchise ownership. This program brings local franchise candidates together with national and local resources to promote increased minority participation in the franchise industry through educational and economic partnerships. Debbie Smith, IFA's Vice President of Public Affairs and Emerging Markets, heads the program.

Franchising, the dominant form of small business ownership today, has grown worldwide because its flexibility allows potential franchisees the choice of the type of business they get into, the type of relationship, and the size of their investment.

Chapter 3

Looking Within: Are You Cut Out to Be a Franchisee?

● ●

In This Chapter

▶ How can you tell if buying a franchise is right for you?

▶ What are the advantages and disadvantages of investing in a franchise?

▶ Franchisee and entrepreneur — are they the same thing?

● ●

*T*his chapter is all about self-evaluation. We won't lie to you. Being brutally honest with yourself is difficult when you're caught up in the excitement of striking out on your own. However, the results of this self-assessment are especially important when the franchise salesperson tells you you're perfect for the opportunity. (News flash: Franchise salespeople want to sell you a franchise, and often they get a commission for doing so.)

So you need to take this part of the process seriously. Making a decision to become a franchisee isn't just about numbers. This part of the decision is about you — your lifestyle, family, likes and dislikes, work rhythms, values, ethics, and even your dreams. Keep in mind this is the real world. Franchising won't make you a new person, and it isn't a self-help game. You need to define who you really are. Your future depends on your honesty.

Operating a franchise is a cross between business ownership and employment. On one hand, you invest in the right to use the business system and the hard assets necessary to start and support the business. On the other hand, while you're responsible for day-to-day operation, you are working under a system provided and, to a large extent, controlled by your franchisor. This duality often can cause some individuals difficulty.

This chapter will help you define who you are and whether you are the type of person who should invest in a franchise. Most individuals looking to buy a franchise have an emotional reaction to the process of selecting one. You may be the type who can stay above the emotional fray and can make investment decisions based only on the merit of the offering. If so, congratulations. But, based on our experience, emotions have a lot to do with selecting a franchise — sometimes not in a healthy way.

It's possible that you'll come away with the feeling that buying a franchise isn't necessarily the answer to your dream of economic independence. On the other hand, you may find that franchising is your ticket to economic security. You need to take the time to find out.

The Advantages and Disadvantages of Franchise Ownership

For many years, franchisors, the trade press, and the franchise associations fueled the perception that franchising was a surefire method of expansion for business and a safe investment for franchisees. Although a well-designed franchise program can be an exceptional method of expansion, poorly designed or operated businesses are not. This isn't just a franchise reality — it's a business reality.

Before you consider whether you're cut out to become a franchisee, you need to understand some of the advantages and disadvantages of franchise ownership.

Advantages of franchise ownership

Your chance of success in franchising can only be as strong as the franchise you select. Mature, well-operated franchise systems generally possess the following traits.

Overall competitive benefits

The public has become accustomed to a certain level of quality and consistency from branded locations (see Chapter 2). What we mean by a *branded location* is a business that has the same name and decor and that the public thinks of as a chain. Whether a company's product is superior or mediocre, if its locations are successful, the secret for its success will likely be in its consistency.

One of the secrets of being a good businessperson is not accepting a poll of one: Just because you find a product or service outstanding or mediocre doesn't mean the rest of the world does.

Regardless of where they are, consumers believe they understand the level of quality they will receive when they shop at a branded location. This often gives new franchisees an established customer base. Branding makes it easier to compete with the well-established, independent operators and even against other franchised and non-franchised chains. The advantage of brand recognition also extends to national accounts. They look at a system that has a network of locations and trust that each will operate at the same level of consistency and commitment. That type of system can service their needs wherever the franchise has a location.

Pre-opening benefits

Although the cost of entrance into a franchise system includes a franchise fee, which is often cited as a disadvantage, the franchisee benefits from, among other things, training, operations manuals, site selection tools, store design, construction programs, and reduced cost of equipment. Additionally, franchisees have their franchisor as a seasoned partner of whom they can ask questions, and they have a network of other franchisees in the system who can also be of assistance.

Ongoing benefits

In exchange for paying an ongoing royalty and other payments, franchisees benefit from periodic training programs and home office and field assistance. Often, through the franchise system's buying cooperatives, franchisees pay less for goods than their independent competitors do.

Franchisees benefit from the purchasing power that comes from joining with others. They benefit from professionally designed point-of-sale marketing material, advertising, grand opening programs, and other marketing materials that independents could never afford. Franchise systems can also afford to modernize through ongoing research and development and by test marketing new products and operating systems.

Each franchisee's spending power is combined with the spending power of all the other franchisees in the local market and in the rest of the system. This combined spending power, on advertising for example, often enables franchises to not only dominate local markets and the established independents but also to compete effectively against large, established chains.

Disadvantages for franchisees

Franchising is not right for every person, and it is important that you understand some of the disadvantages in a franchise relationship:

- ✔ **Loss of independence:** For some people, one of the most serious disadvantages to becoming a franchisee is loss of independence. If you want to make all your own decisions, franchising may be the wrong choice. Franchise systems are structured in such a way that the franchisor sets many of the rules; the franchisee is required to operate the business according to the franchisor's manuals and procedures.

✔ **Over-dependence:** Franchising's loss of independence, if taken to extremes, leads to a further disadvantage: over-dependence on the franchise system. Franchising succeeds when financial and emotional risk motivate franchisees. When they rely totally on the system for their success, their over-dependence can cause problems. Franchisees have to balance system restrictions with their personal ability to manage their own business.

✔ **Other franchisees:** The principal reason for the success of franchising is the public's perception of quality and consistency throughout the system. When the public receives great service at one location, the assumption is that the system has great service. This is also one of the potential major weaknesses of franchising. Franchisees are not only judged by their performance, they are judged by the performance of other franchisees. Poorly performing fellow franchisees or company-owned locations damage a franchisee's business even where they do not share the same market. If the hotel room is dirty in one location or, even worse, if the press were to report that the hotel had rodents, the public assumes the problem exists throughout the system.

✔ **Income expectations:** While good franchisors try to prevent it, some franchisees have unrealistic expectations about the income that they are going to earn. If their expectations are unrealistic, they will regret their investment in dollars, time, and effort and may become a negative influence on the system. Having realistic expectations is important to any investment decision.

✔ **Franchising inelasticity:** Franchise systems are bound together through legal agreements between franchisors and franchisees. Often, these agreements contain restrictions that potentially impact the franchisor's ability to make strategic decisions. For example, if a non-franchisor finds a location perfect for a new store — except for the limitations of finding capital to build the store, it is free to do so. In a franchise system, the franchisor must first look to the legal agreements between itself and the franchisees in the market. If the franchisor has granted the franchisees protected territories, and the new location is in one of those territories, then the franchisor loses that market opportunity — often to a competitor who does not have the same restrictions. The same thing can happen with e-commerce sales over the World Wide Web if the franchisor has provided the franchisee with those rights in the agreement.

It's a double-edged sword sometimes. The restrictions that can make franchising successful can be seen as disadvantages to some franchisees. These can include restrictions on product and services they are allowed to offer, limitations on size and exclusivity of their territory, the possibility of termination for failure to follow the system, the cost of transfer and renewal, and restrictions on independent marketing. Also, the added costs for royalties, advertising, additional training, and other services potentially reduce a franchisee's earnings.

Does Entrepreneur Equal Franchisee?

When you own a franchise, you become your own boss, right? Maybe.

Many media stories on franchising use the words *entrepreneur* and *franchisee* interchangeably, so newcomers to the franchise game may be confused by the reality that being a successful franchisee is not necessarily the same as being an entrepreneur.

Even in great franchise systems, some franchisees do better than others. Quite frankly, even in great franchise systems, there are dismal failures. If franchising is about franchisors providing great systems that can be executed consistently, how is this possible? It's the human factor.

Franchisees are not robots or computers that can be fed a string of commands that they execute flawlessly in every situation. Nor are franchisees true entrepreneurs with the flexibility to make every decision for themselves. If an independent operator is an entrepreneur, then a franchisee is an "entrepreneur lite."

True entrepreneurs are their own bosses, free to make turn-on-a-dime decisions that are full of risk and often full of reward. True entrepreneurs are like captains of their own ships, and sometimes they have a "reefs be damned, full speed ahead" attitude. If that statement describes you, you may not be franchisee material.

Lou Rudnick, partner at Piper Marbury Rudnick & Wolfe, Chicago, IL, explains the difference between entrepreneurs and franchisees like this: "While the opportunity to be one's own boss is a frequently stated reason for acquiring a franchise, the notion of business independence is actually to some extent inconsistent with franchisee ownership. A franchisee must understand that he will be obligated to subordinate a certain level of business independence, and agree to abide by the requirements, restrictions, and business policies imposed by the franchisor to achieve and maintain uniformity in the franchise system."

In other words, when you become a franchisee, you give up some, but not all, of your freedom to run your own show. A clear understanding of the relationship is important.

Consider these potential advantages and disadvantages of the franchising arrangement and gauge your reaction:

- ✔ The franchisor's standards on products and services may seem restrictive, but they provide the public with assurance on the consistency of the brand.

> ✔ Providing you with a limited, protected territory may reduce your market, but doing so allows for the development of other franchise and company-owned locations in the area that can contribute with you to the advertising fund to enhance the local name recognition of your business.
>
> ✔ Additional locations close to yours may seem like competition for your customers. But working together with other franchisees, you can increase your effectiveness against the competition by reducing the costs of goods through buying cooperatives, jointly recruiting personnel, and the improved brand awareness brought on by the fact that customers see the system's trade name more frequently.
>
> ✔ The possibility of being terminated for failure to follow the system may seem unfair, but those same penalties may be imposed on other franchisees who may not perform as well as you. Because franchisees are part of a branded system, customers may view you in the same light as those poor operators. And this can have a dramatic effect on your success.

If you can't let go of the need to run the show, you need to reevaluate your plan to become a franchisee.

Franchisees execute the system the franchisor provides. Great franchisees take that system and improve it: by providing better than the minimum customer service required; by hiring quality people and providing them with training; and by creating an atmosphere in their business that is palpably better than expected by their staff, their customers, their vendors, and the franchisor. Great franchisees enhance the basic system by being "entrepreneur lites."

Are You Willing and Able to Learn New Skills?

The first thing you are going to find out as a franchisee is that there is a lot to learn. The second thing you learn is that every day you are going to have to be both a teacher and a monitor. Teaching your employees how to operate the business and to monitor how well they are serving your customers is going to be your responsibility.

Most franchisors feel so strongly about a franchisee being able to learn the system that they include a clause in their franchise agreement giving them the right to terminate the franchise if the franchisee can't pass the training class. Many will require the franchisee to retake the training until he or she gets it right. Most franchisors even require you to bring any management personnel who will be operating the business to training so that they can evaluate their ability to learn and operate the system.

Part of what franchisors look for is your ability to set aside your preconceived notions of how to operate the business and to focus on how they expect the business to operate. This can be especially hard for those operators converting existing businesses to the franchisor's methods.

Your eagerness to learn new skills is an important attribute of becoming a franchisee.

Would You Rather Give or Take Orders?

Everyone has his or her own ideas about giving orders — and taking them. If you bristle at the thought of being told how to set up your merchandise, how to display the advertising banners, or having to report your sales and expenses every month, you should think about how you'll feel when you are expected to follow an entire system every day. That's day in and day out — year after year.

Successful franchising is based on the principle that following a detailed structure is your best guarantee of success. As a franchisee, part of what you buy is the franchisor's system and knowledge. Your role is to follow the formula the franchisor has developed and to look for ways to improve your operation within the system. That means following the rules, working within the system, and running your business according to the agreed-upon plan. Ask yourself these questions:

- ✔ **Can you follow somebody else's rules, even when you think you have a better way?** If not, independent business ownership may be a better fit for you.

- ✔ **Do you think you can change the franchisor's system after you are on board?** If so, independent business ownership may be a better fit for you.

- ✔ **Do you think that your local market is different from all others in the system and that the franchisor will modify the system just to suit your needs?** They may, but if you're counting on it, independent business ownership may be a better fit for you.

- ✔ **Can you trust (with some honest skepticism) that your franchisor is working for the benefit of the entire system — even when his or her decisions do not necessarily go your way?** If so, franchising may be your ticket.

- ✔ **Are you willing to share financial information and provide required reports each month? Are you prepared to accept coaching and advice on business practices from your franchisor's field staff?** If so, franchising may be your ticket.

- ✔ **Do you have the personal drive to be a great operator?** If so, franchising may be your ticket.

Keep in mind that you won't be a robot doing only what you are told. There are great franchisees and less-than-great franchisees. Everyone starts with the same system. The great ones add their personal skills and personalities to the business. They invest themselves in the job. They successfully manage their personnel (their most important asset). They provide a better atmosphere for their customers (their most important marketing tool). They love what they do, and it shows.

Are You Ready to Say Goodbye to Corporate Perks?

Oh those corporate perks: retirement plans; stock ownership and option plans; paid sick days; paid vacation days; expense accounts; company cars; health, vision, and dental insurance plans. If you are one of the thousands of corporate employees who have lost their jobs, you may start to notice that those perks are now gone because you ended your relationship with your former employer.

Perhaps your company's downsizing, rightsizing, merging, or early retirement program has left you with cash and more free time on your hands than you really want. If so, then this section is about you.

The former corporate middle manager who wants to be a franchisee is a unique breed. This person has a broad understanding of business, knows how to work within a system, knows how to motivate staff, certainly is no stranger to long hours, and now has the capital to make a franchise investment.

In many cases, these former mid-level managers are missing only one key ingredient for running a business: They may never have started one from scratch — without corporate support and corporate financial backing.

Perhaps the biggest adjustment middle managers face as franchisees is the loss of many of the support services they have grown accustomed to. Their secretary probably didn't come with them when they left the 22nd floor. And the copy machines, fax machines, filing systems, payroll clerks, legal department staff, computers, and travel services are probably also at the office where they left them. Although they're not in business by themselves, they may sometimes feel like they are.

Success is no longer measured by the rapt attention that staff or superiors give to those fine PowerPoint presentations. Success is measured each day in performance. In other words, operating a business requires more self-reliance than many middle managers have had to possess.

A structured franchised system replaces some of the support that middle managers have relied on for their success. It's the system, the branding, and the franchisor support that, when coupled with the talents of the former corporate employee, make the transition to business ownership through franchising a success.

How's Your Health?

The demands on a franchisee often require that you have an extraordinary level of staying power. Even when an extra ten minutes of sleep in the morning is what your body craves, you must get up, open your business, and serve your customers. To achieve that level of endurance, you must be in good health.

Can you handle stress? Especially during the early days as a franchisee, as you learn your new craft, things won't always go exactly as you expected. On almost a continual basis, as a business operator you will need to deal with issues and deadlines that will become stressful. How's your coping mechanism?

Do You Like People?

Do you really like people? This question may sound silly. You're probably thinking, "Of course, I like people. Who doesn't?" Keep in mind that we're talking about people relationships, because franchising is based on relationships between and among people. As a franchisee, you need to maintain relationships with your franchisor, staff, customers, and vendors. In addition, your various personal and family relationships can influence your franchise's performance.

You have to handle a lot of relationships at once. You need the ability to communicate and to listen, as every franchisee must interact with a wide array of people during the course of every business day. The essential personal characteristic is simple: You have to like to deal with people every day. A franchise is not a suitable environment for someone who prefers working alone! Your ability to interact positively with fellow franchisees, your franchisor, your staff, and your customers is important every day of your company's operation.

How Much Are You Willing to Invest — and How Much Can You Afford to Risk?

Having just enough money to invest in your franchise and to purchase the necessary equipment and stock is not enough. Even if you are prepared to invest what the franchisor predicts is required, you need to prepare yourself to invest some more, just in case everything does not go by the book.

You've probably heard stories of successful businesspeople who have funded their franchises by maxing out their credit cards — it's part of the mystique of success and entrepreneurship. More often than not, it's really a path to disaster.

It's wise not to risk it all because all may not be enough. Look at your finances, determine what you need to live on if the business cannot support you and your family in the early days, and put it aside. Make sure that you cover the important things, such as food, housing, and college funds for the kids. Franchisees with adequate resources can weather the hard times and have the extra funds available when they need them.

It takes discipline to know what your limits are. It's essential that you work with a financial advisor or an accountant to determine how much you can invest. Ask your friends and neighbors if they know a good CPA who can help you through the process. You can also contact the local CPA association for recommendations. (See Chapter 6 for a discussion on how to find professional advisors.)

How Do Your Family and Friends Feel about Your Franchise Venture?

Buying a franchise is a life-changing decision. Operating a business is more than a full-time job. During the start-up phase, a franchise can become your life. That commitment requires carving out time normally spent with your family and friends and pouring it into the business. If they resent the time you must dedicate to the business, business ownership may not be your thing. Stay an employee. However, we don't know many successful corporate executives who aren't currently putting in 70-hour workweeks. Even for those who punch a clock, between overtime and second jobs, 70-hour weeks may be the norm. Still, you, your family, and your friends must clearly understand and accept the demands on your time before you commit to any business.

Select an industry that meets your personal needs and likes. If you'll be embarrassed to tell friends and family that you own a dry-cleaning business or a janitorial business, even if such businesses are highly lucrative, don't buy one. If working 12-hour days, seven days a week is not your idea of fun, make certain that the franchise industry you select offers better hours. Whether you need $50,000 or $150,000 a year to support your family, make certain that the other franchisees in the system you select make that type of return. And if you're getting groans from family members at the mere mention of franchising, stop right there. Work out the reasons behind the groans and get your family's support before you proceed. Business ownership is demanding — even within a well-developed franchise system.

Personal happiness is the most important factor in buying any business, including a franchise. However, with over 80 different industries and thousands of franchise opportunities available — both in product- and service-related areas — one of them may suit your needs. Examine your feelings toward each one before making a selection.

Include your family in all your preliminary and ongoing investigations into franchising. Get their support for your choice. That way, they'll feel invested in the process and can give you the support you need.

Fact: Both Dave and Michael were franchisees. We worked hard. We dedicated more time than we wished to the business and less than we liked to our families. Neither of us would change a thing. The investment was worth the effort. But, that's us.

Are You Cut Out to Be a Franchisee?

We're not going to tell you whether you should become a franchisee. That's a personal decision. But we are going to ask you to look at yourself and answer the questions we have posed in this chapter before you make your decision. You don't need to score yourself; no one element is more important than any other. You also don't need to get 100 percent to be the perfect franchisee. The questions are for you to ponder and use to make the correct decisions for yourself and your family.

1. Can you follow someone else's rules, even when you think you have a better way?

2. Are you prepared to accept coaching and advice on how you run your business from a franchisor's field and headquarter's staff?

3. If the franchisor turns down your great idea for changing the system, can you live with that?

4. Can you trust (with honest skepticism) that a franchisor is working for the benefit of the entire system — even when their decisions do not necessarily go your way?

5. Are you willing to share financial information and prepare required reports each month?

6. Are you willing, able, and anxious to learn new skills? Can you set aside old habits and beliefs to follow a franchise system?

7. Do you have the personal drive to be a great operator?

8. Are you willing to work whatever hours it takes to make your business a success?

9. Are you willing to give up the corporate perks you have currently to invest in a franchise and operate your own business?

10. Are you self-reliant? Can you work without corporate support?

11. Are you healthy? Do you have the physical ability to meet the needs of operating your own business?

12. Can you handle stress? Do you have the mental ability to meet the everyday needs of operating your own business? Can you handle crisis situations and deadlines?

13. Do you like people? Do you listen? Do you have patience when working and interacting with others?

14. Do you communicate well? Can you be a leader and a trainer for your staff as well as a front person for your business?

15. Can you maintain a positive relationship with the people who work for you?

16. Can you meet the needs of your customers?

17. Do you have the ability to sell — yourself and your products and services?

18. Are you willing to use the advertising and promotional material provided by the franchisor, or do you have to be the creative genius?

19. How much can you afford to invest? How much can you afford to lose? How much will you have in reserve?

20. How do your family and friends feel about your becoming a franchisee? Will they support you in your decision?

These 20 questions are the basic ones you need to consider. Others will come from those you trust for advice and from that little voice inside that will wake you up at night. That little voice deserves to have its questions answered, too.

Chapter 4

Making the Choice: Deciding Which Business Is Right for You

● ●

In This Chapter

▶ Deciding whether to buy a franchise or start your own independent business

▶ Considering the services of a franchise broker

▶ Locating good information about available franchises

▶ Choosing the best franchise industry for you

▶ Considering whether to buy an established franchise or open a new location

● ●

*I*n this chapter, you can stop kicking the tires and put yourself behind a franchise wheel or two. Don't get too excited, though: You're not ready to drive off the showroom lot just yet. This chapter helps you dig a little deeper and get some more specific details about becoming a franchisee.

Franchising, when done right, is a win-win relationship for all parties involved. In order to do franchising the right way, prospective franchisees must get answers to their questions before making an investment.

Franchisees fail — but many of them could have avoided failure if they'd conducted more thorough research at the front end of the franchise selection process. Take your time; don't cut corners. Sure, you want to save money, but at times you'll need to spend money to ensure that you're making the right decision. Just remember that a small investment in getting the facts could save you the pain and expense that comes from making the wrong choice — and possibly losing it all.

This chapter can help you get the information you need to make the right choice — for *you*.

Deciding Whether to Go Independent or Become Part of a Team

You have a choice: You can be an independent business owner *or* you can invest in a franchise opportunity. Which option you choose depends on a lot of factors having to do with your personality, finances, motivation, experience, market niche, product or service longevity, business acumen, and level of tenacity. There is no universally right choice.

Let's look at some of your options.

Starting your own business

If you're the independent type who always wants to run every detail of a project, perhaps you should look into starting your own business instead of buying a franchise.

Keep in mind that most franchisors — like Dave — started out as independent small business owners before franchising their concepts. They plowed every spare nickel and most spare moments into the business — not just for a few months but for a number of years. A dedicated, small independent business owner never gives up and is willing to put everything on the line to see the business succeed. This approach to business offers few safety nets, and the only one making mistakes along the way is you. The support system you have is whatever you can create and sustain on your own.

But if you have an innovative product or cutting-edge service that is currently not being offered to consumers, or maybe just a better way than is available elsewhere in the market, you may want to look into striking out on your own. Business groups, local banking institutions, universities, and area chambers of commerce offer a wide range of support seminars and other group benefits.

In the United States, one of the best places to seek advice is from the folks at the Service Corps of Retired Executives (SCORE). SCORE is resource partner with the U.S. Small Business Administration and provides free counseling to small businesses. As the name says, SCORE is made up of retired business executives who can assist business on a host of issues, including planning, finance, and execution. You can find SCORE's Web page at www.score.org/.

Another terrific program from the SBA is the Small Business Development Center Program, which was developed to provide management and technical assistance to current and prospective small business owners. The SBDC program is a cooperative effort of the private sector, the educational community, and federal, state, and local governments. There are presently 57 centers in the United States, Guam, Puerto Rico, and the U.S. Virgin Islands, with nearly 1,000 service locations located at colleges, universities, community colleges, vocational schools, chambers of commerce, and economic development corporations. The SBA Web page is at `www.sbaonline.sba.gov/sbdc/`.

You have a host of issues (which we address in Chapter 5) to consider in writing your business plan. As you begin the process, you need to keep a few issues in the front of your mind:

✔ Conduct market research to find out whether the product or service you want to sell is in demand. The folks at SCORE and the SBDCs are good places to start. Some college and university business departments also can provide you with low-cost or even no-cost research assistance. And don't forget the Web. That's where the pros go for solid third-party information.

✔ Consider your pricing structures — can you get a reasonable rate of return in sales after accounting for inventory, rent, payroll, advertising, and insurance?

✔ Have you developed good strategic working relationships with local banking institutions?

Meet with your local office of the U.S. Small Business Administration (you can find the number in your telephone directory or at its Web site at `www.sba.gov`) and discuss your ideas with a counselor.

Becoming a franchisee

Becoming a franchisee, with a solid franchisor, removes much of the guesswork of running a business, along with most of the mistakes that independent start-ups make. That's part of what you're buying when you purchase a franchise from a mature franchise system: a proven system of operation with the kinks already worked out for you.

But which franchise system should you invest in? Don't ask us — we're not you. All we can do is provide you with the tools, give you some advice on the process, and hopefully steer you away from some of the dead ends. Research is the single most important activity in making your franchise investment decision — and you're the one who has to do it. We can give you the guidelines, the questions to ask, and the bases to cover, but in the end, you must put in the time, get the information, assess it, reassess it, and make an informed decision. Without adequate information, you may end up making the most costly decision of your life.

Avoiding Franchise Brokers

Franchise brokers are individuals or companies that offer to help you find the franchise that's "right for you." Some of the companies providing these services even offer psychological testing to help you make the right decision. Most of them don't even charge you a fee; they usually get their fees from the franchisor you select. They typically receive a percentage of the initial franchise fee or a percentage of the money you pay the franchisor after you become a franchisee (the continuing royalty payment).

Although there are good and competent brokers, the problem we have with many brokers is that they often only recommend franchisors from their list of clients. Are you surprised? This arrangement is not a multiple listing service, such as residential real estate. But, like residential real estate agents, franchise brokers (no matter how friendly, polite, and helpful they may seem and no matter how impressive their client list) usually work for the franchisor, not you. Little wonder that the right franchise for you — and the one that fits your psychological profile — just may happen to be one of the franchise broker's clients.

No matter how elaborate the process seems to be, using a broker tends to reduce your search, and we believe that it provides little, if any, value. Using a broker may also increase your pressure to buy. It's sort of like using a marriage broker to find you the perfect spouse. Remember, you're making a life-changing decision; don't look for shortcuts. Do the legwork yourself. If you think that you need outside expertise, hire a professional advisor, such as an accountant, an attorney, or a reputable franchise–consulting firm to help you in the process. (We cover finding professional advisors in Chapter 6.)

Finding Good Sources of Information about Available Franchises

Choosing and buying the right franchise takes time, money, and lots of information.

We have found that the best way to gather information is to make lists of questions, write down answers, and set up a method for cross-referencing and cross-checking facts as you proceed. Ask detailed follow-up questions. For example, the franchisor says they provide three weeks of training. "Gee," you say, "that's a lot." However, unless you find out what's included in the curriculum and who's training you, you may simply be working the service counter at a franchisor's company-owned location for 21 days. Or perhaps the franchisor says they have a fully qualified field staff assigned to work with you. Unless you ask, that fully qualified field staff may be a new hire and may visit you only twice a year — possibly only by telephone.

For each franchise system you consider, write down the names of the people you talk with. Jot down the information they tell you so that you begin building a body of information that eventually gives you a pretty clear picture of the business you're considering. In Appendix A, we provide a workbook that you can use in making your franchise decision. The *Making the Franchise Decision* workbook is a simple tool to guide you through some of the key issues you need to evaluate and a way for you to keep track of the information. If you've ever bought a house, you may remember that by the third house you saw, you probably could not remember which house had the big kitchen and which needed the new roof. Selecting a franchise is pretty similar. The workbook helps to remind you which franchise system was the one with the great training program and operating system and which was the one with the 30-page operations manual.

Okay, so where is all this research and information? Fortunately, you can choose from many different ways to get the goods on franchising. Many sources are in print, others are in the form of trade shows, and the newest player in the franchise sales game is the Internet. Don't forget the franchisees in the systems, either. They know firsthand what is working in their system and what is not. Each source of information is worthwhile, but in order to get a complete picture of the franchises you're investigating, we suggest that you take advantage of every resource you can find.

Directories

There are several franchise directories that list most of the franchise companies currently offering franchises. This is the best place to begin your examination because they give you a capsule of information on each company listed.

Just because a franchisor is in one of the directories doesn't mean that the information is complete or accurate. Many of the directories do not independently verify the information the franchisor provides. This is the starting place for your examination. It's the place to get very basic information, such as who is offering franchises today and what industries may interest you. We discuss later in this chapter how to fine-tune the information so that you get a more accurate picture before you invest.

> ✔ *The Franchise Opportunities Guide*, published semiannually by the International Franchise Association, lists the trade association's member companies and nonmember companies, franchise lawyers, consultants, and other suppliers, as well as descriptive sections on franchise statistics, other publications, and educational affiliates. In addition, the publication

contains helpful articles written by professionals in the industry. The cost is $15.00 plus shipping and handling, and you can order the guide by contacting the International Franchise Association at 800-543-1038 or through their Web site at www.franchise.org. This is a particularly good source of information because the members of the IFA tend to be the strongest franchisors in the industry.

✔ Franchise Update Publications publishes a variety of franchise guides, including *The Executives' Guide to Franchise Opportunities, Food Service Guide to Franchise Opportunities,* and *The Guide to Multiple-Unit Franchise Opportunities.* They also publish *Franchise Update Magazine,* a leading trade and management publication targeted to the professionals in the industry. For franchisors, franchise attorneys, and franchise consultants, Franchise Update's publications are a must-read. Prices vary, so contact Franchise Update directly for pricing and ordering information by calling 408-997-7796 or at their Web site at www.Franchise-Update.com.

✔ *Bond's Franchise Guide,* published by Robert Bond, is updated annually and offers a comprehensive listing of franchise companies operating in the United States and Canada. There are detailed profiles of more than 1,000 franchisors listed by name, address, and contact person. They also have a number of other useful books: *How Much Can I Make?* (a compendium of earnings claims included by franchisors in the UFOC — the disclosure document that franchisors are required to provide to prospective franchisees) and *The International Herald Tribune International Franchise Guide.* The cost for *Bond's Franchise Guide* is $29.95, and you can order by calling 800-841-0873 or through their Web site at www.worldfranchising.com.

✔ *The Franchise Annual,* published by Info Press, is updated annually and contains another listing of franchisors. The listing provides the corporate address, contact person and phone number, and a brief description of the business with related investment and fees. The cost is $39.95, and you can order the listing by calling 716-754-4669 or through their Web site at www.infonews.com/franchise.

✔ The *Franchise Handbook* is a quarterly directory of companies currently franchising, along with key information about them; it also offers articles, success stories, and so on. The cost is $22.95, and you can order the handbook by calling 414-272-9977 or through their Web site at www.franchise1.com.

✔ The *International Herald Tribune International Franchise Guide,* published by Source Book Publications, updated annually, is a guide to international franchising. The guide lists franchisors that are offering franchises internationally. The cost is $34.95, and you can order the guide by calling 510-839-5471 or through their Web site at www.franchiseintl.com.

Consumer business publications

Several magazines and newspapers regularly publish franchising-related sections that contain articles and advertising on franchising:

- ✔ *Inc.:* www.inc.com
- ✔ *Entrepreneur:* www.entrepreneurmag.com
- ✔ *Franchise Times:* www.franchisetimes.com
- ✔ *Franchising World:* www.franchise.org
- ✔ *Franchise Update:* www.franchise-update.com
- ✔ *USA Today:* www.usatoday.com
- ✔ *The Wall Street Journal:* www.wsj.com
- ✔ *The New York Times:* www.nytimes.com

Trade shows and expositions

Trade shows and expositions give you an opportunity to meet face-to-face with representatives of many franchise companies at one time. The International Franchise Association (IFA) sponsors the International Franchise Expo.

The IFE is the largest gathering in the world of franchise companies actively seeking new franchisees. These gatherings are also a great place to educate yourself because some of the top professionals in the industry present full-day educational programs on franchising. For information on when and where the next Franchise Expo will be held, call or write to IFA for a show schedule. The IFA is located at 1350 New York Avenue, NW, Suite 900, Washington, DC, 20005-4709; telephone 202-628-8000; Web site www.franchise.org.

Another good starting point that we recommend for people who are looking into franchising for the first time is the U.S. Small Business Administration. They sponsor a host of seminars on franchising through regional Small Business Development Centers (SBDCs). Most SBDCs are located on a college or university campus, and college professors who are well versed in small business start-up information teach the seminars. You usually have to pay a small fee to attend. Check with your local colleges or touch base with your regional SBA office for a schedule of courses. Outside the United States, call the National Association (see Chapter 17). They can give you information on courses and programs offered locally.

A host of regional trade shows occur throughout the year in different parts of the United States. Some of these shows combine franchises and business opportunities. At trade shows, the franchisor usually offers a sense of the business on the exposition floor. You have a chance to ask a company representative questions and, if you're interested, to give some information about yourself as a step toward further discussions.

Trade shows are a wonderful source for brochures on franchise opportunities. Most franchisors give you their brochure and then follow up later by telephone or in writing. Some franchisors even hold seminars (often called *discovery days*) at the show on their franchise and may give you a copy of their Uniform Franchise Offering Circular (UFOC). The UFOC is the disclosure document provided by franchisors to prospective franchisees. It contains a wealth of information on the franchisor. We discuss the UFOC in Chapter 6.

Don't be surprised if they ask you to sign a receipt for the UFOC they give you. They are not only trying to keep track of whom they give the books to so that they can get back to them later. Franchisors are required to keep track of *when* they gave you their UFOC so that they don't potentially sign a franchise agreement with you before the mandated ten-business day cooling-off period. That would be a violation of franchise regulations.

Franchisors like trade shows because the shows give them a chance to strut their stuff, as well as do some on-site prequalification of interested parties. So don't be surprised if they ask you as many questions as you're asking. Good franchisors want to know as much about you as possible as quickly as possible, so no one ends up wasting anyone else's time.

Finally, under no circumstances do you actually *buy* a franchise at a trade show. There are rules about the offer and sale of franchises, and one of those rules requires that the franchisor give you a copy of its UFOC and give you time to review the information. (See Chapter 6 for a discussion of the UFOC.) The franchisor can't legally sell you a franchise — even if you want one — at the trade show. Trade shows are simply another tool for you to use in your research.

The Internet

The Internet is quickly becoming a showcase for franchise companies and can be a useful avenue of basic information. Many companies have their own Web site and list their Web site's address in their advertisements and their franchise brochures or, if they are members of the IFA, on the IFA's Web page, with links to their own Web sites. Most of the companies also are included on various Internet search engines.

The basic categories of information on most Web sites are company histories, press releases, their analysis of their particular industry, management

Will it pass the test of time?

There isn't a single franchise brochure, Web site, or advertisement that's going to say, "We're part of a new fad that may only last a few months." Every franchisor you meet will tell you their opportunity is based on solid market demand that will continue well into Y3K.

Take a close look at the industry. What's the track record for franchisors and non-franchisors? What does the business press say about the future? What impact will technology likely have on consumer demand?

Remember the days when automobiles needed a tune-up every 15,000 miles? Now that many cars need a tune-up every 100,000 miles, we bet the single-service tune-up franchisees are remembering the good old days.

Look at how e-commerce on the Internet is changing how people make their buying decisions. Franchisors that used to offer education programs for children exclusively from fixed locations are now seeing new competitors popping up that offer the same or similar service on the Web. Many of these companies are adapting by adding Internet-based programs.

In Economics 101, they tell you that the weakness of a "banana republic" (a country, not the company) is that they only have one product to offer. When consumer tastes change, or technology makes the product less of a requirement or less attractive, these economies suffer. They have nothing else to sell. It's the same for single-product franchise systems — but worse. Even if the demand for a single-product franchise system's products stays strong, other companies often add the product to their offerings and strip from those companies their major strength — uniqueness. That's what happened to the frozen yogurt industry in the '80s and '90s as ice cream chains and quick-service restaurants added yogurt to their menus.

Look at the companies in the industry you're researching. Have they added new products and services or changed the way they deliver products and services to consumers to ensure that customers will continue to come into their franchisee's doors, or is their location design about as old and out of date as the products and services they sell? What have the historic sales trends been? How are current sales? Are they increasing? Is the company taking advantage of the opportunities e-commerce may provide the system?

Is the company focused on going international, or are they focused on supporting existing domestic franchisees? The hype of international expansion often strips resources from smaller, less-developed franchisors, resources that used to be applied to their domestic operators. This is increasingly a problem.

It's becoming increasingly difficult, during good economic times, to find workers willing to take entry-level positions. Having an available labor force is important.

Have you noticed all of the "help wanted" signs lately? It wasn't that long ago that those entry-level jobs were filled as fast at they opened up. Not today. With a booming economy, every company is hurting for personnel to fill its ranks. If the franchise requires a large pool of entry-level labor, will they be available — in your market — at a rate of pay that the franchise can afford? Even the best system, with the greatest demand, can't operate unless people are available to service its customers. Make certain you will be able to find employees in your market who are willing to work for you at the rate of pay you will be able to afford. We discuss hiring and other staffing issues in Chapter 12.

structure, number of franchised locations, an explanation of their concept, and where to go for more information.

You can use the Web sites to directly communicate with the franchise sales department for more specific questions. Many of the franchisor's Web sites even allow you to complete an application online that can speed up the process of getting additional information or allow you to set up an appointment to visit the franchisor at its headquarters.

Deciding Whether to Buy an Established Franchise or Open a New Location

Suppose you've narrowed your choice to one industry, and within that industry you've further narrowed your choice to one or two franchise opportunities. One franchise company offers brand new store locations only. The other offers new locations but also a selection of existing franchises. What do you do — buy new or used?

Buying an existing franchise

Franchise companies often have existing company-owned locations for sale or keep a list of franchisees that are looking to sell their franchises.

Buying an existing operation from the company or from a franchisee may offer advantages over starting from scratch. You are not evaluating a potential business, but one that is already up and running. It has a history of performance, a reputation in the community, and an existing clientele. You know what the historic profit and cash flow has been and what the trends are for that store. The site is fully developed, and you avoid the burden of looking for a location, negotiating a lease, hiring a contractor, and building and equipping the location. See Chapter 8 for a discussion about establishing a location. The operation may have a trained staff, so you can avoid the hassle of having to immediately recruit new employees and train them before you service your first customer. You can be in business months sooner than if you start the franchise from scratch.

From a franchisor's perspective, your buying an existing location makes sense, too. They may have made a strategic decision not to operate a company-owned store at that location and are looking for a franchisee to buy it. They may have had problems finding people to work for them or could not find a good manager to operate the business and are hoping that a franchisee can do the job better. However, and this unfortunately happens, the store may be a dog that they took back from a failed franchisee and are looking to move quickly — we call that *churning*.

As we discuss in Chapter 6, not every franchisor provides unit financial information to prospective franchisees before they invest in a franchise. Even those franchisors that do not do so are allowed to provide potential franchisees with information on specific, company-owned locations they have up for sale. If you are interested in an existing company-owned location, make sure that you get the financial information about that location.

Franchisors also benefit from franchisees selling their franchises to new franchisees. First, if the existing franchisee is unhappy, getting a new franchisee with new franchisee enthusiasm is a good swap. Second, franchisors typically require new franchisees to sign the then-current franchise agreement. This allows them to alter the terms of the franchise for that location sooner than they probably would have if the franchisee stayed and operated under the old contract. Third, it establishes a selling price for individual locations. If franchises are selling at a high price, that news will get out quickly, and this will increase franchisors' ability to sell new franchises.

Note that we left out the collection of a transfer fee as a benefit to the franchisor. Most franchisors charge a fee for the transfer of an existing location. This fee is usually a percentage of the existing franchise fee or a set amount. Although franchisors do not have to incur the costs of recruiting the new franchisee or helping them find the site, they still incur the cost of evaluating the new franchisee and bringing them up to speed through training and other new franchisee support costs. There are also legal costs associated with transferring a franchise. If the franchisor earns any profit on the transfer fee, it's usually negligible.

Before you buy an existing operation, do some digging for information. Find out why the owner wants to sell. Did the market dry up? Is the location no longer desirable? Did the owner simply want to move on to other things? Is the owner retiring? Look at the store location as if you were starting fresh.

If the business is on the decline for any reason, then buyer beware. Don't assume that you're smarter or a better operator than the existing or previous owner.

Don't assume that just because you're buying a franchise, you have a full term, with renewals available to you. Some franchisors only allow the transfer of franchises with the remaining term of the agreement. Others give you a full term plus renewals. Make sure that you understand not only the business you are buying, but also the franchise you are buying.

The Business Resale Network is a resale network of existing franchises and non-franchises run by *Franchise Update* and *Entrepreneur*. Their Web site contains a database of thousands of businesses for sale and also provides valuable information for the business buyer. You can reach the Business Resale Network on the Web at `www.br-network.com`.

Starting from scratch

Most new franchisees enter franchising by buying a franchise and opening a new location. You get help from the franchisor with site selection, store construction, signage, inventory, grand-opening events, training, and ongoing support during the start-up phase of the business.

The helping hand may seem to be there, but be sure to do some extra pre-buy research to discover the quality of that helping hand.

Take the trip — it's worth it

Ever think about buying a house without seeing it first? How about getting married without meeting your future spouse? When junior went off to college, did you just hope that the school had everything the glossy brochure told you it had, or did you get in the car, board the bus, or hop on a plane and see it firsthand?

Franchising is no different. You need to see the franchisor's headquarters, meet their staff, and evaluate their capacity to deliver the services they promise.

Before the franchisor invites you to visit their headquarters, they will probably have done some preliminary research on you. Most require you to complete a preliminary application that provides them with information on who you are, your background, your employment and education history, and your financial capabilities. Some franchisors run credit checks to verify your finances, as well as criminal background and litigation checks. Good franchisors are as careful in selecting who they award franchises to as good franchise prospects are in selecting which franchise to buy.

Some franchisors may invite you to a one-on-one tour of their headquarters; others may invite you to a group session — called a discovery day — where you have the opportunity to meet with the franchisor and maybe other prospective franchisees. Whichever format you experience, this is the time to get to know the people and the organization that will be your support team. Don't be bashful about your questions. Like your grade school teachers told you: The only stupid question is an unasked question.

During your discovery day, the franchisor may take you on a tour of its stores. Plan some extra time before the program begins so that after it's over you can go see some of the stores that aren't on the tour.

Use the questions in Appendix A as a starting place for evaluating a franchisor.

When professionals in the franchise industry get together and socialize at educational and trade functions, we often talk shop. Who's doing what and when, what's working and what's not. Almost always, somewhere between the first beer and the end of the night, someone uses the phrase "passing the mirror test." Passing the mirror test refers to franchisors that have only two criteria for selecting their franchisees: One, the prospect's check clears and two, the prospect is breathing — and can fog the mirror. It's not a badge of honor to be considered a franchisor in this category. (Some franchisors don't even meet their franchisees face-to-face until they get to training. Their only requirement is the check clearing. We won't even think about what their standards are.) If your franchisor doesn't insist that you visit with them at their headquarters or their regional support centers, beware. If they don't care how well you are going to do as a franchisee, how much care do you figure they took in selecting the other franchisees in the system that will be sharing the brand with you? Making the trip to the franchisor's headquarters may look expensive, especially if you're looking at several franchisors. But it's essential.

If you're married or are going to operate the franchise with a partner, bring him or her along. It's important that your family and partners get to know the franchisor. It also shows the franchisor that you're taking the visit seriously.

Expect to receive a copy of the franchisor's UFOC (disclosure document) if you don't already have one. Also expect to be asked to sign a receipt. Franchise rules require the franchisor to provide you a copy of their UFOC at the first meeting to discuss the sale of a franchise.

Back home — looking at locations

From your research and from the information you receive visiting the franchisor, you should start to get a sense of what type of location you need. If you're set on opening up a franchise in your hometown, you need to make sure that the appropriate real estate is available.

Conduct some preliminary market research. Most franchisors have fairly sophisticated support mechanisms that will assist you later, but you need to know some things before you make the decision to become a franchisee.

Get an idea of the traffic patterns around the sites that you feel meet your needs. Call the city zoning board and planning commissions to get a heads up on future road developments or other significant real estate plans for the area that may end up cutting into your customer base. Check with other merchants who have a customer base similar to the franchise business you're considering and determine whether you have the right traffic at that location. For example, if you're looking at a franchise that markets upscale women's hair care, check with other merchants who sell products to a similar clientele, such as better women's dress shops. This research can give you a good indication of a site's future performance potential.

Don't sign a lease or buy a location for your future franchise just yet. In all likelihood, your franchisor will have to approve the location before you sign the lease.

Get the facts straight from those who know — the franchisees already in the system

Talk to other franchisees in the system and find out exactly how much support they received from the franchisor's home office when they first opened their stores. You're trying to eliminate any surprises down the road. Did the franchisor deliver on the promised support before, during, and after the opening? What about the basic training — was it adequate, or did the franchisees feel they needed more training before opening their doors? How was the sales performance for the first six months of the business? For the first 18 months?

A list of franchisees is provided in the UFOC. Call as many of them as you need until you're satisfied that all your questions have been answered. Call some of the former franchisees listed in the UFOC, as well. Remember that they may have left on a less than positive basis, so you may have to filter what they say. But if they all have the same story to tell, it will be a worthwhile investment of your time. If you are purchasing a franchise outside the United States and your franchisor is not required to give you a list of franchisees in the system, ask for one. You can also speak to an existing franchisee in the system and see if he or she has a list of franchisees you can copy.

The franchisees you call are not obligated to talk to you or give you any information. Even the ones who are willing to give you the information may be too busy running their business to spend the time to chat. Ask them if this is a good time. If it isn't, see if there is a better time to speak on the phone or come to their location and visit with them. They probably get calls all the time about the franchise, so be honest with them about why you are calling. For many of them, it will not have been that long ago that they were making the same calls to other franchisees.

Don't be bashful in the questions you ask. All they can say is no. Ask them about the required investment — especially the working capital. The franchisor will provide you with an estimate of the total initial investment in the UFOC; ask how close it is to reality. Did it take three months, six months, two years or longer to begin making a profit? When were they able to take a salary from the business?

We aren't including every question you should ask here — we just want to get you started. The checklist in Appendix A gives you more.

Going to work

There is a simple and effective way to find out if a franchise is right for you. Try to get permission to work at a location for a while just to see if you like the business. Your investment is your time, and what's three or four weeks if it shows you that you love — or hate — the business?

Nothing can substitute for good, old-fashioned research when you're looking into a particular franchise. Research means getting past the sales hype and getting at the systems, manuals, training programs, headquarters and field support, advertising, and financials. You must also talk to other franchisees in the system.

Most good franchisors stand ready to share this information. They want franchisees who have done their homework and are making informed decisions. That's why spending a few weeks in a franchised operation *before* signing the contract is a good way to find out whether you and the franchise were meant to be together. Words and numbers are fine, but you need to actually get into the business and try it on for size.

A Final Word

A lot of preliminary steps go into making the decision to enter franchising. Each step is important, and each step takes time to complete. But the combined result is worth your efforts. You're investing in yourself, your future, and your level of satisfaction with your life. Taking the time on the front end of the process means achieving the best possible result when the moment arrives to fish or cut bait.

You have a lot of work to do and decisions to make before you select a franchise:

- Decide whether you should become a franchisee or start your own independent business.
- If you want to become a franchisee, do your own research — don't use a franchise broker.
- Learn as much as you can about what franchises are available:
  - Read directories.
  - Read articles in the business publications and look at the ads for franchisors that are offering franchises.

> • Attend trade shows and expositions in your city. Consider going to one of the large shows sponsored by the International Franchise Association.
>
> • Research franchise opportunities on the World Wide Web.

✔ Select the type of franchise that's right for you.

✔ Make sure that, after you invest in the business, you will still have reserves to get you through the early times before the business starts to make a profit.

✔ Don't overestimate how much you can make. Running a franchise is hard work, and there's no guarantee that you'll strike it rich quickly. The road to riches is usually slow.

✔ Make sure that the company has a history of growth and is a good prospect for future growth.

✔ Decide whether you want to invest in starting a new business or whether an existing location is available for purchase.

✔ Don't make a decision on any franchisor before you visit its headquarters and meet the support team.

✔ Review the operations manuals and see whether you can sit in on a training class.

✔ Don't make an emotional decision. Ask questions, do your research, and get advice from professionals and businesspeople you respect.

✔ Review whether locations that are right for the franchise are available in the market in which you want to start your business. But don't sign a lease until the franchisor approves the site.

✔ Make sure that you will be able to hire the required workers at a rate you can afford in your market.

✔ Call and visit as many franchises as you can to get information from franchisees who are currently in the system.

✔ Contact franchisees who have left the business and find out why they left.

✔ Go to work in an existing location — preferably more than one.

✔ Get a copy of the company's disclosure document and franchise agreement. Read it and make sure that you understand what you're being asked to sign.

✔ Before you make a final decision, make sure that you have proper help from professionals. (We discuss whom to talk to in Chapter 6.) Be certain that your advisors (consultants and attorneys) are experienced in franchising.

Chapter 5

Raising Capital: Wowing, Wrangling, and Winning

. . . .

In This Chapter

▶ Taking a look at your current finances

▶ Determining what a franchise is going to cost

▶ Raising the money to buy a franchise

. . . .

*T*his chapter is where you begin to feel the financial reality of franchise ownership. When you decide to buy a franchise, you have to come up with the money, or the deal won't fly. You need to determine whether you have the funds to buy a franchise and to support yourself and contribute to the support of your family (if you have one) for the first year or two of start-up.

This chapter is devoted to the process of finding financing and getting a realistic picture of whether you can afford to become a franchisee. So sharpen your pencil, get out your calculator, and go digging for dollars.

Examining Your Current Finances

Putting pen to paper and taking a good, hard look at your finances can be sobering. You may be tempted to cut corners and gloss over the realities of your financial picture, but having enough capital to get off the ground is not just important; it's vital. If you're heaving a heavy sigh right now, think about this statistical truth: The single most common reason new franchisees fail is that they didn't have enough money going into the investment.

We didn't make up this statistic. The U.S. Small Business Administration and a host of banks and lending institutions have tracked franchisee loan failures for years. Their combined findings show that when franchisees fail, the cause is often that the franchisee was financially stretched during the critical start-up phase of the business.

You won't know whether you have enough money until you start examining your finances. Use an organized approach to your research; make lists of information as you go along. Just to get your financial juices flowing, answer the following questions. This isn't a test and there are no right and wrong answers. It should help you in determining what your resources are, where you can get some help, and the reality of your ability to make a franchise investment.

- ✔ How much cash do I have to invest?
- ✔ What liquid investments do I have, and how much are they worth?
- ✔ What is the equity in my home, and how much can I get from a second mortgage?
- ✔ How much money can I afford to lose?
- ✔ How much money am I willing to lose?
- ✔ Do I want to purchase the franchise by myself or with partners?
- ✔ If I have a partner, can the business I select support more than one family?
- ✔ If I need financing, where do I go?
- ✔ Can I borrow from friends and family?
- ✔ Do I have a good relationship with my bank?
- ✔ Do I have a good credit rating?
- ✔ Can I live off of my spouse's income while I get the business off the ground?
- ✔ Do I need to buy land and construct a building, or will I be leasing space?
- ✔ Does the franchisor provide any financing or leasing programs? If so, how does that option change my investment decisions?

These are the types of initial personal financing questions you have to ask.

Asking for proof of expertise

In the 1960s, I was a franchisee with Kentucky Fried Chicken. I was looking for a loan to remodel our restaurants. I couldn't find a single financial advisor willing to talk with me. After we started having some success, and especially after I started Wendy's, lots of financial advisors wanted to offer me advice on how they could make me more money.

So I developed a rule: When an advisor came to me with a plan, I'd ask to see his or her balance sheet. If the balance sheet was better than mine, I'd listen to the advice. Most of these advisors don't have money but are willing to tell me how to spend mine.

Finding Out What a Franchise Is Really Going to Cost

Opening up a business costs money whether you go it alone as an independent or as a member of a franchise system. Having enough money to get the business up and running and through the period when it stops acting like a cash sponge and begins to support itself is not only important, it's life or death for a small businessperson who's just starting out.

If the only benefit you received from joining a franchise system was an accurate estimate of the costs of developing the business, sources for equipment and suppliers, and the knowledge of how much working capital you needed until the business could support itself, the investment in a franchise might still be worthwhile. This is where an experienced and mature franchise system is worth its weight in gold to a new franchisee.

Franchisors reduce your time and costs on the learning curve. Without a franchisor, for example, you must research equipment options, work with designers on decor packages, research which vendors to use, and so on. Franchising succeeds because the details you may not even think of have already been taken care of. In the franchisor's UFOC (the disclosure document), they provide you with a list of start-up expenses that will make up your initial investment. Regardless of whether you are going to open up a franchise or start an independent business, the following list will give you an indication of the costs.

- ✔ **Finding the right location:** The seller or the landlord usually pays the real estate agent who helps you find the right location. But what about the other costs, such as your time and travel expenses and the costs of obtaining market data, including demographics, traffic studies, and local competitive analysis? These little tidbits can add up because it's likely that the first site you look at won't be the only site you'll need to evaluate. Most mature franchise systems are able to help you in this area, as they often subscribe to outside services that provide them with this information.

- ✔ **Real property and occupancy charges:** If you're going to lease a location, expect the landlord to ask for a security deposit when you sign the lease. If you're buying, add the cost of the land. Don't forget deposits for utility companies and business licenses, either.

- ✔ **Civil and architectural drawings and professional fees:** If you're starting out on your own, you need to develop plans for your location. Even as a franchisee, you need to hire an architect or civil engineer to modify those standard plans to fit your site, although the franchisor will usually provide a set of standard architectural plans. The cost of those revisions, by the way, differ from location to location depending on the changes you need to make and those required by the local municipalities.

✔ **Zoning expenses:** If your dream site is not zoned for your type of business, get ready to spend some money on requesting a zoning variance. Doing so usually requires you to pay fees to the zoning board that considers your request, as well as to the professional who represents you. A rezoning request takes time, and that, in turn, adds cost.

It's starting to add up, and you haven't even dug the foundation!

✔ **Finding a contractor:** Sure, the contractor will work for you and will bid on the job — what cost could you incur in finding a contractor? How about the development of the bid book, initial drawings, equipment lists, professionals to help you put it all together — and don't forget your time. It adds up.

✔ **Improvements and construction:** Now the big-ticket items start. You will need to construct the building and make improvements to the land or, if you're renting, make changes and improvements to your leased location.

✔ **Landscaping:** Someone has to plant those flowers and trees. And you need to install sprinklers to keep the garden green.

✔ **Equipment and fixtures:** Tables, chairs, office equipment, kitchen equipment, trucks, playground equipment (popular in some quick-service restaurants), telephone systems, counters, computer hardware and software, cash registers, and inventory control systems. You have to either purchase or lease whatever you need to operate the business of your choice.

✔ **Decor packages and signage:** Don't forget the lights, signage, pictures, and all the other items you must buy to decorate your location.

✔ **Opening inventory:** Your opening inventory is not just the merchandise you will sell. You need to buy the ingredients and raw materials you will use in making your products. You also need to buy paper goods, office supplies, janitorial supplies, and so on.

✔ **Freight and sales tax:** Much of what will be delivered to your location will come via common carrier. Guess what? Freight is often extra, and sales tax is charged on almost everything you need.

✔ **Insurance:** You need to purchase workers' compensation insurance; liability, property, and casualty insurance; auto insurance; and so on. Depending on your insurance carrier, you may need to pay your first year's premium in advance; if you're lucky, you'll need to make only a deposit.

✔ **Pre-opening labor:** Before you even open your doors, you must pay your manager and staff. Your employees will help you set up and will need to learn how to run the business before that first customer comes in. If you're a franchisee, you may need to send them, and yourself, to training — but we discuss that later in Chapter 12.

✔ **Professional fees:** In addition to your architect and the professionals you hire to help you get through that zoning matter, you need the services of an attorney to help you negotiate your lease and do all the legal work required to set up a business. You also need an accountant to help you set up your books and records.

✔ **Working capital:** Working capital is the amount of money you need to support your ongoing expenses to the extent that they are not covered by your *revenue* (the money your business brings in). Depending on your business, you may need as little as two or three months or as much as two or three years of working capital.

If you're an independent business owner, you and your accountant had better ensure that your estimate of working capital is sufficient to get you through the early days. If you're a franchisee, your franchisor will provide you with an estimate based on experience.

You have to remember when planning for your initial investment that projections — especially when it comes to working capital — are not a guarantee of what you will actually need. They are educated guesses based upon the best facts you have available at the time.

I give this advice about projections to my clients: Projections are based on assumptions about events that haven't happened yet. Even if all your assumptions come true — and they won't — there will usually be differences between the projected and the actual results, and those differences are almost always material. Expect the worst. It's better to be prepared.

In the early days, I would look for the worst-case scenario — that was my downside — if I could live with the downside and feel good about taking the risk. I knew if I made money that I could live with the upside.

Franchise fees

A *franchise fee* is the price of admission to the game, but not the price to suit up and play. That's extra. The franchise fee is the amount you pay the franchisor to offset the franchisor's cost of locating, screening, negotiating with, and training you. It may also cover the costs involved in site selection and development, promotions, grand opening events, and ongoing support during your first months of operation.

Franchise fees vary, depending on the franchisor. They can range from $0 (which is very unusual) to more than $100,000. The franchise fee for most franchisors is between $20,000 and $25,000. Rupert Barkoff, partner at Kilpatrick Stockton in Atlanta, Georgia, offers this advice: "When comparison shopping, pay particular attention to what services you will receive for your franchise fee and what other necessary services have separate charges. The lowest, most appealing franchise fee may not be the best value."

Training costs

Although the cost of tuition for initial training is usually included in your franchise fee, you'll probably have to pay for airfare, hotel accommodations, local transportation, food, salaries, and employment benefits for yourself and your staff who attend training. This is on top of any salary you will lose from your current job while you attend training.

Start-up costs

Total start-up costs vary dramatically, depending on the franchise you select. They can be as low as $20,000 or less, and as high as $1 million. A typical investment for a single-unit franchisee is usually in the $100,000 to $300,000 range, including the franchise fee and all start-up costs. The average investment you need to make is detailed in the franchisor's disclosure document. For more information about the disclosure document, see Chapter 6.

Most franchisors want to see a liquid (read *cash*) capital investment of 35 to 50 percent of the total franchise cost (that's the franchise fee plus all start-up costs). They want to make sure that you have enough money, not only to get started but also to pay your bills, including any principal and interest payments on your loans.

One reason start-up costs may vary dramatically relates to whether it's necessary to own or lease real estate to operate the business. Fixed-based franchises, requiring bricks and mortar, almost always cost more than, for example, a franchise operating from a van or over the Internet.

Raising the Capital: What It's Going to Take

You usually pull together all the financial resources you need to get into business by combining your savings, the collateral in your home, bank financing, loans from family and friends, and possibly money from outside investors. You can cut your overall initial cash requirements by leasing your real estate and equipment rather than purchasing it.

Some franchisors offer a menu of other financing strategies to ease the financial bite. Although not every franchisor makes these benefits available, it doesn't hurt to ask. Here are a few examples of alternative financing strategies:

- ✔ **Deferred payments on your total franchise fee until after you're open for business.** The terms of the deferral can be a few months or sometimes a few years.

- ✔ **Your out-of-pocket costs for training (except salaries and benefits) included in your initial franchise fee.**

- ✔ **A lease from the franchisor on the land and/or buildings.**

- ✔ **Joint ventures between you and the franchisor.** This is when you and the franchisor share in the investment and return on the business — like a partnership.

- ✔ **Supplier financing.** Some equipment manufacturers offer new businesses — especially franchisees — financing on the equipment you buy from them.

- ✔ **Credit systems.** Corporate employees who want to be franchisees can apply profit-sharing credits toward the franchise fee.

- ✔ **Reduced franchise fees for corporate employees who want to become franchisees.** This is a great employment benefit. It gives the employee an opportunity to invest in a franchise at a lower cost and provides the franchisor with a new franchisee who probably knows the system and with whom the franchisor already has a relationship.

Franchisors often establish relationships with a group of approved lenders who are familiar with the business and will provide funding to qualified franchisees. On occasion, the franchisor may act as a guarantor of the franchisee's loans. Sometimes the franchisor provides the loans directly.

Recently, the Small Business Administration set up a program called the Franchise Registry. This registry lists names of franchise companies whose franchisees can get a streamlined review process for SBA loan applications. The SBA has already reviewed the franchise agreements for those franchisors, and prospective franchisees in those systems can get an expedited review of their loan applications. You can review information about the Franchise Registry on the Web at www.franchiseregistry.com.

Avoiding debt

Everyone aspires to avoid debt, but most people deal with it on a regular basis. Going into debt to buy a franchise should not be taken lightly. Before you put your retirement fund on the line or refinance your home, look at a few ways to raise cash in order to minimize your debt:

- ✔ Use money that you've put aside for a future project or a second home.

- ✔ Ask family and friends; they already know and trust you. They may want some equity in the business.

Keep in mind that family and friends are often more intrusive than professional lenders; also, there's a real chance of hard feelings if the investment doesn't go well.

✔ Consider bringing in a partner who can offer money up front or on a continuing basis.

✔ Sell your boat, cabin, second house, scuba gear, RV, jewelry, or any other toy or collectable you don't use.

Don't consider the following sources unless you live on the edge and like added risk:

✔ Don't use your credit cards to get ready cash. Interest rates are too high, and you can run up your credit limit and get into financial difficulty too easily.

✔ Don't use your 401(k), IRA, retirement funds, health-care accounts, life insurance policies, or college funds to start up a franchise. These accounts are for protecting your future and for your children's education.

Creating a business plan

Regardless of where you ask for money (your local bank or your Aunt Edith and Uncle Fred), anyone providing you with funds will want to know something about your business and how you plan to operate it. In other words, they'll want to see a business plan. *You* should want to have a business plan, too.

Think of a business plan as a road map. It gives you and your lender the lay of the land, some directions, and an idea of where your business is headed. You are the mapmaker and the tour guide. You're responsible for helping your lender see the destination and how you plan to get there. Don't fake any of the information — especially the numbers. Lenders and investors hate surprises.

Keep in mind that a business plan may be a pain to write, but it forces you to focus on setting goals and figuring out how to reach them. Take your time and don't be afraid to rewrite. You can be optimistic, but only if your optimism is based on reality.

The best business plan is a living document — meaning that you continually update it. It also is creative, reflects your enthusiasm, and carries solid information.

Among other details, a business plan defines the reasons you need financing, the way you're going to spend the money, and the method you'll use to repay it. It should explain to the reader everything about your location and how you intend to operate it. If you believe that your location will be better than the average location in your franchise system, let the reader know why you think so. Have facts available to support your assumptions.

Your franchisor should be able to assist you with information specific to the business. If you hire an attorney and/or an accountant, ask him or her for input, too. Many, but not all, are used to preparing business plans and can offer valuable advice.

After you have a plan, follow it — don't file it away. Update it as you learn more.

A business plan should include the following elements:

- ✔ **Executive summary:** This is a description of the franchise, products and services, opportunities, risks, strategies, target market, competition, competitive advantage, investment and financial overview, and projected return on investment.

- ✔ **Mission statement:** A mission statement defines the culture of your business. It should describe the fundamental reasons for the company's existence and establish the scope of its activities. It is a reflection of your philosophy as it relates to such things as the franchisor and the system, profitability, professionalism, customers, employees, vendors, and your community.

- ✔ **Overview of the business structure:** This section provides the reader with information about the business, including the date the business began, who the founders were and whether they are presently active in the business. It also includes whether the business was acquired from the founders and when, as well as present financing equity ownership, loans, mortgages, overdrafts, debentures, and so on. Discuss any of your outstanding accomplishments and any setbacks that you have experienced and overcome.

- ✔ **Industry analysis and background:** Next to the executive summary, the industry analysis and background section is the most closely read section. For the company to have a clear direction, you must understand the industry you're in, your competition, and your position in the market. For clarity and comparison purposes, use charts where appropriate to compare your company and its products and services with those of the competition. Describe the industry in which you operate:

  - What is the size of the industry? The reader will want to understand how large the industry is and whether it's growing.

  - Who are the major participants in the industry — in other words, who are your competitors, market leaders, franchisors, and suppliers?

  - Do a few companies dominate the segment, or is the market fragmented among a lot of smaller mom-and-pop businesses?

  - Are there a large number of potential customers, or do a handful account for a high proportion of sales?

  - What factors are important to success in your industry?

- What do published forecasts say about the future growth and profile of the industry?

- What legislation and environmental or business trends will affect your industry?

✔ **Market analysis and strategy:** In this section, you talk about your potential customers, the size of the market, trends in the industry, the existing and emerging competition, the type of location you need, and how the franchisor wants your location to look. It tells the reader that you know about the business in which you will be operating.

✔ **Description of day-to-day operations:** People are your most important asset in any business. In this section, you describe your staffing plans for recruiting and paying personnel and the training programs you or the franchisee will provide. This section also deals with having the proper products and supplies to offer to the public and operate the business. You should also include issues dealing with your suppliers, how they will distribute to you, and how you will deliver the product and services you will offer to your customers.

✔ **Marketing plan:** Every investor, lender, or member of management is interested in how you intend to attract customers to your franchise. In this section, you describe the overall franchise system's strategy for marketing, including any neighborhood and local marketing strategies. Most franchisors also will help you plan your grand opening marketing programs. Let the reader understand how you intend to launch the business. Finally, deal with your pricing strategy. Do you intend to offer everyday low prices, or is your strategy to offer high prices as a standard practice with low promotional pricing for sales?

✔ **Management and organization structure:** Describe the day-to-day management required to operate the business, and if you know who they are, include some biographical information about your managers. Describe the number and type of staff you need to recruit, your compensation plans, employee benefits, and recruiting and retention plans. If you intend to work in the business, make sure to include information about yourself and the compensation you plan to take out of the business.

✔ **Financing:** What is the total start-up investment you require? Will the business require additional funding down the road? Provide the reader with information about your profit-and-loss forecasts and cash flow analysis for five years. Provide a detailed examination of the amount of sales you will need to break even and turn a profit.

✔ **Implementation plan and timetable:** The business plan not only needs to deal with the "whats" of everyday operation, but also needs to include a detailed description of the "hows." If it's an existing business, what changes do you intend to make to meet the plan? What is the cost of implementing those changes, and when do you expect to recoup those costs? If it's a start-up, define the investment, the time frame until opening, and how long before you will break even and get some return on your investment.

> ✔ **Appendix:** The appendix is the place to provide the reader with copies of your tax returns, articles about the company, articles about the industry, information about the community you will be serving, and any other information that will help the reader to understand the business.

For more help in creating a business plan, consult *Business Plans For Dummies,* by Paul Tiffany, Ph.D., and Steven D. Peterson, Ph.D. (published by IDG Books Worldwide, Inc.) or contact your local SCORE office or SBDC location.

This all sounds very scary, but if you truly want to go into business, a business plan is a must. In fact, you should find preparing your business plan a welcome challenge. If not, perhaps you don't have the discipline to own your own business. Often a franchisor will help you prepare or review your business plan, although the franchisor must be careful not to violate federal and state requirements that regulate its ability to make earnings claims. (See Chapter 6 for a discussion of earnings claims.)

Projecting income and cash flow

Most franchisees would rather run their businesses than spend time crunching numbers. Franchisors understand this, and many provide user-friendly accounting programs for the front of the house (customer sales) and the back of the house (bookkeeping, payroll, inventory management, and financial statements).

Unfortunately, bankers and investors want to see a projected income and cash-flow statement before they will invest in your business. The statement reassures them that you've thought through the realistic growth of your franchise. The numbers may not be absolutely on the mark, but they reassure bankers and investors that you're thinking like a person who plans to be in business for a long time.

Developing a successful plan

When I started Wendy's in 1969, I really didn't have a business plan. I had a concept and plenty of operating experience, but I had no five-year plan with a restaurant opening schedule or financing program. (Working with the bankers might have been a lot easier if we'd had a plan!)

Obviously, we have a plan now! Wendy's franchisees follow the plan that we developed over years of trial and error. We want our franchisees to succeed, so following the playbook is really important — and not that difficult: Franchisees need to stay focused and do the basic things day after day to keep customers, employees, suppliers, and neighbors in the community satisfied.

Where do you begin?

A good place to start is to add up all the costs of staying in business for the first 60 months. You want to develop a cash-flow statement by month for the first and second years and at least by quarter for the third through fifth years.

Other franchisees already in the system may be sources for accurate information about actual costs.

Be very careful when you review information that other franchisees provide. Some franchisees may be reluctant to share information with you because you may buy a competitor's franchise and then go into competition with them. Also, the franchisee may be a *shill* — a *plant* — a person the franchisor directed you to call to get bogus information about the franchise that helps the franchisor make the sale.

Most important, is the information you're getting relevant to analyzing your proposed business? Keep in mind that the economics of selling ice cream in Alaska may be quite different from selling ice cream in Manhattan, Florida, or London. Information about units that do match the demographics, size, and location of your franchise may be interesting, but it can also be misleading if you rely on it for projecting future results for your business.

Your accountant may be a source for projecting income and expenses if she or he has any experience in your business.

Ask some of the local franchisees what accountant they use. An accountant who's experienced in the industry and who has a proven track record is your best bet.

Armed with both an annual cost figure and projected sales, you can forecast your needed cash flow. Your accountant can provide you with forms you can use to assemble the information.

The franchisor's disclosure document gives you the projected initial investment. If profit and loss is in the disclosure document, it will tell you how well its operating locations are doing. If your franchisor has included an earnings claim in the information it has provided to you, it should be able to provide you with some of the detailed assumptions it used. This is important; you need to develop your financial projections based on the market in which your business will be operating. See Chapter 6 for a discussion on the UFOC.

If your franchisor doesn't provide earnings information, you may want to take a look at some of the competition. Robert Bond's *How Much Can I Make? Actual Sales and Profit Potential for Your Small Business* provides the earnings claims of more than 150 franchisors. You can order the book for $29.95 by calling 800-841-0873 or at www.worldfranchising.com.

DAVE SAYS

Choosing a banker

I wasn't ready to deal with banks when I took over the KFC restaurants in Columbus, Ohio, in 1962. One of the first things I wanted to do was install air-conditioning systems in the four restaurants because I knew how air conditioning builds traffic. But instead of going downtown to the commercial loan department and talking with someone who knew something about business, I went to the local branch that did our banking. The loan officer there knew about loans for cars and refrigerators but couldn't understand air-conditioning as a necessity of the business. Instead of a loan, I got a lecture on what a lousy risk this was for the bank.

A small businessperson needs a good banker in order to survive and to expand the company. When you pick a banker, don't go after one with the fanciest computer system or the slickest brochure. Choose a bank that has experience dealing with small businesses and that has a good sense of business judgment.

Visiting the bank

Nothing can substitute for preparation. Neither Shaquille O'Neal nor Rebecca Lobo would think of going into a game without first practicing and perfecting a few moves to guarantee a basket. That same attitude works when you approach lenders — only the ball is in their court, and your goal is to convince them to toss it to you.

Local bankers are in business just as you are, and they want to help you succeed. In order to do that, they need information about you, your plans for the future, your business, and franchising overall. Your business plan covers some of the information, but nothing is better than a personal visit to get started.

Just as franchising is based on relationships, so is banking. It's important that you establish and nurture an ongoing relationship with your banker. That commitment means dropping in and visiting with him or her on a regular basis and sharing your progress as you get closer to signing your contract. In other words, your banker wants to be kept informed. No banker likes surprises. The more you share of yourself — your business ideas, hopes, dreams, and goals — the better your banker can assess your loan application when it crosses his or her desk.

If you don't click with your local lender, shop around. Visit a few banks in your operating area and see which one is a good match. Make sure that the bank you choose has experience with small businesses.

If you're in the United States, you stand a better chance of success with a certified U.S. Small Business Administration lender — more commonly known as an SBA lender. These banks have government guarantees on the loans they make to small businesses, including franchises.

Getting a bank's support sounds pretty simple, doesn't it? But few franchisees take the time to establish relationships with their bankers. They show up when they want money. Sometimes they get it and sometimes they don't. Because you may well need to borrow expansion capital at some point in your business future, taking the time now to connect with your banker just makes sense. Consider your banker part of your business team and keep the lines of communication open.

Check with other franchisees and find out who financed their businesses. A banker who has already financed a successful franchisee will be more receptive to your application and will need less education.

Finding an angel

After you have tapped all the available sources of conventional funding — friends, family, personal savings, franchisor assistance, and SBA bank loans — think about finding an angel investor. No, this isn't someone who arrives wearing wings.

Angel investors typically are individuals or groups who offer start-up funds in exchange for a direct role in a new business. They are people with high net worth who want to invest in businesses they know about. Although an angel is usually an individual, angels often form groups that commit larger sums based on the recommendations of one of the group's members.

An angel investor often expects a direct role in advising the new company. This counsel can be an advantage for a new franchisee because an angel can often bring expertise to a new business that the owner can't get elsewhere.

A word of caution: These investors become your partners and may require you to seek their permission before you make decisions. You will probably give up some control, and you will certainly give up some of the profit if the angel takes an equity position.

You can find several directories of angel investors. A new initiative from the SBA's Office of Advocacy is ACE-Net: the Angel Capital Electronic Network. ACE-Net is an Internet-based listing that provides angel investors with information about businesses seeking between $250,000 to $3 million in equity financing. You can visit the ACE-Net Web site at `ace-net.sr.unh.edu/pub`.

The money you need is out there, so don't despair. Just be cautious in your enthusiasm, and don't put everything you have on the line. Spread your risk, combine your funding sources, sell the stuff you don't use, and build those relationships.

Chapter 6

Signing on the Dotted Line: Legal Issues

. . . .

In This Chapter

▶ Understanding the history of the Uniform Franchise Offering Circular

▶ Evaluating the franchise agreement

▶ Finding pros to help you

▶ Negotiating with the franchisor

. . . .

*I*n this chapter, we talk about the Uniform Franchise Offering Circular, or UFOC. (It is also sometimes referred to as a *disclosure statement* or simply the *offering circular.*) The UFOC is important to understand because it is where the franchisor discloses information about the franchise system and the franchise relationship they're offering. The UFOC is designed to give you some — but certainly not all — the information you need in order to make an informed decision about investing in a particular franchise.

The History Behind the Uniform Franchise Offering Circular

Following World War II, franchising entered its modern era. Franchising boomed, fueled by pent-up consumer demand, returning veterans with great ideas and ambition to become franchisors, a GI bill that provided loans to fund new franchisees and franchisors, and a change in the trademark law.

Do you remember where you were when you had your first hamburger from a franchised operation? For the children of the 1950s, the novelty of a hamburger (still warm and wrapped in paper) and some skinny, salty French fries jammed into a small white paper bag is something many of us still remember fondly. Ray Kroc began franchising McDonald's and single-handedly captured the imagination of a generation of consumers — securing a guaranteed market base for decades to come. Such was the magic of franchising in the 1950s. The franchising boom in the 1950s and 1960s achieved almost mystical stature. Companies became household names, as integral to everyday life as homework and housework. Convenience stores started popping up, and the name 7-Eleven became part of the lexicon. Dairy Queen, Kentucky Fried Chicken, Texaco, Hilton Hotels, Marriott, Budget Rent a Car, Duraclean, Midas, and a host of other brand-name franchises were offering their products and services to American consumers who were ready to start spending.

When you're looking at franchisors, look at more than the number of locations they have and their system-wide sales. Look for a system that has that passion for quality, that listens to its customers, and that has a superb team of franchise executives and carefully selected franchisees. That's a system you'll be proud to join. That's a system with a future.

The Wendy's story

Wendy's began in November of 1969 with the opening of the first Wendy's Old Fashioned Hamburgers Restaurant in Columbus, Ohio. A year later, we opened the second restaurant and added some innovations, including a separate grill at the pick-up window to speed delivery. Two years later, in August 1972, the first franchise agreement was signed for Indianapolis, Indiana, and that same year the Wendy's Management Institute was established to develop management skills in our managers and franchisees.

Within five years from when it all began, system sales exceeded $25 million, and the next year, Wendy's went public. By December of 1976, the company had reached 500 locations, and three years later, in 1979, opened restaurant 1,500 in San Juan, Puerto Rico. By 1979, a short 10 years after it had all begun, Wendy's had established itself in the United States, Puerto Rico, and Canada. The growth during those first 10 years dwarfed the first decade of the McDonald's chain, and we accomplished that growth during a period when many thought there was no room for another hamburger chain in the industry.

Today, there are more than 5,600 Wendy's and 1,800 Tim Hortons (Wendy's and Tim Hortons merged in 1995), and system-wide sales exceed $7 billion. We reached this achievement by having a passion for quality, listening to our customers and franchisees, being innovative, assembling the finest team of restaurant and franchise executives in the industry, and, most important, by being blessed with the greatest group of franchisees in the industry.

Our formula was as simple as that.

It would be foolish to think that franchising matured smoothly and without problems. By the late 1960s, the bloom had left the rose. Some franchisors began to focus more on selling as many franchises as they could than on their existing operations. In the process, their existing franchisees often suffered from diminished support from the home office. Another serious problem resulted when some franchisors misrepresented their franchise offerings in an attempt to attract more franchisees. During these darker days of franchising, franchisors sometimes used unscrupulous tactics to lure potential franchisees into buying into a system. Some used celebrity names and endorsements to attract buyers. Some even sold franchises for concepts that didn't exist.

Such fraudulent practices caused several states to enact laws governing the disclosure of information to potential franchisees. California led the way. The laws required franchisors to deliver disclosure documents providing information on the franchise opportunity to potential franchisees. But franchisees only got this protection in the states that followed California's example and enacted franchise disclosure laws.

It wasn't until the summer of 1979 that the Federal Trade Commission implemented a franchise rule requiring minimum disclosure throughout the United States. Since then, the format and content of the disclosure documents have undergone changes that further strengthened disclosure.

Some basics on the law

Franchising is governed primarily by laws that require franchisors to inform prospective franchisees about the system. This information is contained in a document called the Uniform Franchise Offering Circular, or simply the UFOC. Under the federal and state rules, a franchisor cannot offer a franchise until the franchisor has prepared a UFOC. Although franchisors don't need to register and get approval of the UFOC by the federal government, 14 states do require franchisors to register their UFOCs with the state or to notify them that they will offer franchises before they begin to conduct any franchising activity in the state.

The registration states are California, Hawaii, Illinois, Indiana, Maryland, Michigan, Minnesota, New York, North Dakota, Rhode Island, South Dakota, Virginia, Washington, and Wisconsin. Other states, including Florida, Kentucky, Nebraska, Texas, and Utah, require franchisors to file a notice with the state but don't require franchisors to forward a copy of their UFOC to any state agency.

The laws governing the UFOC mainly deal with disclosure of the terms of the franchise and information about the franchisor. However, a second body of law in 18 states and the District of Columbia gives added protection to the franchisee. These are called *relationship laws*. They give franchisees protection from certain actions of the franchisor, including arbitrary termination of the franchise or nonrenewal of the franchise at the end of its term.

Although we miss the days of the handshake agreement, franchising has been strengthened by the rules of disclosure. For the most part, the rules have avoided tampering with the relationship between the franchisor and franchisee. This restraint has enabled franchise systems to compete for franchisees based on the merits of their systems instead of being bogged down by excessive government interference in this vital part of the economy.

Under the disclosure rules, franchisors have to provide prospective franchisees with information about the system. This knowledge allows intelligent buyers to make intelligent decisions. We believe that the lack of significant government interference in the franchise relationship coupled with disclosure of the offering has been a good thing for franchisors and franchisees. The lack of significant government interference in the relationship between franchisors and franchisees has allowed franchising to grow and maintain its place as one of the major economic drivers in the economy today.

On occasion, legislation whose purpose is to set minimum standards of conduct between the franchisor and franchisee has been introduced at the state and federal level. One such piece of legislation, H.R. 3308, the Small Business Franchise Act of 1999, was introduced by Howard Coble, a congressman from North Carolina, and John Conyers, a congressman from Michigan. The goal of H.R. 3308 is to correct a perceived imbalance in the franchisor/franchisee relationship. H.R. 3308 doesn't have much support from franchisors, as it gives government the job of micromanaging how franchisors license their systems. In addition to franchisors, many franchisees also oppose HR 3308 because of the negative impact they believe government regulation of the franchise relationship may cause. Besides the International Franchise Association, other associations, including the U.S. Chamber of Commerce, have come out against H.R. 3308. As this book goes to press, the fate of H.R. 3308 is unknown.

Understanding the UFOC

The purpose of the UFOC is to provide prospective franchisees with information on the franchisor, the franchise system, and the agreements they will need to sign so that they can make an informed decision. In addition to the disclosure portion of the document, the UFOC includes copies of the franchise agreement and other agreements the franchisee will be required to sign, together with the franchisor's financial statements.

Under the guidelines set by the North American Securities Administrators Association (NASAA), franchisors are required to provide specific information about the franchisor, the franchise system, and the relationship between the franchisor and franchisee. Although the Federal Trade Commission has its own form of disclosure, it accepts the NASAA format in lieu of its own.

Almost universally, franchisors today use the NASAA-adopted UFOC format. Under proposed revisions to the FTC Rule, the FTC will scrap the FTC disclosure format in favor of the UFOC disclosure format.

A summary of the UFOC

What appears in the UFOC? In a nutshell, it includes information on the franchisor, the company's key staff, management's experience in franchise management, the franchisor's bankruptcy and litigation history, and the initial and ongoing fees involved in opening and running a franchise.

Also included is information on the required investment, purchases you will be required to make from the franchisor or from approved suppliers, and territory rights you will be granted. You also find information about your legal responsibilities as a franchisee and the responsibility of the franchisor to you.

In addition, the UFOC presents information about the company-owned locations and on the franchisees in the system, including the number of franchises opened, the number closed and transferred, and, most important, a list of existing and former franchisees with their contact information.

It's important that you fully understand the franchise agreement and any other agreements you need to sign. If you don't understand what you're signing, you may find yourself locked into a business relationship that doesn't wear well for you.

Why can't I sign my franchise agreement today?

"I've completed my research, visited the franchisor, gotten the UFOC, read and understood the agreement, and made my decision. I want the franchise now. Why can't I sign the franchise agreement today?" The answer: The law requires a waiting period.

Included in the regulations governing the sale of franchises is a cooling-off period called the *ten-day rule*. Franchisors are required to wait a minimum of ten business days after giving a prospect the UFOC before allowing the franchisee to sign the franchise agreement. This purpose of the rule is to give you time to think about your decision.

You are also legally entitled to have the final franchise agreement — with all the blanks filled in — for at least five business days before you are allowed to sign it. This gives you time to review and consider the terms of the agreement.

The franchise agreement that is provided in the UFOC may contain some blanks that need to be filled in, including who the franchisee is, where your franchise will be located, the size of your protected territory (if there is one), and other matters specific to the franchisee. On occasion, the franchise agreement has to be changed as a result of changes made during negotiations. You must be given a copy of the final agreement — with the changes — at least five business days prior to signing the agreement.

It's a great rule. When you initially make the decision to buy a franchise, your enthusiasm for the deal runs high. The delay allows you time to reflect. By the way, the five-day waiting period can take place during the ten-day period. So if you're in a hurry to get your franchise agreement signed, make sure that you get all the blanks filled in quickly.

The UFOC, point by point

Not counting the cover page, the UFOC contains 23 areas of disclosure — referred to as *Items*.

A few years back, when NASAA was making its last revision to the UFOC format, it added the requirement that "plain English" be used in drafting the UFOC so that it would be easier to read and understand. Although the UFOC may be written in what attorneys consider plain English, it's still written by skilled attorneys who work for the franchisor. Experience tells us that many of the terms used in the UFOC can be confusing to a novice in franchising. Get yourself a qualified franchise lawyer to help you understand what the UFOC means.

The cover page(s)

The cover page(s) of the UFOC contain interesting information that every prospective franchisee should read and understand:

- ✔ It states that the Federal Trade Commission hasn't checked the document and doesn't know whether it's correct.

- ✔ It reminds you to read the entire document, including the contract, when making a decision about a franchisor.

- ✔ It encourages you to take your time in making your franchise decision because it's a complicated investment.

- ✔ It suggests that you show the UFOC and the franchise agreement to an advisor, such as a lawyer or accountant.

✔ It asks you to notify the FTC if you find anything wrong with the document.

✔ It recommends that you find out about the franchising laws in your state.

The second page of the UFOC contains a summary of the franchise offering as well as a summary of the investment that the franchisee is required to make. It also contains information on some of the risk factors that a franchisee should know about before signing a franchise agreement. These include

✔ **Choice of law that governs the agreement.** The franchisor will likely select the laws of its home state to govern the franchise agreement, not the laws in the franchisee's home state. Not all franchisors pick their home state laws, and some states don't allow a franchisor to do so.

✔ **Choice of where the franchisee may sue the franchisor.** If a dispute occurs, the franchisee may have to sue the franchisor in the franchisor's home state, requiring the franchisee to incur the cost of travel and other added costs. Some franchisee advocates believe this gives the franchisor a "home field advantage."

✔ **The inclusion of arbitration as a method to solve disputes.** In some systems, a franchisee may not be able to sue a franchisor but must instead bring the dispute to an arbitrator or use some other method of dispute resolution.

There is also a reminder to the prospective franchisee that just because the state has registered the UFOC doesn't mean that the state has verified the information or is making a recommendation about the company.

The 23 Items

The following are the highlights (not all the subtopics are included) of the 23 items required for disclosure.

✔ **Item 1: The franchisor, its predecessors, and affiliates**

In this section, the franchisor provides a description of the company and the franchise being offered. In Item 1, the franchisor is required to disclose the following information:

- The name of the franchisor, its predecessors, and its affiliates

- The name under which the franchisor does business

- The franchisor's address

- The state of incorporation of the franchisor or the type of business organization (partnership and so on) of the franchisor

> • The franchisor's business and the type of franchise to be offered
>
> • The prior business experience of the franchisor, its predecessor, and its affiliates

✔ **Item 2: Business experience**

Here, the prospective franchisee gets biographical and professional information about the franchisor and its officers, directors, and executives. This section tells you who you will be going into business with.

✔ **Item 3: Litigation**

In the UFOC, you won't find information about all the litigation that the franchisor or the franchisor's management has been involved in. The rules require that only relevant current and past criminal and civil litigation for the franchisor and its management be disclosed.

✔ **Item 4: Bankruptcy**

Sometimes franchisors or members of their management have gone through a bankruptcy. It's important information that every franchisee needs to know because it can tell you whether there is a pattern of bankruptcy by the people and company you will be entering into a relationship with. You'll find this information in Item 4.

✔ **Item 5: Initial franchise fee**

Item 5 provides information about the initial fees you will pay to the franchisor. It tells you what payments the franchisee makes to the franchisor prior to opening the business. It also tells you whether the fees are not uniform to all the franchisees and discloses the range and factors that determine the amount of the fee.

✔ **Item 6: Other fees**

This item provides a description of all other recurring fees or payment that the franchisee must make to the franchisor, including

> • Royalties: the continuing payment the franchisee will make to the franchisor for the franchisee's continued participation in the system.
>
> • Contributions the franchisee will make to the system's advertising fund.
>
> • Requirements for the franchisee to participate in any local or regional cooperative advertising programs.
>
> • Additional training fees that the franchisor may charge.
>
> • Additional fees the franchisee must pay for services or other benefits that the franchisor provides.

- Transfer fees that the franchisee pays to the franchisor when the franchisee sells the business to another franchisee.

- Audit costs that the franchisee may have to pay if the franchisor audits the franchisee's books and records and finds discrepancies between them and the information that the franchisee provided the franchisor.

- Renewal fees that the franchisor charges at the end of the franchisee's term for renewal of the relationship.

You'll notice that we didn't say "for renewal of the franchise agreement." This is because franchisors will usually have made changes to their franchise agreements since the time the franchisee signed their original agreement. In order to renew the relationship, the franchisee usually is required to sign the then-current franchise agreement. The new agreement could have minor or substantial changes from the original agreement.

✔ Item 7: Initial investment

Item 7 is in a table format. The table includes all the expenditures a franchisee is required to make to establish the franchise. In addition to a range of amount the franchisee must invest for each start-up expenditure, the franchisor discloses the method of payment, when it is due, who the payment will be made to, whether the payment is refundable, and whether it is financed. The initial investment usually includes the following:

- Initial franchise fee

- Real estate and improvements

- Equipment and fixtures

- Other fixed assets

- Decorating costs

- Signs

- Security deposits, utility deposits, business licenses, and other prepaid expenses

- Miscellaneous opening expenses

- Opening inventory

- Initial advertising

- Professional fees

- Working capital required during the initial phase of the franchisee

- A total of the initial investment

Item 7 typically has extensive notes that give prospective franchisees additional information about the initial costs included in the table. Read the notes carefully so that you have a fuller understanding of your initial investment. As with everything else, make certain you understand what the notes say.

✔ **Item 8: Restriction on sources of products and services**

The franchisor may have restrictions on what the franchisee can buy for the business and where the franchisee can purchase those items. There are many reasons that a franchisor restricts sources, including a desire to ensure consistency and quality. The franchisee may be obligated to purchase or lease products and services from the franchisor or from suppliers approved by the franchisor. The franchisor may also provide the franchisee with specifications for any of the goods, services, supplies, fixtures, equipment, inventory, computer hardware or software, or other items the franchisee uses in the business. The franchisor usually has the right to approve or revoke approval of a supplier, or to make changes to its specifications for products and services the franchisee uses.

The following tells you the methods the franchisor will use.

- The franchisor is sometimes the only approved supplier. This section tells you whether and in what categories the franchisor is the only approved supplier for the franchisee.

- The franchisor may earn income from the franchisee's purchases. This section tells you the amount the franchisor earns from franchisee purchases.

- Where the franchisor requires the franchisee to make purchases based on approved suppliers or specifications, this section tells you the estimated proportion these required purchases are of the initial investment and the continuing operating expenses of the franchise.

- If the franchise system uses any purchasing or distribution cooperative, you find that information in this section.

✔ **Item 9: Franchisee's obligations**

Item 9 provides a reference table that indicates where in the franchise agreement franchisees can find certain obligations they agree to. The list informs the franchisee of the obligation, where it can be found elsewhere in the UFOC, and where it can be found in the franchise agreement. The details of the obligations are not discussed in Item 9. Not all franchisees in every system have the same obligations. Some of these obligations may be

- Site selection and acquisition fees.

- Pre-opening purchases and leases.

- Site development and other pre-opening requirements.

- Initial and ongoing training that the franchisee will be offered and that they may be required to attend.

- Opening requirements: usually, how much time the franchisee has to get the business open and operating.

- Fees that the franchisee agrees to pay.

- Requirement to comply with the system's standards and policies as included in the Operating Manual and elsewhere.

- Trademarks and proprietary information provided by the franchisor.

- Restrictions on products/services offered by the franchisee.

- Warranty and customer service requirements.

- Territorial development and sales quotas that the franchisee must meet.

- Ongoing product/service purchases.

- Maintenance, appearance, and remodeling requirements.

- Insurance requirements.

- Advertising requirements.

- Indemnification: this section defines the franchisor and franchisee's obligations or duty concerning their rights to seek compensation for losses, damages, or injury sustained due to the actions of the other.

- Owner's participation in the operation, management, and staffing of the locations.

- Records the franchisee must maintain and the reports the franchisee has to file with the franchisor.

- Inspection and audit rights held by the franchisor.

- Transfer requirements.

- Renewal requirements.

- Post-termination obligations of the franchisee after leaving the franchise system.

- Noncompetition covenants that limit the franchisee's ability to go into similar — but unaffiliated — businesses.

- Methods the franchisor and franchisee will use to resolve any disputes.

- Other obligations the franchisee may have.

✔ **Item 10: Financing available**

Some franchise systems provide financing assistance to their franchisees. Item 10 describes the terms and conditions of any financing arrangements offered directly or indirectly by the franchisor.

✔ **Item 11: Franchisor's obligations**

When you invest in a franchise, you expect the franchisor to provide you with certain services. Every franchise system provides different types and levels of service to its franchisees. It's important that you clearly understand what you will get. Included in this section is a description of

- The franchisor's obligations to the franchisee before and after the franchise opens.

- The methods the franchisor uses to select the location of the franchise.

- The typical length of time between signing the franchise agreement and opening the franchise.

- The franchisor's training program, including duration, outline of training, experience of instructors, charges, who is responsible for paying for travel and living expenses, whether the training program is mandatory, and whether any additional training and/or refresher courses are required.

- The franchisor's advertising program, including what media are used; who creates the advertising; the composition of the franchisee advertising council and cooperatives; the specific use of advertising funds, including payment to franchisor or affiliates; and whether different franchisees contribute at different rates.

- The computer or electronic cash register the franchise uses.

- The Table of Contents of the franchisor's manual. Alternatively, the franchisor may elect to allow the prospective franchisee to read the manual before purchasing the franchise.

✔ **Item 12: Territory**

Not every franchisor provides its franchisees with an exclusive territory. When franchisors do make that provision, the exclusive territory will vary for each franchise system and may vary depending on the circumstances within a system. Item 12 provides the prospective franchisee with the following information:

- A description of any exclusive territory granted to the franchise.

- Whether the franchisor has or may establish another franchise or company-owned location in the territory.

- Whether the territory is conditional on achieving certain sales volumes or other performance criteria.

- Whether the franchisor can modify the territory.

- The methods the franchisor will use to resolve conflicts concerning the territory.

✔ **Item 13: Trademarks**

This section provides the franchisor with information about the franchisor's trademarks, service marks, and trade names that will be used.

✔ **Item 14: Patents, copyrights, and proprietary information**

This section provides franchisees with information concerning any patents or copyrights the franchisor may have and how they may be used by the franchisee.

✔ **Item 15: Obligations to participate in the actual operation of the franchise business**

Some franchise systems require franchisees to devote their full time to the operation of the business. Others may allow for absentee ownership, or management by a manager trained by the franchisor. Different franchisors have different requirements concerning the obligations of the franchisee to participate in the actual operation of the business.

✔ **Item 16: Restrictions on what the franchisee may sell**

Item 8 discussed any restrictions by franchisors on suppliers and specification of the products used by the franchisee. This section deals with any restrictions on the goods and services that the franchisee may offer to its customers.

✔ **Item 17: Renewal, termination, transfers, and dispute resolution**

This section provides the franchisee with information, in a table format, concerning the terms of the agreement. Included in this section is information on

- The length of the initial term of the agreement

- The number and duration of the renewal periods

- Reasons that the franchisor or franchisee may terminate the agreement, causes, and any cure period. (A *cure period* is the length of time a franchisee has to fix a problem.)

- The obligations of the parties after the termination of the agreement

- The rights of the franchisor or franchisee to transfer or assign the agreement to another person or company

- The rights of the franchisor to purchase the franchisee's business

- The in-term and post-term restrictions on competition with the franchise system

- How the franchise agreement can be modified — usually the franchise agreement can be modified only in writing

- What methods are provided for resolving disputes between the franchisor — litigation, arbitration, and mediation

- What states or country's law govern the contract

✔ Item 18: Public figures

If the franchisor uses any public figure (celebrity or other public person) in the franchise system's name or symbol, the franchisor needs to disclose the amount the person is paid, the extent the public figure is involved in the actual management of the franchise system, and the public figure's total investment in the franchisor.

✔ Item 19: Earnings claims

This is one of the most important sections to franchisees. If the franchisor provides any information that a franchisee can use to estimate what she or he can earn from the business, it needs to be disclosed in Item 19. This may include specific levels or a range of actual or potential sales, costs, income, or profit for a franchise or nonfranchised location.

Earnings claims are a particularly sensitive area in franchising. We cover them later in this chapter.

✔ Item 20: List of franchise outlets

This section provides information regarding the locations operated in the system. It includes

- The number of franchises and company-owned locations by state

- The names, addresses, and telephone numbers of franchisees

- The estimated number of franchises to be sold in the next year

- The number of franchises transferred, canceled, or terminated

- The number of franchises that have not been renewed by the franchisor or have been reacquired by the franchisor

- The number of franchises that are known to have ceased operation

In addition, the franchisor is required to provide you with the names and last known addresses and telephone numbers of every franchisee who has had an outlet terminated, canceled, or not renewed, or who otherwise ceased doing business under the franchise agreement during the past year.

✔ Item 21: Financial statements

Franchisors are required to include their audited financial statements for the past three years, or for a shorter period if the franchisor has not been in business for three years.

✔ Item 22: Contracts

Item 22 provides you with a list of the franchise agreement or license agreement and all other related agreements that the franchisee will be required to sign. These agreements must be attached as exhibits to the UFOC.

✔ **Item 23: Receipt**

You will be required to sign a receipt that you received the UFOC. Two copies of the receipt form are provided in Item 23.

Understanding some of the key elements in the UFOC

Although your attorney can help you make sense of the UFOC, we think that a few items require additional attention.

✔ Item 7 tells you how much it will cost to get into business as a franchisee — the initial investment. Remember that some of these costs are averages or estimates and that the costs in your market or for your franchise may be different. The areas that may vary the most from the franchisor's estimates are the estimated working capital and the cost of buying or leasing a site.

When you call the other franchisees in the system, get a sense of how much money they needed to support the business in the early days until they became profitable or had a positive cash flow. See how much they were able to draw from the business to support themselves and their families. Try to call franchisees who have been in the system for a year or two, so you'll know their information is current.

✔ Item 11 lists the franchisor's obligations to you. Be sure that you understand what services you will get before you open (training, site selection, development assistance, and so on), what support you will receive for your grand opening (marketing, advertising, and field support), and what services you will receive after you begin operating the business.

Pay particular attention to those services the franchisor is *obligated* to provide and the services they *may* provide. You *must* receive what is required in the franchise agreement; you *might* receive the others. If the franchise salesperson makes a statement about services, such as additional training, additional field support, or special marketing programs (to name a few) and they are not included in the written obligations of the franchisor, this could be an area for you and your attorney to discuss with the franchisor as an amendment to the franchise agreement.

✔ Item 17 discusses renewal, termination, transfers, and dispute resolution, which may be important to you only at the end of the relationship or when a conflict arises between you and the franchisor. This section also includes topics like severability, mergers, and amendments. Attorneys often refer to these items as the boilerplate part of the agreement. *Boilerplate* refers to those sections of an agreement that attorneys usually have already written and stored in their word processor and include in the back of most of their agreements. (It's the stuff many people forget to read.) Boilerplate sections may not necessarily be fair or meet your needs. Take your time to understand what rights you will have and what rights you are giving up. Pay particular attention to any non-compete provisions and your other obligations when the franchise relationship ends.

✔ Item 20 provides you with information regarding the number of company-owned or franchised units that are open and those that have closed or been transferred. This may be the most boring section to read — all it contains is charts and numbers — but it can tell an important story.

Examine how many units the franchisor has taken back and resold. If the number is high, this could indicate churning by the franchisor. *Churning* occurs when a franchisor takes back failed locations from franchisees and then remarkets them — over and over again — to new franchisees.

In addition to the names, addresses, and phone numbers of the franchisees currently in the system, Item 20 gives you information on the franchisees who have left the system in the past year. These are people you want to talk to.

✔ Item 21 contains the franchisor's audited financial statements. If your balance sheet looks better than the franchisor's, what does that tell you about your risk?

✔ Item 22 contains a list of all the agreements, including the franchise agreement that you will be required to sign. Make sure that all the agreements listed are attached to the UFOC — and read every one of them.

Proposed changes to franchise rule

The Federal Trade Commission (FTC) has recently proposed changes to the FTC Franchise Rule, the first changes in 20 years. These changes, if adopted, would alter the format, content, and mechanics of disclosure to prospective franchisees. Here are some of the proposed changes:

✔ "Sophisticated investor" disclosure exemptions would apply to the following: investments that exceed $1.5 million; corporations in business for at least five years and that have a net worth of $5 million; and franchisees who are, or have recently been, officers or owners of the franchisor.

✔ A franchisor may furnish the disclosure document electronically to a prospective franchisee under certain conditions, which include the prospective franchisee's ability to print or download the document as a single, self-contained document.

✔ The proposed changes would eliminate the "first personal meeting" and "10 business day" triggers for disclosure in favor of a 14-calendar-day requirement.

✔ The FTC would adopt the NASAA UFOC disclosure format with some additional disclosure requirements:

- **Item 3:** Disclosure of franchisor-initiated lawsuits against franchisees on issues involving the franchise relationship.

- **Item 19:** Franchisors who don't make an earnings claim in Item 19 will be required to state affirmatively that the FTC permits franchisors to make financial performance disclosures.

- **Item 20:** New table demonstrating unit turnover designed to eliminate double-counting by overlapping categories; disclosure of "gag" clauses signed within the past three years that prohibit franchisees or former franchisees from discussing their experience as franchisees; and the disclosure of an independent, trademark-specific franchisee association.

The proposed changes limit the applicability of the rule to the sale of franchises that are to be operated in the United States, its possessions, or territories.

Source: The Franchise Group of Weily, Rein & Fielding, Washington, DC; www.wrf.com.

How much can I make? The earnings claims

All prospective franchisees want to know how much money they will make if they invest in a franchise. Who is better suited to tell them than the franchisor?

The general rule in franchising is that the only place franchisors can provide you with any information on projected sales, income, profit, or costs of franchised or nonfranchised locations is in Item 19 of their UFOC. This statement of earnings is called an *earnings claim*. Unfortunately, only 20 to 25 percent of franchisors provide you with this written information.

Some franchise salespeople will tell you that franchise law prohibits them from telling you how much you're going to make. That's not true. They're only prohibited from discussing the numbers with you *if they have chosen not to include the information in the UFOC.*

If every prospective franchisee wants this information, why do so few franchisors provide it? Good question. Here are some possible reasons:

✔ We live in a litigious society. If the franchisor's earnings claim contains inaccurate or misleading information, franchisees can sue to get out of the agreement and to recover their losses or obtain some other form of relief.

✔ In some states, the franchisor's officers or directors may be considered guilty of a crime if they give you improper earnings information. Rather than risk the penalties, they choose not to include any earnings information at all.

✔ Franchisors may feel that their system's locations and markets are too diverse to provide the franchisee with any meaningful information.

✔ Franchisors may feel that their locations are all at different stages of maturity and that providing information based on averages and varying levels of operating success makes the information misleading — at best.

✔ Some franchisors fear that because the information their franchisees provide about individual unit performance has not been audited or verified, it may not be accurate.

✔ Some franchisors rightfully worry that because franchisees are often late in providing their financial information, the information may be incomplete.

✔ Some franchisors also worry that information their franchisees provide may not be uniform. They feel there's a high risk that any earnings information they prepare won't accurately reflect the financial performance of units in the system.

✔ Most systems have accurate information on the performance of their company-owned locations. However, they may not have similar information on the franchisee-operated locations. These franchisors believe that providing information based only on company-owned unit performance may not give prospective franchisees a true representation of the performance they can expect.

✔ Some franchisors feel that providing earnings information gives competing franchise systems an advantage because it may contain what they feel are system secrets.

✔ There is no uniform standard for how unit financial information should be provided to a prospective franchisee. The type of information can be as brief as gross sales on the average location in a system. It may be as extensive as full profit and loss statements on every location. Some franchisors include helpful statistical information in their earnings claims. Others don't feel that statistics are particularly helpful. Because earnings claims may differ from franchisor to franchisor, even when those companies are in the same industry, many franchise professionals don't think the information is particularly useful for comparing one franchisor to another.

✔ In some systems, the numbers are so bad that franchisors don't want anyone to see them because, if they did, they wouldn't be able to sell a franchise.

On the other hand, some franchise systems give detailed earnings statements for every kind of franchise arrangement in their system.

Where else can I go to get information?

The debate about whether franchisors should be required to provide mandatory earnings claims disclosure is still unresolved. Meanwhile, if the franchise you are investigating doesn't provide you with an earnings claim, your next best source of information on earning potential is the franchisees in that system. After all, they have the most accurate information on how well their locations are performing and how well the franchisor is meeting its obligations.

Another good source of information on franchisors that are public companies are the reports they make to their shareholders as required by the Securities and Exchange Commission (SEC). These reports contain information that is not required by the Federal Trade Commission but that is required by the SEC. These reports, available from stockbrokers and often available on the Internet, can provide additional insight into the company. The Internet offers an abundance of information — from press releases to articles — that can help you determine the potential earnings of the franchisor of your choice.

As we mention in Chapter 4, Robert Bond has published a collection of earnings claims included by franchisors in their UFOCs. The book is called *How Much Can I Make?* The cost is $29.95, and you can order a copy by calling 800-841-0873 or through the Web site at www.worldfranchisng.com.

Using the UFOC to dig out some of the facts about earnings

Even if a franchisor doesn't include an earnings claim in the UFOC, plenty of information is available in the UFOC to help you start to project your earnings. You may need to dig out the information and combine it with information in some of the other sources we mention, but it's worth the effort. Here are some steps you can take:

- ✔ Examine the franchisor's financial statements contained in the UFOC for information on company-owned unit performance.

- ✔ Look at Items 5 and 6 (initial fee and continuing fee). Often the franchisor has formulas on how the fees are calculated; these formulas can be helpful.

- ✔ Look at Item 7, the initial investment — especially the notes. Besides telling you the approximate size and type of location (from which you can determine what your local rent will be) of the franchise, it often gives you information on the amount and type of staff you will need, the frequency with which the inventory of locations is sold and replaced *(inventory turns),* and how the franchisor calculated the required working capital.

- ✔ Item 8 is a gold mine. It discloses the required purchases and the percentage of your operating expenses they represent.

Even if the UFOC doesn't include an earnings claim, the franchisor is allowed to provide you with information on company-owned units that are for sale. Ask the franchisor whether a company-owned location is for sale in your market, and if so, ask to see the books and records. In addition to getting information relevant to your market, you may find a great opportunity to buy an existing location. However, this exception to the rule isn't a license for franchisors to show you information on locations you're not actually interested in purchasing.

A franchisor who has made an earnings claim is allowed to provide you with a supplemental earnings claim that is different from the one in the UFOC. These are often prepared when the information is about a particular location or other circumstances require it. The information must be in writing, must explain why and how it departs from the information contained in the UFOC, and must be prepared in accordance with the UFOC guidelines. Further, a copy must be given to the prospective franchisee to take with her or him. However, if the salesperson makes earning claims outside of the UFOC — sometimes orally, and sometimes on cocktail napkins or a scrap of paper — these aren't supplemental earnings claims. Don't rely on that type of information in making your purchase decision. But you should save it. You never know whether you will need it during a dispute with your franchisor.

Evaluating a Franchise Agreement

Up till now, this chapter describes what you find in the disclosure section of the UFOC. It's important to remember, though, that while the disclosure section of the UFOC describes the relationship between the franchisor and the franchisee, the franchise agreement — the written contract — governs the relationship. This section introduces you to the franchise agreement and should help you evaluate the contract.

The franchise agreement is more specific about the terms of the relationship than the UFOC. After reading the UFOC, prospective franchisees often believe that they understand the relationship, so they only scan the franchise agreement. This is a terrible idea. Make sure that you read and thoroughly understand the franchise agreement. Unless you're an experienced franchise attorney, you're likely to misunderstand the impact of some of the terms included in the agreement.

Hire an experienced franchise attorney to help you understand the franchise agreement. Although Uncle Alex, who did your last house closing, is cheap, his lack of experience in franchise law and the customs and practices in drafting franchise documents may be costly later on. An attorney who is inexperienced in the nuances of franchise law may be unprepared to help you understand the franchise agreement. Later in the chapter, we discuss how to locate a qualified franchise attorney.

Does the agreement match the verbal promises and the UFOC?

During meetings with franchisors, they often make statements and promises about the relationship and the way they operate the business. If those statements and promises affect your decision to invest in the franchise, make sure that they're included in the franchise agreement. Unless they're included, they won't be part of the legal relationship.

Do you need an attorney or a financial advisor?

As you get closer to making a decision to buy a franchise, getting the right kind of help takes some research on your part. Perhaps you have a good lawyer who handles your current business and private dealings. You may also have a certified public accountant (CPA) who works with you on your income tax preparation. If so, you have a good starting point. If you don't have a lawyer or CPA, don't worry. Connecting with qualified help isn't difficult.

Lawyer

Making your way through the legal language of franchising can be daunting. A qualified franchise attorney can not only help you understand the terms you're considering but also protect you from taking a wrong turn.

Franchise law is a specialty; your franchise attorney should have substantial experience. Attorneys who are unsure of franchise laws and standard practices may review the agreements as they would a lease, thinking that they can make substantial changes to the provisions contained in the agreement. Experienced franchise counsel understands why certain terms are in the agreement and recognizes when others are unusual. As a result, their comments tend to be on the important issues and usually those issues that have the best chance of being changed during negotiations.

For example, the franchise agreement may provide for little or no protected territory. An experienced franchise lawyer might know that most of the franchisor's competitors have protected territories and could negotiate such an arrangement for you. The same goes for additional training or support that would be beneficial to you but that isn't provided for in the agreement the franchisor has presented to you.

If you're looking for a franchise attorney, ask your personal lawyer for a recommendation. He or she may refer you to a partner or associate or may be able to get recommendations from professional colleagues. You can also contact the local bar association, the American Bar Association, or the International Franchise Association for a reference.

The American Bar Association has a Forum on Franchising that can provide you with sources for articles, papers, and information on franchising. For $35, you can also order a membership directory of all attorneys who are members of the forum. The directory is broken down geographically. The ABA Franchise Forum on Franchising has a Web site that you can access by going to www.abanet.org, clicking on "forums," and then scrolling down to "franchising."

Consider asking other franchisees you know for references. A great source is the Council of Franchise Suppliers of the International Franchise Association. (Michael, this book's coauthor, is past chairman of the CFS, the professional arm of the industry association.) The CFS publishes a list of firms that specialize in franchise law both in the United States and internationally in the IFA's *Franchise Opportunities Guide.* Although some of the firms listed represent only franchisors, they can usually refer you to competent lawyers experienced in representing franchisees. You can access an online copy of the *Franchise Opportunities Guide* through the IFA's Web site at www.franchise.org.

Another source is the online *Directory of Franchise Attorneys* published by Franchise Update. The online *Directory of Franchise Attorneys* can be found at www.franchise-update.com.

Consider your franchise lawyer to be a member of your business team and someone you will want to work with in the years to come. For now, though, she or he will walk you through the UFOC and advise you on the overall desirability of the franchise offering. Expect your lawyer to review the franchise agreement and flag any items or issues that could be concerns for you. Your lawyer is your frontline defense against signing up for a franchise relationship that may not be in your best interest.

Financial and business advisor

When it comes to crunching numbers in an unemotional way, who could be better than a professional financial advisor? We're talking about a banker, CPA, or CA (chartered accountant) — someone you trust and you're comfortable sharing your financial information with. You can get directories of qualified CPAs or CAs from their local associations.

Another group of professionals who can provide you with assistance are franchise consultants. While most franchise consultants work primarily with franchisors, several can be of assistance to franchisees. You can locate franchise consultants who are members of the IFA's Council of Franchise Suppliers at the IFA's Web site at www.franchise.org.

In seeking out professional advisors, ask them if they have completed the course of studies offered by the IFA's Educational Foundation and are Certified Franchise Executives. The CFE designation is a relatively new but important industry standard for franchise professionals.

Broker

We have to be honest. We have problems recommending the services of a franchise broker to anyone considering investing in a franchise. Brokers hold out the promise of one-stop shopping, which means that you don't have to go through all the steps involved in researching and deciding on the franchise that's right for you. Someone else is deciding what your future will look like, and we don't think that's wise.

Brokers are typically paid by franchisors to find franchisees and close the deal. Why would you use a third party to find someone you intend to spend the next 10 or 20 years of your life with — especially if the broker's fee is paid by the franchisor? (We discuss franchise brokers in Chapter 4.)

Negotiating with a Franchisor

After you have digested the UFOC, you may think that the next step is haggling with the franchisor. After all, haggling — or negotiating — is the business way, right? In most situations, we would agree. But "striking a bargain" is not a phrase in the vocabulary of most franchisors.

Franchising's strength is its consistency. It's what the public depends on. It's also what you depend on. Can you imagine being in a room with other franchisees who'd signed their agreements at the same time you did and finding out that they got a different deal than you did, simply because they negotiated better? Think about the franchisor trying to manage a system with everyone operating under a different deal. Wasn't that thick document you just read called a *Uniform* Franchise Offering Circular?

Older, more established systems may be less flexible about negotiating terms, and newer systems may be willing to consider certain points as negotiable. If franchisors are willing to negotiate with some franchisees on the significant issues, they are likely to be willing to do so with others. This flexibility may not be a good sign.

Franchisors' reasons for negotiating may be based on their need to sell you a franchise to meet next week's payroll. Even if the need for immediate cash isn't the reason, another word for their flexibility is *inconsistency*. And inconsistency isn't what you or the public wants from a franchise system.

The whole point of buying a franchise is to give you a leg up on the ladder of success because you're buying into an established system. Changing significant parts of that system for any one franchisee may affect the integrity of the entire system.

You should never sign a franchise agreement without clarifying any points you don't understand. Where possible, you should attempt to negotiate the terms of the agreement to fit your needs.

Here are some of the common terms that franchisors may negotiate:

- A change in the size of your protected territory — or even granting a protected territory, if they don't typically do so in their standard franchise agreement
- Additional grand opening support
- Additional training for you and your staff
- Additional field support
- *Intra-owner transfer* — the transfer to another franchisee without incurring transfer fees or changes to the agreement
- Payment terms for the franchise fee
- *Default cure periods* — the time you will have to cure a default in your operation of the franchise. This is important, because if you don't cure a default in a timely fashion, you could lose your franchise.
- Start-up date
- The formula for calculating the franchisor's purchase price for your business on termination
- *Conversion franchisees* (independent operators converting over to the franchisor's system and brand) may be able to negotiate lower fees, or a longer time to liquidate existing inventory or switch to the franchisor's computer system.
- Franchisors may be willing to give up or modify any right of first refusal they may have if you try to sell your franchise before the term of the agreement expires. A *right of first refusal* refers to a franchisor's right to match a bona fide offer you received from someone to purchase your business.
- Although you may form a corporation to own the franchise rights for tax or liability purposes, the franchisor is relying on you personally to meet the commitments contained in the franchise agreement. One of the documents you will be asked to sign will probably be a personal guarantee for performance under the franchise agreements. On occasion, a franchisor may be willing to waive the requirement that you personally guarantee the agreement or may be willing to limit your liability under the guarantee.

These changes have little effect on the system's consistency; some even provide benefits, such as additional support from the franchisor.

However, you should be concerned if the franchisor is willing to negotiate freely about the product or services you will offer to the public, or if the company offers you lower fees for signing immediately. If franchisors are willing to negotiate freely with you, what have they agreed to with others? You and the public are relying on the system's consistency.

Part II

The Startup: Establishing Your Franchise

In this part . . .

To be successful as a franchisee requires that your franchisor provide you with training and other support needed for you to open, operate, and grow your business.

In this part, we look at the types of training provided by franchisors to franchisees and their staff, the assistance provided in making sure that the location selected for the business is right and ways in which you can expect to purchase the goods and supplies you will need to operate your franchise. We will also discuss other services many franchise systems provide to their franchisees.

Chapter 7

Training and Other Services

● ●

In This Chapter
▶ Asking the right questions about training — before you sign the franchising agreement
▶ Getting good training before and after you open your franchise
▶ Finding out about the other services the franchise salesperson promised

● ●

*F*ranchising is most successful when every location delivers the same products or services every time a customer visits the store. Giving customers that level of reliability is what franchisees do every day.

But running a successful business requires more than consistency. You have to find out how to manage the business. Great franchisors make sure that when franchisees begin to operate, they understand how to recruit, train, motivate, and manage their staff. Great franchisors teach franchisees how to manage their finances and how to market their businesses. In short, great franchisors share their formula for success.

This chapter helps you spot the telltale signs of a good training program. After all, you deserve the best chance at success. After you work hard to find the right franchise, you want to get the best short- and long-term value for your money.

This chapter also explains the other services franchisors can provide — before you open for business, during the hectic period of the grand opening, and over the long haul.

Finding Out about the Training Program Before You Sign a Franchising Agreement!

Training is one of our favorite topics — because it's one of the most important aspects of a healthy and profitable franchise relationship. The key to a good franchise business is training, training, training, and more training.

There's a right way and a wrong way

Training our people is the most important thing we do. And the training never ends. We even teach them how to clean the tables. Believe it or not, there's a right way and a wrong way. I also know that the art of teaching and learning goes on forever, and we devote a lot of time and money to making sure that our franchisees get the best information to help them succeed.

A point worth making here is that all franchisee training is not the same. Some franchisors emphasize a strong training effort at the front end — to get you rooted in the basics of the business. Other franchisors believe not only in offering a helping hand in the beginning but in standing by you in the years to come. Clearly, hooking up with a franchisor who wants to stand by you for the long haul is the better choice.

Modern franchising is a complex business, and franchisees require continuous updating and retraining to keep them up to speed and at the top of their markets.

Here are some questions to ask the franchise salesperson about the training program the franchisor is offering:

- ✔ What are the locations, duration, and additional costs of your initial training? Is the cost of transportation and living expenses included in the initial franchise fee, or does the franchisee pay those expenses?

- ✔ Who is required to attend your initial training program?

- ✔ Do you have the option of bringing your staff to the training? How much does the franchisor charge for each staff member who attends? If the franchisee's staff does not come to training, who trains them?

- ✔ How comprehensive is the training curriculum? How much of the training takes place in a classroom? What subjects are covered? How much of the training is conducted in the field? What areas are covered in the field? Do you learn how to manage the operational, financial, marketing, and personnel aspects of the business, or is the training limited to how to make the product or deliver the services? How does the franchisor describe the management training provided?

- ✔ Who conducts the training? What are the trainers' backgrounds? Have they ever operated a location? When? How long have they been in the business? What positions did they hold? How long have they been conducting the training? Do they have any training in conducting these programs? What are their responsibilities in the company when they're not conducting training programs?

✔ As staff and managers turn over, how do the new staff and managers receive training?

✔ In addition to the operations manual, will the franchisor provide any training materials for training new staff?

✔ How often does the franchisor introduce new products and services? When new products and services are introduced, how does the franchisor train the franchisee, managers, and staff on the new products and services?

✔ Are training programs continual and regularly scheduled? What types of additional training are provided, who can attend, what is the cost, and where does the franchisor conduct this training?

✔ Do any members of the headquarters staff or field staff provide hands-on assistance during the pre-opening, grand opening, and initial period when the franchisee is beginning the operation of the business? What type of assistance does the franchisor provide, who provides the assistance, what is the duration, and what is the cost?

✔ What is covered in the operations manual? Are you allowed to see it before you sign the franchise agreement? When was the operations manual last updated? How often is it updated?

✔ Are you allowed to attend one of the training sessions before you sign the franchise agreement?

✔ How does the franchisor communicate with the franchisees? How do the franchisees communicate with the home office?

✔ What happens if you have an emergency problem or question — maybe after regular hours or on weekends?

Getting Good Training Before and After You Open Your Franchise

A good franchisor insists that you learn the business and that you keep learning as the system changes — and market conditions evolve. Most franchisors train at their offices, at established operations, or at franchisee locations. Follow-up support is usually handled through the area field representative, who acts as the liaison between you and the home office.

Getting good initial training

Expect to cover a lot of ground during your initial training. Initial training should be aimed at teaching you and your staff how to produce and deliver the franchisor's product or service the same way every time. But good training is more than simply learning how to make the product.

Franchisees should learn

- ✔ Standards and operating procedures
- ✔ Food safety (if the franchise is a restaurant or a store selling food products)
- ✔ Technical operations on products and services (non-food franchise)
- ✔ Leadership and business management
- ✔ Problem solving
- ✔ Tips for understanding the customer experience
- ✔ Brand positioning (how the franchisor wants the public to think and feel when they hear the brand name)
- ✔ Merchandising and pricing methods
- ✔ Marketing and advertising
- ✔ Labor management, including recruitment, supervision, and motivation
- ✔ Techniques for training staff
- ✔ Cleaning and maintenance
- ✔ Safety and security
- ✔ Vendor relations, purchasing, receiving, stocking, and inventory management
- ✔ Financial management and business plan development
- ✔ MIS/POS systems. A *management information system* (MIS) is the computer system used to manage business matters (accounting, payroll, and so on), while the *point-of-sale system* (POS) is used to manage sales activities (cash registers, pricing, and inventory).
- ✔ Communications, both internal and external
- ✔ Site selection, construction, landscaping, and store design

Good training instills in the franchisee the franchisor's brand philosophy, teaches franchisees everything they need to know from opening the business in the morning to closing at night, and gives them the sources for additional or emergency support.

Most franchise systems begin training after you sign the franchise agreement and pay your initial fee. Many provide training in segments such as the following:

- ✔ Initial training to assist you in site selection and development
- ✔ Training for the franchisee and his or her management personnel

✔ Training for your initial staff

✔ Continual training that introduces your staff to new products and services

✔ Training for your replacement staff when employees leave the franchise

How much training you can expect depends on the industry, the complexity of the business, and especially on the franchisor.

If the industry historically has a high turnover of staff — and the franchisor requires you to send your staff to the franchisor's training program and then charges to train your replacement staff — this is an additional cost of turnover. It's also a good inducement to recruit and retain good employees.

In some systems, you can expect only a few days of training, and often this time is spent working in operating locations. In others, you can spend months in training, both in class and on the job in training locations, and then the franchisor provides continual training for innovations, new products, and your replacement personnel. The length and scope of the training you will receive are detailed in the Uniform Franchise Offering Circular, or UFOC (see Chapter 6). Make sure you feel confident that the training is sufficient for you to operate your business.

Ensuring that you receive effective ongoing training

Once your franchise is open, expect the franchisor's field staff to show up armed with operational, marketing, and organizational support. For example, Wendy's is a big franchise, so field support in the United States is provided by one of the five regional offices. Smaller franchise systems may use the headquarters staff to provide you with your training and ongoing support.

Operating a franchise in today's economic climate means staying on your toes all the time. You can't do that by yourself. As a franchisee, you should expect the franchisor to provide you with more than initial training. You should also expect the company's help with the rollout of innovations, such as the preparation of new products or the operation of new equipment. The hallmarks of great franchisors are offering new products, updating research, implementing new-product development, installing state-of-the-art technology, introducing better methods of customer service, and repositioning franchises in the market. These services keep a company more than one step ahead of the competition, such as Wendy's did with its Service Excellence program (see the sidebar "Managing innovations").

DAVE SAYS

Managing innovations

Managing innovation is one of the most demanding tasks a franchisor can face.

Wendy's leads the industry in providing great customer service. The speed, efficiency, and accuracy of our operations lead the industry. In 1998, our drive-through pick-up window was rated by *QSR* (quick-service restaurant) magazine as number one in the industry for speed, accuracy, menuboard, and speaker clarity. But we thought we could be better.

We introduced a new program called Service Excellence to further improve our customers' experience. Service Excellence was created in our Western Region, and we're rolling out the program throughout the company.

Service Excellence tracks the service we provide to our customers. For customers using our pick-up windows, the program tracks the time from when they order at the menuboard, to the window where they pay, and then to the window where they pick up their food. The timers provide us with a breakdown of operational performance and timing for each segment of our customers' experience. This study provides the data that enables our managers to improve customer service and speed. Since introducing

Service Excellence in our Western Region, service times at our pick-up windows in many restaurants have improved by more than 100 percent.

The Service Excellence program involves more than simply giving timers to the locations. The program is supported by a comprehensive set of operating principles and continual training that gives store managers the analytical tools to measure results and the skills to coach the restaurant crew, reward their outstanding results, and improve morale.

By improving the speed at which customers are served while maintaining the accuracy of their orders and the quality of the products, franchisees are able to provide better service to their customers. Better service is one way to keep them coming back. By improving staff efficiency, you reduce the number of staff you need for your existing customers and reduce the number of staff you have to add as the business grows. Not surprisingly, when personnel are working efficiently, a lot of the normal customer hassles go away. When the hassles go away, the staff is happier, and retention is up.

Training your employees

Let's face it. You can be the best-trained franchisee in the system, but if your full-time and part-time employees don't know how to provide the product, ring up sales, keep the store clean, and offer a positive shopping experience, you're not going to get happy — and repeat — customers.

So a question worth asking is this: Who trains the employees? Plan to get a lot of different answers to this one. Some franchisors pass on the responsibility to the franchisee, and other franchisors do the initial training and expect the franchisee to follow up with day-to-day reinforcement.

What's the best way to train your employees? You won't find one right answer to that question. Some franchise systems work best if franchisees handle all the training. If you're buying that kind of franchise, make sure that your franchisor teaches you how to train your employees. That advice may sound convoluted, but think about it. How can you teach your employees about their job duties if you've never been taught how to teach?

Teaching someone how to do something is a skill, and maybe even an art. Simply saying, "Here, watch me" isn't adequate training. It's important, therefore, that franchisees who are expected to train their staffs receive "train-the-trainer" instruction. This training gives them the skills they need. Great franchisors also provide franchisees with training aids to make their job easier.

Some franchisors use the Internet to provide training to their franchisees through distance learning programs. This training technique enables franchisees and their staffs to access the franchisor's training program online when they have the time to devote to learning. It also enables the franchisor to know who is being trained and how well franchisees and their employees are scoring on the tests that are often provided.

Franchisors such as Wendy's provide franchisees with a host of training materials, including train-the-trainer programs, videos, workbooks, and certification programs. Before any employee performs a task, he or she is trained and certified according to the franchisor's standards.

Find out whether you're on your own if an employee needs some extra training. A good franchise field staff can help with retraining and refresher courses, so check on that option, too.

Finally, no matter how much help you get from the franchisor's headquarters or field staff, the day-to-day follow-up and supervision of your staff belongs entirely to you. Your employees are your front line — they create the first impressions your customers have of your store. And those first impressions are lasting ones. So your employees need your ongoing attention and input — they're an important part of the recipe for successful franchising.

Evaluating Other Services: What Support Can You Expect from Headquarters?

Every franchisor is different — and the services franchisors provide their franchisees vary widely, based on a company's philosophy, maturity, and fees.

The franchise agreement defines the services the franchisor provides. The services are usually divided into those the franchisor provides pre-opening, such as initial training, and those that continue throughout the life of the franchise, such as field staff support.

If the franchise salesperson makes a promise that you're relying on, make certain that promise is contained in the franchise agreement. For more on franchise agreements, see Chapter 6.

The following sections mention just some of the services you can expect to receive in addition to training.

Services before you open your franchise

Before you even open the doors of your franchise, a franchisor can help you by providing the following services and information:

✔ Site selection criteria, selection assistance, prototype plans, construction assistance, interior and exterior design and layout, fixtures, equipment, and sign specifications.

✔ Operations manual.

✔ Plan-o-grams that give instruction on where and how to display merchandise. Plan-o-grams also provide information on promotional displays, seasonal displays, and even the *end-caps* (that's what they call the merchandise displayed at the end of the row).

✔ Information on conducting a grand opening marketing and public relations program.

✔ Help with coordinating store-opening activities.

Services after you open your franchise

You can expect your franchisor to provide some services on an ongoing basis, throughout the life of your franchise. The following are examples:

✔ Updates to the operations manual

✔ National, regional, and local advertising programs and materials

✔ Research and development of new products and services and system enhancements

✔ A franchisee advisory council and other methods of communications

✔ Field support

✔ Continuing, advanced, or replacement training

✔ Group purchasing programs for inventory, supplies, insurance, equipment, and so on

✔ Enforcement of system standards and protection of the trademark

Your franchisor should have systems in place to instantly communicate data on inventory, personnel, and financial reports — such as point-of-sale (POS) systems and management information systems (MIS). Look for monthly newsletters and/or an *intranet* (like an Internet newsgroup, only private to the franchise system) to transmit company news, industry information, and local market data. Some franchisors use voice mail to personally reach you.

Although the franchisor provides you with services to support your business, keep in mind that the primary purpose of any continuing service is to enhance and protect the value of the franchisor's trade name and related trade and service marks. So it's important that you work with the franchisor and its personnel to seek out and use the services they provide. The support, after all, benefits both of you.

Time to call home

Suppose that you buy a terrific franchise in a great location and your customers love you. As a new franchisee, you completed all the training your franchisor offered and finished with flying colors. You have a sharp staff, which you trained, and right now your monthly sales are strong. The future looks good.

Then a problem pops up, and you need your franchisor's help.

At this point in the game, you find out that what you thought were promises of future hands-on support from headquarters were nothing more than part of the sales sizzle. You may find yourself alone in a very nasty business situation. It's too late to amend the franchise agreement to force the franchisor to respond. For example, suppose that a key member of your management team quits without notice. Back when you were buying the franchise, the franchise salesperson told you about a great program in which the franchisor provides temporary replacement managers to franchisees should just this type of event happen. When you need such a program, you find out that it was only a test program and the franchisor no longer offers that service. If that service is not in your agreement, the franchisor may not have any obligation to provide that unique service. The time to find out whether you can depend on your franchisor through the bad times as well as the good is before you buy a franchise. When the unexpected happens in a good franchise system, franchisors may not have a legal obligation to help the franchisees, but they help anyway. Wouldn't it have been nice for the franchisee in the preceding example to find out that, although the program had been canceled, the franchisor was going to help out anyway? That's why we continually remind you to check with other franchisees before you buy the franchise. Make sure that when you call for help, your franchisor will answer the phone and take action to see you through the rough spots.

What's the difference between a field consultant and a general manager?

Is there a difference between a field consultant and a general manager? You bet there is.

In most cases, a general manager is an employee of the franchisee operating multiple locations. Sometimes the general manager may be the franchisee. A field consultant works for the franchisor and is your primary support person in most systems. When franchisees buy a franchise, they buy the right to operate the business under the franchisor's system. The system provides them with the tools to operate to the franchisor's standards, training to ensure that they know how to do so, and follow-up support.

Field consultants, field representatives, and territory managers (or whatever the franchisor calls its field staff members) are a franchisee's first line of continuing support. They visit franchisees and call them on the phone to provide them with advice on operations, merchandising, and promotions. They also evaluate how good a job franchisees are doing in offering the products and services to customers. This attention ensures that franchisees are in compliance with the system's standards. In most food-related businesses, the field staff members also assist you in evaluating food safety. Ensuring that standards are met protects everyone's business.

However, as long as a franchisee is in compliance with system standards, the franchisee and the franchisee's general manager are responsible for making the decisions — not the field consultant.

The general manager, on the other hand, is a decision maker. He or she is responsible for sales, customer satisfaction, personnel, management, marketing, financial management, legal compliance, safety, security, and so on.

Remember that the general manager is the franchisee's employee, but the field consultant answers to the franchisor. Therefore, franchisees should not expect their field consultant to manage their business. That's the role of franchisees and their general managers. The field consultant is there to ensure compliance and to give advice — sort of like an accountant or attorney.

Chapter 8

Establishing a Site: Location, Location, Location

*H*aving a good location is important, but having a good, or even a great, location won't make up for a bad operator. Given the choice between that old tired chant of location, location, location and an equally one-dimensional chant of operations, operations, operations, we opt for neither — but lean toward the latter.

High-Visibility Locations — Always the Best Choice?

For some businesses, getting the best corner in town — with high visibility and terrific customer access — in a strong, anchored center is not only unnecessary but also the path to rapid disaster. Carpet cleaners, janitorial services, building repair services, direct mail companies, lawn care services, pest control businesses, moving companies, tool delivery services, and home inspection services, among other service providers, don't usually need high-visibility retail space and can't afford it, either. Their needs run more to good-looking trucks, delivery access, access to postal facilities, highway access, warehouse facilities, and good telephone service than to locations where their customers shop. After all, most of these service providers go to their customers; the customers don't come to them.

DAVE SAYS

Location, location, location

I don't know whether there are any really bad locations. But I can tell you, there are some really bad operations that you can turn around into good operations. If people live or work near your location or drive by it and they can get in and get out of your store, you can develop the store into a good operation. If you have a good operation and you screw up, then you end up with a bad operation. You can't really blame your problems on the location as much as you can on operations. In other words, you can change bad operations; it's tough to change a bad site.

In considering the criteria for your businesses location, you need to first establish the criteria that's important for your type of business. But regardless of whether location is important, operations is the ingredient necessary for success.

Finding Out What Constitutes a Good Site

We won't kid you: Finding a good retail or restaurant location in today's market isn't always easy. Many of the best spots have already been taken, and competition for the available real estate is brisk. Given rapidly changing consumer traveling patterns, opening your franchise in the right location does matter because if your operations and your location are great, you have the best of both worlds.

This section can help you recognize a good site.

Getting some general advice about site selection

You may think the best place to open your doors is where the crowds are right now, such as in a shopping mall or adjacent to a busy highway. You may be right — for now. But you may not know about plans on the drawing board for another mall development just down the road or a highway bypass that will take your customers down a different route — away from your franchise.

No one can offer a stock definition of a good site because different businesses require different kinds of locations. Some generalities do hold up, however. If you're investing in a retail franchise, focus your search on a location that gets in your customers' faces. If it's in the path of people commuting to work, near an entertainment arena, or in an office complex, customers can see your business and more easily buy your products and services.

The emerging markets

The emerging markets of the United States represent one of the economic jewels for businesses today — especially for franchise systems. The opportunities to satisfy local demand are staggering. When a franchisor opens locations in emerging inner-city markets, franchisees create jobs, train young people to work, create paths for career advancement, and, best of all, create opportunities for local wealth.

Some of the golden opportunities today are in what may be called the *emerging American markets* — the inner cities and downtowns. Many of these urban areas are still underdeveloped for branded quality goods and services. The potential return for franchisees that are able to meet local demand can be enormous. Plus, some inner-city franchises may qualify for tax credits on equipment and employee salaries.

You may luck into a site just by driving through town on the lookout for "for sale" or "for rent" signs. Or you may opt to use a real estate broker. Another resource is the exhibitions where shopping center developers lay out their construction plans. Contact the International Council of Shopping Centers at 212-421-8181 or at its Web site at www.icsc.org.

Using specific data to evaluate a site

Investigating a site for your franchise is very much like following the scientific method. Suppose you hypothesize that a given site may be a good location. You need facts to support your hypothesis before you can reach any conclusions. Here are some factors you need to put under the microscope.

Most demographic studies present information based either on census tracks or on a radius measured in miles from a center point. For franchisees, what is important to you is how large an area you should measure. It doesn't do you any good to measure five miles out when your customers are primarily within walking distance of your location. The franchisor usually can give you assistance in determining how large your trading area is. The *trading area* for a location is the area it draws the majority of its customers from.

I've always tried to keep the search for real estate simple for Wendy's — we look for where people work, live, or play.

Here are some factors to consider:

✔ **Population density:** How many people are in the site's trading area? What are their ages, incomes, ethnic backgrounds, family sizes, and marital status? What is the expected short- and long-term growth in the area? Do the people live in houses, or do they rent apartments? Do people in the area buy enough of your particular product or service to maintain your business? Are new residential or business developments going up nearby?

Several companies in the United States can provide you with demographic reports. Two sources are CACI/Information Decision Systems, phone 800-795-7483, Web site www.infods.com; and National Decision Systems, phone 800-866-6510, Web site www.natdecsys.com. Many franchisors are subscribers to one of the demographic companies and may be able to provide you with the report.

✔ **Traffic generators:** Is the site in close proximity to activity centers — such as malls, office complexes, factories, government centers, schools, hospitals, and housing developments — that draw customers? Is the location near a tourist attraction or site where special events are held periodically?

If you are in a retail business, you want to be in a center that draws customers to your site. If you are looking for heavy consumer traffic (we call that *frequency*), would you rather be next to a major supermarket or a furniture store? People shop for groceries several times a week; they replace their mattresses once every ten years.

Who's located to your left, your right, and behind you? Can your concept feed off theirs? Will you be able to do cross-promotion with other tenants? (*Cross-promotions* is a marketing strategy in which two or more business — with similar customers — work together on a promotion. Take a look at Chapter 11 for more on this.)

Is the site in a professional, downtown office building that allows you to draw off the people coming to and leaving work? If your concept, however, draws from an evening clientele and the downtown is dead at night, maybe the office building doesn't work for you. But if most of the tenants are small businesses and you're a Mail Boxes Etc., this could be a perfect location.

In a mall or strip mall, who are the anchor tenants? Anchor tenants such as grocery stores and major department stores draw people to the center. If it's a new center and you plan to live off of the anchors' customers, however, you may not want to open your business before the major tenants — who generate the traffic — open theirs. At an existing location, are the tenants economically healthy?

Determining the economic health of the rest of the tenants is important. The simplest way to find out is ask them. Talk to the existing merchants and see how business is, who their customers are, and where people are shopping. Look at their locations — both inside and outside. Are the facilities tired and do they look old? Are they in need of maintenance and upgrade? If the answers are yes, these are signs that the center is economically distressed. You can also talk to the local chamber of commerce and banks. They usually know what's happening in their neighborhoods.

✔ **Traffic count and accessibility:** How many cars drive by the location, or how many people pass by on foot? Both kinds of traffic are desirable. But if the cars are traveling at 60 miles per hour and can't stop at your location, traffic count doesn't really matter. Is traffic heaviest during the time of day you are open, or does it substantially drop off on the weekends when you are supposed to be the busiest?

Can your customers safely get in and out of the site's parking lot and the location itself? Is it convenient to highways and public transportation? Is accessibility hampered by restrictions such as "no left turn" or "one way"? Where is the traffic signal in relationship to access to your location? Can target customers reach your business within a reasonable amount of time during rush hour and at other times? Do pedestrians have to cross a major street? Are any road construction projects in the works? Do any barriers exist that might make customers drive or walk right by? Is the site on the right side of the street to support your business? If you're selling donuts, for example, you may want to be on the side of the road where traffic is heaviest in the morning. However, if your clientele stops in after work, say to pick up dinner or their dry cleaning, perhaps the side of the road on their way home is better.

✔ **Competition:** Where is your competition located? Are plans for more nearby competitors on the drawing board? Some landlords try to limit direct competitors in the same center. Others don't care about the tenant mix in their centers but want to restrict any franchise that has a location in their center from opening up five or more miles away. Many concepts benefit from being next door to similar business — ever notice how QSRs (quick-service restaurants) are clustered together? Printers, who may depend on walk-in customers, on the other hand, like to be the only one in the neighborhood.

✔ **Saturation:** Given the competition — both established and proposed businesses — does the area still need your product or service?

✔ **Security:** Is the site safe? Who provides security for the center?

✔ **Potential employees:** Do you have a potential pool of employees available to staff your franchise? For example, is the franchise near a college, in case you need part-time workers? If the only jobs you have available are entry-level positions and there isn't a kid in the neighborhood who isn't driving a Porsche, labor may be tight. With everyone vying for a limited number of employees, pay scales can go through the roof.

✔ **Size:** Is the property appropriate for your needs? Is it zoned correctly? Can you get the right size building? Does the property have enough parking spaces?

✔ **Appearance and tenant mix:** If the site is an existing one, what condition is it in? Is the parking lot paved and striped? Is the landscaping attractive? (Watch out for big trees that block your visibility from the street.) Is it well lit at night? Is it in a safe area? Who are the other tenants? Do they enhance the standards of your business? Is their signage attractive? If there are a lot of empty locations, what's happening to the businesses in the center — is there a high turnover?

If the center has a location that meets your size requirements, can it be easily retrofitted to the franchise standards? If it can be, you may have a leg up, because necessities such as sanitary hookups, storm drains, and electrical power are already in place.

For new centers, your concerns are similar. What is the reputation of the landlord when it comes to keeping the center attractive? Do the landlord's other properties tend to have branded upscale tenants, or do their centers deteriorate rapidly until the only merchants open are the local charity's used clothing drop-off center and Bureau of Motor Vehicles?

✔ **Visibility:** If the site is a retail location, can potential customers clearly see it from all major roadways and access routes? If motorists can't see your location until after they have passed the entrance to your center, building a clientele will be a slow process. Are the landscaping and trees attractive but so large that they block your signage? Most landlords don't look kindly on tenants who play lumberjack at night. Drive past the location from all directions and count the seconds of visibility. The longer your signage can be seen, the better.

✔ **Signage:** Customers have an easier time seeing that you're in a center if you can use the signs, logos, and colors that they identify with your brand. However, some landlords like to have all the signage uniform — same size, same colors, same lettering. It is important, therefore, that you check to see whether the landlord or the town's zoning board has any signage restrictions. This issue is important if you want to benefit from the franchisor's consumer brand recognition. Franchisees need to check that their signage is welcome at the location. Be certain that if you expect to use illuminated signage or signs on poles outside your location, you will be allowed to do so.

✔ **Zoning:** Is the site appropriately zoned for your type of business? Do you need the town's zoning board to make an exception (or variance) in your case? How accommodating is the local zoning board? Are zoning changes in the works that may affect you or change the character of the neighborhood?

✔ **Other limitations:** Do the area's ordinances, statutes, or codes restrict building colors, parking spots, signage, or building heights? Is selling or consuming liquor restricted? Does the community regulate the type of equipment you can use or goods you can sell? For example, a restaurant that by concept depends on open-hearth cooking is asking for trouble if it opens in a community that restricts wood burning. Talk to the local zoning board and your real estate agent — they should be able to help you with the facts. Also verify with the landlord that what you *intend* to do in the location is actually something you *can* do.

✔ **Environmental concerns:** Is the soil clean? Are any contaminants present inside an existing structure? Will the subsurface support a structure? Is the land appropriate for construction? Does it require excavation or tons — and we mean tons — of fill? If you need to install underground tanks, will you be able to do so? What about grease and waste lines? Are they adequate? Specialized engineering and consulting firms conduct these types of services. Your architect and builder can assist you with locating local firms. Most times, your franchisor can also provide you with information on how to find the proper professional assistance.

✔ **Title:** Who owns the property? Is the landlord in good financial condition, or in bankruptcy? Is the title to the property free and clear, and can the landlord afford to keep the property up? Does the property conform to the boundaries specified in its legal description? Check with a local title company, which can do the proper research for you. Your attorney, banker, or CPA can help you locate title companies they have worked with.

✔ **Land and building purchase and/or rental or leasing fees:** Is the cost of the site within your budget? Is the cost in line with the competition and what the franchisor said you can afford? Is the payment subject to increases? Are you responsible for any improvements? Are the lease terms flexible?

✔ **Hidden costs:** Do you have to pay common-area maintenance and insurance charges, merchant association fees, or mandatory advertising contributions? Is the developer responsible for upkeep? Are there restrictions on the hours of operation? Are they likely to affect you, for better or worse?

Not all of the above factors will apply to you, and there may be other criteria we haven't covered. You may be able to work through some potential problems. If your site potentially violates zoning ordinances, perhaps the zoning board will be sympathetic to your cause — especially if you're bettering the quality of life in the community. Franchisors can help you determine which criteria are important for you. They may have a site selection manual, training program, or staff available to help you. It's a good idea to also hire your own realtor, who can help you in your search.

Building successful locations

When I took over Kentucky Fried Chicken's four stores in Columbus, Ohio, the locations were not the greatest. Actually, the operations were terrible. The management lacked necessary skills and exercised no consistency in following the system. I fired the management, and over time, I rebuilt those four stores into good operating units. Once sales were better, everybody started saying, "Hey, how did you get those great locations!"

Look for any red flags. A location that keeps turning over or that has been on the market for a long time should raise your eyebrows. If anything — and we mean anything — smells fishy, investigate further before you sign a lease. Don't let your desire to find a site and open your store trap you into selecting the first available location.

Choosing a Good Site

One of the best things about owning a franchise is that in most good systems you get all kinds of support from your franchisor. You still, however, need to double-check any information the franchisor supplies against your own research. Think of this as a check-and-balance. You check on the accuracy of the data, and your information provides a balance to what the franchisor offers.

Getting help from the franchisor

When you're dealing with location issues, most franchisors can offer one big advantage: experience. The staff at a mature franchisor can help you identify the kinds of locations that usually work — and those that don't. For example, staff members know whether a franchise can be effectively home-based initially or even long term, whether an office attracts more business in a generic, white, two-story building or with a Park Avenue address, or whether a retail franchise fares better tucked inside a mall or flaunted center stage on a main thoroughfare. So your first step in the process of selecting a location is to discuss viable options with your franchisor. The company may allow a variety of locations or may stick to only one type.

Exploring your location options is a big part of your franchise research. Start-up costs for a home office versus a freestanding site — and everything in between — can vary by hundreds of thousands of dollars. How's that for hitting you in the pocketbook? Defining your location is also a vital part of your business plan. Anyone who's financing your venture — even your moneybags uncle — will want to know where the cash is going, including what the site will look like, why it will attract customers, how much customer traffic will pass the site, and who your competitors are.

Okay, so now you know the kind of site you need. What's next? A good franchisor points you in the right direction. The franchisor's staff can fill you in on demographic secrets, especially the chain's *target market* — the profile of your potential customers. How many customers do you need, say, of a particular age and income within a certain radius? How far are customers willing to travel to buy your goods or services? How much are they willing to pay for what you sell?

Many franchisors bombard new franchisees with *site criteria* — a list that spells out specifications for a particular franchise — inside and out, so that the site meets the franchise system's standards. You may be required to have X number of parking spaces, X number of seats, X number of grills, and so on.

Retail and restaurant franchisors, especially, expect their franchisees to comply with their design standards — without variation. On the other hand, an office-based franchise may not care whether you have wood floors rather than carpeting or mahogany desks rather than oak. A consistent look at each of the locations may have no importance to them as long as it meets their overall quality standards.

Will your franchisor ultimately help you find this crown jewel of a site? Franchisors usually educate you about their site criteria, provide you with site criteria forms, and ask you to find the location and do the required research — before you present the site package to them for review. They will then evaluate your information and visit the location before approving or disapproving your choice.

As for actually finding the site, some franchisors provide considerable help, some provide guidance only, and some leave you on your own. Look at your franchise agreement to find out what your franchisor will do for you. Ask the other franchisees in the system how good the franchisor's site selection assistance actually was.

Typically, the franchisor will approve a general area for your location and expect you to search within those boundaries for a location, unless the franchisor already has a site in mind. Once you find it, the franchisor's role is to accept or reject the specific site you select.

Other franchisors — especially start-up franchisors — may physically accompany you on your site hunting; the staff may jump in the car with you, plot demographics, and talk to landlords.

Some franchisors may already have located the site, built the building, outfitted it with equipment and fixtures, and made it available for you to buy or lease.

One thing is virtually a given: Once you select a site, you probably need the franchisor's final approval. Check your franchise agreement to see whether and how the franchisor must approve a franchisee-selected site and the time limit for the franchisor to render a decision. Standard contracts allow a franchisor to accept or reject your request to open at a particular location. This decision, like everything else in franchising, reflects the need for consistency.

In almost every franchise agreement, the franchisor is only approving or not approving a site, not guaranteeing it. This is true even if the franchisor found the location for you — you didn't have to accept it, did you? The franchisor's approval does not indicate anything other than that the site is acceptable. Ultimately, the selection of the site is your responsibility.

The reason franchisors distance themselves from the final decision is their potential liability. If they selected the site — even if it fails because the franchisee did not operate the franchise properly — a good franchisee advocacy attorney will claim that the business failed because the franchisor picked a bad site.

In the end, selecting and accepting the location is your responsibility, not the franchisor's. Understand your franchise agreement.

Avoiding encroachment

One thing that gets people talking in franchising is *encroachment*. You'll hear the term, and we suggest that you understand the concept before, not after, you sign your franchise agreement.

Suppose that your franchisor has granted you a protected territory stretching one mile around your location. That means the franchisor is prohibited from allowing another franchisee or company-owned location from opening closer than one mile from your store. But it doesn't necessarily prohibit the franchisor from selling over the Web. It depends on the language in the agreement.

Suppose that you open a franchise on the corner of 5th and Main. A year or five years later, another franchisee from the same system opens a franchise on 4th and Main. The new franchise is so close you can see your customers going in and out of the new location. That's what we call encroachment.

As in this example, encroaching can come from another franchisee or company-owned location opening in your protected territory. But it can also happen if the franchisor begins to sell products in other locations — such as a supermarket or a convenience store within your protected territory. It can also happen if the franchisor allows others to offer the same services you sell in your neighborhood. Encroachment can occur through catalog sales (from catalogs mailed into your market) or through the Internet, if customers can buy through e-commerce the same products you sell in your location. It depends on what the franchise agreement says about your protected territory. Encroachment is like someone stepping on your toes — only the person doing the stepping is your franchisor, who you thought was your "partner." Ouch, that can hurt!

Obviously, encroachment can pose a big risk to your business. Carefully examine the language of your franchise agreement. Are you getting a protected territory, or do you have no territorial rights? If your franchise grants you only a site franchise (your protected territory is no bigger than the four walls of your store), the franchisor could conceivably establish other locations nearby that will compete with you. Some contracts specifically state that a franchisor may establish other units and/or sell items through other channels of distribution in direct competition with a franchise. Since Internet sales don't require the establishment of a location, e-commerce may not legally be encroachment, unless it is specified in the agreement. Don't assume you have rights not provided in the agreement.

You need to know — before you sign the franchise agreement — whether the franchisor will be able to open locations in your market area. Joyce G. Mazero, lead franchise attorney at Jenkens & Gilchrist in Dallas, Texas, cautions, "Contracts normally tell you what the franchisor is granting, such as the right to operate a site, but don't always plainly tell you what it is not granting — such as no right to exclusivity outside of the site, no right to conduct business on the Internet and no right to prohibit the franchisor or another franchisee from operating from a site close to your site. What you are getting is just as important as what you are not getting."

Don't rely on a franchise salesperson's statements about what the system generally does or doesn't do regarding its locations. Even if the salesperson makes sense when saying that the franchisor would never open a location so close to you that it would adversely affect your business, when it comes to locations and protected territories — as with everything else that's important — get it in writing in the franchise agreement.

Even where the franchise agreement allows the franchisor to establish new locations close to an existing franchisee, some franchisors establish procedures — adopted internally or with their franchisee advisory councils — to review the impact of encroachment on existing units. If the encroachment is significant, they may decide not to allow the development of the new location. If the encroachment is minor, they may allow the unit to be developed but may compensate the affected franchisee for the lost sales. One possible remedy the franchisor could employ is called a reverse royalty. A *reverse royalty* is when a franchisor pays directly or indirectly to the affected franchisee a percentage of the other franchisee's sales.

Other franchisors simply cite the terms of the affected franchisee's agreement and allow the unit to open — regardless of the extent of the impact.

Find out what the franchisor's policies are concerning protected territories and encroachment before signing the franchise agreement. Read your franchise agreement; speak to other franchisees in the system, and talk to your attorney.

Doing your own market research

When you sign your franchise agreement, you will be granted an area to locate your franchise in. It could be within a zip code or within a larger area such as a city or a county. It's up to you to determine where in the area you will finally locate.

Your franchisor should be able to give you criteria for choosing your site, and you should know how big your protected territory is, if it is protected. Get a list of locations of other franchisees in your system and find out from the franchisor whether any other franchises are under development. By plotting these locations on a map, you should be able to begin localizing your search.

You can find a great deal of information on the areas you have selected at your local library, city hall, chamber of commerce, and on the Internet.

We suggest that you tackle demographics first. Local chambers of commerce typically keep updated demographic data from the Census Bureau and track local business activity, employment levels, local retail sales, and the area's long-term economic health.

In the United States, you can get census data directly from the U.S. Census Bureau's Web site, at www.census.gov. This site provides information on population in your targeted neighborhood that you can use to determine whether the area has a population that can support your business. Shopping center and mall developers may also have this information, which is generally free if you are looking in their center.

Much of the demographic data is based on Census Bureau findings, which are assembled every ten years. Unless the data you use is fresh or has been adjusted for the passage of time, you may be making your plans on 9- or 10-year-old data. Make sure that the information you are using reflects the most current information available.

Your franchisor may subscribe to a demographic service or may be able to give you the names of commercial services to use, such as National Decision Systems and CACI/Information Decision Systems.

Visit the local police department to find out about traffic and pedestrian safety in the area. Check with the city engineer and the local and state transportation departments to see whether they've logged car counts on particular roads. You can spend thousands of dollars to commission your own study, but that may not be necessary. Instead, do your own visual inspection. You probably counted red cars, blue cars, white cars, and so on just for the heck of it when you were a kid; make believe that you're a kid again, but this time get down to business. Park yourself in front of your target location and count the vehicles that pass by. Make sure that you do your counting on different days and at different times to get a true picture. Be observant. If you're looking for children, look for car seats. If young teenagers are your target, look for teens on bicycles. If you sell home medical equipment and wheelchairs, how many and how frequently are the spaces reserved for handicapped drivers filled? Anything that gives you information about potential customers in the area can help you pick a better site. We're sure that you're dying to know about the competition.

State retail associations are a terrific place to get statistics on the number and size of competing retailers. Check the local yellow pages or call the National Retail Federation at 800-673-4692. In addition to real estate brokers, local bankers and community development corporations often keep lists of regional shopping centers, strip malls, and other developments.

Chat with local business groups, local merchants, and suppliers to get a sense of what running a business in town is like. Then pound the pavement again. Stop in on the owners of similar businesses in the areas you are examining to cull behind-the-scenes information on police protection, zoning board involvement, seasonal fluctuations, merchant or professional group activities, and competition. Is there enough business to go around? Do you get the sense that you'll be welcomed into the fold or driven out of town?

To find out about future development, check with city hall, real estate developers and brokers, and the folks at the local zoning and planning department. Investigate road construction projects and future housing and business developments. Find out about any zoning proposals or done deals. You may even want to sit in on a zoning board meeting to see whether the board members are flexible in approving variances to businesses.

An experienced real estate attorney can hold your hand through this process — or you can do some of the work yourself. Start by going to the town or city hall and meeting with the planning department. Let the employees there introduce you to the people in the zoning department and meet with them — get a feel for what is important to them and what isn't. Go to the zoning board meetings and listen for how they determine whether to make changes for other folks looking for variances. This research takes some time to do alone — that's why experienced real estate attorneys can be worth their weight in gold.

Also, find out whether you can benefit from locating in an economically depressed area. In the United States, if you settle in a rural or urban empowerment zone or enterprise community (these are areas defined by the federal government for special federal funding assistance), you may be eligible for federal tax benefits on equipment purchases and wage tax credits for employees. For more information, contact the Department of Housing and Urban Development, Economic Development Initiative, at 202-708-0380.

Some franchise systems, banks, and the Small Business Administration have special incentive programs to encourage franchisees to open locations in economically depressed areas. Ask about them.

This process sounds pretty time-consuming, doesn't it? Research for a freestanding building can easily take 90 days to a year. But it pays not to cut corners. Actually, once you start the research, piecing together a composite picture of your future market becomes kind of fun. You'll be happy you went through the process, because it will likely improve your chances of selecting a great site.

Considering Specific Site Options

Depending on your franchise, you will be confronted with a host of different types of locations in which to establish your business. Good franchisors look closely at successful operations in the system and provide franchisees with profiles of what they consider ideal locations. Some franchisees rent office space in high-rise office buildings; others work from home; but most select sites in malls, shopping centers, or freestanding locations. Here are some of the types of locations you typically will be looking at:

- **Malls:** Malls are large, enclosed shopping facilities anchored by two or more major retail stores and servicing a large geographic area. A mall is typically easily accessible by automobile via major arteries or interstate highways.

  Selecting a well-developed mall requires a franchisee to balance the benefits and the drawbacks. The principal drawback is the cost, which includes not only the rent but a host of additional expenses, such as common-area maintenance — your share of caring for the public space. Malls also charge merchants association fees, which are used for advertising for all the tenants in the mall. You also usually have to operate during the hours that the mall is open. On the plus side, malls are natural draws and attract large numbers of potential customers.

- **Major shopping centers:** Major shopping centers are similar to malls except they aren't enclosed. A trend in many markets is to convert some of the underproducing enclosed malls to major shopping centers, because people like the convenience of the regional malls but prefer the ability to park in front of the store of their choice.

✔ **Shopping areas:** A concentration of stores serving a local community is considered a shopping area. "Downtown" is a shopping area and benefits from the traffic from office workers, visitors to downtown, and people who live in the downtown area. Because of the traffic and their prime locations, in some cities, these sites can be expensive and often suffer from lack of parking for their customers. Since most of the traffic in the downtown areas is usually created by office workers, the hours during the weekdays are busiest, with most customers coming in before work, during lunch, and after work. This inconsistent traffic pattern makes staffing a bit problematic. Except for a few cities that have re-created their downtowns as entertainment destination areas for residents from the suburbs — as Baltimore did — these areas are quiet in the evenings and on weekends and holidays.

✔ **Neighborhood centers:** A supermarket or a discount store — or both — typically anchors a neighborhood center with a variety of small retail and service stores. These centers usually provide the most reasonable rents and draw from a trade area of from one to three miles, depending on population access and concentration. Most neighborhood centers have few restrictions on signage — although the upscale centers can be as tough as the regional malls and are the type of location that most retail and service franchise systems target for their franchisees.

✔ **In-line centers:** In-line centers have become more popular in recent years. If you've ever been to the center of a small upscale town in New England, you've seen a typical in-line location. These sites are attractive to merchants selling higher-priced, impulse items requiring lower traffic counts, and to merchants selling lower-priced items that would benefit from high foot traffic. The amount of traffic depends on the area where these centers are located. These areas have one significant drawback — a shortage of parking — but in major urban areas, this problem is overcome by public transportation.

✔ **Strip centers:** These are neighborhood centers of three or more stores, generally anchored by small grocery or convenience food stores.

✔ **At-home sites:** Although maybe home locations aren't sites in the traditional sense, more and more franchisees are opting to work out of their homes. We discuss home offices in the next section.

✔ **Nontraditional sites:** Airports, ballparks, and cobranded locations are all types of nontraditional sites. We discuss these locations in some depth later in this chapter, as they represent significant opportunities for many franchisees today and are a growing trend in franchising.

Working from home

Many franchise systems, especially service franchises that never have customers coming to their offices — for example, carpet cleaning, janitorial, maintenance, and repair services — not only allow their franchisees to work from their homes but actually encourage it.

Working at home reduces a franchisee's cost of doing business and is convenient. For many franchisees, it's perfect. If they like, they can get up early, do their paperwork, and plan their day — all before taking a shower and getting dressed. In the evening, after dinner, they can relax in their office, watch some TV, and prepare for the next day. And since they don't have any other office, they can deduct the costs associated with their home office on their tax returns. (You should check with your accountant and tax preparer to determine what is deductible.)

This arrangement does have its downside, though. Working and living in the same place often gives franchisees the chance to spend more and more time at work and less and less time with the family. If the office is in a family area, you may be taking away space that the family used for other purposes — like watching TV together. Some communities have zoning restrictions on whether you're allowed to operate out of your home. Although many communities ignore home businesses that do not put up signage, others are sticklers for the rules. You also need to be disciplined. Running the family errands, mowing the lawn, and picking up the kids may be more than distractions; they can rob you of the time you need to do business.

Still, if your franchisor allows such a location, and you enjoy the informality of a home office, it can be a terrific way to operate.

Opting for a nontraditional site

More and more franchisors are expanding their systems by allowing franchisees to open in locations that are not where you typically expect to find them. These locations are called *nontraditional sites,* and they are popping up wherever people congregate — gas stations; convenience stores; hospitals; airports; train and bus stations; colleges; large department stores; and movable kiosks at sporting arenas, ballparks, and malls. These sites are often also referred to by people in the industry as *mass gathering locations,* locations that provide a "captive audience."

One of the biggest benefits of setting up your site in a mass gathering location is a guaranteed flow of potential customers, whether you advertise or not. The biggest drawback is that your business success is tied to the ebb and flow of people in the host environment. In other words, when the ballplayers go out on the road or when the season ends, you're out — of luck. Colleges are governed by the academic calendar, so get ready to twiddle your thumbs during summer vacation, unless many students attend summer school.

Some other nontraditional locations are called *dual-branded locations.* In this arrangement, your franchise shares common space with another brand, for example, in a food court at a mall. If your business brings in traffic in the morning hours and is less busy during the afternoon, partnering with another brand that has a heavy afternoon business but a weak morning business may make sense. You can save on the cost of real estate and, possibly, equipment. And you have the ability to use your staff more effectively. Check with your franchisor to see whether any dual-branding opportunities are available to you.

If you choose a nontraditional site, you're still buying a franchise, paying royalties, and remaining accountable to the same standards. Make sure that your franchisor offers equipment, signage, and design specifications to fit these new locations. Compare the costs — and sales/profit potential — with those of traditional locations. These sites are usually tucked inside another location and take up less square footage. The smaller space usually means less staff and possibly lower overhead. Some of these franchises operate seasonally. But just because they're smaller doesn't mean they're cheaper. Some — such as highway travel centers — are on prime properties, and the bidding can be fierce.

So has a nontraditional site caught your eye? Many of the same criteria that you use to check out a traditional site apply here — and then some. Is it heavily traveled? Is it visible to patrons? Are there signage restrictions? If an airport location opens up, there's a big difference in the number of road warriors if it's located in a main terminal, concourse, or food court as opposed to a terminal for the smaller, less traveled carriers, in small regional airports. Not every mass gathering opportunity is the same — you need to do your homework. Where would you rather be, in a sports stadium where the home team fills the stadium each game or in a sports stadium where the home team can invite the spectators to share the bench with them — and still have room? You get the point.

Understanding a lease

When it's time to sign a lease, you've already decided on a location. You should be in the process of contacting the real estate or mall management company that manages the property to determine space availability, specific occupancy costs and lease terms, and to complete your site review package for your franchisor.

Does the center have an adequate amount of space available for your business? While you don't want to squeeze into a space that's too small, you also don't want to pay for space that you will never need. Square foot costs can vary with overall size; often, the larger the space, the lower the square foot cost. However, even with a lower per-foot cost on a larger space, the maintenance and development costs will be higher. Evaluate size based on your needs.

The occupancy cost typically consists of the following:

✔ **Base rent:** This figure is usually stated as a square foot cost. Evaluate the base rent against the rent other tenants are paying, as well as what comparable space in the area is going for.

Example:

Location size:	2,400 square feet
Annual gross rent:	$48,000.00
Base rent:	$20 per square foot

✔ **Common-area maintenance:** This cost can be stated in a variety of ways, but it is the business's share of the cost of maintaining the center or the mall — including snow removal, parking lot maintenance, security service, common-area utility costs, exterior lighting, common signs, and so on. The share is generally based on the business's square footage as a percentage of the total square footage of the entire center. These costs can vary considerably from center to center. Pay attention to them. Ask other tenants whether the common area is being maintained.

✔ **Leasable versus leased:** Mall charges other than rent may be calculated one of two ways:

> **Leasable:** The total basis is your square footage divided by the total number of square footage in the center or mall.

> Example: 2,400/500,000 = 0.0048

> **Leased:** The basis is your square footage divided by the number of square feet actually leased.

> Example: 2,400/435,000 = 0.0055

Using the leased method is always to the landlord's advantage. This method means that if stores are closed or not leased, their portion of the charges is spread among the existing tenants. Always try to use the leasable method.

✔ **Real estate taxes:** Typically, you will pay your square-foot share of the center's tax bill.

✔ **Cost of living escalator:** Some centers try to increase the rent based on increases in the Consumer Price Index or some other economic measurement. Because these indexes can be volatile and unpredictable, especially in a period of inflation, it's better to reject this method of generating excess rental payments.

✔ **Percentage rent:** Many strip centers expect a percentage of sales beyond a certain stipulated amount that relates to base rent. The percentage is determined by the information you give to the center management and by its estimates of the business's potential. Obviously, it is to your advantage not to have a percentage rent or to keep the percentage as low as possible and the sales point as high as possible.

✔ **Merchants association:** These associations are usually the province of malls and are used as contributions to the mall's promotions. The fee is usually based on a square-foot share, paid quarterly, and normally adjusted based on some economic index or formula.

The occupancy cost is made up of a group of economic factors and must be viewed in total. The ultimate cost of a location may have little resemblance to the base rent. When comparing locations and negotiating a final lease, compare the *total cost* of the space.

Building a location

Sometimes the only site you can find in the area that is perfect for your franchise is an empty lot. What do you do now? Build.

If building a site is going to be your choice, make sure you touch base again with the local zoning board and building department before you even close on the property and certainly before that first shovel of dirt is moved. You want to be in compliance with everything — down to local ordinances that set the hours that you can hammer and saw to your heart's content. You also want to determine whether the town needs to approve any *variances* (which give you permission to do something on the land that's different than the zoning rules allow) for the property and whether the site will support your needs for things like utilities and parking.

Although your contractor or architect usually does the legwork, it's your responsibility — not the franchisor's — to see that it all gets done.

Your contractor needs to obtain the following:

✔ Permits for construction, utilities, signs, *curb cuts* (those indentations in the sidewalk that let the cars in), and environmental matters

✔ Variances, if you need the town to approve some specific violation of the zoning requirements for your site

✔ Certificates of occupancy, which allow you to occupy the location

There's more. You also have to prepare preliminary plans and specifications for site improvement and construction, and usually — big surprise! — submit them to your franchisor for approval.

Understanding the layout

Every retail and restaurant franchisor has a floor plan (footprint) that is excruciating in its exactness. Even if you think that a counter should be 2 inches longer on the left side, you have to follow the franchisor's plans — or get the franchisor's permission for a change. Even if you know for a fact that menu signs are more readable if they're placed 12 inches lower to the floor than the required 90 inches, you still have to follow the plans. You need to get these specifications and standards so that you can review them with your architect and contractor.

Franchisors usually provide prototype plans for every location. Your architect must develop plans for your site that meet local ordinances as well as the franchisor's standards. Don't assume that you can add improvements to the design, such as a bigger *back of house* (the kitchen and storage area). Check with your franchisor before making expensive changes that you may have to reverse.

All this specification from the franchisor is intended to ensure consistency. That's great, but what if your particular community has some type of restriction that runs counter to your franchisor's building plans? Make sure that you notify your franchisor so that the two of you can discuss the required changes. If it's important, the franchisor often personally contacts the builder or city planner to discuss the changes.

Wendy's provides one standard building plan for freestanding locations. Wendy's also has plans for remodeling existing locations and restaurants in strip centers. The company offers design services — including site plan layout and preliminary equipment plans — for nontraditional units. The company's engineering department develops the specifications and standards for the building products and equipment based on Wendy's experience with building design, maintenance, and quality assurance.

Selecting the contractor

You're probably groaning by now, remembering the last time you hired a contractor to fix up your family room or enclose the patio. But selecting a reputable commercial contractor who has experience with meeting deadlines and the quality requirements of a franchisor isn't difficult. And doing so is only common sense.

The following checklist is a useful guide for selecting a contractor.

- ✔ Get the names of several contractors from your franchisor, architect, other franchisees, and other merchants in the community.
- ✔ Check the contractors' reputations with the local building inspectors, consumer affairs department, and Better Business Bureau.
- ✔ Ask for the names of at least ten prior customers and call several of them. Ask the following questions:
  - Did the contractor start on time as promised?
  - Did glitches or surprises crop up during the building process?
  - Did the contractor finish on time and within budget?
  - Was the contractor fair about any extras?
  - Were the workers reliable?
  - Was the contractor familiar with local building code, and did he have a good relationship with local building inspectors?

- Did the contractor follow laws and take safety precautions?

- Were actual materials and workmanship as specified?

- Did the contractor cut any corners?

- Was the work area maintained?

- Did the contractor listen to your concerns?

- Have any structural problems (for example, leaks or cracks) occurred since completion?

- Did the contractor deal with any problems that occurred after payment was made?

- Are you happy with the quality?

- Would you use this contractor again?

✔ Visit some of the locations where the contractor has completed work.

✔ Verify that the contractor is licensed, has adequate insurance, and is bonded.

✔ Make sure that no court cases or actions are pending against the contractor.

✔ Prepare with your architect and your franchisor's construction department the completed RFP. Make sure that the RFP is detailed and includes brand, model, color, quantity, size, and so on of all equipment included.

✔ Get written proposals from at least three contractors, using the same specifications.

✔ Review all proposals with the contractor to make sure that you have a clear understanding of the proposal.

✔ Review the proposals with your architect and your franchisor's construction department.

✔ Make a decision based on the quality of the contractor's work, ability to meet deadlines, and reputation for correcting problems quickly. Price, though important, shouldn't be the overriding criterion.

Building your own location can be tedious and demanding. But if you select the site based on your franchisor's criteria, plan the job, select your contractor carefully, and monitor the job closely, you will have the exact location that you need.

Chapter 9

Getting the Goods: Merchandise and Supplies

In This Chapter

▶ Getting supplies from the franchisor or franchisor-approved vendors

▶ Buying supplies through a cooperative

▶ Choosing your own vendors

▶ Taking delivery of your merchandise

▶ Maintaining your inventory

*I*n this chapter, we look at the way franchisees purchase and maintain inventory and supplies. One of the main benefits you are looking for in a good franchise system is the ability to combine your purchases with those of the franchisor and the other franchisees. Working together, you hope that you can get the best price, the best products, the best equipment, and the best service from suppliers. A good franchisor has also made certain that the suppliers want to participate in this beneficial relationship simply because it's good for their business, too. Probably no benefit is more important to a franchisee than the potential strength in numbers the system brings to controlling the quality, consistency, availability, and exclusivity of the equipment, supplies, merchandise, and raw materials used by its franchisees.

All franchises need merchandise and supplies of some kind. Some franchise systems require franchisees to buy certain goods direct from the franchisor. Some systems specify that franchisees must purchase from approved suppliers. And some systems allow franchisees to choose their own vendors. The method or combination of methods depends on the type of industry, the products or ingredients the franchise uses, the size of the system, the size of the region the franchisor serves, and the available delivery methods.

Which method or methods the franchisor uses often depends on the philosophy of the franchisor management in how it wants to service and sometimes control the system. It may also depend on whether the franchisor earns money from the purchases made by its franchisees.

When you're looking at different franchise opportunities, you can tell in advance what methods the franchisor uses by reviewing the franchisor's Uniform Franchise Offering Circular (see Chapter 6). The UFOC tells you which methods the franchise system uses and whether the franchisor earns any income on the franchisees' purchases. Finding out in advance is important because some systems with a lower royalty rate may actually cost you more money than a system with a higher royalty rate, because the difference may be more than offset by the income the franchisor earns from your purchases.

 There's nothing wrong with a system that earns money every time you purchase goods from a supplier. After all, it costs the franchisor to set up and maintain these supplier relationships. It's also important for franchisees to have a financially strong franchisor who can provide them the services they need and want. However, in a perfect world, you want to find a franchise system in which the "blended" costs of being a franchisee (royalty and other costs) are the lowest, while the services provided by the franchisor are the highest.

Following the Rules: When Your Franchisor Directs Your Purchasing

Suppose that you've purchased a maid service franchise. You've hired a first-rate staff, and they're ready to get busy scouring, wiping, dusting, and polishing. But elbow grease isn't enough; they need cleaning products. You may not have the option of hopping over to the local warehouse store and loading up a cart. Your franchisor may require you to purchase products directly from the company. Or your franchise agreement may specify that you use only franchisor-approved suppliers or authorized products. These rules ensure that the supplies you use meet the franchisor's standards. A bonus to you is that, because the franchise system may buy in large volume, prices may be lower.

Buying goods direct from your franchisor

When franchisors elect to be the exclusive suppliers to their franchisees, the requirement usually extends only to items that are proprietary (read, secret recipe) or that contain certain key ingredients. These products may be ordered directly from the company, or in most systems, the franchisor has provided the products to the distributors that serve the system.

Merchandise and supplies that aren't proprietary are another matter. Even if the franchisor distributes them, they usually aren't the exclusive suppliers, and franchisees have the option of making their purchases from either approved suppliers or from their own chosen vendors. (Sometimes, the purchases must meet standards or specifications set by the franchisor.)

At Wendy's, for example, there are no products or services for which Wendy's and/or its affiliates are the only supplier. However, at Tim Hortons — the coffee and fresh-baked donut chain that Wendy's acquired in 1995 — franchisees are required to purchase certain products such as coffee, sugar, flour, and shortening from one of the company's subsidiaries. Tim Hortons distributes products to its locations (from six warehouses located through-out Canada) in a fleet of Hortons-owned trucks and trailers.

Many of the legal disputes over the past two decades have resulted from fran-chisee perception that they are getting gouged — that is, the products they must purchase from the franchisor are excessively marked up. This makes them less competitive. Rupert Barkoff, Partner at Kilpatrick, Stockton in Atlanta, Georgia, warns, "Beware of franchisors who require that certain products be purchased through them. It is easier for a franchisee to digest the franchisor's decision that products must be purchased from the fran-chisor when the product sales are not a profit center for the franchisor."

Although the methods the franchisor uses for supplying products are in the UFOC, the franchisee usually gets additional information on supplier relation-ships at training.

Getting merchandise and supplies from approved and required suppliers

Rather than inventory all the merchandise required for a network of fran-chisees, some franchisors give franchisees a list of approved suppliers from whom they can buy their items directly. As long as the approved suppliers sell only the merchandise approved by the franchisors — without unautho-rized substitutions — franchisors can maintain control over the quality of the products sold under their brand.

A good franchisor is the keeper of the brand. In that role, the franchisor's rep-resentatives identify, screen, and approve suppliers to the system. Suppliers come in all shapes and sizes, and your franchisor has hopefully sifted through the best of them for you. Before you chafe over having to use only a franchisor's choice of suppliers, curb your entrepreneurial spirit and read on.

A good franchisor wants to keep your operational costs as low as possible to help you make as much money as you can. If a franchisor has gone to the trouble — and expense — of finding good suppliers for you, take advantage of that effort! Of course, ask your fellow franchisees whether they're happy with their suppliers. (Make sure that you ask this question before you buy the franchise. You don't want to be surprised.) If they are, be thankful that finding good suppliers is one less item on your to-do list.

Supplying goods the Wendy's way

Wendy's franchisees can take advantage of arrangements we make with suppliers. Programs set up by our purchasing department can help make sure that products meet our quality standards and are available when our franchisees need them. At the same time, our franchisees can buy at a lower price because of volume buying. We provide the purchasing service free of charge to our franchisees. It's not a profit center for us. It's another way we ensure consistency in the Wendy's brand. I think a good franchisor should offer this service for the franchisees because it's the right thing to do.

We have a whole staff of people who go into our suppliers' operations and audit their facilities.

Our staff members check on the entire production line and make sure that the company is doing everything the way we want it to. We even check our products by pulling them from the suppliers' facilities and the distribution centers around the country and sending them off to an independent laboratory for evaluation. We want to make sure that all the food safety measures are in place and being used. With all the recalls in the food industry, you have to be aware of exactly what the suppliers are doing, what's going on at their production facilities, and what environment our products are being produced in.

Franchisors worth their salt negotiate with manufacturers for the lowest net prices on goods, for marketing support, and for other benefits. Check with your franchisor about the way rebates are handled in your system. The procedure is far from uniform among franchisors or among suppliers. Also, if you discover that a supplier in your area meets your franchisor's criteria and is less expensive than the franchisor's authorized suppliers, make sure to pass the information on to the franchisor's headquarters.

Buying products authorized by the franchisor

All franchisors — big, small, or in-between — require consistency in the products sold under their brands. Product standards and specifications are one of the keys to controlling product consistency.

Franchisors set product standards and specifications, which means that they tell their franchisees what type and quality of products to buy. As long as franchisees follow these rules, they can choose their own vendors. This practice is common in small franchise systems, but even big franchisors often allow franchisees to buy items locally, as long as those products meet the standards. A recent study of the quick-service restaurant (fast food) segment by FranData (a research and information firm based in Washington, D.C.)

focused on 12 franchisors, and all required that franchisees' purchases meet set standards and specifications. Most franchisors required that their franchisees buy only from suppliers that had been approved.

Buying Goods through Cooperatives

Several franchise systems use *cooperatives,* or buying groups, to purchase products, marketing, advertising, insurance, leasing, credit, and other goods or services.

Cooperatives are by no means uniform in how they function and whom they represent. Many are started by franchisees, and the franchisor isn't part of the buying group. Other cooperatives include both company-owned and franchisee-owned locations. Still others represent members from several franchise systems.

The value of joining a cooperative is that group purchasing lowers prices. This method gives you a competitive advantage over those who can't buy as cheaply. Also, large buying groups often get better access to new products, better allocation when products are scarce, and better service from suppliers when things go wrong.

Franchisees and/or franchisors purchase membership in the cooperative and commit to buying a certain percentage of their requirements through the cooperative. Cooperatives are controlled by the members, typically on a one-member one-vote basis, with members determining the officers, directors, policies, and procedures adopted by the cooperative.

Cooperative members may also share in what are called *patronage dividends.* Patronage dividends, like stock dividends, are distributions of the earnings of the cooperative. However, patronage dividends differ from stock dividends in one major way: Stock dividends are based on the number of shares you own, while patronage dividends are based on the amount of your purchases from the cooperative. The more you buy, the more you get back in patronage dividends.

Of course, when you purchase through a cooperative, you still must meet the standards and specifications your franchisor has set for your location.

Finding Your Own Suppliers and Goods

One key advantage of buying a franchise is that you can be part of a larger network that includes your franchisor, fellow franchisees, and regional support staff. But if you're one of the first franchisees in a system or your franchisor isn't large enough to have national or regional distributors, you may have to do some of the relationship building with suppliers that a franchisor in a larger system would do for you.

If your franchisor doesn't provide you with a list of authorized suppliers, you're going to have to choose your vendors yourself.

Selecting vendors

Work with your field consultant and your franchisor's purchasing department to see whether they can help you identify suppliers in your markets. Visit other similar businesses and ask what suppliers they use. Your local chamber of commerce may also have a list of suitable suppliers.

In deciding on a supplier, you need to do some preliminary homework:

- ✔ Define your specific needs. Make sure that you have a list of authorized products from your franchisor (if your franchisor sets standards and specifications).

- ✔ Know what you want and how much you need *before* you call a vendor. You need to be as specific as possible when you talk with vendors. Being decisive increases your credibility and, as importantly, reduces the chance that a good salesperson will be able to sell you a substitute product, additional products, or a larger quantity than you can possibly hope to use during a reasonable time period. Your franchisor or other franchisees are the sources for this information.

- ✔ Identify and talk with more than one vendor before making a final decision. Each vendor has its own strengths and weaknesses:

  - Pricing

  - Scheduling of deliveries

  - Emergency deliveries

  - Delivery charges

  - Market research

  - Merchandising assistance (plan-o-grams)

  - Rebate management

- ✔ Obtain written qualifications, bids, and quotations. Get references from several of the vendor's other customers.

Evaluating vendors

When you review bids and quotations from vendors, make sure that you understand the total charges. Some vendors quote a low price on a product but make up the loss with additional handling and delivery charges. Look for these hidden charges when you compare pricing.

Price is certainly one of the prime considerations in selecting a vendor. However, basing your decision solely on price can be a mistake. A good price on items constantly out of stock or a good price from a vendor who is continuously trying to dump outdated merchandise won't help you build your business.

If your franchisor offers a supplier-evaluation questionnaire, get it — and use it. If not, you need to make one up yourself. In addition to competitive pricing, look for the following attributes when you select and evaluate a vendor:

- On-time delivery

- High quality standards

- Consistent product quality

- Prompt order processing

- Professional sales force

- Professional advice about local pricing, what products are hot, and so on. This is especially helpful if you are selling a "commodity" — milk, bread, and cigarettes — where knowledge of what others are charging for the same commodities can be extremely helpful.

- Reasonable credit terms

- Exceptional customer service

- Meaningful reports about your purchasing trends (seasonality and periods of greatest need), returns (items you tend to order in excessive amounts), and so on. Why returns? If your manager is overordering merchandise that isn't selling, it's a good thing to know. You don't want your shelves full of items that don't sell and that take up valuable shelf space. With knowledge of what is being returned, you can replace slow-selling merchandise, or merchandise that is not selling at all, with hot items. But make certain you speak with your franchisor before changing your product mix.

- Timely and complete information on new products

- Merchandising assistance. Some suppliers actually come into your location and unpack the merchandise they sell you. Some also lay out your shelves based on a *plan-o-gram* (a layout of how the shelves should look) supplied by the franchisor or, if a plan-o-gram isn't supplied by the franchisor, based on one they've developed.

> ✔ Effective promotional assistance and participation
>
> ✔ Fair and honest financial practices (for example, passing on the full amount of manufacturer rebates and allowances)
>
> ✔ Documented insurance and financial stability
>
> ✔ Sufficient staff and resources to grow with your business

Receiving Merchandise

If you own a franchise, the first thing you have to figure out is how to manage your receipt of merchandise. You must properly check, log in, and store all merchandise entering the store. You can negotiate lower prices for your merchandise, but you won't save any money if you don't notice unacceptable quality or shortages in shipments. To avoid these losses, you or the store manager must establish a regular receiving routine for your store. Having a routine helps to monitor vendors and reduces the chance of shortage.

Your franchisor should provide you with a list of recommendations and procedures for maintaining your inventory. Follow it.

If your franchisor doesn't provide inventory procedures, the following sections offer useful guidelines.

Receiving deliveries

Suppose that you've just purchased a convenience store franchise. The new site has been built, and you're standing inside your brand-new building. The only problem is that the shelves are empty. Soon you'll need to begin scheduling and receiving deliveries, but you may not have any experience in this process. Follow these general tips for receiving merchandise at any type of franchise:

> ✔ Make sure that deliveries are scheduled in advance. Accept deliveries only during specified hours. When the location is open and operating, you want the merchandise to come during off-peak hours so that you can concentrate on accepting the delivery.
>
> ✔ Don't allow vendors to park in front of your business. Require vendors to park in an out-of-the-way spot. The front of your business is for customers.
>
> ✔ Have the delivery driver bring all products into the building before you check the items. (Some systems want their own employees to bring merchandise into the store.)

✔ Make sure that the merchandise you receive is for your business.

✔ Check all vendors *in* and *out*. Be sure to physically see every item; don't just take the driver's word. Check all cartons and boxes when the vendor is leaving to make sure that they're empty, that no merchandise is being carried out of the store. Unless absolutely necessary, vendor check-in should be done *away* from that vendor's display and away from merchandise you already have on hand. Don't allow a vendor to both stock shelves and remove boxes unless you check both before the vendor leaves.

✔ Watch helpers. Some vendors have helpers whose main job is to distract you during the check-in process.

✔ Immediately put away all perishable products.

Checking the goods after they're in your location

A truck pulls up at the back door of your franchise, and a flurry of activity follows. Suddenly, you are surrounded by boxes. The driver is completing the paperwork for your signature. This situation doesn't have to be scary if you know what to do. Check the quality and condition of the merchandise before accepting it. Here are some additional tips:

✔ Examine every box for obvious signs of damage, such as tears, broken cardboard or crushed areas, signs of tampering, rattles, damp or wet cardboard, bad odors, dented cans, substitutions of standard items, and so on.

✔ Before signing for the boxes, open any cartons that have been opened and resealed or that you suspect have internal damage. Note any damages on the receiving record.

✔ Always check the date code on the product when it is delivered. Make sure that the product is within the code and that you can reasonably expect to sell it before the code expires.

Verifying invoices

Attending to paperwork may be the least entertaining part of franchise ownership, but in the case of delivery receipts, it can be rewarding. You can avoid financial losses by ensuring that you're getting what you pay for. Check out these tips:

✔ Before accepting delivery, check each item on the delivery receipt against the product that has been delivered and then compare against the product ordered. Quantities received need to be checked against quantities ordered. Count the number of cartons delivered and compare this number to the number on the driver's record or freight bill. Never sign for more cartons than you receive. Any discrepancies must be noted on the freight bill or receiving record, or corrected before the vendor leaves the store.

✔ Never give the delivery receipt back to the vendor. Obtain the delivery receipt when the vendor walks in and under no circumstances return it to the vendor. Manipulating the delivery receipt is one of the most common ways that some vendors steal from franchise locations.

✔ If a substitution is made, call your franchisor's field consultant to verify that the substitution is valid and acceptable. Inform the driver and note on the invoice that substitutions that aren't approved by your franchisor are subject to return for full credit.

✔ If any item that appears on the delivery receipt is not received, have the driver clearly mark the item "short" along with the quantity not received. The driver must then sign the delivery receipt before you sign it.

Maintaining Inventory

Your franchise training manuals teach you all about maintaining your inventory. Procedures vary widely, depending on the type of franchise you own. Your franchise may not even have any inventory, and in that case, you can skip this section. (There's no test at the end of this book, and nobody but you will know.)

Back of the house

The *back of the house* is also known as the *stockroom*. It's literally in the back area of your business, and it's where you keep all the items not currently in use. If you need more vitamins, you go to the back of the house — or the back room, or the stockroom — and get them. Back of the house is also where you store perishables or frozen items, which means that it can also be the location of a refrigerator or freezer. You'll be expected to know what you have in the back, too; but again, franchisors already do a lot of the work by providing a plan-o-gram for the back of the house, just as they do for the front.

Your franchisor should provide detailed back-of-the-house storage procedures. Follow them.

If your franchisor doesn't provide information on back-of-the-house arrangements and procedures, here are some procedures to consider.

Dry storage practices

Dry storage may actually be wet — sorry. It's a term used for items that don't require refrigeration. If you're a health food franchisee, your vitamins and sports drinks are both dry storage items.

✔ Store products at least 6 inches off the floor on clean surfaces to permit the cleaning of floor areas and to protect from contamination and rodents.

✔ Don't store products under exposed sewer or water lines, or next to sweating walls.

✔ Store all poisonous materials — including pesticides, soaps, and detergents — away from food supplies, in designated storage areas.

✔ Store all open packages in closed and labeled containers.

✔ Keep shelving and floors clean and dry at all times.

✔ Schedule cleaning of storage areas at regular intervals.

✔ Date all merchandise upon receipt and rotate inventory on a first-in-first-out basis (place the oldest products in front of the newly received merchandise).

✔ Locate most frequently needed items on lower shelves and near the entrance.

✔ Store heavy packages on low shelves.

✔ Don't store any products above shoulder height.

Refrigerated storage practices

Make sure to place anything that requires refrigeration into your cold storage as soon as you can.

✔ Any food or other product removed from its original container should be enclosed in a clean, sanitized, covered container and properly identified.

✔ Don't store foods in contact with water or undrained ice.

✔ Check refrigerator and freezer thermometers regularly.

✔ Store all foods to permit the free circulation of cool air on all surfaces.

✔ Don't store food directly on the floor.

✔ If you're a business that needs to store products under refrigeration, make certain that the temperature setting is appropriate for the product.

✔ Schedule cleaning of equipment and refrigerated storage at regular intervals.

✔ Date all merchandise upon receipt and rotate inventory on a first-in-first-out basis (place the oldest products in front of the newly received merchandise). Doing so is particularly important with refrigerated products, as their shelf life is usually short.

✔ Establish preventive maintenance programs for equipment.

Front of the house

The *front of the house* is everything that's not the back of the house. This is the area that customers see when they enter your store. Obviously, how the front of the house looks is more important for locations that are frequented by customers and less important for locations that customers never see.

If you're a retail location, you will handle your merchandise differently than if you were a restaurant. Still, at all times, the front of the house is your showcase — it's what customers see every time they visit your store.

Retailers need to place merchandise on shelves so that it's attractive to customers and induces them to buy. Restaurants and other businesses that sell food also need to keep their locations attractive. If you have reach-in refrigeration accessible to your customers or if you have items on display, how they are displayed is just as important to you as it is to a retailer. Your franchisor should provide you with a plan-o-gram for that purpose.

✔ Follow your system's plan-o-gram.

✔ Your shelves and *merchandisers* (displays for your merchandise) should be kept stocked, clean, and dust free.

✔ Use proper product rotation by placing the oldest product in front of the newly received merchandise (first-in-first-out).

✔ Identical items should be priced the same. One benefit of modern point-of-sale technology is that you don't have to reprice each item when prices change — all you have to do is change the price in the computer and on the shelf's price tag.

✔ Make sure that you have adequate space between displays, as required by your local code.

✔ Use only signage that is acceptable in your system. If your franchisor requires you to use professionally prepared signage, don't use hand-written signs. As important, make sure that you remove the Christmas posters before Labor Day.

✔ Keep your floor area free of empty boxes, unless they're part of your design concept.

The Americans with Disabilities Act requires you to keep your store arranged in a manner that makes it usable for individuals with disabilities. As a general rule, provide enough space for easy passage of a wheelchair throughout the store, make certain that the lines to your registers are accessible, and don't display merchandise in a way that makes it difficult for people with disabilities to shop. If you have no choice about how you merchandise the store, make certain that your staff is actively available to any customers who may need assistance. Remember, it's the franchisee's responsibility to comply with all federal and local laws.

Part III
A Well-Oiled Machine: Operating Your Franchise

The 5th Wave   By Rich Tennant

"That new fella's acting crazy again. I'm gonna go fog him, and when he calms down I'll flick him out the window."

In this part . . .

Franchising is about relationships and your ability to work with people.

In this part, we examine four key relationships: your relationship with your franchisor, your fellow franchisees, your employees, and your customers. We look closely at how franchisees and franchisors relate and communicate with each other — during the good times and the bad. We discuss methods you can use to attract and maintain customers and, most importantly, we will talk about how to recruit your staff, which is the most important asset for any business.

Chapter 10

Working with Your Franchisor and Fellow Franchisees

*T*his chapter, perhaps more than any other, talks about people. People will give you plenty of directions for operating your franchise. People will look over your shoulder to ensure consistency. And people — lots and lots of people — will make up the franchise team. You need to know how to deal with them and what to expect from them. This chapter provides that information.

Playing by the Rules

Franchisors and franchisees show confidence in each other by signing the franchise agreement and agreeing to work together. But others are also part of this bargain — the other franchisees in the system. How well you operate has a direct impact on them. If you don't follow the system, your operation is likely to suffer, and you may fail. If you fail, the value they have built up in the goodwill of their businesses is reduced. It's really very simple. The whole team is counting on you to play by the rules.

Meeting franchise system standards

When you become a franchisee, good franchisors hope you will do so with pride. Franchisors are going to show the same pride by drilling into you the chain's standards — at training sessions, during franchisee meetings, in the operations manual, and in franchise newsletters. They will do it every chance they get — all in an effort to maintain the value of the brand and to support the pride everyone has in it.

Maintaining a system you can be proud of requires that everyone meet the system standards — at every franchisee operation and at every company-owned operation.

Violating system standards poses a threat to the system, and franchisors take it very seriously. So do the franchisees who work hard every day to maintain the quality of their locations.

Violations occur; most are corrected as soon as the franchisee is alerted to the problem. If violations continue, most of the time (unless the violation is creating a public hazard or the violation is considered extreme) franchisees will be contacted by their field consultant (the franchisor's employee assigned to your location) and counseled again to stop any unapproved actions.

Typically in mature systems, franchisees are also offered assistance in returning to operating standards. Franchisors usually beef up the oversight of the location to ensure that the corrections have been made and monitor it to ensure that it stays that way. This process goes on in every mature franchise system. If the violations continue, though, the remedies included in the franchise agreement kick in, an action that could ultimately terminate the relationship. Nobody benefits then.

Supporting and watching the system

In franchising, big brother, or sister, is watching. This oversight is for your benefit — and protection — and may take many forms, including those described in the following sections.

Field support staff

The field staff — sometimes called field representatives, field consultants, or regional managers — are the real troubleshooters in franchising. They are the members of the franchisor's staff who work directly with franchisees. Field consultants and franchisees must develop a relationship of mutual confidence and respect in order to maintain a positive working relationship.

Of the various names franchisors use to describe their field staff, *field consultant* is the most accurate because the major role of the field staff should be to act as a consultant to the franchisee. Their primary job should be to help franchisees improve the performance of their operations. The field consultants stay in regular contact with the franchisees by phone, e-mail, or in person to identify problems, answer questions, and hopefully bring solutions and new ideas directly to the franchisee. In some systems, the field consultants are also involved in local training.

DAVE SAYS

If I were a franchisee

If I were a franchisee, I'd expect field consultants to help me, not hurt me. I'd want a field consultant to come in and tell me what's wrong with my restaurant. If I had a problem, I'd want the consultant to help me solve the problem. I'd want the consultant to be professional, and I'd want the consultant to treat my people with respect.

Field consultants are not dictators, and they're not reporters. They don't come in and "write you up."

If I had a problem with my training, for example, I'd want a consultant to come in and tell me what's wrong. That's part of what franchisees pay for. Our franchisees pay Wendy's 4 percent in royalties (the continuing fee paid to the franchisor that is usually calculated as a percentage of gross sales) to help them become successful.

The field consultant's job is to conduct regular inspections of the franchisee's location, discuss any deficiencies, and make recommendations for improvements. Perhaps the franchisor's standards are not being met, the staff is not in uniform, or the merchandise displays are empty or dirty. Perhaps the franchisee's sales are down, and the location's payroll is up. The job of the field consultant — in good systems — is to help franchisees improve their performance.

In some systems, field visits are few and far between. Infrequent visits from field consultants are not a badge of honor for those systems. In some systems, every franchisee is visited on a set schedule. Others vary visits depending on a host of factors that may include the franchisor's analysis of the franchisee's financial and operational indicators. In mature systems, the franchisor obtains this information from reports and other information that the franchisee routinely sends (usually electronically), as well as from other sources. Depending on the industry, the ratio of field staff to franchised location could be as low as 1 to 8 or as high as 1 to 100, but the average is probably closer to 1 to 40.

Mystery shoppers

Mystery shoppers are usually employees of companies that specialize in "shopping" a chain's location and reporting back to the company what the customer experience is really like. Mystery shoppers are used not only in restaurants or retailers; franchisors rely on mystery shoppers to help them evaluate carpet cleaning, haircuts, gas stations, automotive repairs — just about every segment of franchising uses mystery shoppers.

That woman in the red dress may look like the other women in line, but she's really under cover to check out your staff and operations. The mystery shopping company and the franchisor work out a checklist about the shopping experience — and those reports are sent to the franchisor, who then discusses the report with the franchisee. To keep it fun, some franchisors have contests and give prizes — including trips — to the staff persons at system locations identified as doing an outstanding job. The hope is that all customers will be treated as if they were mystery shoppers.

Fellow franchisees

Your fellow franchisees can also be the eyes and ears of the system. Don't be surprised if they approach you with concerns about how you're operating your business. The biggest enemy to a franchisee is the other franchisee down the road who's doing a poor job. Customers may not know and certainly don't care that each location is individually owned. They'll just assume that the product or service is bad all over.

Often a franchisee's best advisor is a more experienced franchisee. After all, they're in the trenches together. Some franchises have "senior franchisees" whose role is to assist franchisees in certain circumstances. Who better to get advice from than a peer who understands the reality of day-to-day operations and knows the tricks?

On occasion, one franchisee will report another franchisee to the franchisor if they see that a fellow franchisee is not complying with the franchise system's rules and standards. Franchisees don't think they're interfering in someone else's business. Each unit is part of the whole; they're just protecting their interests.

Franchisees are part of the support team. Look over your own shoulder. Periodically review the operations manual and any training materials to ensure that your business is up to snuff. Ask for help if you need it. The franchisor may not know that you have a problem unless you tell them.

Keep one thing in mind, though: All knowledge and assistance do not flow from the franchisor's well. The franchisor is licensing you a system — not operating your business.

So if you need help, you can and should seek professional, outside advice: local accountants to help you improve your record keeping so that you can have a better handle on the business; marketing experts to help you create cross-merchandising opportunities with other merchants in the industry or to help you develop ways to target new customers; mystery shoppers who can tell you how well you really are doing — on a more frequent basis than the franchisor. Attend management classes at the local university. You can also send your manager and assistant managers to class — after all, they're running the show when you're not there. Remember, your success is your responsibility, not the franchisor's.

Changing the system

Ideally, every system should encourage ideas from franchisees. After all, franchisees are the ones on the front lines and may see ways to tweak the system.

Newer chains may be most receptive and may say yes immediately or fine-tune the suggestion further before rolling it out system-wide. Older systems also embrace great ideas but typically use caution before rolling them out. They may conduct focus groups to see how customers will perceive the change and will test it for ease of preparation, cost, and other factors in their test facilities long before they bring a new idea to market. Even then, they launch it conservatively in a few test markets before introducing it to all of the locations.

You have a much better shot at having your changes accepted if the new idea improves the system, fortifies the brand, doesn't infringe on the system's goal of uniformity, and enhances a franchisee's profitability. You improve your chances for success if you present your proposal in a professional manner and garner the support of other franchisees and your field consultant before approaching the franchisor. Some franchisors have new product committees as a subset of their franchisee advisory council. In those systems, talk to members of the committee to determine what criteria they use for recommending approval of new products and services.

The well of innovation

Many of Wendy's best ideas have come from our franchisees and from our Franchisee Advisory Council (FAC). Our FAC meets regularly to discuss issues that affect our franchisee community. Members of the FAC are a sounding board for changes or improvements that we plan for our stores. For Wendy's to be successful, we must all work together toward a common goal: to serve the best-tasting hamburgers in the business.

Franchisors want consistency, but they also should have flexibility in certain areas. Franchisors should develop a partnership relationship with their franchisees. (Franchisors may not be partners in the legal sense, but they should respect their franchisee's advice. They are, though, the senior "partner" and need to make the final decisions.) Franchisors have to remember that sometimes, to buy their franchise, franchisees have signed over their houses, taken out loans, put their kids' futures in jeopardy, and so on — so they must recognize that franchisees are a big partner in the business. At Wendy's we may have a basic menu, but we bring on different items from time to time, many of these proposed by franchisees.

If you have what you think is a great idea, speak up. But don't be insulted if the franchisor says no. A franchisor has to look at the overall system and how it serves the customer. Your great idea may not fit into the overall scheme of things. The franchisor's job is to make the hard decisions, and sometimes the decision is no. If, however, the idea is approved, most franchisors consider that improvement their property and reserve the right to use it in the rest of the system — without paying the franchisee any compensation.

Be wary of franchisors who willy-nilly approve all suggestions, especially those that compromise product lines and quality standards. That lack of discretion is evidence of a weak system and can destroy the basic concept that you're buying into.

Building a Relationship with Your Franchisor

In franchising, as in any relationship, you're bound to have ups and downs. The key is to be part of a system in which the seesaw tips toward the higher end.

We're not going to fool you: The love-hate relationship between the franchisee and the franchisor can turn nasty. You need to check out any past or present litigation involving the franchisor; this history must be disclosed in Item 3 of the Uniform Franchise Offering Circular (see Chapter 6). If the franchisor has been involved in a number of lawsuits, check out the lawsuits before you buy into that franchise system.

Being a team player

If you sign a franchise agreement, you're committing to a relationship for a long term. You're promising to uphold your end of the bargain (pay royalties, abide by the operations manual, and so on), and the franchisor is also promising to meet certain obligations (support services, brand identity, and so on). That's the relationship drawn on paper by the lawyers.

The real relationship begins from the very first moment you meet the franchisor and continues through initial training, the grand opening, field consultant visits, phone calls, e-mail, newsletters, continuing training, updates to the operations manuals, and annual meetings. Communication is a two-way street. Taking part in communication with your franchisor keeps you current, keeps the relationship fresh and open, and helps you move forward as the system evolves.

The relationship with your franchisor should be based on mutual trust and respect. It doesn't hurt if your relationship grows into a friendship — a franchise relationship is a long one, and it's better to work with people you like.

Some chains are so convinced that personality contributes to a successful relationship that they compile behavioral profiles on franchisees. So don't be surprised if franchisors put you on the proverbial couch. Their assessments are usually based on the profiles of top-performing franchisees. (Yes, some franchisors might reject your franchise application if you don't meet their preferred profile.) The franchisors aren't therapist wannabes. They simply figure that if they know how you tick, they can make sure that you fit the culture. The support staff will also be in a better position to help you.

Being a team player usually tops franchisor's most-wanted list of franchisee traits. That's because you have to be willing to abide by the premise of the ongoing franchise relationship: The franchisor is the coach — the designer of the plays, the person responsible for the whole team. You're the superstar — the one who makes all the plays work, the person whom the rest of the franchise team relies on to perform well. This basic relationship, where everyone depends on everyone else, doesn't change even as you mature as a franchisee.

Don't overdose on support and expect the franchisor to manage your business from afar. It's your responsibility to run your business. The responsibility for your success or failure is yours, not the franchisor's.

Getting what you need from the relationship

As a consumer, you want to get what you pay for. We all do. So as a franchisee, whether your business launches slowly or fires up like a rocket (we hope the latter is the case), you want to have gotten your money's worth each time you mail your royalty check.

I like to say that there's no "I" in Wendy's

Wendy's starts with "We," and "We" can do almost anything together.

We have staff who have been with us for 25 years, and they still look on us as a team. We all discover what works best together. Nobody's an expert. We have a system, we know that we have a good product, and — if franchisees do it right — we know the concept works. But we always have to ask, "How can we improve; how can we make the system better?" Wendy's is not unique in franchising — great franchisors don't have I's — they have We's.

What you really get for your royalties is the right to use the franchisor's trade name and membership in its system, factors that should translate into brand identity and consistency. If you believe that the franchisor's ultimate success is tied to yours and that of the other franchisees, then the services you receive are as much a benefit to the franchisor as they are to you.

As franchisees mature in a franchise system, their need for support changes; they certainly shouldn't need the level of handholding in year five that they received in year one. What doesn't change is that every week or every month they write their franchisor a check for their continuing royalty payments. And, as sales go up, usually so does the size of the checks. This could be a formula for dissatisfaction by the franchisee — they need less support as they mature in the system, yet the size of the check is bigger. They can ask, "What's the franchisor done for me lately?"

Mature franchisees understand that they have prospered in the system in part because the franchisor is working in partnership with them. They may not like to admit it, but they may not be in the successful position they are without the system, the brand, and the support they received by being a member of the franchise.

You want to stop and pause every once in a while and look at your ongoing relationship with your franchisor. Ask yourself, for example: Is the franchisor telling me what I need to know? Is the franchisor listening to what I have to say? Am I getting what I need? Am I following the procedures and meeting the standards of the system? Am I available when the field consultant wants to meet with me, and have I established a good relationship with the consultant and the franchisor's headquarters staff? The franchise relationship should be give-and-take.

How can you tell whether your franchisor is looking out for your future needs? Ask yourself some simple questions about the franchisor's focus:

- Is the franchisor's staff doing research and development into new products and services?

- Is the franchisor working on new ad campaigns?

- Is the franchisor ahead of the technology curve to keep you competitive?

- Is the franchisor examining opportunities to expand business through e-commerce?

- Could the franchisor turn on a dime in response to changing customer demands and market conditions?

- Does the franchisor have an active franchisee advisory committee, empowered to help improve the business and look at new opportunities?

- Are franchisees involved in strategic planning for the franchisor?

A franchisor can't afford to be complacent with the system and the services it provides to its franchisees. In today's competitive environment, franchisors must be the active shepherds of their brand — committed by their actions and their resources to improving the competitive performance of the franchise system.

The following sections discuss a few support services that franchisors typically provide.

Research and development

Great franchisors keep their franchisees one step ahead of the competition.

One function of a good research and development department is to understand changes in the market, see opportunities for new products and services the franchisee can sell to the public, and introduce those new products and services to the marketplace.

E-commerce is the next horizon for many businesses — including franchise systems. For some franchisors, that means establishing a Web site only for the purpose of attracting new franchisees. Good franchisors whose products and services have potential on the Web are dedicating more and more resources to establishing e-commerce channels — some that benefit their franchisees' bottom line as well as that of the franchisors. E-commerce sites enable the franchisor to keep the brand in front of the consumer, thereby strengthening the overall system.

Most franchisors use their company-owned stores as test locations before they try out new products or methods on their franchisees. Others, working with their Franchisee Advisory Councils, also test new products and procedures with their top-performing franchisees.

In launching new products or services, good franchisors typically go through an elaborate process that includes the following steps:

- Seeking franchisee input
- Gathering consumer research
- Examining other industries and competitors for ideas for new products and services or other uses for existing products and services
- Lining up suppliers needed for the new product or service
- Determining ease of preparation or assembly, ability to achieve consistency, time required to deliver product or service, and so on by testing products or services in test facilities
- Determining what existing equipment or technology will be used and what new equipment will be needed
- Developing training materials on the new products

✔ Determining inventory requirements

✔ Planning advertising and promotions

✔ Verifying economic viability

✔ Testing in company-owned or franchisee-run facilities

Even great franchises begin to lose market share when the public gets tired of their products, their look, or their services — or the public just wants something new. They also lose market share when competitors introduce new products and services that are simply better, or are sold in a way that customers prefer — today that may include e-commerce. Although many new products and improvements come straight from the franchisees (after all, they're on the firing line with consumers every day), the responsibility to keep the concept fresh rests with the franchisor.

Office support

At some chains, your royalty payments buy nitty-gritty back-office support. For example, some chains maintain a toll-free hotline for your customers or divert phone calls placed to your local franchise to a main switchboard. This way, a person — not a machine — answers the phone when you're out, making you appear much bigger than a one-man show. Other franchisors also take care of billing customers and handling employee payroll. Such administrative services are most commonly found in commercial/residential cleaning and employment franchises.

DAVE SAYS

Timing is everything

I really believe in research and development. I also believe in letting the Wendy's organization take the time to do things properly. The timing would have been wrong for a lot of products that I would have rolled out.

For example, I would have rolled out our new bun six months earlier, but doing so probably wouldn't have been right because it wouldn't have been the best product we could have provided to the franchisees and may have raised their labor costs. So I let the R&D people do what they do best — work on improving it. You have to let the organization work.

We're totally committed to research and development. We commit our money to it and have

done so for years. We'd be nuts not to. I think that franchisors today who don't look at R&D as a major part of the future of franchising aren't focused on keeping their companies competitive. When we work on new products or product enhancements, we get all the other departments involved so that we understand how it affects our entire system. We include the folks in charge of operations and training, the people responsible for sourcing and purchasing new equipment and ingredients, the people who will plan the marketing strategy, and the accountants who can tell us what the financial impact on the system will be. We also include the Franchisee Advisory Council. We don't isolate the process.

Other perks

Most modern franchisors have moved away from an à la carte–type support system where you pay for services as you go. The reason for this change is obvious: The franchisee who needs the service most, such as additional field support, may not be willing or able to afford it.

Don't assume that all types of support are included in your royalty payments. Additional fees are common in many systems for a host of things, including further training of managers and employees, reservation systems (for hotel or car rental franchises), proprietary software, marketing, and special field support.

At times, you may think that the franchisor should offer you more support. You may expect additional service because the franchise salesperson told you to expect it. The key is to look at your original franchise agreement (see Chapter 6). It lays out in black and white the franchisor's obligations. Strong franchisors, however, often go beyond their spelled-out obligations, doing more than they have to. In practice, it's really very simple: A franchisor's job is to help franchisees be successful. But even with a franchisor's help, it's your responsibility to be successful. That's one thing a franchisor can't guarantee.

The franchise agreement is the key to understanding the obligations of the franchisor and the franchisee. Just because one party to the bargain wishes more services or they choose not to do something they have committed in the contract to do, it does not create an obligation on the other person to do those additional services or ignore the other party's obligations. If you're getting more services from your franchisor than what the agreement requires, say thank you. Such support shows that your franchisor cares.

Dealing with Change

Time for a wake-up call. Does everything with your franchisor seem same old, same old? Or has something changed while you were snoozing? Just as people pass from infancy to adolescence to adulthood to old age, franchises go through stages, too. These phases can greatly affect the franchisee-franchisor relationship — for better or worse.

Changes in a company's growth, financial state, support staff, and even competition can all contribute to subtle or blatant swings in support services, communication, operating requirements, and other aspects of your relationship.

When the system's size or focus changes

Regarding a chain's size or focus, consider this: If a franchisor adds more and more units nationally and even internationally — or even begins to offer another type of franchise or begins an e-commerce business — but doesn't increase staff or services, the support you will get from the franchisor will suffer.

Consider this example. You joined a franchise system that sells a product manufactured by your franchisor. Since the beginning of your relationship, your field consultant has visited your retail store each month spending four to six hours with you, going over marketing, operations, scheduling, and other important matters. Then the company begins to offer franchises internationally, and your field consultant is assigned the added responsibility of overseeing the development and support of locations in a country you can't even pronounce. The consultant visits you quarterly rather than monthly and spends only 30 to 40 minutes with you before rushing off to another franchisee.

Here's another example — same franchisee, same system. Instead of going international, the franchisor begins franchising another product or diverts attention to the development of an e-commerce business on the World Wide Web. The franchisor uses the training, operations, and field personnel from your franchise system to support the development of the new e-commerce business or the new franchise system. Same results: The support you came to rely on is no longer there.

Read your franchise agreement. You were probably never promised weekly or monthly visits that lasted four to six hours; you only grew accustomed to them. Still, a reduction in the frequency and length of meeting with your field consultant is no reason to be complacent. You may want revenue from e-commerce activities, but you may not legally be entitled to it. (See the next section, "When conflicts occur.")

In looking at a franchisor, don't be overly impressed about their entrance into foreign markets or that new store that just opened up on the other side of the country. Although a growing chain adds to the brand's value, it doesn't necessarily contribute much to what you should be interested in — franchisor support for your location.

Ideally, as a franchise chain grows, the size of the support organization also grows. For example, if the optimum ratio of field consultants is 1 to every 30 franchisees in a system, and the franchisor does not add a new field consultant to service new franchisees, the number of units that field consultant is responsible for will increase, and the consultant's ability to service each franchisee will decrease.

Technology, however, can allow a field consultant to handle additional locations effectively. Many mature franchisors now use cell phones; e-mail;

automated sales reporting; Internet training, distance learning, and CD-ROM-based training; video-conferencing; and so on to make their field consultants more efficient and effective. Higher density of units can also make it more efficient to get from store to store. And multi-unit franchisees often need less handholding.

But, absent changes in technology, if as the number of locations increases, field consultants are added so that the ratios stay basically the same, that's franchising at its best.

When conflicts occur

Smart franchisors work hard every minute of every day to forge lasting partnerships with their franchisees. Franchisees need to have confidence in their franchisors and vice versa. The recipe doesn't get any more wholesome than this: honesty, integrity, and open communications.

Communication has to flow in both directions to work. You may have a problem and are angry that the franchisor isn't helping you. Does the franchisor even know that you have a problem? If something is on your mind, call your field consultant. If you've spoken to your field consultant and the problem hasn't been taken care of, call your franchisor's regional or headquarters personnel. Franchisors may not know something is broken unless you tell them.

 Despite your best efforts, sales have been down for the past two months, and you're looking at a potential cash problem in the coming few months. You're upset and worried about meeting your financial commitments to the bank, to your suppliers, and to your franchisor. Don't wait until you have no money in the bank and are in default to ask for help. Call your franchisor and ask for advice. But don't demand that the franchisor waive your royalties simply because you have a cash problem. The franchisor didn't sign up to be your banker or your guarantor.

What franchisors can do is look at your operations, see whether they can find the problem, determine whether there is a quick fix, help you prioritize your cash flow, lend you some other support, and maybe — but not often — work with you on a temporary deferral on your royalty.

When changes occur that affect you negatively, speak to your franchisor. Find out whether the change is permanent or temporary. See whether you can work out a compromise position that satisfies both of your needs. Talk to the other franchisees who are affected. Talk to the leadership of the franchisee advisory council. Often, when franchisees come together to talk to a franchisor about a problem that is occurring, the franchisor and the franchisees work it out together. Sometimes, however, they don't, and that's often when the relationship between the parties begins to experience difficulties.

Although it's better to work through the chain of command, don't be afraid to voice your concerns to a higher level if you don't get a satisfactory response. Good franchisors need to know when their field consultants and other personnel are not responding or performing. Also, consider putting your serious concerns in writing. Your written communications don't need to be nasty or threatening, but a letter often helps you to convince your franchisor of its staff's inadequate performance if that ends up to be the case.

Open communication between you and the franchisor may avert or quash any friction. Your goal should be to resolve any disagreements in the least costly, least time-consuming, and least adversarial ways if you want to continue being a franchisee.

Disputes that can't be worked out between the franchisor and franchisee happen. Before going to blows in a lawsuit, many franchisors require that (as provided for in the franchise agreement) franchisees first meet with them and an impartial mediator. Some franchisors, instead of going to outside mediation, have set up internal mediation units that include other franchisees, and some have appointed an *ombudsman* (an employee of the franchisor who is paid to be an advocate for the franchisees) to look into disputes.

Several franchisors in the United States have joined the National Franchise Mediation Program, which is a formal mediation program endorsed by the International Franchise Association.

We've talked a bit about franchising involving a team: the franchisor, the manager, you, and other franchisees. As a team member, you will often turn to your fellow franchisees when you need help.

Reaching Out to Your Fellow Franchisees

Your fellow franchisees are a big part of the team, and as the newest recruit, you want to hear their take on the game, the coach, and the other players. Think of existing franchisees as the "live" version of an operations manual; they live and breathe the system every day, so they know what playing by the franchise system's rules is like.

Building a relationship with other franchisees goes beyond simply tapping their knowledge. They're also great sources of inspiration because they usually have confronted the same issues you may be facing. Finding out how someone else has successfully dealt with a problem that has been keeping you up at night and learning what to do and what not to do is not only helpful but also inspirational.

Franchisees who share a geographic area often get together to chat about common issues. Good franchisors encourage this type of communication. When staff recruiting is difficult, they often work together by getting a booth at a local job fair. Need a cup of sugar — or is it a case of carpet cleaner? That's what neighbors are for. Franchisees get together to plan local promotions, create local buying cooperatives, or just to update each other on what is working in their business and what is not. In short, other franchisees provide a valuable support network.

The International Franchise Association has established a monthly networking group for franchisees, franchisors, and suppliers. These meetings are held in about 30 cities around the United States. Many franchise associations internationally have similar networking groups. The great thing about these meetings is that you get to meet franchisees and franchisors from not only your own system but other franchise systems. It's another place to build a support network of franchisees and learn from them. Many of the suppliers who come to the meetings can also provide you with advice. Contact the IFA at 202-628-8000 and ask whether a networking group meets in your city.

Even if you don't make an effort to reach out to your fellow franchisees, they'll find you. You'll meet at regional meetings, annual conventions, Franchisee Advisory Council or association meetings, perhaps even on the Internet, or maybe on the intranet that the franchisor has set up for the system.

How do you go about getting to know other people who share your franchise name?

Most franchisors will be happy to provide you with a list of your fellow franchisees. Ask for it.

Go to the franchisees

If you came to me and wanted to know about Wendy's, I'd tell you to go talk to our franchisees. Let them tell you the story of Wendy's. Let them tell you whether we're doing our job as a franchisor.

In the early, early days of Wendy's, when the chain was just a handful of restaurants, I put prospective franchisees on a bus and drove them to an existing franchise in the city. I let them see all the lines, the store, and the lunch business; and I talked to them. After the lunch rush was over, the franchisee opened up the books and showed the group how much that particular franchise made. This was a real, live, working restaurant. And visiting this operating location, this living laboratory, was the fastest and most truthful way to sell a franchise to a prospective franchisee. Prospective franchisees saw not only the success but also how hard a franchisee really has to work.

Staying in touch

After you meet these franchisees, don't just take the knowledge and run. They're a valuable resource for more information, brainstorming, and camaraderie down the road.

You have their numbers. So call them again when you want to ask a question, devise a new way of doing something, simply chat, or share good or bad news with someone wearing the same uniform that you wear.

Some franchisors publish periodic company newsletters about the system. Often, they include the latest news about fellow franchisees. Read them regularly to hear about the latest recruits, significant milestones in a franchisee's business, or franchisee suggestions. You may be able to use this information in operating your own franchise. Most franchisors welcome your input for the newsletter. You may even see your own name in print!

A chain's regional and annual meetings provide a lot of opportunities for networking both with your franchisor's staff and with your peers. You don't have to make the meetings all work and no play. Often, spouses and friends are welcome; cruises, games, or entertainment are often part of the getaway.

In a more recent trend, some franchisors are formalizing franchisee contact by setting up mentoring programs. These programs are powerful tools for passing on knowledge. MAACO Auto Painting and Bodyworks uses such a program. MAACO assigns a new franchisee to an experienced operator at the company's annual convention; the relationship usually matures after that via phone and e-mail.

Even if no formal mentoring program exists, you may want to consider asking the franchisor to start one or scouting around on your own for a powerhouse franchisee who is willing to adopt you as a little brother or sister.

Joining advisory councils and associations

Franchisee advisory councils and franchisee associations (don't fret, we'll explain the difference) give order to the franchisee universe. They're communication vehicles — among franchisees, and between franchisees and franchisor. As a franchisee, you *want* representation. And you *want* a system that welcomes quality input.

Franchisee advisory councils

A *franchisee advisory council* is a committee established by the franchisor and composed of franchisee representatives. It may also have representatives from the franchisor-operated units.

Its purpose is purely advisory. Here are some of the ways a franchisor can use the council:

- ✔ To bounce new ideas off franchisees before rolling them out system-wide
- ✔ To solicit suggestions on improvements to products, services, and system support
- ✔ To review marketing and advertising strategies
- ✔ To assist the franchisor in looking at conflicts in the system

Franchisees can use the council to influence the company's direction, network with peers, and voice complaints. In a council, franchisees are heard more loudly and clearly than they're heard as individuals. Even if you don't sit on a council, you can raise your points by contacting one of the council's members, who can then speak for you.

Wendy's set up its Franchisee Advisory Council because Dave believes that everyone has a role to play, and the franchisee's role is to give Wendy's guidance and relay what needs to be done better.

The structures of franchise advisory councils vary from one franchise system to another:

- ✔ In some systems, the franchisees and franchisor jointly establish a council and agree on the membership, meeting dates, voting rights, and other rules. In other systems, the franchisor establishes the council and draws up the bylaws.
- ✔ Some franchisors pick up the cost of the franchisee attending council meetings, while others pick up a portion of the cost, and others pick up none. There are no hard and fast rules.
- ✔ Some councils will have franchisor-operated locations represented. Others won't.
- ✔ Some councils have franchisees elected by their peers, others are appointed by the franchisor, and some have a combination of both.

Often, a franchisor will establish criteria on who may sit on the council. If a franchisee is in default, for example, they're usually not invited to the big table.

Councils often spin off other committees, such as an advertising committee that provides input into advertising decisions and a buying committee that looks at cooperatives or other joint efforts for purchasing products and services for the system.

When you are speaking to the franchisees of a system, ask about their views on the advisory council. What does it do in their system? Do they get reports on the council's activities? Get from them or the franchisor the name of the head of the council or the local representative and give them a call. You want to understand if the council is well run and empowered by the franchisor to have a meaningful role in the system.

Franchisee associations

Unlike franchisee advisory councils, franchisee associations are usually independent organizations, made up of dues-paying franchisees who come together when there is no franchisee advisory council or the council is not viewed as adequately promoting their interests. They may function like a council, but franchisee associations set their own rules, membership requirements, and agendas. Membership dues usually fund them, while the franchisor more often than not picks up the tab for its franchise advisory council.

Historically, many franchisee associations were started because of a systemic crisis. For example, the franchisor may have been on the verge of bankruptcy or introduced a radical new product or service into the system without adequate testing. Or a change in management may have occurred, or the franchisor may have dramatically revised the terms of its new and renewal franchise agreements. Franchisee associations were also frequently formed on the verge of system-wide litigation.

Today, many franchisors have recognized that an independent association is not a bad idea and may make a positive contribution to the system, as long as its leadership acts responsibly and listens to the legitimate concerns of its constituency. Although franchisors have no legal duty to "recognize" a franchisee association, like a company would recognize a union, many franchisors have cautiously developed procedures to include them as part of the process to maintain and grow their systems. In some systems — Holiday Inn and Sylvan Learning Systems, for example — the franchisee associations are granted specific rights under the franchise agreements. Holiday Inn, for example, has agreed to run certain proposed changes past its franchisee association; the Sylvan Learning System franchisee association owns 50 percent of an entity that controls that system's marketing fund.

It is not unheard of for a franchise system to have both a franchisee advisory council and an independent franchisee association.

Being number one

All this concern about interacting with other franchisees is well and good. But what if you're *it?*

When you're the first franchisee in a new chain, you don't have another franchisee to check with about a franchisor's follow-through — or anything else, for that matter.

Some buyers find being number one exciting, anticipating a great surge in their franchise's value as the chain grows.

You have reason to be cautious, however. Just because a company has a Uniform Franchise Offering Circular does not make it qualified — in a business sense — to be a franchisor. (Chapter 16 discusses franchisability.)

Without the input of other franchisees, you need to scrutinize the company much more carefully, because the network you're joining — for the foreseeable future — may just be you.

If the management of the franchise system you're looking at also operates another franchise system, feel out the franchisees in the other system to at least get a sense of the company's management.

If you're thinking about being the first franchisee, you need to weigh the potential risks against the potential rewards. Support services may be lacking, systems may still be evolving, and buying cooperatives to give you lower prices may not be available. In fact, almost everything the franchisor will know about operating a franchise system and franchisee performance will come from working with you. You're about to pay for the privilege of being a guinea pig.

But as the first franchisee, you may be able to get your pick of location, negotiate a better franchise agreement, and get concessions that subsequent franchisees won't get.

You may consider a form of a prenuptial agreement. Part of what you're expecting is that the franchisor will grow and you will be part of a franchise system — with all the benefits. What happens if a year from now you're still alone or, if in five years, it's just you and one other franchisee? Not all new franchise systems grow — in fact, based on our experience, many don't. Negotiate a walk-away clause that gives you the option to leave the system before your franchise term is finished if the franchisor can't grow the franchise system. Pick a number — a good one is the number that the franchise salesperson has been telling you the system will grow to during the next year or two. Have your franchise attorney discuss other options with you.

Being a franchisee of a new system is a toss-up. (Dave was an early franchisee of Kentucky Fried Chicken, and it worked out for him.)

You may be getting in on the ground floor of a great opportunity or joining the crew of the *Andrea Doria*. (Everybody uses the *Titanic* as a metaphor for disaster; however, we thought as franchise executives we should be more innovative.)

Chapter 11

Attracting and Keeping Customers

You're probably familiar with the movie *Field of Dreams,* in which a starry-eyed Midwesterner transforms a cornfield into a baseball field so that Shoeless Joe Jackson could come back and play ball. Despite skeptics, the farmer believes, "If you build it, they will come."

We bet you have that same twinkle in your eye. And that's great. Optimism is a necessary ingredient if you want to have success. But you have to build a foundation for your business to be successful. You have to fill *your* stadium — regardless of whether it's built on a concrete pavement in New York, farmland in Iowa, or the West Bank of Paris.

This chapter explains how to attract customers in the first place and then how to give them a winning experience so they turn into real fans.

Like a Beacon in the Night: Promotions, Marketing, and Advertising

We begin with a few definitions. Many people use the words *marketing, advertising,* and *promotion* interchangeably, but they mean different things. The savvy business owner knows the difference:

> ✔ **Marketing:** This is the big picture of selling our products and services. It involves all aspects of getting a product into the buyers' hands, which are often referred to as the four Ps: product (having the right products and the right quantity of products available to meet consumer demand); price (discount, competitive, or premium); promotion (getting your offer and message to consumers); and place (distribution and delivery to the customer).

✔ **Advertising:** A paid, nonpersonal communication that attempts to persuade, inform, or create an image. Advertising messages are distributed to consumers through various media (television, radio, newspaper, magazines, direct mail, Internet, and out-of-home).

✔ **Promotion:** The offer presented to entice customers to take action. Promotions generally run for a specified period of time. The most common offers involve pricing: individual unit discounts; two-for-one specials; buy one, get one free; and so on.

Common sense tells you that customers won't show up at your door unless they know you're there. A marketing method can be as simple — and as cost-free — as mentioning your new franchise to your golf buddies, former coworkers, or Grandma Frieda who tells the women at the bridge game who tell their hairdressers who tell their clients, and so on. On the other end, a marketing plan can be as outrageous — and as costly — as parading a cavalcade of elephants draped with your company's banner throughout town. But to be successful, marketing has to be targeted to the right audience, planned in a way that the audience will see it, and cost-effective so you can sustain it.

Creating an effective marketing plan

Successful marketing campaigns are a unique blend of science and art. They present the right product to the right audience in the right manner at the right time. They require research, planning, and creativity.

Here are some suggestions for developing an effective marketing plan:

✔ Do your homework. Learn everything you can about your product, your concept, your customers, your marketplace, and especially your competition.

✔ Create an offer that features the attributes of your product that your primary customers want the most and that provides them with an incentive to buy that is too good to refuse.

✔ Create an advertising and promotion message that speaks directly to your target customers and clearly defines who you are and what you're offering with a sense of excitement. If your franchisor uses an advertising or marketing agency, those who work on your business must thoroughly understand your concept, your market position, and your goals and be able to create and communicate an effective message to your target customers.

✔ Once you have an effective message, make sure that it is properly delivered to your audience. Messages may be delivered through traditional media, including TV, radio, print, out-of-home (billboards and so on), and direct mail, or through community involvement, sponsorships, and public relations activities. Which method or methods you select depend on your concept, your offer, and your message. Remember, what works for one franchise may not work for another.

✔ Keep your name in front of consumers. Television is still the medium with the most impact — combining sight, sound, and motion with great entertainment value. Studies show that an average consumer has to see a TV commercial at least three or four times before having any recollection of the message. (Because consumers watch a variety of programming, your commercial must run many, many times to ensure that your target audience sees it three times.) Other media require even greater frequency.

✔ Don't talk to people who can't buy your product. We don't want you to be rude, but remember, broadcast media cover vast geographic areas. If your customers come from no more than five miles around your location, paying to advertise to a wider audience is a waste of valuable ad dollars — advertising types call this *waste circulation.* Talking frequently to those people who can benefit from your message is certainly more polite.

✔ To keep your name in front of your target audience, select media that you can afford to use with adequate frequency. Consider the cost of producing the commercial or ad and how much money you will have left to actually run your ad. A print campaign run every week in a local paper is more effective than a TV commercial that runs only a few times or late at night when your target audience is asleep.

✔ Pool your resources with other franchisees. By combining advertising dollars, you can afford a stronger advertising plan and get "more bang for the buck."

✔ Check out local media discounts. As a local advertiser, you may be eligible for local advertising rates that aren't available to large, national advertisers.

✔ Monitor your results. Do more of what works and change what isn't producing the results you want.

✔ One approach that can pay off is using spokespeople to market a product or service. Dave is proof, as we discuss in the sidebar "Wendy's way of advertising." The key is that spokespeople have to strongly believe in what they're selling in order to be credible. Okay, we know that Dave's a hard act to follow, but you can be an effective spokesperson for your own franchise. Making a personal connection with customers strengthens the business. So the more you become identified with your company in your local community, the better off you'll be. (Someone may even ask for your autograph!)

Wendy's way of advertising

Wendy's is virtually a household name, thanks to the power of national TV. Or should we say, thanks to the power of successful marketing campaigns on national TV? The company's had three hits in a row. As a result, customers are tuning in more and more to the brand, and franchisees are riding the campaigns for all they're worth.

In 1977, Wendy's took to the tube with its "Hot 'n Juicy" campaign, featuring its Hot 'n Juicy hamburgers. They're so Hot 'n Juicy that the campaign's spokesman, Jonathan Winters, used napkin after napkin after napkin.

Next up: "Where's the Beef?" Clara Peller and her sidekicks turned these words into a sizzling expression. The commercials netted three Clio awards for creative advertising.

Then, in 1989, Dave appeared in America's living rooms. He's been featured in 700+ commercials, flying in hot air balloons, riding camels, playing on hockey rinks — you name it, he's done it — for the sake of different promotions. If not for Dave, would anyone have heard of the 99-cent value menu? Only his ad agency knows for sure where he'll turn up next.

The national exposure's paying off. Sales at the average Wendy's restaurant are up 30 percent since Dave started acting — really just being himself. Advertising awareness of Wendy's has risen 200 percent. And catch this: 92 percent of Americans who watch TV know who Dave Thomas is — by name or in relation to Wendy's.

Franchisees are taking notice. They contribute to a national marketing fund that backs the creation and placement of these heavy-hitting commercial spots. A national marketing committee made up of elected franchisees and franchisor representatives decides how to spend the money. Franchisees must spend at least 4 percent of gross sales on advertising. They used to contribute 2 percent for national advertising. Again in 1999, franchisees voted to kick in another 0.5 percent for two years — reallocating 2.5 percent to national campaigns and 1.5 percent for local/regional marketing. That willingness to contribute money says it all about the success of Wendy's national campaign.

The way a franchisor wants customers to think about the brand is perhaps the biggest component behind an effective marketing plan. One method that advertising agencies use to determine the image conjured up by consumers when the brand name is mentioned is to create a "brand personality." If your brand were a person, what would she or he be like — happy, fun, serious, old, young, adventurous, or studious? These personality attributes are then translated into the advertising message, which creates an image of the brand in the consumer's mind. (Other pieces are customer expectations and pricing strategies.)

Tissues. Petroleum jelly. Photocopies. You know how we often call these products by specific brand names, even if other companies manufacture them. (We're sure you're guilty, too!) That trend just confirms our belief that the power of the brand is critical to long-term success. Brand identification makes it easier for new franchisees to compete against well-established chains and independent operators. The brand is more powerful than any individual franchisee — so it makes sense to keep it front and center. It's also the reason that franchisees need to follow the system: so that the message in the ad is the reality when the customer comes through the door.

Brand marketing often boils down to dollars and cents. Franchisees of larger chains gain an edge because their collective advertising dollars can support national ad campaigns. Smaller chains have to work harder because they lack the financial muscle. In either case, you, as a franchisee, have to do your part, too.

Evaluating national and local advertising strategies

Don't worry if you're not the creative type. That's where franchisors come in; they'll help get the word out. Many chains spearhead regional and national advertising campaigns, organize advertising cooperatives with franchisees in your area, and provide a wealth of marketing materials. At a bare minimum, franchisors should offer marketing guidelines and suggestions — if not the materials themselves — to help with your own local advertising efforts.

When you look at advertising, divide it into national and local levels. We discuss the national picture first.

The franchisor's national ad campaign: Your fee dollars at work

It'd make life easier if we could tell you that there's only one way advertising contributions work in franchising. Sorry. What *is* likely is that you'll be bound in some way to contribute some dough.

Many franchisors — especially large ones — administer national advertising funds. They most commonly charge a national ad fee based on a percentage of sales or revenues, ranging from less than 1 percent to 10 percent. Some franchisors charge a flat dollar amount or a fee based on each transaction; others don't impose any ad fees, or they collect only a regional/local fee. The requirements and recommendations often depend on a chain's size and industry. Make sure to ask the franchisor about your obligations and review them in the franchise agreement. And talk to other franchisees about the franchisor's approach, the effectiveness of the chain's campaigns, and the franchisees' individual marketing strategies.

Franchisors typically charge an advertising fund contribution based on sales/revenues/margin or some other criteria.

According to a survey by the International Franchise Association's Educational Foundation, the following is true:

- ✔ 49 percent of the respondents required a national advertising fund contribution.

- ✔ 27 percent of the respondents required no fee.

- ✔ 17 percent of the respondents required a regional or local advertising fund contribution.

- ✔ 7 percent used another method.

Of the 570 franchisors who charged a national advertising fee based on a percentage of sales/revenues, 405 (or 71 percent) of them charged a fee ranging from .01 percent to 2 percent. Only two systems charged more than 10 percent, and only 3 percent of the franchisors charged more than 5 percent.

Some franchisors cap the minimum or maximum real-dollar amount — such as 2 percent of gross sales with a minimum of $1,000 and a maximum of $2,500 per month.

Don't waste your advertising dollars simply because you have a few dollars to spend. To be effective, advertising has to be seen — and seen often. Franchisees in a market area look at the amount of money they have in their ad fund to spend collectively on advertising. If the duration and frequency they can buy with the ad dollars won't be effective, should they spend them anyway? Probably not, but many do.

A more effective way of spending your advertising dollars is first deciding what a minimal effective flight of advertising will cost. Then look at the budget available. If the franchisees in the area have been working together as a team, they often decide to contribute additional money — on a store-by-store or other basis. (We call that *supplemental contributions.*) The supplemental contribution made by the franchisees, when added to the money available in the ad fund, ensures that the ads they run will be seen with enough frequency and enough duration and therefore will be effective.

Not all advertising funds operate the same way. Their structure, including decision-making power, could greatly affect the end result — and your bottom line. Ideally, franchisees should have input. Some companies set up national marketing/ad committees or councils, most commonly made up of franchisee and franchisor representatives. In other cases, franchisors make all the decisions. Funds can really get a boost when the system's vendors and suppliers also make contributions. Consider whether your franchisor has that kind of clout.

Look for some safeguards to ensure that you're getting value for your money. The franchisor should use the advertising fund only for the purposes that it states. For example, if the fund's purpose is to market the brand, it shouldn't be used to recruit franchisees. However, because the franchisor is administering the fund and may have personnel working on the marketing, most franchise agreements allow the franchisor to charge the fund for its administrative costs. You should be aware of how much and what kinds of administrative expenses the franchisor is charging to the fund. Also, if the franchisor is operating company-owned locations, do those locations contribute to the fund just like the franchisees? You would hope so, but not all of them do.

Many franchisors don't provide audited financial statements to their franchisees on their advertising fund. Many don't provide even an unaudited report unless the franchisee requests it. Often, the request must be in writing. Read your franchise agreement carefully to understand what your franchisor is obligated to provide to you. You, your Franchise Advisory Council, or your franchisee association (see Chapter 10) should routinely ask to see an accounting of the system's advertising fund. Understand where the money is being spent and make certain that everyone who is supposed to be contributing is contributing and that all expenditures to the franchisor from the fund are appropriate. Look closely at the expenditures made by a franchisor's in-house advertising agencies (these are ad agencies set up by franchisors). Be certain that the in-house agencies are actually performing services for the fund that are appropriate under the franchise agreement.

Be aware that franchisor policies can change. In their disclosure documents and franchise agreements, some franchisors specify an advertising contribution, but in practice, they suspend collection (usually because of the chain's small size). Others reserve the right to impose an advertising fee and fund at some later date. The agreement should state the exact or maximum fee. If the mandatory fees are described only as "reasonable" — or worse, not described at all — beware: You may find yourself in a potential bottomless pit. Franchisors may also ask franchisees from time to time to *voluntarily* boost their contributions or shift the national/local allocation. To protect yourself, look for fee caps and majority voting requirements should the franchisor wish to increase your advertising contributions.

Get the following information:

- ✔ How much are franchisees required to spend on advertising locally, and what is the national/regional/local allocation?
- ✔ Does the ad fund pay for the franchisor's pubic relations efforts? Are public relations focused on getting new franchisees or getting new customers?
- ✔ Do all franchisee-owned and company-owned units contribute equally to the ad fund?

✔ Does the franchisor contribute to the fund, such as matching contributions or a lump sum to kick it off?

✔ Is the franchisor's contribution voluntary, and at what rate does the franchisor contribute to the fund?

✔ What happens to any remaining funds at year-end?

✔ Can the franchisor change the contribution requirements, and do franchisees have input into this decision?

✔ Who decides on the creation and placement of the ads?

✔ Does the franchisor have a national marketing or advertising committee or council, and who sits on it?

✔ Is the council advisory only, or does it have decision-making power? Can the franchisor veto the decision?

✔ Can the franchisor change or dissolve the council?

✔ Is there separate accounting of the advertising funds?

✔ Is the fund independently audited?

✔ How much of the fund goes to administrative expenses?

✔ Does the franchisor receive rebates on ad placements or product rebates, and do franchisees share in them? Are they contributed in whole or in part to the system's advertising fund?

✔ How often do new ad campaigns appear?

✔ How often does the franchisor develop new creative material?

✔ Is the effectiveness of the campaigns evaluated and shared with franchisees?

✔ Does the franchisor provide materials to tie in local campaigns with national ones?

✔ Do you need franchisor approval to conduct your own advertising or create your own materials?

✔ What are the plans for future advertising campaigns?

✔ Does the franchisor have an internal advertising agency, and does the agency perform any services for the fees that it is collecting?

Times change, and so do franchise systems. When systems first start, franchisors often establish an advertising fee structure that turns out to be too small. Then they often need to go to their franchisees and request that they voluntarily increase their advertising contributions. The ad fund is set up for the benefit of the system. If the franchisor requests that you increase your contribution — and has a good case for making the request — work with your other franchisees to do so. Make sure, though, that if you're increasing your contribution, the company-owned locations are as well.

Getting in on the ground floor

Some chains don't have a national advertising fund because they don't have enough units to make national, or even regional, advertising efficient. Remember that the science of advertising is getting the right message to the right audience. Reaching an audience beyond your geographic or demographic profile is a wasted effort. People will only travel a certain distance to buy your product — no matter how good your offer. And people outside your target demographic group are unlikely to purchase as well — not many teenagers have a need for adult diapers.

If your chain isn't large enough to need an ad fund, stay tuned — you can still buy prime time on a local basis. And your franchisor may establish a fund as the need arises. That was the case with Mail Boxes Etc. It had grown to 2,500 units worldwide when it set up its first national media fund in order to kick off its brand awareness campaign. Since the beginning of its media fund, the chain has advertised on the Super Bowl several times.

Local advertising options

Now we get to the local scene. Here's your opportunity to strut your stuff.

Often, a franchisor requires or recommends a level of local advertising expenditure — again, either a flat amount or a percentage of sales or revenue. It may organize — and you may be required to join — regional or local advertising cooperatives among franchise-owned and company-owned units. Pooling local money enables you to afford bigger buys on radio, TV, out-of-home, print, direct mail, and so on.

It also helps to keep a consistent message in front of consumers. Imagine 15 franchisees in your city, each advertising a different offer in a different manner, as opposed to everyone's advertising sending the same message. Which approach does more to promote the brand?

As with national ad funds, ask about a cooperative's structure — membership, administration, financial oversight, and so on. You may be able to split your local dollars between your own advertising and cooperative advertising.

Some chains give franchisees lots of flexibility to create local campaigns. They figure you know your community and customers better.

 Before you do your own thing, try to be objective. Do your materials maintain brand identity? Are you confusing customers, sending a different message than the national campaign? Does this *really* sell your product/service? Can you afford to create new materials instead of using those provided by your franchisor? Spending local dollars to create advertising means you have less to spend on advertising time. Make sure that the local ad you want to make is worth the cost of making it.

In essence, the sky's the limit in promoting your franchise in your own market.

Most franchisors require some form of approval over ads that franchisees create. Check with your franchisor about the system's policy.

Here are some suggestions on how to promote your franchise:

- ✔ Sponsor a Little League team. Provide T-shirts with your name on the back. (Your mom probably still has your first Little League shirt in the attic!)

- ✔ Hand out discount coupons, free products, or award certificates to students who earn high marks or record good attendance in school.

- ✔ Send out newsletters announcing new products/services or highlighting accomplishments of employees at your franchise.

- ✔ Telemarket. Make sure that you abide by the Federal Trade Commission's Telemarketing Sales Rule, which requires certain disclosures and prohibits misrepresentations; call 202-326-2222 for more information. If you're calling consumers who may not be your current customers, you also have to comply with the Telephone Consumer Protection Act, which, for example, limits calls to between 8 a.m. and 9 p.m.; contact the Federal Communications Commission at 888-Call FCC (888-225-5322) for more information.

- ✔ Do cross-promotions. Hooking up with other local businesspeople cuts the advertising expense and adds credibility if you're the new kid on the block. Years and years ago, even Dave used cross-promotion when he was a Kentucky Fried Chicken franchisee. Once, he made a deal with a local car dealer, hawking, "Test-drive a new car and get a chicken dinner free!" Cross-promotion is an old gimmick, but it still works great today.

  Make sure that your cross-promotion partner is a reputable businessperson and that your brand is enhanced by the association with the company and the product. Promoting your gag and gift shop with a funeral home is not a wise idea.

- ✔ Participate in charity promotions. As a franchisee, you'll find that participating in a community event or charity works wonders to promote your franchise. It builds goodwill, and it can build sales. Many franchisors encourage franchisees to support charitable causes that are most appropriate for their local communities. The key is that they *suggest*, not *mandate*. See whether your parent company offers guidelines. It's smart business, for example, to steer clear of any controversial or political issues that could polarize a segment of your customer base.

  Certain causes have won the hearts of some franchisors. As a franchisee, you can get involved as much or as little as you want. For example, Wendy's provides ongoing corporate support for the Dave

Thomas Foundation for Adoption (Dave was adopted — in fact, his proceeds from this book go to the Foundation); more and more franchisees are getting involved on the local level.

Even though you'll participate in charity promotions out of the goodness of your heart, check whether the cost of sponsoring a charitable event gets credited to your local marketing expenditure requirements. It probably does. Discuss this with the franchisor's marketing department.

Before taking any of these steps, make sure that your plan is in compliance with your franchisor's policies. Any advertising or promotional materials that involve the franchised business and include the franchisor's trademark must almost always be submitted to the franchisor for approval. Franchisors are vigilant about protecting their trademarks.

Franchisors take local advertising seriously. Most likely, you will have to document advertising expenditures. Your operating manual should specify what counts — and what doesn't count — toward these markers. At Wendy's, local radio, TV, outdoor billboards, newspaper and magazine ads, coupon offers, direct mail, in-store materials, and sponsorship of community events all get a thumbs-up. Logo T-shirts? Nope. Hiring your nephew as a marketing assistant? No way.

When you need to arrange for local marketing, see how your franchisor can help you out. The company should have demographic profiles of the typical customer base, and you can supplement that with your own market research. Perhaps your community has a slightly older population, for example, that would prompt you to push a certain product over another.

Ask your franchisor for guidance on appropriate mediums (for example, whether to buy airtime or newspaper space) and analysis of marketing costs in your local area. Advertising on a talk show with a well-known but offensive host can be expensive and turn off customers, while funneling your dollars into a family-oriented channel might click with the wholesome image you want to project. In addition, the franchisor should help you evaluate the effectiveness of any promotions or campaigns. You don't want to wait until the end of the promotion to find out that it's a dud. If it's broke, fix it as you go. A minor adjustment to your offer or message could save the day.

Most franchisors also prepare advertising materials for use by franchisees — sometimes for an additional fee, sometimes not. These usually include the following:

- Advertising, publicity, and promotional kits for the grand opening
- Direct-mail pieces
- Outdoor billboards
- Point-of-sale materials, such as window and floor signs

✔ Promotional contests

✔ Public relations kit

✔ Newspaper, yellow pages ads, and coupons in modular form that can easily be adapted to your local market

Your franchisor may give you the actual materials needed for print advertising or provide you with the components on CD-ROM or via the Internet or intranet. Most often, print ad layouts are modular so that you can tailor your exact offer while maintaining the overall "look" associated with the brand. There usually is also space for your name, address, telephone number, and hours of operation. Your local newspaper or direct mail house can handle the production for you.

Broadcast advertising is similar. Your franchisor will give you a tape of a radio spot or television commercial with time allotted for your local identification. Your local TV or radio station can take it from there.

When using local media companies to tailor your ads, make sure that you proofread and double-check the changes before the ad runs. They don't know your business the way you do.

A lot of additional interest occurs if you tie local advertising and promotion to your franchisor's national campaigns. Just look at how franchisees can catch the wave: When Wendy's ran its national contest to unearth a Dave look-alike, a Memphis franchisee jumped in on the excitement. He brought in the winner, a sheriff from a nearby town, to make personal appearances. He sure fooled the folks! Likewise, during a cross-promotion with Coca-Cola involving motorsports, Wendy's offered franchisees life-size cutouts of famous race car driver Dale Jarrett to rev up local sales.

You may be able to whip up your own local advertising strategies — instead of or in addition to using the franchisor's materials and approach. Here are some scenarios when brainstorming may make sense:

✔ The franchisor's materials may not work exactly right for your store.

✔ The featured product doesn't meet your local demand.

✔ Your own creative juices are overflowing, and you can concoct what you think is a better formula.

Ultimately, you need to remember who your customers are, what media reaches them, and what will make them take action. One big mistake is to assume that your customers think like you — unless they mirror your profile. A campaign built around the good old days may bring back fond memories to your bridge club members but do nothing for your business if your customers are from Generation X. And while we're at it, if you air your radio spot on the local classical station, you'll hear it, and it will warm your heart, but it will completely miss your customers if they're country music fans. In short, don't waste your advertising dollars talking to yourself.

The importance of local advertising

Wendy's intent is to always speak with one voice. If we're running a spicy chicken campaign nationally, we strongly encourage spicy chicken for local campaigns. Why would someone advertise grilled chicken and spicy chicken at the same time? The consumer would be confused.

There are periods when we're not on national TV. Even Wendy's, with all its muscle, is not on national television 52 weeks a year. That's when it's really important for franchisees to do local advertising. Wendy's is outspent by our major competitors by four to five times, so we say to our franchisees: When we're on nationally, save your money; when we're off, spend double. That way, they get more bang for their buck.

Can't wait to get started? Hold on a minute. Dave is adamant that franchisees — of whatever system — must have their operations and management systems down pat before they do any marketing. If you don't run your business right, telling people who you are and where you are won't do you any good. You'll just disappoint your customers, which means that ultimately you won't have any.

Don't be a franchisee who has to pass up the parent company's advertising campaign because it's great and your franchise isn't. This probably sounds strange, so we'll explain. Suppose that a bread company develops a really great color ad; it portrays spotless ovens, counter people in military-crisp uniforms, and rows of breads baked to perfection. Mr. Smith sees the ad and, with mouth watering, rushes in to the local franchise — only to find grease-stained equipment, rumpled uniforms, and burnt bread. The standards are not up to the message, and the disappointed customer is turned off to this store and the entire chain.

We know this example is extreme — and a good franchisee would never let quality fall so low — but we're making a point. Had the franchisee been following the system, he or she could have followed a powerful marketing campaign, too. Attracting customers is important, but keeping them is a franchisee's top priority.

All Hail Customer Service

Excuse us for putting this bluntly: When it comes to customer service, the last thing you want is a *selfish* franchisor. Is yours?

Take this simple test to find out. Who comes first — the customer or the company? If it's the customer, give your franchisor an A+ in customer service; if it's the company, watch out.

In today's marketplace, a franchisor must pay attention to the customer *first* and the company *second* so that it can meet and then surpass the customers' expectations. Putting customers first means giving customers what *they* want — not what *you* want to give them.

Doing otherwise could be an expensive mistake.

Knowing your customer

Knowing your customer is a major step in customer service. Their wants, their needs, their buying habits, their ages, their genders, their lifestyles, their pocketbooks, their time schedules — all this information provides the clues you need to serve them better.

No doubt, this census sounds like a daunting task. It really isn't. Keep in mind that you're part of a team. Your franchisor will help you capture this information — without having to knock on every door in town. You can supplement this demographic information with a narrower study of your local area (see Chapter 8).

Once customers storm your franchise (and they will, because you've done such a great job of marketing), you can cull even more insight. Tech-savvy franchisors require computerized point-of-sale (POS) systems that store customer profiles, buying habits, and other information. Some larger franchisors have private-label credit cards and frequent-buyer cards to track purchasing trends. On a more human note, you and your staff should be observant. Paying attention to your customer lets you know what customers crave and helps you anticipate their changing desires.

A critical part of customer service is giving your customers a good and fair product or service. Customers want true value each and every time they shop at your store. Dave has a famous saying: "You should always make the hamburger you'd be proud to serve to your best friend." That goes for any product or service. We're talking about total quality. You can't cut corners. And you must — absolutely must — keep a keen eye on operations, every minute of every day. It's really a no-brainer: If you give your customers the best service and the best product, they'll be back.

Finding out why it's not nice to fool the customer

Honesty and integrity: These are two traits you wanted in a franchisor, remember? Well, what goes around, comes around. Customers look for the same traits in you — in your franchise. If you don't demonstrate honesty and integrity, someone else will swoop your customers up. You're a step ahead of the game if your brand already portrays this image.

Customers expect consistency from franchises. They expect to receive the product or service your franchise is known for. And they expect to receive it in the way it's been portrayed to the public, through advertising or other means. Your job is to give it to them so that the reputation of the brand doesn't get tarnished. For example, just imagine what a mess it would be if all franchisees personalized their franchises — Dorothy's Wendy's, Alyssa's Wendy's, Charlie's Wendy's. The public wouldn't know whether the product in each location was the same or whether Dorothy added a new ingredient to the chili to make it Dorothy's chili. Imagine trying to advertise a consistent message when the name isn't consistent. Dave never wanted to personalize Wendy's and make it Dave's Wendy's because doing so would weaken the brand.

Staying true to your mission

Sometimes you have to listen to your gut more than to the customer.

Wendy's has a Frosty. It's thick. You can't drink it; you have to eat it with a spoon. The Frosty was created because I wanted hand-dipped milkshakes like you'd get at the old-fashioned soda shops and drugstores. I didn't believe Wendy's could consistently offer this product, so we created the Frosty. People wanted vanilla; people wanted chocolate. We couldn't decide which to use, so we just mixed them. A Frosty is half vanilla and half chocolate.

Throughout our 30 years of existence, there have been customers who have adamantly said, "I want a vanilla" or "I want a chocolate" or "I want a strawberry." But we have not done this.

Part of our decision is based on our understanding of how much of a market there is for this product. We're in the hamburger business; the Frosty was offered as a dessert. We're not in the Frosty business. Creating three, four, or five varieties of Frosty would divert our focus from hamburgers. So I had to stay true to my conviction, which was this: I'll give you three different types of hamburgers because that's the business I'm in. But I can't complicate my operations by giving you three types of Frosty. There aren't enough people out there who are going to buy a Frosty every day, but there are enough people who are going to buy hamburgers every day. By diverting attention from hamburgers, you can lose focus. Never lose sight of your top-selling product.

Another means of fooling or confusing the customer is with "express units" that don't offer the full line of products. If customers are used to buying a product at a full-line store and then go into an "express unit" without realizing the difference, they will be disappointed when they can't buy what they came for. Smart franchisors make sure that customers know the difference between their full line and limited units. (The "express" units may not even get the customer out faster — they may just get out with a substitute for what they came in for — if they make a purchase at all.)

Be careful about introducing new products. If you're constantly changing the operations and focus of your business, you're putting undue stress on your own operations, and you have the potential of confusing the customer. The customer will forget what you really stand for.

It's likely that your franchisor has conducted consumer research that shows what customers are looking for. For example, at quick-service restaurants, patrons want economy, convenience, filling and satisfying food, and a familiar and predictable experience. If you don't fool with any of those factors, you're right on target in customer service.

Consumers purchasing automotive aftermarket products (such as sunroofs and sound systems) or repair services (tires, brakes, and glass repair) want knowledgeable salespeople and well-trained technicians. They want their problem fixed the first time they bring the car in, at the agreed price, and they want the work completed on time. They don't want to wait for parts to be ordered or deal with out-of-stocks. A car is a large investment, and they want to be able to trust those who work on their car.

If you're having your carpet cleaned, you want assurance that the technician knows the difference between a wool carpet and a nylon carpet and between a wine stain and common dirt. And you want to know that the technicians know how to clean each type of carpet and remove each type of stain. It's not a good feeling to think that the new guy is learning the business on your family room carpet.

Another reason why it's not nice to fool customers is that they have good memories. They remember what ads say, and they remember what a business actually delivers. If there's a discrepancy between the two, say good-bye. So when you make a claim, you'd better live up to it.

Keep this in mind, too: Customers tell twice as many people about a bad experience as they do about a good one. So if you maximize customer satisfaction, you'll reap a positive domino effect. It's the best advertising in town. Customers will visit again and tell others to visit, too.

Make the best of your mistakes

Everyone makes mistakes. The key to success is recognizing those mistakes and doing something about them. Customers don't like the fact that mistakes are made, but they will accept that fact if you do something about them.

What's important is how a complaint is handled, either in person or on the phone. Your franchise is only as perfect as the person addressing the customer. If you or your employee has a bad attitude and a bad frame of mind, the customer picks up on that mind-set. If you have a good attitude and a good frame of mind, your customer recognizes that, too.

The loyalty factor is diminishing today. So clearly, you have to be sensitive to customers, and you have to keep them happy. You're not guaranteed to get them every day, so you'd better treat the customer like your job depends on it — because it does.

Is the customer always right? You and I both know that the customer isn't always right. But sometimes, the issues aren't about who's right and who's wrong. It's about building long-term customers. That philosophy is part of the Wendy's culture.

Doing a reality check

You'll face all kinds of customers at your franchise. Some will look at the glass as half full, and others will look at it as half empty. Their perspective makes a difference in your franchise's success. Suppose that you run a computer training franchise. One day, a customer comes in and finds the latest equipment working without a hitch and instructors who really know their stuff. The next time that student shows up, the computers keep crashing and the teachers are fumbling. If the customer views the glass as half full, he may remember the first experience more and give your franchise another try. If he sees the glass as half empty, you really have a lot of making up to do.

The message we're giving you is this: Be on your toes at all times, and try to change a customer's negative experience into a positive by correcting your franchise's mistakes and resolving any conflicts.

Any blunder is a signal to look inward. Strip apart your operations and see what needs improvement. Go back to the franchise operations manual — it most likely addresses your particular problem. Seek help from regional or corporate support staff if you need it. Maybe you need to retrain employees in customer service. (In Chapter 12, we discuss employee training.)

To salvage relationships with customers, your best bets are to

- Respond quickly.

- Listen to what they have to say — without interruption.

- Apologize and then apologize again for any errors.

- Be polite and make eye contact.

- Put yourself in your customer's shoes; think about how you'd want the problem resolved.

- Promise your customer a correction — free product or services, discounts on future sales, shifting employees, extra attention, and so on.

- Prove yourself the next time.

Be aware that very few customers verbalize their complaints to employees or management, especially if money isn't involved. Unfortunately, the way you find out about poor customer service is when it kicks you in the stomach: Customers don't come back, and sales plummet.

Save yourself grief and do a periodic reality check.

There are two ways to check customer satisfaction — inexpensively and expensively. The cheap but effective approach, of course, is simply using your eyes and ears, listening to and watching customers and employees. Here are some additional ways:

- Read your mail — from fans and foes.

- Make comment cards easily accessible so customers can fill them in; using these feedback cards is low-cost and easy.

- Many franchisors solicit input from customers on the company Web site and can pass on that information to you.

- Periodically, speak directly with customers to make sure that all's well — or to cut off a small problem before it becomes a bigger one.

- You can also do informal one-on-one surveys and random phone surveys with your customers.

- Some sophisticated tools that you may already use at your franchise, such as cash registers that capture sales and customer information, can facilitate customer surveys by providing the names of customers and what they have purchased.

- Or go the extra mile and hire local research organizations to gather quantifiable research on your franchise's performance. If you want to hire outside experts, talk to your fellow franchisees about combining forces and splitting the cost.

The hands-on approach is best

We strongly encourage Wendy's franchisees to be on the front lines on a regular basis and talk to their customers. Doing so is the best way to get immediate feedback.

In addition to not having enough money to fund their businesses, another reason franchisees fail that's equally relevant is absentee ownership.

If you're going to be a franchisee and rarely show up at your location, you're an absentee. And if you're an absentee, you don't know what your customers are thinking and how they're interacting with your staff.

You must have hands-on involvement to truly understand the pulse of your business.

Looking beyond your cash register

Every part of your business makes an impression on the customer. Sure, the customer can't wait to dip his spoon into a Frosty, or slip into a freshly detailed car, or find the perfect health care aide. No question, the end product or end service offered by your franchise is why customers come in the door to begin with.

But customers *do* notice things like the wallpaper, employee appearance, friendliness, equipment, and restrooms — most definitely restrooms. Paying attention to details is a big part of customer service. It's also a big part of employee service; nobody likes to work in a junky or dirty environment. The job of both you and your franchisor is to set tough standards — because customers do.

Obviously, franchisees in various industries have to inspect the premises a little differently in order to meet the needs of their specific type of business. Here are some general guidelines to make sure that your business is in ship-shape:

- ✔ Are employees friendly, helpful, and well-trained?
- ✔ Are problems resolved quickly?
- ✔ Is service prompt, dependable, and consistent?
- ✔ Is the location in good condition, clean, and welcoming?
- ✔ Can your customers see your quality as they drive by? What does the outside of your store say to your customers?
- ✔ Do customers or employees have concerns about security or safety?

✔ Is equipment updated?

✔ Are products in stock?

✔ Are you offering all the products the customer expects from your brand?

✔ Are the needs of the physically challenged customer being met?

A perfect score is reachable. It just takes time and teamwork. A big part of that teamwork must come from your staff.

Chapter 12

Hiring, Firing, Training, and Other Staffing Decisions

*Y*ou're about to add the last spoke to your franchise's operations wheel: staffing. Every employment decision you make has far-reaching implications — on your franchisor's brand, your budget, your competition, your aggravation level, and, of course, your customer satisfaction. Human resource executives and business owners agree: If you want to be customer-focused, you have to be employee-focused.

In this chapter, we give you tips on how to hire employees, how to train them to the nth degree, and how to motivate them with incentives.

The Best Interviewing and Hiring Techniques

As desperate as you may be to staff your franchise, it doesn't make sense to hire just anyone who walks through the door. You want to hire only the best. By developing the reputation of being a great place to work, you'll attract quality candidates. The result will be better customer service, less employee turnover, reduced cost of recruiting new employees, reduced cost of training new employees — in short, more profit.

As an employer, you need to be conscious of one more thing: the law. You have the right to be very fussy, but you also have to be fair.

Following EEOC guidelines

If there's one word you don't ever want to hear while operating your franchise, it's *discrimination*. We urge you to become extremely familiar with the employment laws that were written to prevent discrimination. Discriminatory practices include bias in hiring, firing, promotion, and job assignment.

The U.S. Equal Employment Opportunity Commission (EEOC) enforces these federal statutes. You'll want to be in touch with this agency only to find out about the laws, not because you're in noncompliance.

These are the major statutes:

✔ Title VII of the Civil Rights Act of 1964 (Title VII) prohibits employment discrimination on the basis of race, color, religion, sex, or national origin. Sexual harassment and harassment on the basis of race and/or color or national origin violate this act. An amendment to this act, the Pregnancy Discrimination Act, bans discrimination on the basis of pregnancy, childbirth, or related medical conditions. Title VII applies to employers with 15 or more employees (including part-time and temporary workers).

✔ The Age Discrimination in Employment Act of 1967 (ADEA) protects job applicants and employees who are 40 years of age or older from employment discrimination based on age. The ADEA applies to employers with 20 or more employees (including part-time and temporary workers) and employment agencies.

✔ Title I of the Americans with Disabilities Act of 1990 (ADA) bans employment discrimination on the basis of disability. It applies to employers with 15 or more employees (including part-time and temporary workers).

A few other statutes are also worth noting:

✔ The Equal Pay Act of 1963 (EPA) prohibits discrimination on the basis of gender in compensation for substantially similar work under similar conditions. It applies to most employers.

✔ The Immigration Reform and Control Act of 1986 makes it unlawful for an employer to hire any person who is not legally authorized to work in the United States. Employers must verify the employment eligibility of all new employees. It also prohibits smaller employers not covered by Title VII from discriminating based on national origin and citizenship status.

If applicants or employees file discrimination charges with the EEOC, you'll hear about it. The commission will send you a copy of the charge, and if it finds there's a legal claim under EEOC-enforced laws, it will investigate. Remedies for unlawful practices include hiring or reinstatement, a court order to eliminate discriminatory practices, and damages.

For more information, contact EEOC's headquarters in Washington, D.C., or any of its 50 field offices in the United States, or visit the EEOC at www.eeoc.gov. Some state and local laws provide protection to groups not covered by federal statutes. Check with your local department of labor or state attorney general's office.

Discrimination is not only against the law; it's a bad business practice.

Asking the right questions

An interview presents the perfect opportunity to discover the human being whose name tops a résumé or job application. This process can be challenging. Many of today's job candidates are very well polished, including those who have been coached by outplacement firms or how-to books. Your job is to understand the position you're looking to fill, ask fair questions, maintain control of the interview, and project a sense of confidence. You may want to ask human resource personnel at your franchisor's corporate or regional headquarters for guidance.

Most franchisors today include a human resource section in their operations manual and training programs. Make sure that you have the most up-to-date version. The manual should have information on the following:

- Job descriptions and staff responsibilities
- How to anticipate your management and staffing needs (these needs vary depending on your volume, type of location, and the maturity of your business)
- The profile of candidates you should be looking for
- Features and benefits of the job you can use in recruiting candidates
- Recruiting tools — brochures, ad slicks, letters, in-store signage, and so on
- Recruiting sources
- Recruiting techniques and strategies
- Interview preparation
- Interview questions and techniques
- Telephone techniques for recruiting

- ✔ Hiring evaluation
- ✔ Applications and other hiring tools
- ✔ Reference checklists
- ✔ Recommended pay plans and bonus plans
- ✔ Human resource paperwork

If your franchisor doesn't provide this information to franchisees, ask the franchisor to begin the process of developing a human resource guide.

When you're interviewing employees, be sure to put your best foot forward and to communicate clearly:

- ✔ Always be professional.
- ✔ Be natural and comfortable. The candidate knows when you're faking it.
- ✔ Be flexible. Every candidate is an individual. Don't feel obligated to follow the script line-for-line. Be spontaneous when necessary. Asking follow-up questions that aren't on the list not only gives you more information about the candidate but also makes the candidate know you're interested in her or him.
- ✔ Understand that your body language communicates loudly.
- ✔ Greet the candidate. A firm handshake and a smile set the tone for the interview.
- ✔ Make and keep eye contact throughout the interview — but don't stare.
- ✔ Face the candidate.
- ✔ Show respect and interest.
- ✔ Be relaxed but make certain that your posture reflects your attention.
- ✔ Don't use any inappropriate hand gestures. (You know the type — they're the ones your mother told you not to do when you were 5 years old.)
- ✔ Explain the purpose of the interview.
- ✔ Explain the interview format.
- ✔ Give the candidate your full attention.
- ✔ Keep the meeting as private as possible.
- ✔ Don't conduct other business during the interview — you'll miss important information, and doing so conveys to the candidate that you're not entirely interested. Besides, focusing on other business is simply rude.
- ✔ Listen to what the candidate has to say before you form or ask the next question. Listening should be 75 percent of what you do in an interview.
- ✔ Acknowledge what the candidate says — either in words or gestures. (Even an "uh-huh" is better than silence.)

✔ If you take notes, make sure the candidate knows — through your words and gestures — that you're still listening.

✔ Leave your biases at home. Don't project your own values or prejudices.

✔ Be supportive. The candidate should not feel threatened by your actions or statements.

✔ Be professional and respectful. If a question makes the candidate uncomfortable, change or rephrase the question.

✔ Act secure. The candidate wants to know that you're in charge and what to expect from the "boss" after being hired.

✔ Be fair. This isn't a power play. Don't make yourself feel important at the candidate's expense.

✔ Understand that your gut reaction may be wrong. Probe for information.

✔ Don't let your need for a body to fill the position undermine your need to hire the right person.

You need to remember that when you're conducting an interview, you're not only representing the brand but also making an important investment decision. If the candidate becomes an employee, you want that person to understand your passion for your business and the way you expect them to perform as an employee. Even if a candidate doesn't join your team, they still have the ability to talk about you and your operations from an insider's viewpoint. Remember, they can influence others — both potential employees and potential customers.

Hiring, training, motivating, and retaining employees cost time and money. Neither is a commodity that you can afford to waste.

You need to select — not just hire. You want the best candidate for the job. Having just any warm body filling a position places your investment in jeopardy. Every employee has an effect on how customers view your operation and helps them decide whether to come back or to recommend your services to other customers. Invest the time and money it takes to put together a team of employees who take your investment seriously.

To do the job right, you've got to have the right tools. If a prototype application form is included in your operations manual, photocopy a big stack.

Review the application before you meet with the candidate. Look at all the answers — placing the greatest emphasis on dates of employment, reasons for leaving, salary history, positions held, and references. You'll have time before you make the job offer to verify the information. During the initial interview, simply accept the answers as facts that you can use to ask probing questions.

During the interview process, all your questions must be specifically job-related. Consider the value of each question and ask questions accordingly. Base hiring decisions strictly on the requirements of the job and the behavior and personality necessary to perform it — according to your standards, of course.

During an interview, don't ask questions the law forbids you to ask. If you're not sure whether you're crossing the line, double-check with your attorney, your local department of labor, or your state attorney general's office. Your franchisor likely also has a do's and don'ts list in the operations manual.

The first general principle of interviewing is to ask open-ended questions whenever possible. Open-ended questions are questions that can't be answered with a simple yes or no. They encourage the candidate to talk and provide a basis for interaction. An interview that uses primarily open-ended questions is more lively than an interview that goes from one staged question to the next. Open-ended questions are those that usually begin with action words, such as *why, who, where, how, in what way, describe, tell me about,* and so on.

Closed-ended questions, those that can be answered with a simple yes or no, or factual statements are useful for gathering factual and objective information. These questions provide specific information about such things as skills and experience. For example:

- ✔ What was your title in your previous position?
- ✔ Did you graduate from high school?
- ✔ Do you have a driver's license?

Open-ended questions are more far-reaching; they encourage applicants to express their ideas, goals, values, and feelings. For example:

- ✔ What would you like me to know about you, Jackie?
- ✔ What did you like most about your last job?
- ✔ What are the characteristics of great customer service?

Often, candidates will tell you about their families and their hobbies. This information offers hints about what excites and motivates them and whether they'd be happier, say, behind a desk or out on sales calls. Reading between the lines can give you a sense of their interpersonal skills, strengths and weaknesses, and willingness to be a team player.

Here are some more examples of open-ended questions:

- ✔ What did you like most about your last position?
- ✔ Tell me about the skills you learned on your last job.
- ✔ How would your previous supervisor describe you?

✔ How would your fellow staff members describe you?

✔ Describe the work environment in which you are the most productive.

✔ Please describe yourself to me.

✔ What rewards do you look for in a job?

✔ What would you like to be doing one year from now?

✔ What actions, if any, should be taken when a fellow staff member fails to arrive for work on time?

✔ What would you do if you saw one of your fellow staff members taking money from the register or stealing products from the store?

These questions open up the interview for dialogue.

Remember that there are areas of questions you don't want to explore because they violate the law. Make sure that your open-ended questions and dialogue with the candidate don't cross the line.

If the candidate tells you that he didn't learn anything on his last job and that his supervisor was constantly on his back for not coming in on time, you have to look further to see whether the candidate understands what it means to work as part of a team.

If the candidate thinks that petty theft is okay, do you think you can trust her?

Look past the surface answer and probe until you get an understanding of who the person is and how well she or he will fit into your team.

Some people like to hold second interviews. Depending on the job and the tightness of the job market, this can be a good technique. However, remember that hourly wage, entry-level employees may want to go to work today. By tomorrow, they may be working for your competitor.

If you have the luxury of holding second interviews, treat the first interview as a screening process. The second interview — the hiring interview — can outline the tasks involved in the position and determine whether the applicant can meet your requirements in areas such as available shifts and full- or part-time hours. In today's job market, compressing the entry-level, hourly employment interviews into a single session is likely to be your preferred method.

Once you find a qualified applicant, it simply makes good business sense to check references — personal and business — before you make an offer the applicant can't refuse. Background checks go beyond job skills to reveal other qualities. Is the applicant conscientious? Does she have integrity? Is he arrogant? Is she a perfectionist?

Obviously, some people will get cut. You may, however, want to keep their applications on file for a year in case a job opens up that fits their skills.

You represent the brand in everything you do. Just because a candidate doesn't fit your needs today or you don't fit theirs doesn't mean you have to part enemies. Candidates may have friends who need a job and fit your requirements better. They may know coworkers at their current jobs who are perfect for your opportunity. They may love your product or service and tell their family and friends. Even in a job interview, you represent your brand.

Screening your applicants

Running a business is like being onstage, and you are the stage manager. You control the environment:

- ✔ Set the tone for the interview. Conduct the interview in a quiet location with limited disturbances. Your goal is to establish rapport with the applicant so that you can gather information to guide you in making your decision. Always give candidates your undivided attention. They deserve this courtesy.

- ✔ Introduce yourself and explain your function within the business.

- ✔ Always refer to "we" rather than "I" to instill a sense of belonging. Making certain that candidates know "we" includes them if they join your team makes them feel they're joining an organization that is inclusive and that cares about them, the team, and their work environment.

- ✔ Review the employment application and the times and days the applicant is available to work. See whether these match your needs.

- ✔ Determine the applicant's wish list — in terms of position, desired shift, part-time or full-time work, pay, and opportunities for advancement. Do the applicant's needs concerning pay and hours match your needs? If not, the applicant probably won't take the job; if he does, he'll be unhappy.

- ✔ Often class schedules, second jobs, a spouse's or lifemate's job schedule, or child care affect an applicant's availability. Ask about availability, because doing so may identify a candidate suitable for split shifts or part-time hours — which can reduce your payroll costs. (Make certain, however, that your questions do not violate EEOC guidelines.)

- ✔ Assess the applicant's appearance, attitude, character, and desire for the job.

- ✔ Determine the applicant's potential. What is the candidate's education background? Has the person had a career that shows progression in responsibility? Do the applicant's speaking ability and demeanor command respect? The answers to these questions can identify traits you should be looking for.

- ✔ Make a decision to continue or close the interview.

Continuing the interview

Remember that your role in the interview is to find the best candidate for your operation. Here are some tips to help you reach that goal:

✔ Ask open-ended questions.

✔ Listen more; talk less.

✔ Maintain eye contact.

✔ Avoid expressing personal opinions.

✔ Establish a candidate's background, personality, and potential.

- Does the candidate have a sincere desire to work?

- Does the candidate want to work with the public?

- Will the candidate's experience benefit the franchise?

- How will the candidate represent the franchise?

- Does the applicant have leadership abilities and the potential to become a member of your management team?

- Would you want this candidate to serve you if you were a customer?

- Does the candidate's job history reflect stability?

- Because you'll be investing in training, will the candidate provide long-term benefits to your organization?

Explaining job requirements

Job seekers are eager to please and may give you answers they think you want to hear. You can avoid feeding them answers if you ask your questions first. After you've covered your preliminary questions, it's time to hand over the necessary job information so that the candidate can make a decision.

✔ Provide the candidate with a complete job description, including duties, available shifts, hourly wages, benefits, training, and so on.

✔ Let the candidate know your policies and expectations.

✔ Discuss your dress code and grooming requirements.

✔ Let the candidate know your scheduling requirements. What shift will she be on? When does she need to be at work? Does she need to be on call? Are there times of the year she can't have vacation or time off because it's your busy season?

✔ Stress that the atmosphere is one of teamwork and why this is important.

Answering the applicant's questions

The applicant will have questions. Respond to them. The candidate needs to make an important decision and, just like you, should want to have all the relevant facts. Allowing the candidate to ask questions may open up a line of thought you hadn't considered before. By making sure that a candidate understands what's what, you'll reduce the risk of turnover due to misunderstandings and unrealistic expectations.

Effective Leadership

In any business, effective leadership is critical. In franchising, there's another layer: Effective franchisors lead to effective franchisees, which lead to effective employees.

There's no passing the buck here. A franchisor should give you intensive training and operations guidelines to help you hire and train your staff. You can read Chapter 7 to find out about franchisors' training programs.

Regardless of what a franchisor suggests in its manuals or its procedures, your employees are your employees. Your actions are your own — and are not the responsibility of the franchisor. Carefully verify all your employment procedures and policies with your attorney or other advisors.

Next, a franchisor should clearly communicate its corporate culture so that you can transmit it down the line. The corporate culture must be the central focus of the system. It defines your brand and is included in your promotional messages, in your local and community image, in your quality and consistency, and in how your employees interact with each other, consumers, vendors, and everyone else who comes in contact with your business.

Familiarity with the corporate culture can help your staff make decisions. For example, suppose that you have a store manager who has never met the franchisor and is wondering how to handle a certain situation. That manager may find the answer by asking, "What would the franchisor do in this situation?" Your leadership will convey to the staff what the culture really means. It must be the rallying point or, better yet, the "fabric of the system" that transcends the manuals, the forms, and the written procedures. It generates in every staff a level of ownership in the brand and loyalty to the system. The power of the culture is there.

Finally, a franchisor should lead by example. If a franchisor maintains high standards, that tone will be set for franchisees. Then — you guessed it — you'll be the role model for your employees.

DAVE SAYS

A good manager

A good manager is flexible enough to help out with whatever is needed in the restaurant — lending a hand at the window, cleaning tables in the dining room, or greeting customers. He or she just has to be very observant of what's going on — and keep the lines moving. It's really a lot of fun. If you stand behind the grill all the time, you're not being a good manager.

A good manager thinks. It's not how hard a manager works; it's his or her ability to get other people to work hard. Is he a good motivator? Does she know her people? I mean, you've got to have the right person at the cash register. You

have to cross-train, of course, but you'll still have some people who are better at certain tasks than others, at making sandwiches, for example. You have to be very fast to do that, and only certain people are good at it. The manager's really got to say, "Okay, this person is best and happy at this job." That's part of management. You've got to know your people.

Me, I like to work the grill. I don't like the cash register at all. If I had to go in and take over something, I'd want to go in and take over the grill.

One more thing. Until now, you've been relying on your franchisor a lot. But employment is one area where franchisors have to step back a bit. From a legal standpoint, it's unclear how much franchisors can tell franchisees what to do in regard to human resource issues, so they steer clear of making certain things a requirement. These are *your* employees.

There's a silver lining behind this cloud, though. Franchisors can make suggestions, and when they own corporate units, they can show actual case histories — of recruitment strategies, wages, bonuses, training, promotions, work schedules, filling out government forms, and so on. Many operations manuals contain EEOC policies, interviewing guidelines, and sample recruitment materials. (Some do not, because franchisors are sensitive to the potential liability of looking like coemployers to your employees.) Plus, you can always tap your fellow franchisees to see what's working for them. That's plenty more information than you'd get as an independent business owner.

Finding the right employees

Are you resourceful? Good. You've got to be for this job. Finding employees boils down to putting in time and effort, thinking creatively, and, usually, spending some money. In a tight labor market, you've got to try everything and anything once, and then four more times to see what works.

Before recruiting, have an idea of how many employees you need and when you need to bring them on board. Operations and training manuals should help with this; you're a step ahead if your own business plan spells out these guidelines. Also have clear job descriptions (hopefully, your franchisor has helped you out here). Franchisors also typically provide franchisees with information on employee profiles to look for and to avoid. Although not perfect in every situation, the employee profiles can provide you with a good tool to work with as you learn the business.

Word of mouth is a great way to start your search. Just as with marketing, talk up your business to friends, relatives, neighbors, and other businesspeople. People are often in the market for new jobs or know someone who is.

You never know where you may find potential employees, so always be on the lookout for them. Maryann Spencer, director of training at Express Personnel Services, an Oklahoma City temporary help franchisor, perks up when she's shopping and notices a sales associate wowing customers with superior customer service skills. She's not shy about handing over her business card. Her feeling: "You can train almost any skill, but you can't train a servant's heart."

When you hire your employees, you've begun a referral network. Happy employees are your best marketers; they love to bring in others — especially when there's an added incentive. Many franchisees offer rewards, for example, cash, concert tickets, or other prizes, for every referral who's hired. Advertise the program on bulletin boards, in newsletters, and at employee meetings.

You can also use your site to give customers a heads-up; they're the perfect captured audience! Wendy's uses outdoor billboards, counter cards, crew buttons, tray liners, job posting centers, and recruitment messages on carry-out bags.

Also tap your community — churches, community organizations, schools, and colleges. In some areas, employers can claim a tax credit for hiring at-risk youth and other hard-to-employ residents. Contact the Department of Housing and Urban Development at 202-708-0380 to find out whether you're in a federally designated zone. Government agencies, local chambers of commerce, and nonprofit groups can help you locate senior citizens and the developmentally disabled. (Dave feels these are some of his best dining room employees.) Some Wendy's restaurants in metro areas recruit students in high school Spanish classes. The pitch: Help us train Spanish-speaking workers, and we'll give you real-life experience in speaking Spanish. It's a win-win situation.

So far, you've probably gotten away cheap. Now get ready to open your wallet. Classified ads are the most popular hiring tool. See whether your franchisor offers recruitment ad slicks that you can use, and can guide you on the appropriate media.

Recruitment ads, just like every other advertisement you use in your business, need to be professional and designed to be effective. Many franchisors produce advertising material that you can customize for your location.

Some of these ads may be posted in the help wanted sections of your local newspaper. Others may be targeted for school publications, senior citizen centers, trade journals, hospital and other employers' internal newsletters, and so on. Let your franchisor help you spend your recruiting dollars wisely.

Employment agencies and executive recruiters, which typically charge a flat fee or percentage of salary per hire, may work for some positions, such as management or positions that require certain skills or licenses.

Other options are hosting open houses or so-called Discovery Days, contacting your local department of labor, and participating in career fairs.

Networking within your franchise system can also pay off. Consider this: A wonderful employee at a franchise in Florida is relocating to Tempe, Arizona — exactly where your franchise is located. You've just hit the jackpot: You get not only someone with glowing references but also someone who knows the system.

In recruiting, your message can make all the difference. Make sure that the language you use in your recruitment materials is in compliance with EEOC guidelines. For example, to avoid discriminating against older job candidates, nix words like *young, recent graduate, boy,* or *girl.*

Recruiting sources

It's your responsibility to keep an eye out for potential employees. The following sources can help you in the recruiting process:

- ✔ School and college placement offices
- ✔ Staff referrals
- ✔ Newspaper advertising
- ✔ Religious advisors
- ✔ "Help wanted" sign in window
- ✔ "Homemakers — Spare cash for your spare time" ads or window signs
- ✔ "Students — Spare cash before and after classes" ads or window signs

- ✔ Word of mouth
- ✔ Other neighborhood stores or retailers
- ✔ State and local government employment offices
- ✔ Current applications on file
- ✔ Vocational and trade schools
- ✔ Community agencies
- ✔ Private employment agencies
- ✔ Walk-ins

The job opportunity may come across as more inviting if you convey a personable image. As a job seeker, which would you choose: a mega-supermarket that has a stark white sign in the window with "Help Wanted" printed in black ink, or a full-color poster or billboard with pictures of happy workers that urges you to "Join Our Team — it's not a job, it's your future."

In addition, emphasize — go ahead, even boast about — how you stand out from the crowd. People like to work on a winning team. Perks such as bonuses, child-care reimbursement, and career advancement could make you the employer of choice.

Training your team

Now that you have your rookies, it's time to transform them into team players. Just suiting them up in the right uniform won't do it. Training is what scores points here — big points.

Employee training is part vocational, part philosophical. Sure, your employees need to know their specific tasks, maybe even be cross-trained in several roles. But they also need to understand the chain's vision and culture, especially its thoughts on customer service — the lifeblood of any business.

Wendy's franchisee Tim Hogsett of Albuquerque, New Mexico, understands that the reputation of the brand, the way an employer treats its employees, and the possibility for advancement are important in recruiting new employees. He says that he's been able to hire people away from other organizations "simply because the culture at his Wendy's is better than elsewhere."

Be prepared to train everyone you sign up. Even if someone has experience in the business, that's not good enough. You're in franchising now. Everybody has to learn the system. Training should be simple, fun, and consistent — and continually reinforced.

Who's the teacher? It depends on the system and often on the specific job. Check your UFOC (see Chapter 6) to see whether the franchisor offers initial or ongoing training to any of your employees. Is there a limit on how many, say, managers can be trained over time? Is only a certain level of employee included? Are there additional training costs? In any event, expect to pick up transportation and lodging costs. And unless you're obsessed with racking up frequent flyer miles, find out whether continuing training is available at a closer, regional office so that you don't have to trek to corporate headquarters.

Most franchisors provide some training at your site when your franchise first opens so employees can get in on the act. Later on, ongoing training may be available at your site, probably for a fee. A few franchisors even broadcast training via satellite or over the Internet directly to a unit. If you're a multi-unit owner, you may be big enough to hire your own training staff; for consistency's sake, it's likely that they'd have to be certified by the franchisor's trainers.

Expect to do a lot of your own training. Fresh out of Franchise U, you're full of knowledge that's worth passing on. And, hopefully, your franchisor has taught you how to pass it on. (The same goes for your manager, if you have one.)

If your franchisor takes training seriously (like a franchisor should), you'll be loaded up with training manuals, pamphlets, checklists, and audiotapes to ensure consistency. High-tech tools such as videotapes and CD-ROMs sometimes lighten the training program with everything from rap songs to interactive games; the best part is that they can continually be popped into a VCR or computer to train new employees or refresh memories. Many are reinforced with printed materials and online training over the World Wide Web — we call that *distance learning*.

To do it right, plan on including lots of role-playing in your training. "What if's" — including nightmarish scenarios — help your employees survive sticky situations and go miles toward achieving great customer service. Then move on to real life. Ride with your employees out of the corral — accompanying them on a sales call or coaching them through a register ring-up.

Expect your franchisor to address some training issues at your chain's annual meeting. Franchisors usually welcome managers and employees at continuous training, including some national and regional training seminars.

Training is like a song that never ends. It keeps playing on and on because there are always new employees, new things to learn, and information that needs to be reinforced.

When you're training a new employee, avoid a sterile, lecture-like approach. Encourage the new employee to ask questions and get involved. A new employee may have the right attitude but lack the experience and skills necessary to work effectively.

Manual skills are best taught by a simple four-step method:

1. **Prepare the employee.**

   Explain to the employee the task he will be doing. The employee simply observes someone else doing the skill and asks questions.

2. **Present the information to the employee.**

   Let the employee do the task. Slowly lead him in the process while you explain how to do each step.

Training never ends

You can't expect your employees to do things they don't know how to do. That's a major mistake bosses make. The boss knows how to do it. The boss may have learned how to do it over a significant period of time — maybe after years and years of experience. It may have taken you six months to learn a new trade, yet you want to teach your employees in six days because you think you get more efficiency that way and you don't want to invest the time.

Training is nonstop, never-ending. It has to be. It has to remain a priority in your business because, one, you have turnover, but two, you can always improve.

If you and your staff have the attitude that you can continuously improve, you have a good training program because the day you think you understand it and have it, your competition will come up with a new way of doing it.

3. **Let the employee practice.**

   Have the employee do the task, but this time let him explain each step while performing the task at half-speed. Provide the employee with coaching and advice as needed.

4. **Follow up to see what the employee has learned.**

   Have the employee perform the task at full speed, without any coaching or assistance. This tells you whether the employee is ready to work independently and with your customers on that specific task.

   Congratulate the employee when he has mastered the new task. Doing so instills pride in doing a good job. Go back and observe the employee periodically to make sure that he's still doing the task correctly and hasn't picked up any bad habits.

   Remember to break the skill down into easy-to-understand portions. If the skill is to learn how to clean a restroom, work on sweeping and washing the floor separately from cleaning the mirrors, the washbowls, and other fixtures. The job may be cleaning the bathroom, but the task is the individual components of the job.

Holding on to your employees

Look at how much time you've already invested in rounding up your employees! Now you have to figure out ways to make sure that they'll stick with you. Today, a paycheck alone isn't good enough. You've got to motivate and offer incentives. We all appreciate a pat on the back.

DAVE SAYS

Keeping the job diverse and interesting

Particularly in our business, the tasks that the staff performs are pretty much the same day in and day out, so it becomes important for employees' mental well-being that they're cross-trained so they can get diversity in their work; otherwise, employees will get bored and leave. The days of assembly-line mentality are changing.

Labor shortages also make it necessary for employees to understand how to work more positions. If you have a staff shortage in one area, you can easily slide employees over from other areas.

Now there are some that will argue, yeah, but the employee never gets good at a task if he's constantly being moved around. I disagree with that because there aren't a hundred tasks to do — you may be moving around between three, four, or five tasks.

The best approach is to make recognizing your employees a priority — throughout the day, not just at the end of the day. You have to delegate. You have to empower. You have to give respect. You have to relate well. Express your expectations to employees and communicate with them, via such methods as rap sessions, anonymous employee surveys, and information — positive only, please — posted on bulletin boards.

Dave learned a lot about making employees feel good early in his career when he worked at the Regas Restaurant in Knoxville, Tennessee. When he made mistakes, the Regas brothers never belittled him; they'd explain what he had done wrong and how to correct it — leaving him feeling good. From that, Dave developed his Regas Rules for Restaurants (for any business, actually):

- ✔ Back your employees when the situation calls for it.
- ✔ Build your people's confidence. Tell them what they're doing right, and make it easy for them to learn from their mistakes.
- ✔ Reward motivation and determination.

One of the greatest motivators is making employees feel that they contribute to your franchise. If they don't feel respected, they'll leave no matter what you pay them. Are you giving people responsibility? Do you recognize and reward good deeds? Do you bounce ideas off employees? Do you let them mentor newer employees? Do you encourage them to voice complaints?

Employees also get energized if you offer them some diversity in their responsibilities. That's a big reason to include cross-training in your training program. If employees feel skilled and confident at their tasks, they'll be more likely to stay on.

Also, remember that employees like to be valued — especially in ways that affect their lifestyle. At Wendy's, when a general manager catches an employee performing extra-great, he'll throw her some "bonus bucks" cash or paper money that can be redeemed for prizes like pizza parties or CDs.

Think of some incentives that will work in your market. In Alexandria, Virginia, franchisee Liz Daus of The Maids International has an employee wellness program that includes seminars on domestic violence, financial management, and self-esteem.

Here are some other perks to consider:

- Reward an employee for attendance, appearance, or overall store performance with cash bonuses, concert tickets, and trips.

- Link raises and extra vacation time to profitability.

- Recognize employee achievements, birthdays, and other milestones in company newsletters or with special dinners.

- Start a savings club that matches employees' withholdings from their paychecks if they stay a certain length of time.

- With students, dangle cash for high grades, award scholarships, or offer tutoring.

- Consider getting involved in employees' pet charities.

- Participate in regional rallies that your franchisor organizes. These might include prizes, games, and other rewards for employees.

- Offer partial ownership in your franchise. Giving up some profits may be tough, but there's no better motivator than owning a piece of the pie. Isn't that what's making *you* work so hard?

Obviously, even with your best efforts at retention, you will probably have some turnover; someone may move or become a stay-at-home mom. Or misconduct, customer complaints, or poor job performance may be so severe that, despite warnings, an employee's got to go. Even if you have a great staff and your turnover has been low, maintain a strong staff-recruiting program. You never know when you may need it.

A Good Work Environment

Franchisees always talk about making customers happy. That's absolutely a top priority. But if your employees aren't happy, how can your customers be happy? A big step towards employee satisfaction comes from creating a good workplace environment. That doesn't mean plastering smiley face stickers on every wall; it means concentrating on those aspects of your operation that make employees feel they're being treated fairly and safely.

Service Excellence

We have a program at Wendy's called Service Excellence. It's real simple. It's about cross-training people, motivating people, and giving people the best service and the best product so they will come back. In our pick-up window, for example, we're running 100 seconds from ordering to delivering, and we've increased our percent of total restaurant sales coming from the pick-up window from 50 to 65 percent of the operation. That's where the gravy is.

Restaurants run so much better when we have incentives for our crews. We have parties, football tickets, concerts. We do this on a consistent basis so that when people come to work, man, it's fast, it's working, we're getting things done, it's cross-training, and it's fun.

We get our crews to have fun and take care of our customers. And our customers are having fun coming into our restaurants. So that's where the push is right now.

To create this feeling among employees, you have to do three things. One, you have to establish and enforce policies on antidiscrimination compliance. Two, you have to follow the franchisor's safety and security guidelines. And three, you should encourage employees to speak up about any of their concerns on these issues.

Complying with federal regulations

Some employers get into trouble with federal regulations by making assumptions. Consider this: Sixty-year-old Sally won't fly as a salesclerk because she's set in her ways, won't be able to report to her 25-year-old manager, or is likely to check into a retirement community soon. Wrong. If you base any employment action on these age-related assumptions, you're violating the Age Discrimination in Employment Act.

When you're dealing with people with disabilities, you may ask applicants about their ability to perform specific jobs, but you may not ask them about the existence, nature, or severity of a disability. Also, you must make reasonable accommodations if it wouldn't impose an undue hardship on your business. Accommodations include modifying work schedules, adjusting training materials, and making existing facilities readily usable. Smaller employers may qualify for funds from the State Vocational Rehabilitation Services Program (202-205-8719). Also available for small businesses are tax incentives to offset costs, and a tax credit for hiring individuals classified by local employment agencies as "vocational rehabilitation referrals"; contact the Internal Revenue Service at 800-829-1040.

Here are some suggestions the EEOC makes to help you comply with Title VII of the Civil Rights Act.

- **Regarding sexual harassment:** Clearly communicate to employees that sexual harassment will not be tolerated.

- **Regarding race/color discrimination:**

  - Do not institute a "no-beard" policy, which may discriminate against African American men who are predisposed to severe shaving bumps, unless the policy is job-related.

  - Stress that ethnic slurs, racial "jokes," and derogatory comments based on an employee's race/color are unacceptable.

- **Regarding religion, unless these would impose an undue hardship on your business:**

  - Schedule exams or other selection activities at times that don't conflict with an employee's religious needs.

  - Allow observance of a Sabbath or religious holiday.

  - Offer flexible schedules, job reassignments, and lateral transfers.

- **Regarding pregnancy:**

  - Provide modified tasks, disability leave, or alternative assignments — just as you would for other temporarily disabled employees.

  - Do not limit pregnancy-related fringe benefits to married employees.

- **Regarding national origin:** Don't institute a speak-English-only rule unless you can show that such a rule is necessary for conducting business and you communicate that rule to the employee.

Set up an internal system to handle employees who complain of discrimination or observe instances of discrimination, and develop appropriate disciplinary action.

Ensuring workplace safety

Smart franchisors provide you with reams and reams of paper on recommendations for safety and security. You should be looking for this kind of commitment. You also need to review the Occupational Safety and Health Act, which is administered by the Department of Labor's Occupational Safety and Health Administration (OSHA). The act regulates safety and health conditions and may require employers to adopt certain practices to protect workers. All this material may be tedious to read through, but it's worth your time. Preventing mishaps directly corresponds to employee and customer retention — and profitability.

Take care of your equipment

Wendy's has guidelines on everything, down to taking apart the Frosty machine. We tell employees not only when to take it apart but also how to take it apart, how to clean it, and how to put it back together. Part of the reason we have to cross every *t* and dot every *i* is not only the safety of the equipment but also the safety of the food.

Now, service or other non-food businesses don't have to worry about food safety, but they do have to worry about the safety and durability of the equipment. Proper maintenance is critical to getting the maximum results out of your equipment, and a lot of people don't worry about that.

Maybe you have a ceiling fan in your house. The instructions may tell you to lubricate it every six months. Nobody does that, and then they get upset when the thing breaks after five or six years. Well, if you never oiled it, what do you expect?

The same point can be made about the maintenance of your equipment. You have to follow a maintenance program; you're investing a lot of money in the equipment.

Safety concerns vary by business, of course. But some safety issues are pretty standard, such as properly using the equipment, correctly handling material, knowing where you store fire extinguishers, and preventing burns, falls, and other accidents. Nobody wants to see an employee or a customer fall on a sidewalk that should have been cleared of ice. You should have certain procedures down to an exact science — for example, how often you should clean the bathrooms and mop the floors, and how to lift heavy objects. In the restaurant business especially, food handling, storage procedures, and cleanliness are a major priority for safety and health reasons. Remember that you want to have happy employees. Well, no one will be happy working hard and long in a dirty place.

Safety and security are your responsibilities, not the franchisor's. Whether the franchisor gives you guidelines or not, whether they include comments about safety and security on their field reports to you or not, it's your responsibility to operate your business in a safe and secure manner.

Security issues are a whole other story. As an employer, you could face a wide range of problems, from employee theft to armed robberies. Find out what your franchisor recommends in terms of alarm systems, closed-circuit TV systems, and door controls. Check with local experts and the police on what you can and should do to make your location safe. Safety and security are your responsibility to your customers, vendors, and staff.

Carefully check out an employee's background — to the extent that you're legally able to.

Then train your employees to be on high alert. Instruct office or store managers to call the police immediately, for example, if they see a crime in progress or someone disturbing customers or employees. Instruct employees in simple security precautions; for example, advise them to leave a restaurant after dark only if they're accompanied by another worker.

We're sure this advice sounds like common sense. Still, you need to have security precautions in place and procedures for reporting all crimes. You don't want to get caught without them.

Part IV
Times Change: Deciding What to Do Next

The 5th Wave   By Rich Tennant

"We're hoping to franchise six more of these over the next three months, but... who knows?"

In this part . . .

In this part, we talk about your growth options — buying additional units from your franchisor or investing in additional franchises with other franchisors. If you're successful as a franchisee, owning just one franchise may not be enough for you.

At some point, your relationship with your franchisor is likely to come to an end. This part also prepares you for that situation.

Chapter 13

Acquiring Other Franchises

. . . .

In This Chapter

▶ Complying with your franchise agreement: Are you allowed to buy more than one franchise?

▶ Exploring the purchasing options

▶ Evaluating personal and financial resources

▶ Weighing the pros and cons of multiple ownership

. . . .

For some franchisees, jingling just one set of keys is fine. For others, one franchise is just the beginning.

Some franchisees open one location and it's years before they approach their franchisor with a request for a second or a third. Others enter franchising intending to open multiple franchises so that when they drive through their town every one of the locations that carry their franchisor's brand is a place they can point to as their own. Still others dream of becoming *master franchisees* — that's when they obtain the rights from the franchisor to recruit their own sub-franchisees that will operate under the franchisor's brand. Their goal is to become sort of mini-franchisors. (For details on master franchising, see the section titled, "Acquiring an area," in this chapter.)

This chapter shows you how you can buy another franchise — or even multiple franchises — and how to make sure you're making the right choices along the way.

Checking Your Franchise Agreement: Can You Buy Another Franchise?

Before you get charged up about buying multiple franchises, make sure that multi-unit ownership is an option in your franchisor's system. Companies have different philosophies on expansion.

Some franchisors say that one's the limit — period.

Other companies encourage you to expand, expand, and E-X-P-A-N-D some more. Still others embrace only multi-unit development, turning their backs entirely on the little guy. Some franchisors have a set waiting period before you can open another location or another territory. (Population or geographic area typically defines territories.) These companies may want to make sure that franchisees can operate their first business to system standards and do so profitably before they will consider letting them purchase number two. Make sure that you're aware of the franchisor's restrictions and requirements.

Your franchisor's policy may be spelled out in their disclosure document — the Uniform Franchise Offering Circular (see Chapter 6). Even if it's not, check with your franchisor to determine what the franchise fees and other fees are for expansion. Some franchise systems charge lower fees — at least up front — for franchisees willing to commit to opening multiple locations

Understanding Your Purchase Options

First things first: You have to decide how you want to expand. Depending on the rules of your chain, you may be able to open up new locations only one at a time, or you might be allowed to go for multiple locations, acquire an entire territory, or convert an existing operation.

Then you have to deal with *where* to establish your next franchise.

Go back to the drawing board and diligently pursue site selection with the same gusto you did the first time around. You may think that you know your market inside and out if you've already been operating a franchise, but you need to be aware of other considerations. For example, a location in a different neighborhood or even on a different avenue in the same neighborhood may have totally different dynamics than your current operations.

Traffic patterns will likely differ, your customer base could change, and even the side of the street you select will have to be considered. Your franchisor should help you with site selection guidelines. Check demographics, traffic patterns, zoning laws, competition, and so on (see Chapter 8).

Buying a franchise from another franchisee in the system

Sometimes you want what you can't have — like your neighbor's location. Well, maybe you can have it.

She may be chugging along day after day, never thinking of selling until you bring up the idea. Or maybe that franchisee has the franchise on the seller's block because she is planning to retire or cash out while the business is thriving. Perhaps the business is failing, and you're sure you can turn it around.

Don't rush headlong into the deal. Find out what the franchise contract says. Usually the franchisor will consent to a transfer, but the company may reserve the right to disapprove a proposed transfer to an existing franchisee based on specific conditions. You need to read the fine print in the agreement and discuss expansion criteria set by your system. If your existing locations are not meeting system standards or are performing poorly, it's likely that your franchisor will be reluctant to see you open another location. Maybe you're already in default under your existing agreements. Do you think the franchisor wants to see you possibly default on other agreements?

A franchisor may also have the right of first refusal over any location up for sale; that is, the franchisor can match any bona fide offer and purchase the seller's interest. (See Chapter 15 for more information on selling out.)

How do you find out if existing franchises are for sale? The first place is straight from the horse's month. You should always stay in touch with the other franchisees in your system — especially franchise owners in your market area. By doing so, you're likely to know what other franchisees are planning and which one has a location that might be up for sale.

Your franchisor might approach you about acquiring an existing franchise, but you don't have to wait for them. Call the franchisor's headquarters or speak to your field consultant about possible opportunities they might know of. Many franchisors operate active resale networks, sometimes for a fee but usually for free. After all, it's in the franchisor's interest to help someone who wants out of the system to leave, especially when an existing good operator wants to expand.

Buying an additional franchise takes analysis, perhaps even more analysis than starting from scratch. Before deciding to purchase, consider the other franchise's proximity to your current site. Is the site so close to your existing store that you won't get any real benefit, or is it too far away for you to properly manage? Maybe the area it's in has changed since it was opened, and the change is having a negative effect on the operation.

Find out whether the other franchisee's business meets your franchisor's standards or whether you'll have to do significant remodeling to bring it up to standards. The good news is that you know the business, know how a franchise should be performing, and will be able to look at an existing operation to understand its potential advantages and faults.

Proximity

The first consideration is the franchise's proximity to your existing business. You don't want to invest a great deal of money only to find that you're splitting, rather than adding to, your customer base.

Life is easier if you expand nearby, so you can still be a hands-on manager. Time spent driving long distances or even flying to a second location is time that could be better spent on operations. Of course, the location shouldn't be right next door, either. So how close is ideal? There are no hard and fast rules. You could have one location two miles away that hurts your current business; another one that's a half a mile away could have no negative impact if it's separated by a river or a major street that divides the town or trading area. The bottom line: Look carefully at your trade area.

Remember, though, that the business is already in existence. If it's already affecting your existing operation, whether it continues its operation in your hands or someone else's, the impact will probably still be there.

Just because you have a unit in a mall doesn't mean you can't develop a successful location nearby — even right on the pad in the mall's parking lot. You may be drawing from a completely different population of customers.

Even in franchising — the king of duplication — your second site doesn't have to be an identical twin of your first. If you have a freestanding location now, perhaps a nearby strip center or a nontraditional site (such as a kiosk that sells the same merchandise you carry or in a food court) is a better choice for your next purchase. (Turn to Chapter 8 to find out more about nontraditional locations.)

Franchisors are not allowed to provide you information about unit financial performance in the United States unless they do so in their disclosure documents — the Uniform Franchise Offering Circular (UFOC). However, this restriction does not exist when you buy a location that's up and running. You can and should always ask to see the actual operating results for the location you plan to buy from your franchisor or from another franchisee.

Other questions to ask about an existing business

When you buy an existing franchise, you need to be aware of some issues and examine them closely before you make the purchase. Ask yourself the following questions to help uncover any costly and time-consuming problems:

✔ **Does the location meet your franchisor's current standards?** You don't want to make additional investments in the business that you didn't count on, such as remodeling, adding new equipment, expanding the parking lot, or building an addition. Remodeling costs can increase significantly if the facility doesn't meet the standards of the Americans with Disabilities Act (ADA).

On the other hand, if the building is intact — and the utilities, sanitary hookups, and storm drains already exist — remodeling may be less expensive than building a whole new site. Be sure you know what you're buying, and factor it into your purchase offer.

✔ **Is the business profitable?** If not, are the problems fixable, and do you have the time and talent to make it all work?

✔ **If you have to make improvements to the site, how soon do they have to be completed?** Does the franchisor have any financing programs to help you modernize? Are there enough years left on the franchise rights to allow you to amortize your added costs? Talk to your franchisor.

✔ **How has the franchise scored on the franchisor's periodic reviews?** What were the problems? Can you fix them?

✔ **How good are the employees?** Is the management team trained? Are they experienced? Do you have managers in your other locations who can be transferred to the new franchise?

✔ **Are employees willing to stay on?** Are their current salaries and benefits in line with what you're willing to offer? Do they have any labor issues that could cause you problems in your other locations?

✔ **Does the location have a good reputation with the public?** If not, can you really expect that new management will be enough to regain customer loyalty? Does the current customer profile even live in the area anymore? With older systems, this is often a problem.

✔ **Does the current owner keep a list of all of their customers?** Is the list current? Will they give it to you when you buy the business?

✔ **How much time remains on the real estate lease and equipment leases?** Do you have the option to renew? What are the terms of the leases?

✔ **Does the owner have any legal problems that could affect the business later?** Is foreclosure a possibility? Does the government hold any tax liens against the property?

✔ **Is anything happening in the area — such as a new road under construction or a new competitor — that could lessen the franchise's performance?** Do at least the same amount of site due diligence as you would for a new site — title, survey, environmental, and so on (see Chapter 8).

Retrofranchising: Buying a company-owned location

Often, franchisors own locations that they operate themselves. Sometimes the franchisor will build locations with the intention of operating them for the long term; sometimes they build locations so they can sell them to prospective franchisees, and sometimes they buy them or take them back from franchisees that may have left the system.

Franchisors sell these existing operations for many reasons:

- They need the proceeds from the sale to pay down debt or for other corporate purposes.
- They want to exit one market so that they can build additional units elsewhere.
- They changed their strategy and no longer want to operate company-owned locations anywhere.
- The location was built with the intention of selling it to franchisees.
- The only reason they have the location is that they acquired it from a former franchisee with the intent to sell it to a new franchisee.
- The location is losing money, and they want to get it off their books.

Often, franchisors will look for franchisees that are willing to buy the location and are willing to invest in additional locations in the same market.

Let's assume the franchisor determines that for the market to be a success, it requires five locations — we call that *critical mass.* Critical mass is important because it gives the brand a stronger presence in the market and allows advertising costs to be spread over more locations; therefore, more advertising can be purchased. Critical mass enables the franchisor to more easily provide support to the locations in the market, because more franchisees bear the cost of the market visits that the field staff makes. (We call that *leveraging the costs.*)

By tying the sale of the company-owned location to an obligation to build out additional locations — and create the desired critical mass — the franchisor benefits the system.

Retrofranchising locations is often good for both the franchisor and the franchisee:

- The locations are up and running, and you can see their track records and performance.
- Franchisors may be willing to sell these businesses at a discount or finance some of the acquisition costs if the franchisee is willing to invest in additional locations.
- The franchisor gets to use the money for other company needs.

Refranchising is different from churning. *Churning* occurs when a franchisor takes back a location from a franchisee and then resells it repeatedly, knowing that there is a strong possibility that the subsequent franchisee may also fail at that site. This scenario, while infrequent, can happen when the original franchisee can't make a go of the location or is not able to operate to company standards and so is terminated.

Snapping up opportunities

If the financial deal is favorable, sometimes a franchisor develops a location that offers a unique opportunity — regardless of whether a franchisee is waiting in line to purchase the site. The franchisor may run the location as a company unit until a new franchisee buys it. Or the franchisor may offer the site to an existing franchisee. Getting the location is the first priority, and then the franchisor can work out who will operate it.

This situation happens often with nontraditional units because these opportunities are few and far between. There may be only one high-volume hospital in town. So if a location becomes available in the hospital, you'd better grab it because another one might not be available for 20 years. If franchisors don't want to operate the location themselves for the long term, they have the option of offering it to new or existing franchisees.

If the poorly performing location was owned by a nonfranchisor that did not have the opportunity to refranchise it to a new operator, they would likely be forced to close the poorly performing location. In the hands of some franchisors, though, these poorly performing locations can stay alive — while succeeding new owners attempt to operate them and go out of business trying. While churning is not a common practice, there are a few franchisors (thankfully, very few) that do it — you need to be careful.

Make sure you look at the financial performance and ownership history of a location. If it was a bad location in another franchisee's hands — and if your franchisor has a habit of flipping bad units from one franchisee to another — the fact that you're a great operator won't magically turn a failing business into a success.

Converting a competitor's location

If you're looking in your market area for expansion opportunities but there's no available site that fits your needs, check out competitor's locations. Acquiring an existing location from a competitor that meet your requirements is a way of finding sites and knocking out the competition in one fell swoop.

Sometimes, this opportunity can be a no-brainer. An independent may beg you to buy him out. A lot of independents feel like David up against Goliath when franchises charge into town. If franchising is working right, your powerful name recognition, national advertising, and better prices (thanks to a chain's volume buying power) are pushing the competitor's customers to your doors. Consequently, he may be about to close his business.

Buying a competitor's site is another case where you won't be starting from ground zero. Hopefully, you can pick up the competitor's customers. You may be able to retain, but retrain, some employees. Who knows — the former business owner may want to be your new manager.

Making the transition, however, won't be easy. Since the competitor's location probably has a different design than units in your franchisor's system, you'll probably have to remodel the location to meet system standards. You'll have to hire an architect and contractor to make the changes. If the location was being used for the same type of business, zoning probably won't be a problem. In addition, your cost for developing the location should be lower than building a new location, because the building is up and the electricity, water, and sewage are probably in operation. To convert the location to your system's brand, you'll be changing the layout, hanging new signs, changing the décor, and possibly adding new equipment.

Ask your franchisor's real estate and development department to work with you on this project. These professionals can help you determine whether the savings you expect from buying an existing location is likely to happen. For example, the site may have plumbing but it may be in the wrong place and you'll have to move it. There will be electricity, but it may not be sufficient for your needs. The building may be zoned correctly, but it might not have enough parking spaces. Engage their assistance before you make your purchase.

If you're buying a location that has been operating under a different franchisor's brand, consult your attorney to make sure you can acquire the location without violating the other franchisor's rights. The existing operator's franchise agreement may prohibit or hinder the sale. Also confirm that your own franchise agreement allows you to expand and that the competitor's location won't encroach on another franchisee's territory or — in the opinion of the franchisor — negatively affect sales at your existing location.

Starting from scratch

You always have the option of simply going through the same process you did when you opened up your first franchise: Purchase a franchise from the franchisor, locate a new site, and develop it fresh from the ground up. That's how most franchisees go from being single-unit operators to multiple-unit operators — building one unit at a time.

Buying multiple units

It's becoming more common today to find franchisees that decide right from the start of their relationship with their franchisor that single-unit ownership is not for them. These franchisees plan for multi-unit ownership right from the start. Many of these new franchisees are investor groups, and some are even public companies that are larger than the franchisor.

By the time a franchisee purchases four or five franchises, she will probably start creating some of her own administrative and back office operating systems. Franchisees often set up training stores; their trainers will probably be trained by the franchisor. They'll add supervisory personnel, such as store-level managers and a district or general manager. Ideally, managers will receive training similar to the training provided to franchisees when they first joined the franchise system. (We discuss training in Chapter 12.)

After purchasing several franchises, franchisees often begin to feel the need to increase or fortify their "back of house" support capabilities. They will typically have an accounting department, human resource personnel, a training department, and a team responsible for developing local advertising. Even when they get this big, franchisees still need the franchisor. Besides getting the almighty brand, franchisees can take advantage of the franchisor's expertise in national marketing, research and development, and field support.

Acquiring an area

If you have big dreams from the start of being a franchise tycoon, you may want to consider franchisors that offer the whole package: *area development rights*. These rights allow a franchisee to expand exclusively within a specific territory, according to a schedule — X number of units within a certain period.

In a twist on this method, some chains sell an entire territory to a franchisee, and, based on a schedule, allow the franchisee to open units herself, or sell unit franchises to other operators, called *subfranchisees*. This approach is called *master franchising*.

The master franchisee recruits new franchisees into the system and often provides them with many of the services other franchisees get directly from the franchisor. In exchange for recruiting and supporting the subfranchisees, the master franchisee retains a portion of the initial fee paid by the subfranchisee (franchise fee) and also retains a portion of the *continuing royalty payments* (a continuing fee paid by the unit franchisee to the franchisor, usually based on a percentage of gross sales). This arrangement is very common in international franchising but is becoming less so in the United States. (In Chapter 17, we explore international expansion.)

Some franchise systems expand only via area development or multi-unit development. Theoretically, by dealing with fewer but larger and hopefully more sophisticated franchisees, they can manage their systems with more ease and focus their efforts on support, new products, services, and other areas besides franchise sales.

Other chains use a multi-unit strategy only in their core or larger markets and sell single franchises only in their smaller markets. The method depends on the system and its growth strategy.

For franchisees, an advantage of acquiring an area is that you lock in a territory in which you can develop multiple locations without having to worry about how many other franchises are being developed and how close those locations are to your sites. In contrast, if you buy franchises one at a time, you risk getting closed out of parts of your area because other franchisees or company-owned locations have been developed.

Before striking a deal for area development rights, consider the following:

- The number of stores you ultimately want
- The amount of money you can invest or raise to develop those stores
- The number of locations the market can support
- The additional costs and savings you will incur

Be prepared to pay substantial money up front. Area development rights typically command either a flat fee — that could be even hundreds of thousands of dollars — or a fee per franchise you commit to develop. For example, if the franchise fee is $40,000, you might fork over the entire franchise fee for the first unit and a $15,000 deposit on each additional one; the remainder would be due upon opening.

If you default on the development schedule, you may lose your deposit — plus the exclusive rights to the area. Check to see how strict the franchisor is regarding the default option. Some franchisors will amend the agreement to accommodate late construction schedules or other problems. Franchisors may also extend the opening date. (Sometimes they charge the franchisee an extension fee.) The development schedule may include grace periods. Many franchisors don't have a set policy. How they respond often depends on whether the franchisee has been trying to get the units open and whether, despite their efforts, unforeseen obstacles have arisen. The flexibility of the franchisor may depend on whether the franchisee and the franchisor have a good or bad relationship. Check with other multi-unit operators to find out what the franchisor does in a crunch.

Franchisors often offer a lower per-unit fee to an area developer than they do to a franchisee that's only committing to opening one site. There are many reasons for this disparity, but they all rest on two basic issues:

- ✔ The franchisor reduces its costs by having one individual or company own multiple locations. They save on having to recruit additional franchisees to open the locations. They save on the time, cost, and effort of providing support to individual locations; with an area developer, they work with only one franchisee for all of the locations.

- ✔ The franchisor recognizes that the area developer makes a commitment to the system and takes a sizable financial risk. They feel that the commitment should be rewarded in some fashion — lower fees is often the reward.

The amount of the fee discount usually depends on the franchisor, the number of locations being committed to, and the time it will take to get the units up and running. Franchisors usually limit any fee reduction to the initial franchise fee and rarely reduce the continuing royalty rate. From the beginning, make sure that the development schedule is reasonable. If it's not, should you need to negotiate later with the franchisor for an extension of time, you may find that you have to make certain concessions, such as a reduced territory.

You're probably thinking that area development is for gamblers. In a way, it is. These franchisees are betting that their units — and the franchise chain — will strike it rich. The gamble is the same, but the stakes are higher than with a single franchise. Instead of going to the $2 blackjack table, franchisees that acquire areas are sitting at the $20 one. If they make the wrong bet, they're out of luck; but if they make the right bet, they're very happy that no one else can touch their entire franchise area.

Reviewing Your Personal and Business Resources

Having one franchise unit is far different from having 2 or 10 or 20. Buying another franchise is like having another child — the entire dynamic of your family structure changes. You need to deal with issues on a whole different scale — including hiring staff, training, product purchases, and marketing. You might know the old adage: small children, small problems; big children, big problems. But don't forget — growth can also bring big rewards.

We hate to recommend more paperwork, but we suggest that you develop a tactical plan before you make a decision about owning multiple franchises. Don't worry — your plan probably doesn't have to be as grandiose as one a Fortune 500 company would develop.

Looking in the mirror: Are you ready for multiple ownership?

Brace yourself — it's time to look in the mirror. You need to do a thorough self-assessment to see whether *you* are ready to own multiple franchises. That's a totally different issue from whether *your business* is ready to expand; we cover that issue in the section titled, "Taking a hard look at your business and finances" in this chapter.)

Successfully shifting from a single- to a multi-unit operator depends largely on your personality and personal issues:

✔ **Are you a team player?** The more units you own, the more staff you'll need, including some in managerial positions. Be sure you can handle coaching a much bigger team. Be sure that you are able to give up some decision making to employees whom you have hired, trained, and trust.

✔ **Are you an operator or a manager?** It's easy to say that you want 50 stores; it's another thing to understand what it takes to manage that many. Single-unit owners worry about opening the business in the morning, taking care of the events of the day, and closing at night. As single-unit owner, you might be used to greeting your customers, training your employees, and taking care of many of the hands-on tasks yourself. Become a multi-unit franchisee, and you're forced to be even more of a manager. You'll have to build and rely on a support organization.

✔ **Can you delegate responsibility?** No question, it's tough to let go; after all, the franchise is your baby. Being in two places at once (unless you know something we don't know) is impossible, so you must develop staff and delegate responsibilities — comfortably. You'll probably spend a lot of time nurturing each new unit, and then focus your attention — more or less — on your other franchises as different issues arise.

✔ **Are you organized?** You'll have to be. You might be at a construction site on Tuesday morning and a staff meeting at your existing location in the afternoon. Assuming responsibility over different locations, with different problems and somewhat differing obligations, will make you feel like a juggler sometimes. Depending on the number of units, you'll have to set up internal support systems, such as hiring a general manager, bookkeeper, and administrative support staff to free up your time to let you handle more than one location.

✔ **Is the timing right?** Look at your personal life, and determine whether you can devote time to another project and still maintain your desired lifestyle.

✔ **Do any family members want to get involved?** Perhaps your spouse wants in. Perhaps you want your children to earn their own gas money, with an eye on succession. (In Chapter 15, we discuss leaving your franchise to your children.)

✔ **Do you think big?** If you do, you probably won't be content with a solitary site for very long. But you also have to know your limitations. You have to *be able* to expand, not just *want* to expand.

Taking a hard look at your business and finances

If you already own one franchise, you probably conducted some research before you made that purchase. Before you make the leap to multiple-unit franchising, we recommend that you examine your existing business and your finances.

Asking the right questions about your own franchise

Answer these questions before you move forward and become a multi-franchise owner:

✔ **Are your employees ready?** We hope you've been grooming your employees for promotion. It's a great motivator (see Chapter 12). But right now, your highest-level employee is probably an office or store manager. Now that you'll likely need more managers — and perhaps even a district or general manager — responsibility goes up a notch. Can your existing managers move up to general managers? Is your crew good enough to assume new duties? Will you have to retrain or hire new employees? Can you let go a little and trust them to make decisions?

✔ **Do you have your operations perfectly down pat?** Are you carrying out operations according to the franchisor's rules and standards? Although you probably won't be an absentee owner (we never suggest that), you can't possibly be as hands-on when you purchase an additional business.

✔ **Are you feeling competitive pressures?** Perhaps a competing chain has steamrollered into town, quickly erecting one unit and plopping down construction signs elsewhere. If you don't catch up, it might gain market share by its sheer number of locations.

✔ **Will expansion affect customer satisfaction?** Suppose you've harnessed a steady stream of regular customers, but recent highway construction projects are hindering your customers' access to your franchise. Rumor has it that some customers may take their business closer to home. If you open a second location in another part of town, maybe you can salvage the relationship. Conversely, if you're no longer at your current location all the time, will customers miss your personal touch?

- ✔ **Is another franchise location in your chain up for grabs?** This idea isn't so far-fetched. Consider this: The perfect site is available in your market, and your franchisor wants its name on it. Your franchise agreement doesn't give you an exclusive territory, meaning that anyone else — company or franchise unit — can move in. If you don't grab it, someone else will. Is this a prime site?

- ✔ **Does your franchise agreement restrict you in some way?**

- ✔ **Do you have the money?** Hands down, your existing unit should be profitable first. Many franchisees dip into cash flow from one franchise to fund part or their entire next unit, and finance the rest. No matter how many units you have, you can't make money if the individual locations are losing money. What are the costs involved? Will you have to pay additional franchise fees?

Crunching the numbers

This section offers more tips for evaluating your financial readiness to expand.

How much you'll have to pay the franchisor for a second location varies according to your franchise agreement. Some chains charge the regular franchise fee for a second unit; some reduce the fee and slash it even further for subsequent ones.

The last thing you want to do is rob Peter to pay Paul. You don't want your second — or seventieth — unit to unduly or unexpectedly impact the ones that came before. So to plan for growth, it's essential that you look at your financial picture. (Be sure to review Chapter 5 to avoid financial pitfalls.)

Review your franchise's overall financial condition:

- ✔ **The balance sheet:** This document includes your assets (cash, real estate, inventory, depreciated equipment, and accounts receivable) and your liabilities (outstanding bills, including tax obligations and loans).

- ✔ **Return on investment:** Are you outperforming other investment opportunities? It makes some sense to calculate whether the return you're getting from your investment in your franchisees is better than you could get from investing in something else. For example, if all you are earning on your investment in the franchise is 3 percent, and your bank is paying 6 percent, you have to decide whether buying more units is a smart decision.

- ✔ **Budget:** This group of numbers projects income and expenses for the coming year, which you can then compare to actual income and expenses.

> ✔ **Profit and loss statement (referred to as a *P&L*):** This document summarizes your income and expenses: your profitability or unprofitability.
>
> ✔ **Cash flow:** This figure tells you how much cash you are generating from your existing operations.

These tools can help you identify whether you can afford to expand — using your current cash flow or by seeking financing. Find out whether your franchisor will lend you expansion funds. (Chapter 5 guides you through financing options.)

You must weigh other money matters, too. Will your bank support your growth? If you'll need financing, what's the current interest rate? Rates might have been low when you took on a loan last time; higher rates could dramatically alter your investment strategy. Also, escalating costs of real estate and construction could mean you might need to borrow more money.

Consider all your initial costs — the franchise fee and other start-up expenses. Don't assume that you'll pay exactly the same amount as you paid the last time you bought a franchise. Some costs may be lower — such as a reduced franchise fee for subsequent units or diminished advertising costs because you can share promotional costs. But some expenses may be higher. It's possible the franchisor has chosen a new design, décor, and equipment package making construction more expensive, or that the prospective site requires a zoning variance — which requires lawyers' fees and possibly more construction costs later.

Also figure this factor into your budget: As you acquire more franchises, you may be able to buy inventory and secure other services at better rates because of volume purchasing. These savings should help boost profitability. You may incur additional expenses, though, because you may need to hire higher-skilled personnel.

If you're buying area development rights, remember that you typically pay a portion of the franchise fee up front for unopened units — way before they pull in any revenues. The fact that this prepayment will not be earning you any immediate money could have a profound impact on your profits.

Just because you're operating a unit successfully, don't mistake yourself for a financial maven. Review your financial state of affairs with your franchisor's development staff, your lender, your lawyer, and your accountant before making any firm decisions.

Identifying the Pros and Cons of Multiple Ownership

Suppose you're a franchise owner and from where you sit, everything looks rosy. Your franchise is doing great. Your franchisor loves you — your royalty payments are rising and paid on time. Your banker loves you — you're paying back your loan and meeting your payroll, and bill collectors aren't camping out at your doorstep. You love you — you're in the black, baby; you might even kick off your shoes and take that cruise to the Caribbean.

Just for a moment, stop patting yourself on the back (even though you really deserve to) and ask yourself the big question: Will expansion change all this? The reality is that acquiring more units can have advantages and disadvantages.

Benefits

You don't have to be a rocket scientist to figure out that the more businesses you own, the more potential you have to make money or lose money. You're building equity in your business — and possibly in real estate. Just as at the franchisor level, sheer size should bring you better prices on supplies and services. It might also yield favorable financing; the common wisdom is that lenders are more interested in multi-unit operators. Also, as you get a reputation for being a great multi-unit operator, expect the real estate community to notice. They will start to offer you locations — even before you asked for them.

Remember that you will have more at risk than the smaller franchisee that may also have locations in your market. His or her performance will affect yours. Make sure that you keep abreast of how neighboring franchises are doing.

Find out whether you can save any labor or product costs by setting up a *commissary* (a central location where you can prepare some products for all of the locations) and ship products to all of your locations in a prepared or semi-prepared fashion. This approach is acceptable in some franchise systems and taboo in others. Check with your franchisor.

Expansion can also help you with marketing. It's difficult to justify — let alone afford — radio and television spots when you have only a few units. When you cluster your franchises in a regional market, however, the mass media costs start falling into a realistic range on a per-unit basis.

Purchasing additional franchises has an impact on employees, too. With size, you'll likely attract higher-quality employees. They can envision career growth opportunities. You may qualify for lower rates on insurance plans, enabling you to offer better benefits. You might not have to reject good job applicants; you have more placement choices now. A candidate who hails from a small town may not be happy in, say, Los Angeles but might thrive in a surrounding community where you own another franchise.

Having multiple units close to each other often lets franchisees float staff between units as the need arises. The same can be said for unit management. Sometimes, one skilled manager can direct three or four units, while the day-to-day responsibilities are met by a less expensive, but still talented, assistant manager.

Perhaps the greatest benefit to multiple ownership is sharing. Multiple units are great for swapping employees in a bind. And imagine this scenario: The new manager at your pizza franchise makes a mistake with the cheese order and runs out of cheese on the very day that all the town's soccer teams are having pizza parties to mark the end of a brutal season. What does she do? She rushes to another one of your units to replenish the supply — and satisfies lots of little customers (who will grow into big customers someday). You can take the same approach with staffing. If one franchise is overstaffed and the other is understaffed, you can shift employees to meet your needs.

Consider pricing, also. Because franchisors can't tell franchisees what to charge for their products and services, prices may be inconsistent in a region dotted with individual owners. If you own all the units, presto — uniform pricing and less customer confusion.

Remember those other franchisees in the market. Don't talk to them about pricing. Price fixing, whether it's between the franchisor and franchisee or between franchisees, may violate the anti-trust laws in the United States.

In general, the more franchises you own, the more clout you will wield with the franchisor. That's not to say that chains don't have small, successful owners who aren't very influential. But it's human nature to listen most to the people with the loudest voices — those with the greatest economic power.

Drawbacks

Although you may be enthusiastic about future development, you must weigh the cons along with the pros.

The greatest risk is not having the operational and financial capabilities to effectively be a multi-unit owner. Perhaps you're growing *too* fast. Without leadership, management skills, and a financial cushion, your new empire could sink — like the Titanic. That's why we again encourage you to really investigate yourself and your business before moving forward.

Think about bringing in partners or establishing a workable joint venture with people or businesses — or even the franchisor. This approach may make your financial share smaller, but a smaller share of success is a whole lot more than 100 percent of a loss.

Getting carried away by your business size is another potential drawback. You run the risk of thinking you don't have to have your hands in the business anymore because you've built an organization. That assumption is far from the truth.

As you purchase more franchises, you may conceive of new ways of doing things. You'll be more tempted to tamper with the system — only to get frustrated by the fact that, although there's some room for change, you have to work within the franchisor's system.

It's possible to turn these negatives into positives. Just proceed with caution.

Chapter 14

Acquiring Other Brands

. . . .

In This Chapter

▶ Expanding or not

▶ Reviewing noncompete clauses

▶ Doing your due diligence

▶ Buying more concepts from the same franchisor

▶ Diversifying your portfolio

▶ Wearing many hats

▶ Setting up a one-stop shop (also known as *co-branding*)

. . . .

*O*nce some folks discover franchising, they just can't get enough. If you want to own more than a single franchise of the same concept, head over to Chapter 13; it discusses acquiring multiple franchises within the same chain. But if you're after more than one unit and more than one brand, stay put. This chapter covers expanding outside your current franchise concept.

Don't feel guilty if you want a little variety. It's the spice of life, right? Touting multiple brands may seem odd, because we've compared the franchisee-franchisor relationship to that of a family. Let's just say that in the franchising world, in some instances it's not like you're cheating on your spouse if you marry into another system without divorcing the first. For the most part, you can step up to the altar repeatedly. (We discuss the exceptions later in this chapter.) Given the thousands of franchise concepts, in your future relationships you may end up with partners from the same industry or from totally different ones.

In most instances, franchisors don't allow you to acquire another business in the same industry — hamburgers to hamburgers, sneakers to sneakers, and so on. In fact, some limit the percentage of a "competing" business you are allowed to own. It's important to seek legal advice very early in the process of looking at other franchise systems. Even having discussions with other franchisors can sometimes lead to problems, especially if any of your current system's confidential information or trade secrets are discussed or jeopardized in some fashion.

Gearing Up

If you thought buying your first franchise concept was a big deal, here's a news flash: Buying multiple franchise concepts is an even bigger deal. Unlike round one, though, you have a head start this time. You know what it's like to be a franchisee, and you grasp the franchisee-franchisor relationship as an insider.

Round two is different. You're starting over with a new concept and, most likely, a different franchisor. (Read about companies that franchise multiple concepts in the next section.) This time, your decision can have a domino effect on your original business. Say you've worked your tail off and your first franchise is humming along smoothly. Now you add a second brand. It's only logical that your new franchise steals some of your time, energy, and money from your first venture. Any expansion can hurt — just as easily as it can help — your other franchise or franchises.

So before you diversify, do your homework. Explore the risks and rewards of tackling another concept, whether you're limited in any way from expanding, and which franchisor to hook up with.

Check your current franchise agreement. Some require you to spend 100 percent of your time on that business. Others limit the types of other concepts you can operate or even invest in. Then get ready for a balancing act. If you've ever tried juggling, you know that keeping your eye on the ball when you're tossing more than one takes a lot of concentration. Mix different shapes and sizes and, boy, is it hard to keep everything in the air.

Expanding

Before you start juggling, make sure that you can handle this new venture emotionally, operationally, and financially. Franchisees who expand within the same chain go through basically the same analysis, so turn to Chapter 13 to see what you should consider.

With the added dimension of diversification, we've added bonus questions:

- What's your existing franchisor's philosophy on multi-concept franchisees?
- Is there a strategic similarity between the concepts?
- Will you be able to divide your attention between more than one concept, let alone more than one location?
- Who will operate your existing business while you're away at training for your new franchise?

✔ Can your existing business survive your absence?

✔ Can you use skills you learned at your original franchise (customer service, management, recruiting, and vendor relations) at the next chain?

When you move from brand A to brand B, you certainly can use many of the skills you've mastered, but confidentiality requirements may preclude sharing of proprietary information.

✔ Will you mind writing more than one royalty check each month?

✔ Can you deal with more than one franchisor and more than one set of rules?

✔ Will you play favorites?

✔ Are you willing to expend all that start-up energy again?

✔ Will you listen to new ideas and training, because not all operating methods are transferable?

✔ Is one franchisor more mature than the other? Will the new franchisor meet your expectations on franchisor services?

✔ Do you have existing managers who would be perfect for the new operation? Who do you have to replace them if they move to your new concept?

✔ Are you better off selling your existing brand and focusing all your time and attention on the new brand?

✔ What happens if one of the concepts fails — especially if they are sharing the same location?

✔ How do you intend to structure the ownership of the multiple franchise rights: one company, parent/subsidiary, holding company, brother/sister? Talk to your attorney and your accountant to find out which structure can work best for you.

✔ Can you realize any overhead or other cost savings by being affiliated with two or more brands?

So you think you can be a chameleon, switching back and forth from one concept to another. The real question is: Why should you?

Just as you did when you bought your first outlet, look at general market trends and demand for a particular product or service. A few factors may prompt you to acquire other brands:

✔ **Silver bullet for a shrinking market:** You want to add franchises, but your territory already is saturated with your first format. So if you want to keep all your businesses close to home — it's easier to manage that way — your only option may be to develop another brand. A newer concept, in particular, may have wide-open spaces.

✔ **No room for expansion:** Although the market may have room for growth, local zoning restrictions, which make affordable or available locations hard to find, may stunt or delay your growth.

✔ **Defensive play:** You own the only chicken joint in town. Customers flock to your restaurant. But will they fly the coop if one of your competitors rolls into town? You decide that it's not worth the risk to have someone else clawing at your niche, and you open the other chicken brand yourself. Although you may cannibalize your own sales, you'd much rather divide sales between your own units than lose market share to a stranger. Keep in mind, though, that you may or may not be allowed to do this under your current franchise agreement. (We cover noncompete clauses in the section titled "Reviewing legal issues" in this chapter.)

✔ **Diversify risk:** Consider yourself lucky if your franchise always runs smoothly. More likely, your business goes on a roller-coaster ride every now and then. It may dip or rise according to competition, economic conditions, seasonality (ice cream and skis), trends, or the state of your franchise concept. Operating more than one brand may get you through these cyclical flows. You may even be able to cross-train some of your employees to balance ebbs and flows in seasonal businesses. The bottom line: Diversifying spreads your risk and could give you better use of your staff. Of course, if the business cycles coincide, the result may be disaster.

✔ **Economies of scale:** Adding units may bring economies of scale. Obviously, a lot depends on the synergies between the concepts. You're a big spender now. If product lines match up and you're not restricted by the franchisor, you may net better deals from suppliers. The same goes for print, TV, and radio ads. You may be able to leverage an office, computer and phone systems, accounting departments, and warehouse space. And if you locate your franchises under the same roof, you may be able to slash utility, real estate, and other fixed costs. (See the section titled "Co-Branding" for details on operating multiple brands in shared space.)

✔ **Cross-marketing momentum:** If the multiple brands are complementary, you can pitch your marketing to the same customers. You already have a market base with one concept. Customers know and trust you. So it may follow that sales take off quicker with the next brand.

For example, say your original business is a carpet-cleaning franchise like Rainbow International (a franchise offered by The Dwyer Group). Also suppose that your choice for a second business is a plumbing franchise like Mr. Rooter (also a franchise offered by The Dwyer Group). You may have a natural cross-marketing opportunity. Your Rainbow International customers already know you and trust your work at cleaning their carpets. Now when you launch your Mr. Rooter franchise, you can notify those customers about your new venture, possibly jump-starting your new business off your existing customer base. Better still, as customers use one of your business services, you can offer them a discount on your other services. That's one way to continually reward your customers of both brands.

✔ **Prime locations:** With more concepts, you can respond to more real estate opportunities. Say a prime spot in a mall or strip center opens up. It may be too small for your original concept but perfect for brand B. Or maybe the center already has stores that compete with brand A; you can put in brand B instead. For example, if you are a franchisee of Play It Again Sports and Once Upon A Child, both consignment-type franchises offered by Grow Biz International, you have flexibility when that perfect spot opens up.

✔ **Employee retention:** As a one-concept franchisee, you may not be able to satisfy an employee's desire for more hours, diversification, or career advancement. Once you add units, opportunities open up. For example, the assistant manager at your auto-detailing shop does a bang-up job, but your manager is here for life; open up a brake repair franchise, and the assistant manager is a perfect candidate to run it. It's a win-win situation: You retain a known commodity, and your employee gets to move up the ladder.

✔ **Pure excitement:** You feel like a kid in a candy store. A franchisor is marketing a hot concept, and you absolutely must get a piece of the action. You want a challenge. Or you've been successful, you've earned a bundle, and you feel primed to do it again.

Any or all of these reasons may prompt you to speed ahead. We must flash a cautionary yellow light, however. Think twice if you want to acquire other brands. Doing so could

✔ Reduce your focus on your original business.

✔ Hurt your financial situation.

✔ Overtax, not leverage, management and existing systems.

✔ Cause friction between you and your current franchisor.

✔ Take time away from you and your family, just like your first franchise did when you got started.

Franchising is an inelastic business. By that we mean that when franchisors grant territorial rights to one franchisee, they often preclude other franchisees or the franchisor from establishing new locations in the market — even when market demand exists and competition requires it. This is considered one of the biggest weaknesses of franchising when compared to traditional, nonfranchised businesses. Traditional businesses can deal with the market; franchisors also need to deal with the contracts they have with their franchisees — and those contracts can limit market development.

If you're satisfied with your current operation and are looking outside the system only because no free territory is suitable for development, consider buying existing operations from other franchisees or the franchisor. Consider contacting your franchisor in advance and sharing your plans. You may be able to gain your franchisor's support in restructuring your agreement into an area-development arrangement. This allows you, once you acquire the other locations, to establish new locations in areas previously restricted from development because of other franchisees' territorial rights.

Reviewing legal issues

Before you begin a double shift with another chain, dust off your franchise agreement and make sure that you can do so, legally. Lest you forgot, franchising includes ties that bind you.

Most important, review your existing franchise's and the new franchise's noncompete clauses. Typically, these clauses prohibit you from branching out into a competing business or in the same industry during the term of the franchise agreement. Geographic restrictions range from not competing anywhere to not competing in a specific market. Noncompete clauses are enforceable as long as they're reasonable.

Talk to your attorney early and get his or her opinion. Remember, when you bought your first franchise, you probably were not contemplating investing in another opportunity from a different franchisor.

Remember, a noncompete clause in the same business or industry is in the typical franchise agreement. Some noncompete clauses go to opposite extremes, however. Most liberal hotel franchisors do not restrict franchisees at all (it's just sort of evolved that way). So they can operate competing brands — even right next door. At the other end, a few chains forbid franchisees from participating in any type of business — competing or not — during the term of the franchise agreement.

 When you renew your franchise agreement, the new agreement may read differently. If the noncompete clause changes or product lines differ, you have cause for concern: You may be holding a hot potato — another franchise that's now "competitive," even though it wasn't before.

If you find yourself in this situation, you have three choices:

✔ Don't renew your original franchise agreement.

✔ Divest yourself of one of your franchise affiliations.

✔ Try negotiating with the franchisor.

You should also speak with your legal advisor to determine if you have any legal rights that would preclude the franchisor from making these types of changes to the agreement.

Other contractual clauses may affect your acquisition plans. Franchisors may restrict the goods and services you can sell. And, typically, you can't use your franchise premises for any other purpose without the franchisor's okay. So, before you set up the sugar cones and sprinkles, check out whether you can add an ice cream business to your hamburger franchise.

You want to be familiar and predictable to the consumer. We don't allow our franchisees to open up, say, a Dairy Queen inside a Wendy's, because it's not our business. And it's confusing to the customers because they would see this Dairy Queen here and then they would go to a Wendy's 5 miles away and wonder, well, why doesn't this one have it? The whole purpose of franchising is to be predictable to the consumer.

Even if it's clear sailing to jump aboard another chain, many franchisees confess their expansion plans to their existing franchisor. It's not that they need their blessing; they just feel that frankness avoids muddying the waters. It's all about being part of a team. Others think it's none of the franchisor's business as long as they're abiding by their franchise agreement. You might also want to tell the new franchisor about your current business. (It'll probably be on the franchise application anyway.)

Doing your due diligence — again

Each time you expand, you need to get back to the basics: researching the franchise concept, the franchisor, its franchisees, and its competition. Franchises — even from the same franchisor or within the same industry — can be as different as night and day. So even if some of the faces are the same, the old rules still apply: investigate, investigate, investigate.

Now that you're in the game, you do have some advantages: you know the ins and outs of being a franchisee. And you've purchased a franchise once, or more than once before, so you know what to look for in a chain. (See Chapter 4 for information about choosing a franchise.)

Plus, since you're already a franchisee, feel free to tweak our formula a bit by investigating some areas more than others or asking questions based on your own experience. For instance, if your franchisor offers great product discounts, see if you'll get the same royal treatment again. Or if franchisee-franchisor relations are rocky at your existing chain, you know how disruptive this can be on a franchisee's operations. This time, because of your experience, you are better able to dig into the issues that are important to you.

Don't get complacent if you're buying another brand from your existing franchisor who happens to also sell other concepts. Obviously, you know the franchisor. But this may be a good opportunity to take a fresh peek. And, of course, you still have to examine the individual concept. Think of each brand as a company within a company. Scrutinize the staff and support. Also, your core franchise concept may be tops in its industry, but another concept may be trailing, raising a whole new set of challenges. For the inside scoop, contact existing and former franchisees of the sister concepts and talk to headquarters employees assigned to this arm of the company.

If you buy two different concepts from the same franchisor, watch out for the so-called *cross-default provisions.* For example, if you are behind in your royalty payments under one franchise agreement, this may be a default under your other franchise. Check your agreements carefully. The easiest way to avoid this dilemma is not to buy into two concepts offered by the same franchisor if this cross-default provision could affect you.

Whether you're dealing with the same or a different franchisor, scout out a few multi-concept franchisees in your current chain and the new one. The more similarities to your situation, the better. This may be like finding a needle in a haystack, but the trick is to get the sharpest possible picture of what it's like to own multiple concepts. A good source for this type of information will be members of the Franchisee Advisory Council of both systems. They are likely to know the players and who's doing what.

You're a franchisee; we know you're busy. But don't cut corners in your investigation. Being successful once doesn't guarantee success again.

Mixing Industries, Mixing Brands

If you're thinking expansion, don't just jump in the car and go. You need to be headed in a specific direction. One big decision you need to make is whether you want your second — or subsequent — venture to have any connection to your existing one. Here are some possibilities:

- ✔ Do you want your franchises to be in the same industry? Lots of restaurant franchisees add other food concepts, for example. A recent survey by *Restaurant Finance Monitor,* Roseville, Minnesota, shows that 76 of the nation's top 200 restaurant franchisees (by revenue) own and operate more than one restaurant concept.

- ✔ Do you want the brands to be complementary so you can overlap some of your operations or marketing? On the other hand, do you want to run them separately? Picture an automobile repair center where you own the franchise rights to a quick oil change franchise, a muffler or brake franchise, and maybe a body shop concept. Your customers never have to leave your lot — except to drive home.

- ✔ Do you want to stick with the same franchisor or switch to another company?

Your strategy may depend on your willingness to return to the trenches — to learn new skills, operating methods, and industry and brand terminology; to retrain or hire new management; and to work with a new franchising partner.

Buying more from the same franchisor

You're not the only one talking multiple concepts. Franchisors are, too. More companies than ever are franchising more than one brand. Of 1,167 franchisors in 1999, 33 have two concepts, 4 have three concepts, 2 have four concepts, and 7 have five or more concepts, according to FranData Corp., a Washington, D.C., franchise information service. And some conglomerates have various incorporated entities that sell franchises — like The Dwyer Group, which includes seven service-based franchising companies.

Multi-concept franchisors are starting additional brands from scratch, acquiring companies, or both. Given the feverish pace of mega-mergers, it's no wonder this trend is hitting franchising, too. So even if your franchisor has only one concept today, it may have more under its umbrella tomorrow. Keep your eyes open: Franchisors typically introduce new concepts to existing franchisees first.

Usually, a multi-concept franchisor's brands are within the same industry or complementary industries; however, some are unrelated. Here's a glimpse of what's out there:

- **Wendy's** also franchises Tim Hortons, a coffee and fresh-baked donut chain that hails from Oakville, Ontario, Canada. (Wendy's acquired the chain in 1995.)

- **Grow Biz International of Minneapolis** offers lots of concepts involving mostly used and consigned merchandise, such as sporting equipment (Play It Again Sports), computers (Computer Renaissance), and children's clothing (Once Upon A Child).

- **Moran Industries,** Midlothian, Illinois, sells several transmission repair brands and other auto-related services, such as Alta Mere, Milex, and Mr. Motor.

- **The Dwyer Group,** Waco, Texas, offers seven service concepts: Rainbow International (carpet cleaning), Mr. Rooter (plumbing), Aire Serve (heating and air conditioning), Mr. Electric (electrical repair), Mr. Appliance (appliance repair), Glass Doctor (automotive glass), and Worldwide Refinishing System (bathroom and kitchen remodeling).

✔ **The Service Master Company,** Memphis, Tennessee, offers seven franchised concepts: AmeriSpec (home inspection), Furniture Medic (residential and commercial furniture repair and restoration), Merry Maids (home maid service), Rescue Rooter (plumbing), ServiceMaster (janitorial, commercial carpet cleaning, residential carpet and upholstery), Terminix (pest control), and TruGreen (lawn care). Busy company. They even have a nonfranchised company called American Home Shield that provides home warranties.

✔ **The Franchise Company, Inc.,** Etobicoke, Ontario, Canada, is different; its concepts encompass diverse franchise companies, from Stained Glass Overlay, Inc. (decorative glass products), to College Pro Painters Limited (student painters), to Paul W. Davis Systems, Inc. (restoration services).

You can check with the International Franchise Association at 202-628-8000 or at the Web site `www.franchise.org` for other companies that offer multiple franchise brands.

What does this mean to you? For starters, expansion opportunities may be right under your nose. If you're happy with your franchisor, it's natural to look to acquire more of its brands, rather than an outsider's — as long as its other concepts catch your fancy. You'll still deal with one company. You know its business philosophy, its strategic plan, its management, how its system functions, and its support services. There's a comfort factor and stability, and it could shorten the learning curve tremendously. And you increase the odds of greater negotiating leverage with your franchisor when you have more units of its brand or brands.

Another possible value is brand synergy. If a franchisor's multiple concepts complement each other, you could gain volume-purchasing discounts, central customer service systems, and cross-selling opportunities.

Some franchisors act on these synergies. For example, they may cross-market concepts, helping you move sales between the brands. But just as important, some don't capitalize on these synergies or even allow cross-merchandising. If you're buying a franchise from a diversified company because of its scope, make sure it doesn't just sit back. Otherwise, it'll be up to you to produce cross-marketing materials or to hook up with franchisees of sister chains on your own; you can still use these synergies to your advantage — it just takes more effort.

In dealing with multi-concept companies, don't just assume that what succeeded once will succeed again. Not all concepts — even from the same franchisor — are winners; numerous multiconcept franchisors have squashed or sold some brands that didn't work out. And not all concepts get equal attention from a franchisor. Beware of so-called *franchise factories* — companies that spit out concepts with the sole intent of selling franchises rather than servicing franchisees and their customers.

In evaluating franchises, Robert L. Purvin, Jr., chairman of the American Association of Franchisees and Dealers (AAFD), San Diego, California; 800-733-9858; www.aafd.org, a franchisee advocacy group, counts any multi-concept franchisor "as a potential strike against a franchise system." Although conceding that there are exceptions, he cautions, nonetheless: "The warning flags should go up all the faster and all the greater when you're dealing with a multiconcept company. Support services might not be there. The company's dedication to growing the business may be lacking if it diverts its resources to the other concept. The goal has to be to invest in a franchise system in which the franchisee is the essential vehicle through which the franchisor reaches its ultimate customer — the consumer." Purvin's concern, however, could exist with respect to any system run by any company that has other business interests, franchised or not. But Bob's warning needs to be taken to heart. If the franchisor does not view its franchisees as the "essential vehicle" and does not put its resources into support of the franchisees, then the opportunity for success by the franchisees may be weakened.

Kay Marie Ainsley, former director of international development for Domino's Pizza and Ziebart International, and managing director of Michael H. Seid & Associates, feels that "Many franchisors that choose to offer multiple concepts do so because they have the expertise as well as the resources required to support additional brands." She also feels that "Many of the multi-brand franchisors find that there are synergies between their existing brand and their new concepts and these create opportunities for efficiencies that would not be available otherwise."

What you want is a franchisor that pays attention to each of its concepts (or, selfishly, at least the ones you're buying). In other words, they don't play favorites. Is there good management? Is there dedicated staff for each brand? Are support services as mature for both? Is the franchisor actually cross-marketing? A franchisor should maximize its management and resources, not stretch them as it adds to its family of franchises. It's no different from when we tell you that you concentrate as you expand.

Be on the lookout for lower prices if you buy more than one brand. Not all franchisors give preferential treatment to existing franchisees, but some reward their own. For example, Blimpie International, Inc., Atlanta, Georgia, gives a break to franchisees who buy more than one of its concepts, and The Dwyer Group discounts based on a franchisee's years in business, up to 50 percent for five years or longer.

One more thing: Just because you're an existing franchisee doesn't mean you're a shoo-in with a sister concept. Franchisors still give you the once-over, and some even set tougher qualifications for expansion. For example, in many instances, The ServiceMaster Company hasn't offered a second brand to franchisees because it wasn't "in their best interest," says Jim Wassell, vice president of marketing at ServiceMaster Franchise Services. "We want to make sure that the person with the original brand is really developing that brand aggressively and exploiting that brand as best they can before we encourage them to split their attention to another brand," he says. "It's certainly not for everyone."

Starting fresh with a new company

One big reason to join forces with a different franchisor is because it has the brand you're after. It's that simple. It's no different from switching to another pet store because they have healthier treats for Taffy or to a new clothing boutique because they have exclusive fashions from the next Calvin Klein.

You may also want to spread your wings to grab perks that your franchisor doesn't offer. Maybe another franchisor negotiates better discounts, and you can ride those coattails for both of your ventures. Perhaps another chain offers superior training, giving you a franchise MBA that you can apply to all your businesses.

By splitting loyalties, you might gain negotiating power with franchisors. Consider this: You have limited capital resources to develop more franchises, and a prime site emerges. Should you put in brand A or brand B? A franchisor, knowing that you're weighing the two concepts, might agree to lower fees or grant other concessions if you give priority to its brand. Hey, it's worth a shot.

Finally, call us doomsayers, if you must, but you may want to diversify your risk. Say you've bought two or three brands from the same franchisor. If that company tumbles into legal or financial trouble, all your franchises may go down the tubes along with it. Stay diversified and, hopefully, some of your concepts will remain intact if the others crack up.

Meeting the challenge

There's really only one way to effectively wear multiple hats: focus. Be prepared to toil like you did the first time, and put all your energies into your new venture. But at the same time, be careful that you don't lose sight of your original concept — the one that brought you here. Having a start-up business that needs all your energy and dealing with a formerly successful business that is on the decline because you were not around to manage it is a guaranteed recipe for disaster.

Successful multi-concept franchisees build up strong management teams. They oversee all their brands, and they assign managers to each entity. This requires two skills: You have to be able to shift gears, and you have to delegate even more than before.

Diluting your focus

Must a Wendy's franchisee have our permission to open a franchise of a noncompeting chain? No. Would we like to talk to them about it? Yes.

Wendy's has learned from experience about diluting focus. If you want to develop a second chain, how are you going to do it? Will you take some of your best operators from Wendy's and move them over to the new place? Will you run it yourself? Will you take 20 percent of your workday and go work on this other chain?

When you started Wendy's, you devoted your time — morning, noon, and night — to making it a success. Why would it be different when you

buy into another franchise? You're still going to have to devote morning, noon, and night to making it a success. How will you do both?

We want our franchisees to go in with their eyes open. We don't want them to dilute their focus and risk losing their success rate at Wendy's. We also want to make certain they haven't forgotten what it's like to open the very first store, and the time commitment and attention that are necessary.

Tread gently when it comes to advertising multiple brands. Focus on maintaining brand identity for each concept. In cross-marketing, you don't want to confuse the customer.

REMEMBER

Generally, franchisors won't be very happy if you jointly market brands of different parent companies; some companies don't even want you to link their own brands. Franchisors control their trademarks, so they can police any such tie-ins. Read about the do's and don'ts of marketing in Chapter 11.

Co-Branding

If you flip through any directory of franchises, you'll quickly see that franchising responds to consumer demand. Pick a need, and there's probably a franchise to fill it. It's not surprising, then, that when harried consumers began craving convenience, voilà, a strategy called co-branding appeared on the franchising scene.

Co-branding is when more than one brand operate in a single location. It may be two brands *(dual-branding)*, three brands *(triple-branding)*, or any other multiple *(multi-branding)*. For simplicity's sake, we'll refer to this tactic as co-branding.

No doubt, you've seen these kinds of partnerships. We bet you've probably dropped some dollars at them, too. The most visible are travel centers along the nation's highways, combining fast-food franchises, gas stations, and convenience stores. In one fell swoop, you can fill up your belly, your car, and your pantry. Shopping malls, airports, and stadiums host co-branded food courts — the ultimate smorgasbord of franchised concepts. And look around Main Street in your own town. There are bound to be some two-in-one franchises, perhaps a combination dessert/convenience store or sandwich shop/car wash. If it's not there yet, believe us, it'll be coming soon.

Setting up a one-stop shop

You're reading this chapter because you want to acquire other brands, right? Well, co-branding certainly offers you the opportunity to do this in a couple of ways:

- **Buy the franchise rights to each of the concepts you bundle under one roof from either the same or different franchisors.** Taking this approach lets you control the whole operation. Expect to sign separate franchise agreements and pay separate franchise fees for each concept.

- **Stick with just one concept but take advantage of co-branding at the same time.** This tactic may sound contradictory, so listen up. You can

    - **Own a franchise and share space with a franchisor, franchisee, or franchisees — even an independent businessperson — who operates different concepts.** You could be the quick service restaurant (QSR) inside a convenience store operated by a major oil company. Just make sure there are enough profits to go around in this kind of arrangement.

    - **Lease space.** You buy the franchise rights to a concept and lease space, say, in an airport or a hotel. Mail Boxes Etc. (MBE), San Diego, California, has a concept called MBE Express. You'll find these locations at airports such as Chicago's O'Hare or inside hotels such as Marriott. Some of the locations are staffed by franchisees and provide a full level of MBE services such as shipping and copying. Others have no on-site staff because card-swap technology enables customers to make copies and fax documents. MBE found a way of moving their locations closer to their customers.

See whether the franchisor sets different fees or net worth requirements for co-branded locations as opposed to traditional outlets. Also, find out if you get a break by buying more than one concept from the same franchisor.

So where should you hang your multiple banners? Co-branding today occurs everywhere. You'll find Tricon's three brands (Taco Bell, Pizza Hut, and KFC) sharing space in *pad locations* (freestanding locations in parking lots) outside

Leveraging locations

By combining Wendy's and Tim Hortons in one building, we're saving close to 25 percent in development costs. This means we can buy more expensive land because it's cheaper to build. And that creates an opportunity in some expensive city neighborhoods and on major intersections or highway exits where the cost of land might be too high for either a Wendy's or a Tim Hortons alone.

We share a dining room and front door. Wendy's is on the left side and Tim Hortons is on the right. We have separate counters, separate cash registers, separate drive-thrus, separate kitchens, separate deliveries, and separate staffs. They're two separate businesses, and we keep it that way.

of malls, just as you will find other franchisors setting up shop inside ballparks, arenas, and airports.

Wherever you choose to set up, check out the site just as you would for a single franchise, including demographics, traffic patterns, competition, and accessibility. (Chapter 8 discusses site selection.) Then add the co-branding factor. With multiple concepts, you might be able to secure a better location. A landlord may have a prime 2,000-square-foot location, but you can only use 1,200 square feet for your brand. But if you co-brand with another concept, together you might be able to use the entire location. In addition, because the cost of developing two brands under one roof is typically lower than building two separate locations, you might be able to afford more expensive land, because you'll be dividing the development costs.

In selecting a site for a co-branded unit, consider these issues:

- ✔ Is the site conducive to operating more than one brand?
- ✔ How much will you save by developing one building, not two? (Consider the sharing of land costs, taxes, and maintenance fees.)
- ✔ Will your brand be front and center?
- ✔ Will there be adequate room for signage to maintain brand identity?
- ✔ Can customers easily gain access to, say, the counter space and cash registers for each brand?
- ✔ Are common areas large enough to accommodate customers of multiple concepts?
- ✔ Do both concepts benefit from the same traffic patterns?

Beneficial duality

We have franchisees that have Wendy's and Tim Hortons as a dual brand. It really works with the right people.

Co-branding helps both businesses. The reason for that is in most instances, Wendy's does not open for breakfast. And Tim's does the largest percentage of its business from 6 a.m. until 10 a.m. Tim Hortons is traditionally slower at lunchtime when Wendy's is the busiest, and then they're slow at dinnertime when we have a rush. So people coming in at lunch for Wendy's can get dessert at Tim Hortons, or people who are coming in the afternoon for an iced cappuccino at Tim Hortons might get fries or a hamburger at Wendy's.

Tim Hortons is bringing in people who may not be regular Wendy's customers, and we get them for an extra visit a week or an extra visit a month. And Tim Hortons is picking up a Wendy's customer who needs a dessert for their meal. It's truly helping both, because it's drawing off each other's customer base without competing for the same customers.

You may not be lucky enough to get equal treatment for every concept in every location. (After all, doesn't someone always end up with the short end of the wishbone?) If you're the stronger brand, try negotiating a more prominent position. In any case, you don't want to be overshadowed or hidden by another brand, or be inaccessible to your target market.

Combining your resources

Co-branding is taking off because there's strength in numbers. With more choices, customers have a reason to stay longer and buy more during each visit. When co-branding is effective, you draw new customers, boost brand awareness, increase market share, and reduce start-up and ongoing costs.

Here's how to jump aboard this hot trend:

- **Find a partner.** This is no time to just pick out of a hat. The other brand should complement your brand, not cannibalize sales. It should add value for a customer. Combine a breakfast concept with a lunch/dinner concept, and there's something for everyone throughout the day. (In industry lingo, this is called *balancing day parts*.)

  When picking a partner, you can look to brands from the same franchisor or different franchisors. Some multiconcept franchisors such as Tricon and Wendy's are integrating their concepts into co-branded sites. Others are forging alliances with co-branding partners; in other words, they're doing the legwork for you.

Be aware that not all franchises belong together. Buddying up with another brand that is equal to or stronger than your brand sends good vibrations to consumers — and can steer sales your way. But a weaker brand or a concept that doesn't have your standards can pull your business down. You want to add, not take away, credibility. You also don't want to confuse a customer with too many concepts in a single location. The same advice is true for picking a location, by the way. If your franchise strives to give a wholesome, clean environment to your customers and the center you select has trash in the parking lots and the common bathrooms are filthy, guess what — it affects what customers think of your brand.

✔ **Look before you leap.** Make sure your franchisor lets you add a specific concept on your premises; refer to the section "Reviewing legal issues" in this chapter. Also, think ahead: If you operate a single-brand unit and your franchisor's new strategy is co-branding, you might be pressured by your franchisor to co-brand in the future.

✔ **Reconfigure the real estate.** You can either develop a co-branded location from scratch or retrofit an existing location. Obviously, size is essential. With some renovations, you may be able to squeeze another concept into an existing unit. Blimpie International allows franchisees to mix and match its brands: Blimpie Subs & Salads, Smoothie Island, Pasta Central, and Maui Tacos. A Blimpie franchisee can easily carve space for a Smoothie Island; it requires only 70 square feet for blenders, ice, and a "frozen" table. In contrast, Pasta Central requires 700 square feet, so franchisees tend to co-brand that from scratch.

In arranging your co-branded unit, you should have two goals: first, to have each concept maintain its own identity and, second, to reap economies of scale. So, with a co-branded food franchise, you'll probably want — or your franchisor may require — separate counters, signage, and cash registers. You ring in the overhead savings by sharing a parking lot, rest rooms, and dining area. Be sure to configure the concepts to grab customers' attention, making it conducive for them to purchase brand B even if they only came in for brand A. These are the incremental sales at the root of co-branding.

Some franchisors may allow you to share space but not equipment or employees, so be sure to factor this in.

✔ **Work out the details.** If you twin with another franchisee (rather than own the multiple brands yourself), determine how you're going to split the cost of utilities, insurance, repairs, landscaping or snow removal, and cleaning common areas. And if the franchisors or the operators have different standards of cleanliness and service, you must address these issues, too.

Sometimes partnerships look better on paper than in reality. If you're sharing space with someone else, make sure you can live with this stranger — and his or her habits.

✓ **Staff up.** Ideally, you want to identify separate staff for each concept to maintain brand identity. To save money, you might be able to have one manager oversee all the concepts. Franchisors have various staffing requirements at co-branded units. Some mandate entirely separate staff. Others have few standards and might allow an employee to throw on a branded hat and apron over a gas station uniform to make a bologna and cheese sandwich, and then run back to the pump. It's important to know that the standards for each brand match up.

If you cross over employees between multiple concepts, you may be able to offer them more hours of work. This often helps recruit and retain better employees.

✓ **Decide on your "menu."** Depending on the concept, you may have some leeway to adjust your product offerings. Wendy's requires all its locations — including co-branded units — to carry a full-service menu. But of the hundreds of Tricon two-in-one units, many offer the full KFC menu and a limited menu of Taco Bell products, and some offer the full KFC menu and limited Pizza Hut items.

✓ **Cross-market.** Signage helps you cross-market various brands, so make sure it's clear to consumers. Is there equal billing? In addition, many co-branding partners share the costs of traditional advertising and offer coupons that drive traffic from one concept to another. Through co-branding, you could also get a free ride on national advertising if, say, your partner's chain does national advertising and yours doesn't. You could also consider training cashiers or other employees to recommend additional purchases from the other concepts.

Building an empire through the addition of other brands is becoming more popular. Markets are maturing, and new concepts are constantly being developed that may just suit you. But remember, you have to do your homework:

✓ What impact will the new brand have on your current operations?

✓ What impact will expansion with the new brand have on you financially? Are there other opportunities that may suffer?

✓ Are the synergies between your existing franchise and your new franchise real?

✓ Does either franchise agreement place restrictions on you that could cause you problems during or after the term of the agreements?

✓ How strong is the new franchisor you will be joining? Do they have the support programs you have become used to from your existing brand?

Growth is the goal of every businessperson. But don't shortchange the process of investigating your opportunities. Take your time, do your homework, and verify that you've made the right choice.

Chapter 15

The End Has Come

*I*t may seem odd that we want to talk about ending a franchise when you're just about to begin one. But, as the expression goes, all good things come to an end. Bad things, too. In franchising, you're not locked in for life. When your franchise agreement expires, you may or may not want to renew. Or there may come a time — any time — when you want to sell out. That's okay. The hope is that someone — your children, a fellow franchisee, your franchisor, or a complete stranger — wants to pick up where you've left off.

We want to be completely honest with you. Sometimes franchisees leave a system because their business has failed or because the franchisor terminates them for, say, withholding royalties or violating other aspects of the franchise agreement. But lots — lots and lots — leave the ranks because they want to, not because they have to. Perhaps your franchise caught on like wildfire, and you want to take the money and run. Perhaps your spouse got a great job offer out of state, and you want to ride her or his coattails. Perhaps you've brainstormed a new business (even want to become a franchisor), or this was your final hurrah before retirement. Or perhaps you've rolled one too many bagels, heard one too many complaints from customers, or butted heads with your franchisor one too many times.

Whatever the scenario, THE END doesn't have to be as ominous as it sounds. It could be the start of a whole new world.

Renewing the Franchise

On a franchise journey, there's no open-ended ticket. You're leasing the right to use a franchisor's brand name and system for a specific period of time. Depending on your franchise agreement, your rights may last 5, 10, 15, maybe

20 years. The clock usually starts ticking on day one. So at some point, you'll have to — happily or unhappily — end the relationship.

At the end of the term, you have a few options.

If you've had enough, you can simply thank the franchisor for the ride — and move on. You'll relinquish the brand name, and the franchisor may resell rights to that particular area to a new franchisee. You'll also probably sell your building, equipment, and other assets, or return them to the lessor.

You might sell the business to another person who could sign a new franchise agreement with the franchisor — that is, if the franchisor wants to sign a new franchise agreement.

Depending on your franchise agreement, you may choose to stay in the game, but as an independent. You could take down the brand you have been leasing and put up your own brand and continue as you did before. In most instances, though, doing so won't be an option.

If you think the trip's been too short, there's some good news: You most likely can renew your franchise agreement and "go around again." Usually, you have to notify the franchisor in writing within a specific time period of your intent to renew. You need to check your original franchise agreement, but notice is usually required six months before your existing agreement expires.

The ball is not entirely in your court, however. Even if you're gung-ho on renewing, franchisors can say no. Some franchises are for one term only and do not permit renewal. That was the agreement you made with the franchisor at the beginning of the relationship. Those franchisors who do permit renewal can turn you down. Typically, there must be extenuating circumstances. They may not welcome you back into the fold because you are behind on royalties, have defaulted on your agreement during the term, or refused to comply with remodeling, training, or other conditions of renewal. Franchisors usually want their good franchisees to renew — but you can't fault them if they don't want to renew franchisees who haven't met the terms of the initial bargain.

Getting the goods

Just as with the first time around, when you renew, you obtain the rights to use the franchisor's trademarks and operating methodology in a certain area for another specified period of time. Every franchisor puts its own spin on renewal agreements. Many renewal agreements are for the same number of years as the original agreement (such as 10-10); others are for a shorter period of time (such as 10-5-5). Some franchisors offer unlimited, continuing renewals (we call them *evergreen agreements*); others permit only one renewal term. Don't assume that the brand is yours to use for life. Be aware of the terms when you sign the original franchise agreement (see Chapter 6): Fully understanding the agreement helps you plan your business — and your life.

Renewal fees also are across the board. Some franchisors don't charge a renewal fee. (Many franchisee advocates think that's the way it should be.) Other franchisors require either a flat amount — typically ranging from several hundred to several thousand dollars — a percentage of the then-current franchise fee, or the same fee they charge for new franchisees.

It makes sense for franchisors to encourage their franchisees to renew. The job of closing locations, locating new franchisees, and training them puts a burden on the system, is expensive, and over time can damage the competitiveness of the brand in the market. It also strains relations with the remaining franchisees when they see others leaving the system. By placing a modest fee to cover administrative costs, or no fee, franchisors tell their franchisees that they are valuable members of the system and that retaining the relationship is important.

Wendy's has an extremely high renewal rate. Our franchisees are obviously happy with their investments. Obviously, if you're not making money and not enjoying your investment, you're not going to renew. Our franchisees know what the new fees are at the time of the renewal, and if they were too high, they wouldn't renew. Right now, for the people who are renewing, the $2,500 fee is dirt cheap. We have it that low because we require a lot of money to be put into the facility when the franchisees renew their agreements to upgrade and modernize. And we want their money to go there. Right now, the royalty fee is the same as for the old agreement, so franchisees have no reason to object.

However the renewal fee is figured, it shouldn't be anywhere as steep as your initiation dues. That's because you're not starting from scratch this time. The franchisor's job is a lot easier because you've already mastered operating the franchise. There's no need for initial training. No need for site selection. No need for inventory advice. You've already been there, done that.

Still, don't be surprised if you're required to undergo some training. Say that the franchisor requires you to install a new computer system and proprietary software upon renewal; you may have to go to corporate headquarters for training. You may or may not have to pay for the training, but you can pretty much count on travel expenses.

Even though you're older and wiser now (and maybe a bit grayer, too), by renewing your franchise you're entitled to continue receiving ongoing support. Will the support be the same as with the old deal? Maybe not.

Putting together a new deal

Will the deal be the same as the original agreement? Not usually. Five, ten, or twenty years have passed since you signed the original agreement. The system and marketplace have evolved and changed — and, in most cases, so have the terms of the agreement. At renewal, expect to sign a new franchise agreement — typically, the then-current franchise agreement for new franchisees. It's logical that franchisors adapt over the years, which could mean a change in fee structure and operating system, new products or equipment, or different territorial rights.

The new agreement may differ substantially from the one in your hip pocket. This may work to your benefit — or detriment. An agreement that works to your detriment probably doesn't sound fair to you, right? After all, you've paid your dues all these years. But, as you know by now, franchisors want consistency, and renewal brings the old franchisees into compliance with the terms of the deal now being offered.

Many franchisees are surprised, and sometimes angry, at the differences between the arrangement they have and the one being offered at renewal. The royalty and advertising fees may have changed, the size of their territory — or even having a protected territory — may have changed, and the cost of bringing the location to the "then-current design" (a common feature of renewal agreements) may be high. You have to make a decision when the time comes, but you should be prepared for, not surprised by, the changes. During the term of your franchise, keep abreast of the changes that your franchisor is making to new franchise agreements. Discuss them with your franchisor. Keep in mind, though, that times do change and the needs of the system change as well.

A limited number of states have laws that limit a franchisor's right not to renew your franchise. Rupert Barkoff, a partner with Kilpatrick Stockton, Atlanta, Georgia, says, "If your franchisor has informed you that your franchise will not be renewed, you should immediately consult with your attorney as to your rights. One way to avoid surprises is to try to negotiate limitations on the franchisor's ability to change the deal at renewal time before you sign the original franchise agreement."

Be on the lookout for changes in the following:

✔ Royalty and advertising fees

✔ Territorial rights

✔ Remodeling requirements

✔ New equipment and signage

- ✔ Training requirements
- ✔ Renewal terms
- ✔ Material business terms of the relationship

You may face a hike in royalty and advertising fees, especially if you got in on the ground floor of a franchise; royalty and ad fees may have swelled in line with the system's growth. This isn't cut-and-dried, either, as some franchisors carry over their existing royalty structure for renewing franchisees.

Very often, you have to make remodeling changes. Typically, franchisors require renewing franchisees to do anything that the majority of existing franchisees must do. Perk up your ears, however, if the franchisor requires excessive remodeling. Reasonable upgrades are understandable because, again, franchisors want consistency. You have to define "reasonable." For example, would you like to live with the same bright purple paint for another ten years when the walls at new franchises are bathed in lavender? So you may have to paint, lay new carpet, put up new signage, redo the seating area, install new equipment, or add a drive-through window. A franchisor may offer a cap on remodeling costs (limiting the amount of money a franchisee is required to spend) or a monetary incentive. Find out whether any offers are on the table.

If you're a smart business owner and the new location design is having a positive impact on new store sales, consider remodeling your store even if the franchisor doesn't require it, and even if your term isn't up.

Again, some franchisors are more strict about conformity than others. At American Leak Detection in Palm Springs, California, a franchisee simply has to be a team member in good standing to renew. Nothing more, nothing less. But although the company constantly updates its electronic equipment to detect water, air, gas, and oil leaks, renewing franchisees do not have to trade up at renewal. Any required changes — especially those that impact your bottom line — could affect your decision to renew. Say that a franchisor requires a hefty remodeling upon renewal and offers only one, five-year renewal term. Is the significant investment worth it for such a short operating period? The answer takes some number crunching. So gather the troops. Make sure that you, your attorney, and your accountant review all the paperwork before making any future commitment.

Franchisors typically ask for some other things upon renewal. They want evidence that you can continue to occupy the same or a different location — in other words, a lease, rental agreement, or deed. After all, they don't want you frying chicken in the middle of the street. And you typically have to sign a general release of liability of all claims under the prior franchise relationship. The concept behind that release is this: If you've got a claim against us, raise it now.

Your attorney must carefully screen the new document for any language that's different from the original contract or that releases your franchisor from valid claims you may have under the old agreement. When it comes to franchise contracts — any contracts for that matter — substitution of just one word can make a big difference.

Watch for any substantial changes to the material business terms of the relationship. One big issue today is the method used to resolve franchise disputes. Perhaps a franchisor now requires mediation with a neutral party; that's a whole lot different from requiring you to bring legal action in the franchisor's home state (see Chapter 10). Another hotbed of controversy is encroachment, or when someone sells products or services in your operating area (read about this in Chapter 8). Make sure that the rules haven't changed — or that you can live with them if they have.

Times have really changed. When many franchise agreements were originally signed, alternative locations may not have been as popular, and competition from Internet sales certainly wasn't even considered. However, since e-commerce doesn't require the establishment of locations, those Websites may be required to keep the brand competitive and may not be included in the franchisee's territory. Make sure that you understand the full impact that such changes may have on your business. Understand, though, that in the age of the Internet, where your competitor may not be down the block but in another country, in some businesses the idea of protected territory may start to seem as quaint as waiting for the town crier to give you the week's news.

Negotiating change

You feel like you've been a loyal soldier all these years. Shouldn't the franchisor cut you some slack at renewal? You'll never know unless you ask.

One area worth a try is release of liability. A typical agreement provides for a general release of all claims in favor of the franchisor. Many franchisees end up negotiating a mutual release of liability — claims against the franchisor and against the franchisee.

You may also try negotiating changes to territorial rights, training, renewal fees, changes in royalties, and remodeling requirements. Perhaps you can strike a deal that places a cap on refurbishing costs, if no such limit exists. Or maybe you can split the royalty increase.

Although negotiations in changes to territorial rights, training, renewal fees, and additional capital costs are not all that uncommon, changes to the then-current royalty rate and advertising fees are. It makes a great deal of sense if you think about it. When you entered the system, the costs for operating the system and supporting the franchisees were at one level, and time may have changed those realities. When it comes to advertising, *grandfathering* (giving a benefit to a defined group) older and often lower fees to renewing franchisees puts a strain on the system's advertising budget and could have an ill effect on the franchisor's relations with other franchisees who may be paying a different and often higher fee.

Strength in numbers may help here. If you truly feel that the changes in the new agreement will have a detrimental effect on your business or simply are not fair or justifiable, speak to other franchisees and get their feelings. Often a good place to work through negotiations is the Franchisee Advisory Council or a franchisee association. (Read about the role of these groups in Chapter 10.)

If your negotiating efforts foundered when you were a fledgling franchisee, take heart. Joyce G. Mazero, lead franchise attorney at Dallas-based Jenkens & Gilchrist, says that renewing franchisees may wield more negotiating power, "only if the franchisors are making money from the relationship. Leverage is the key here. You don't have a lot of leverage going in."

Too often, franchisees make the mistake of hiring an attorney to do battle with their franchisor rather than simply sitting down with the franchisor, discussing their concerns, and coming to a negotiated resolution. The only people who benefit from unnecessary legal conflicts are the attorneys and some of the advocacy groups whose only way of remaining in business is to ferment disputes between franchisors and franchisees. Discuss your concerns with your franchisor first. There is always time to bring in the legal troops if the concerns can't be resolved.

Exiting Gracefully

We're going to tell you what you should not do if you want to exit your franchise: simply turn out the lights, lock the door, and vanish. Leaving in this way would be wasting all the sweat equity — and real equity — that you've pumped into your business all these years. Even if you want to disappear, your business doesn't have to. There's value there, and you should reap it.

When you want out, you can "sell" (or "assign" or "transfer" — or whatever the legal language is in your agreement) your interest in the franchise agreement and sell your assets (such as the building, fixtures, and equipment if you own them). Doing so can add up to a big chunk of change.

Timing is everything

There's a reason you open your store at 10 a.m. sharp, hire more employees to service the evening customers who pick up their vitamins or get their hair cut after work, and insist that your employees greet the customer within 20 seconds of their entering the door. Timing. Running your franchise according to the clock makes sense. The same goes for selling it.

There are right times and wrong times to exit. The time all depends on inner and outer forces.

"Inner forces" means you. It's critical to put yourself under the microscope. Investigate why you want to cash out and when doing so would make the most sense.

If burnout is the culprit, can you do some things to rejuvenate yourself? Maybe you just need a long vacation to recharge your battery. Or are you so far gone that getting out is the only solution? If the burnout is real, you may want to get out sooner than later, before the telltale signs really start to affect the value of your business. Remember: Bad reputations spread faster than good ones.

Maybe you're just downright miserable. Everyone knows someone who unhappily dragged his feet to the same job day in and day out. After 25 years, he was rewarded with a gold watch. After another 25 years of dragging himself to work, he was treated to a blowout retirement dinner (with lobster and champagne, if he was really lucky). You vowed you'd never stay that long if you were unhappy.

Perhaps the business has outgrown you: You lack the skills and money to take it to the next level. Or maybe selling your franchise never crossed your mind until you became seriously ill. In both cases, it may make sense to leave now, before the business — and subsequently, the price — begins to suffer.

Say, though, that you want to sell because you're focused on the future — a new racket, relocation, or retirement. In these cases, financial factors are critical. Do you need to hold out for a certain price to fund the new venture or to secure a worry-free retirement? Do you have to sell within a certain time to kick-start your new life?

Of course, even the best-laid plans can go astray. Maybe you anticipate retiring in five years, but an unsolicited — and incredible — purchase proposal lands at your feet. That may be reason enough to hang your hammock now.

Okay, now for the "outer forces."

Zero in on the economy. Good times are conducive to buying and selling a business. When interest rates are low and financing is plentiful, more buyers jump into the pool. Even if you're thrilled by your business, if the right offer comes by, can you afford not to take it? Maybe with the proceeds from the sale of your existing business you can relocate to a place you've always wanted to live and invest in a new franchise — maybe even one from the same franchisor.

Also look around the area in which your franchise is located. Are new businesses coming in? Is the area undergoing revitalization? Is the landlord beefing things up? If the answers to these questions are yes, that could bolster the price of your business. In contrast, if the surrounding neighborhood is starting to look shabby, you may have missed the boat. Try to get out before, say, a new super bookstore sets up near your little bookshop or before a business-unfriendly local law takes effect.

Then look at your industry. If it's thriving, it could be your ticket on the gravy train. You want to cash out before a market is saturated, before a fad fades, and before new technology makes your business obsolete.

Finally, consider the state of your franchisor. We know you did all that due diligence about the company before coming into the franchise, but things change — for better or worse. If same-store sales are starting to get soft because new and innovative competitors are entering the market, maybe it's time to bail out before the news becomes generally known. Maybe, though, you learned that the franchisor has developed a new product line and it's going to be a big hit. In that case, it may be time to invest in more locations. Market leaders command higher value; declining systems get you less.

Take a look at the marketplace and decide the following:

- ✔ Are competing companies adding new products or extensions to existing ones while no changes appear on the horizon in your system?
- ✔ Has the third president in the past two years just joined the system?
- ✔ Has the franchisor filed Chapter 11 (that is, bankruptcy)?

"Yes" answers to the preceding three questions won't help the selling price of your business.

There's an opportunity for a new buyer to grow if

- ✔ The brand is strong because of new products and great marketing.
- ✔ The brand is strong because the system is growing and is focused on establishing critical mass.

✔ The brand is strong because customers love to come to every store in the system.

✔ Potential purchasers want a franchisor who's financially strong, franchisee-friendly, and forward thinking. Does yours fit the bill?

If trouble is brewing or unknowns lie ahead with the franchisor, it could scare off buyers or drain the value of your business. Pay attention to such developments as franchisee lawsuits, uncontrolled growth, sagging system-wide sales, unprecedented franchise closures, unacceptable changes to the new franchise agreements, management shake-up, or an acquisition of the franchisor.

Just like potential home buyers, potential franchise buyers want to know why you're selling. Your reason could affect the sales price. If a buyer senses urgency, you can bet your bottom dollar that he'll try to squeeze out the lowest price. If a buyer understands that you're in an industry that's flying high, she'll pay extra for the privilege of taking over.

Leaving it to your children — maybe

Little Johnny has swept the floors at your franchise since the broom was taller than he was. Little Jane has stuffed marketing coupons into envelopes since before she could write a complete sentence. Sound familiar? It's not at all unusual for your franchise to be your children's second home. But have you ever thought of them as not just helping hands — but as potential successors?

Growing numbers of franchisees have that very mind-set.

Your children have worked hard, love the business, and have helped you build up value. Who better to pass the business on to? Like any parent, you probably think that your kids can do anything. But because we're not talking independent business here, you have to convince your franchisor of their greatness. In a franchisor's mind, children aren't always chips off the old block.

Franchisors normally reserve the right to approve transfer of ownership — even to family members. If an owner dies, some franchisors allow assignment of the franchise to a spouse or heirs without approval; others require approval within a certain time period — say 12 months; and others require approval immediately. Some franchisors waive a fee for transfer of ownership to a spouse, parent, or child; others don't.

Specific approval criteria are not usually laid out in a franchisor's documents, so you may want to feel the franchisor out in advance to see what's likely to be required. It also may help if you gradually acclimate your son or daughter to the franchisor. Take your child, at an appropriate age, to franchise conventions and training, for example. Some franchisors "preapprove" your children or your spouse as future franchisees if they satisfactorily complete the required training program now.

One reason people go into business is to establish something of value for their heirs. One of the best things that parents can give their children is a business that's going forward. Being a franchise business operator, they're not subject to the perils of corporate takeovers and downsizing. The children are getting something of value. Certainly, we encourage transferring the business from parents to their children. Family members are acceptable franchisees if they're willing and able to do what is required to operate the franchise. When a Wendy's franchisee wants to transfer ownership to a family member (more and more kids are getting involved!), we must give our okay. We look at the same issues as we do with a sale to a third party: Who will be the franchisee? Who will operate the business? Have they been trained? Is the business well capitalized? Then, in recognition of the family connection, we almost always waive the $5,000 transfer fee for family members (unless it's a really complex situation).

Passing on or selling a franchise to your children is not as easy as giving them a shiny new bicycle on their tenth birthday. You must plan to transfer a business. It takes time. Lack of planning can significantly affect whether a family business passes smoothly into a new generation. Don't assume that your franchise will be in your estate. Understand your rights contained in the franchise agreement by knowing the answers to the following questions:

- ✔ How much time is left on the franchise?

- ✔ Do you have the right to transfer your franchise in the agreement? In most instances, it's no different from your rights to sell your franchise; check with your accountant concerning how you value the franchise and any tax consequences.

- ✔ What renewal options are available? Who has to execute them to get the most benefit?

- ✔ Does the franchisor require the new owner of the business to sign a new franchise agreement with terms that are different from the ones you're currently operating under?

- ✔ Does your franchisor have a right of first refusal to buy your business if you try to transfer it to your children?

- ✔ Are your children acceptable franchisees to the franchisor? They usually have the right to approve who the new franchisee will be.

Before handing over the reins, it's critical to develop estate plans, which include the current fair-market value of the business; succession plans, which should include personal, financial, and business goals and time schedules; investment plans; and written strategic plans.

Transferring a family business has financial, legal, and tax consequences. You can pass down the business through estate planning or sell some or all of your interest, or a combination of the two. Consult with accountants, estate attorneys, investment advisors, insurance agents, and family business consultants. Your franchisor may offer succession-planning advice. Nationwide, about 100 family business centers that are affiliated with universities provide education on family business topics. The Family Firm Institute, a Boston-based professional association of advisors to family businesses, can connect you to family business centers, consultants, and other information sources; you can reach the institute at 617-789-4200 or www.ffi.org.

A successful transition depends a lot on your mind-set as an owner. In order to tackle succession planning, you first have to recognize your own mortality. You also have to be willing to let go. Pass down your knowledge (although your kids will likely still have to go through training when they become franchisees) and recognize that they'll probably run things a little differently than you. Let them learn from their own mistakes. And don't push the family franchise on your children; the decision has to be theirs. The feelings that you transmit about the business — from around the dinner table to when you're standing behind the counter — influences them from the time they're off the bottle. Moan and they'll moan, too; be positive and watch the good feeling spread.

Your kids have to do their share, too. It might be easy for them to just work the family business and never have to go on job interviews or wear a suit to the office. The lack of a well-rounded work background doesn't work well for succession. Outside experience adds credibility and kills a "boss's son" attitude among employees.

Who's the best kid for the job? You can avoid getting caught between sibling arguments about succession if you stay out of it. Many experts suggest that you let the siblings decide among themselves who's the most competent; they can also get input from employees and an outside board of directors, if one exists. They're the ones who have to live with their decision.

Selling Out

Smart franchisees orchestrate their exit strategies meticulously, from the overture to the finale. They devise a personal business plan, plotting when and how they want out. In this way, they can continue to have one foot firmly in their franchise while the other foot is inching out the door.

It makes sense to begin preparing several years before your target date. You'll want to take steps to boost the value of your business — and doing so takes time. You also need to investigate and then select an appropriate sales vehicle. Once you put your franchise up for sale, it could get swept up right away, or it could take weeks, months, or even years to sell. You also have to insert another element in the timeline: the franchisor, who gets a voice on several items before the deal is done.

The word on the street is that 20 percent of companies on the market sell right away. The other 80 percent don't, because they're overpriced or the owner didn't get the company in shape. So start preparing — and good luck.

Getting the most out of your business

Selling a franchise is very much like selling a house. Obviously, you don't have to light a fire in the fireplace or fill the air with the aroma of freshly baked apple pie. Still, you want to make your business look, feel, and be its best before potential buyers cross the welcome mat. What you put into the selling process affects what you'll get out of it.

The first place to start is with your finances. There's no question that a prospective buyer's biggest concern is your bottom line. Is your business profitable? The only way anyone knows for sure is if your books are in tip-top shape — clean enough to pass the strictest military inspection. Give yourself at least three years lead time to start keeping accurate records. By accurate, we mean bumping your Cadillac, artwork, and other personal assets that you used to minimize taxes off your financial statements. Your books should reflect only the business's true expenses and revenues. Set up your records by using generally accepted accounting principles and consider including audited annual statements. Try to settle any financial obligations, liens, and claims or lawsuits from suppliers, customers, or other parties. Also talk to your accountant and attorney this far in advance for financial planning purposes — such as setting up charitable trusts — so that you don't get slammed in post-sale taxes.

Have other papers in order, too. Prospective buyers see value in such things as business plans, employee records, supplier contracts, operational diagrams, and of course, organized franchise support materials. Keep all your operations and training manuals as well as any additional information that may come in handy — such as materials from seminars or conventions, surveys, the title, and environmental information.

Next, cosmetic changes may be in order. You should already be in good shape because you've had to meet the chain's standards all along. Still, any business could probably use some spit and polish in some nook or cranny. Be your own worst critic; attack things that a customer — and therefore a buyer — would see. Low-cost, routine maintenance pays off here. You may want to get new blinds, paint some walls, and straighten the pantry.

Bigger investments take more thought. For example, should you upgrade equipment or remodel to meet current standards, or should you let the new franchisee deal with — and pay for — these requirements? Will your investment or noninvestment impact the sales price or the sale? The answer depends to some extent on how far in advance you're starting to spruce up (will you benefit from the improvements before the sale?) and the extent of the franchisor's requirements upon transfer.

Now is no time to put blinders on. No matter why you're leaving, rev yourself up and continue to build the business and operate in a way that maximizes value. Make sure that your employees are performing, pay attention to customer service, keep inventories well stocked, and continue marketing to bring in new customers. The more business-as-usual, the better chance you have of selling.

In the end, much of your preparation work in buying a franchise pays off when you're selling. Site selection was quite a chore, right? Here's the payback: Many buyers consider physical location a primary factor in determining value. Real estate leases that have several years remaining and renewal options are selling points; leases on, say, obsolete equipment are not. Remember the amount of time you spent on employee training? Perhaps the prospective buyer is so impressed that she wants to keep some of your employees. And how about your devotion to customer loyalty? Supplying the new owner with an organized data bank of customer names gives her a head start.

Finally, you can sweeten the deal to make your business worth more at resale. One legitimate concern of a buyer is whether you plan to open a similar business nearby in the near future. His wheels are spinning, figuring that you can easily duplicate your success — and potentially cut in on his turf. The point is moot if you're bound by a noncompete agreement with your franchisor. Otherwise, calm the buyer's fears by striking your own noncompete deal. You might also offer some type of financing arrangement or help train the new owner for a specified period. These latter conditions tie you to the business a little longer, but if they help get you where you want to go, do it.

Valuing the company

At this point, you probably want us to talk dollars. Just how much can you get for your franchise? Answering this question isn't so easy. In the past, many business consultants and brokers were quick to rattle off formulas — usually, a multiple of cash flow. But they've wised up and realized that too many factors go into valuing a business to make it so generic. Every business has to be valued by itself.

Here's another reason why rules of thumb don't work. Say that you're basing a valuation purely on gross sales. Well, there's a huge difference between a franchise that's sunk from $1 million to $500,000 in sales and a business that's grown from $250,000 in sales to that same $500,000. There's also a big difference between a franchise with 3 years remaining on the contract and one with 23 years.

Valuations are based on the financial facts of the business, the current state of the industry, the business's position in the industry, the location of the business, and timing. The key to valuation is that the numbers have to be accurate, and the ultimate value is based on cash flow, assets, and the return on investment anticipated by the buyer.

You can set a higher value on your business if you have time left on the agreement than if you're at the end of your last renewal period.

When you transfer the franchise, many franchisors require the new franchisee to sign the then-current agreement but may not provide them with a full-term and renewal period(s) as they would for a new franchisee. The agreement is modified to provide only the remaining time and renewal periods unexpired from the original agreement. The difference between 3 years and 23 years of remaining life can have a dramatic effect on the selling price of the business. Determine what your franchisor will do concerning the length of time available to the new franchisee. Franchisors often consider an early renewal, especially when there is only a short period left to run on the franchise agreement, or provide the new franchisee with a full term.

You can certainly ask the franchisor and other franchisees what comparable franchises have sold for, but don't expect your franchisor to help you set a price. Doing so could be a conflict of interest if the franchisor has a right of first refusal to buy your business. Doing so also could open the franchisor up to other potential liabilities should the selling price the franchisor sets for you be lower than you could have reasonably expected.

Having your business appraised is worth the expense. It's best to seek out an independent third party to do the valuation. This third party could be an appraiser, business broker, accountant, attorney, or business consultant — as long as the person you choose isn't connected with the deal. Obviously, credibility is important. In the buyer's mind, if the broker who's selling the business values your business, the price has probably been marked up. Find out what your business is worth — and why it's worth that price — before you list it with a broker or other source.

The cost of a valuation varies. The cost depends on the company, the condition of its records, and the number of locations. The Institute of Certified Business Counselors offers this range: $1,500 to $4,500 for a company that sells for under $2 million. Figure that a valuation takes about 30 days — and plug that into your time line as well.

Again, just as with selling a house, don't expect your asking price to be your selling price. Be prepared for negotiations and be willing to compromise. Try to understand the buyer's motivations and to view things from the buyer's perspective. We know that it's tough to let go of something you've put your blood, sweat, and tears into, but being calm, rational, and friendly throughout the selling process pays off.

Playing by the franchisor's rules

When selling a franchise, you're not a free agent. Even if a buyer tosses you a great offer, you can't officially catch it until you check out some details with your franchisor.

First, most franchisors have what is called a *right of first refusal.* This term means that whenever a prospective buyer makes a bona fide offer to purchase the franchisee's interest in the franchise agreement or assets, the franchisor has the right to purchase it on the same terms and conditions within a specific time period. Review your franchise agreement to see what rights the franchisor has reserved for itself, how you're required to notify them of the possible sale, the form of the notification, and how many days they have to respond.

In other words, your franchisor may end up buying your franchise. Many franchisees have a problem with this provision. Rightfully so. They feel that such a provision hurts their sales efforts. Consider a sophisticated buyer who spends months checking out your franchise and makes an offer — only to be pushed aside because the franchisor moves in, matches the price, and buys it right out from under them. Trust us, this person will not be pleased.

Some sophisticated buyers will not even begin to negotiate with you or do their due diligence on the business if they have to go through the expense while there's a good chance that the franchisor will simply match their offer. Discuss this issue with your franchisor and determine what their intentions are before you begin to market your business. If your franchisor decides that it isn't interested in executing on its right of first refusal, get it in writing. Such proof allays the potential buyer's fears.

Then there's the issue of approval. Most agreements give the franchisor the right to approve all transfers of ownership. Think of this right of approval as a prospective groom asking the father of the bride-to-be for permission to marry his daughter before he asks for her hand in marriage. Some provisions add that the franchisor can't unreasonably withhold consent. The word "unreasonable" can be open to debate, however.

Look at your franchise agreement so you can plan carefully. The general rule for transfers typically goes like this: If you're transferring control of the company to an individual or group, whether a family member is involved or not, the franchisor reserves the right to approve or disapprove the new owners. If you're transferring less than controlling interest, whether it includes a family member or not, a franchisor may not have to approve it. Some franchisors, however, leave the transfer issue completely open and have the right to review any type of transfer.

Typically, a new franchisee must meet the franchisor's qualifications, fulfill ownership requirements — such as training and remodeling — and sign a then-current franchise agreement.

The franchisor also receives a transfer fee (usually to cover legal and accounting costs). Not all transfer fees are identical for all buyers, so be aware of the exact fee before you start negotiating the purchase price. Instead of charging a flat fee, some franchisors charge a percentage of the then-current franchise fee or even the sales price. Others reduce the fee if the buyer is an existing franchisee or an employee of the franchisor or franchisee.

Transfer fees, training costs, and even the cost of remodeling requirements can all be bargaining tools in the negotiating process — from your end or the buyer's.

Also expect your franchisor to eyeball the purchase agreement between you and the buyer before anyone signs on the dotted line. Franchisors basically are looking for the following:

- ✔ Any inconsistencies between the purchase agreement and the franchise agreement
- ✔ Debt structure and leverage
- ✔ Overall viability of transaction
- ✔ Structure of ownership and operations
- ✔ Condition of the facility

Obviously, an attorney should be involved in drawing up a purchase agreement.

American Leak Detection, for example, is concerned about the responsibilities of buyer and seller — such things as who handles bad debts, who returns calls on jobs prior to the transfer, and reimbursement for insurance or yellow pages advertising already in effect. Questions about these issues may seem intrusive, but the company requires approval for the buyer's protection. "We don't want buyers to go in with their eyes closed," says Sheila Bangs, its director of franchise sales. "Once the seller is gone, the buyer is now our franchisee. We want it to be the same as if they bought directly from us."

Franchisors also tend to put in their two cents about a seller's obligations upon transfer. Three typical conditions of transfer are that (1) a franchisee must pay all monies owed to the franchisor and its affiliates, (2) a franchisee must sign a general release of all claims against the franchisor, and (3) a franchisee must sign a noncompete agreement. Sometimes the noncompete agreement has already been built into the franchise agreement.

In addition, some companies suggest, highly recommend, or mandate that the existing franchisee remain on board for a certain amount of time to smooth the transition. They may also require the existing franchisee to stay on as a guarantor of the franchise if the company has concerns about the buyer. These stipulations have both pros and cons. The need for such requirements and how well they work out may depend on the expertise of the new buyer and the personality of the seller. Obviously, just as when you're asked to train a new replacement in corporate America, watching someone fill your shoes is a little awkward. It's even more awkward if someone starts messing with your tried-and-true methods. There's also the risk of separation anxiety — for you and your employees.

On the plus side, in-house mentoring, a consulting agreement, or personal introductions to suppliers and customers should raise the sales price. Purchasers may view your willingness to stay on as an admission that you're not hiding anything. And, if the new franchisee's a gem, it may give you peace of mind — seeing for yourself that your baby is in good hands.

Many franchisors are reluctant to get involved in the sale — especially when it relates to commenting on the selling price. The reason is that if the selling price is high, but the buyer is willing to pay, the selling franchisee may sue the franchisor for stopping the sale. On the other hand, if the franchisor doesn't tell the new franchisee that the price is excessive, and the new franchisee is unable to meet their debt service, the new franchisee may sue the franchisor later on. It's a troubling aspect of the relationship. Many franchisors have worked out formulas concerning debt service to cash flow ratios, which they make available to their franchisees. Although not guarantees, these formulas can avoid problems later on. However, several legal precedents suggest that as long as the franchisor is acting in good faith, the franchisor may refuse to approve a deal where the price is seen as too high. Sometimes the franchise agreement specifically makes an excessive price an acceptable reason for the franchisor to refuse to approve a sale.

Selecting a sales method

Okay, this is it. You're ready to let go. You're convinced the timing is right, you know what your business is worth, and you're aware of your obligations to your franchisor. All that's left is actually putting it on the block.

We suggest that you don't try to market it yourself. Doing so is draining. Besides, you're a franchisee, not a broker or negotiator. Leave the selling to a professional and concentrate on running your franchise so that you have something to sell.

The most logical place to start is to contact your franchisor. Because franchisors typically have the right of first refusal, it just makes sense to first see whether they want to take the business off your hands. Selling to a franchisor usually yields the fastest — but not necessarily the highest-priced — deal.

From the moment you buy your franchise, be alert for signs that your franchisor may be interested in a sale when the time comes: Is the franchisor establishing a pattern of buying back units? Is it repositioning itself with more company-owned franchises? Is it selling pieces of company units to employees in lieu of stock? Is it looking to edge in on your particular market?

Reason number two for going to the franchisor: If the franchisor isn't interested in buying, it probably knows who is. Potential candidates logically flow through corporate offices. These can be either existing franchisees or new candidates just dying for your territory, or — in some systems — any territory. The franchisor considers these leads "qualified" if they're in its database, which should speed the process along.

Adding to the pool of qualified buyers, some franchisors have programs that specifically groom employees to become franchisees. For example, at AlphaGraphics Inc., in Tucson, Arizona, employees at franchised units and corporate headquarters can earn up to nearly $40,000 in credits over a three-year period that can be applied toward the purchase of an existing franchise. The company's succession planning program also includes business valuation services using an outside consultant (cost: $5,000), guidance on how to improve the value of the business, and marketing services.

We give a lot of our own people who are already working in our stores the opportunity to own a Wendy's, over just somebody walking in off the street. We give a franchise to some people who have been with the company for a long time. We can't guarantee whether the employee will work out as a franchisee, but we hope they do, and we'll do everything we can to help.

Many franchisors are turning informal grapevines into formal resale networks. They've assigned salespeople exclusively or nonexclusively to handle sales of existing units. They're marketed through newspaper advertising or the Internet. Check whether the franchisor charges a commission for this service.

Sometimes it's easier for a franchisor to sell an existing franchise than a new one. That's because an existing franchise is an open book. If a franchisor doesn't make an earnings claim in its UFOC (see Chapter 6), buyers of new franchises may have some difficulty projecting earnings. But if a franchisor is selling a "live" business, the potential new owner can check out its financial health firsthand. As a result, someone who comes in thinking "new" may realize that "used" can work out just as well — if not better.

Don't rely only on your franchisor to get to existing franchisees. Tap your chain's Franchisee Advisory Council (see Chapter 10). Put out the word yourself on the chain's intranet, and talk up your franchise at conventions and other meetings. If you're active in your system — which you should be — you should know which franchisees are on the prowl for acquisitions. Usually, existing owners more heavily critique your operation and your books, but they also tend to pay more to corral another unit of the same chain.

Beyond your franchise community, try marketing your franchise on a resale listing service on the Internet. But be careful, because this sales technique also opens your information to your managers and staff. Owners and brokers pay to post franchises and other business opportunities for specific time periods. The big plus is that the networks — thanks to the power of the Internet — expose resales all over the world, 24 hours a day. Prospective buyers can search for free — by city, state, listing price, and category. They may be put in touch with a broker or the owner, or the listing service may pass the prospective buyer's name to the seller. Try the Business Resale Network at `www.br-network.com` (provided by Franchise UPDATE and *Entrepreneur* magazine) and the business resale listings on the Web Site `www.usatoday.com` (a service of *USA Today* and Franchise Solutions).

Another way to go: List your franchise with a business broker, the equivalent of a real estate broker for businesses.

We mention several times throughout this book that we don't recommend the use of a franchise broker when you purchase or sell a franchise. A business broker is not the same as a franchise broker. A business broker typically handles the sale of individual businesses, whether franchised or not, brought to them by sellers. A franchise broker, on the other hand, is in the business of marketing franchises for their clients — the franchisor.

Use a business broker with a national and international network, because the buyer may not come from around the corner. If the business broker is familiar with franchises, all the better. Fees vary by location and sales price. For referrals to a broker in your area, call the Institute of Certified Business Counselors, Eugene, Oregon, at 541-345-8064 or the International Business Brokers Association, Reston, Virginia, at 703-437-4377 or `www.ibba.org`.

Whichever sales method you choose, confidentiality is critical. You don't want to let the cat out of the bag unless the buyer is serious and prequalified in some way.

The Party's Over

You've just completed Life as a Franchisee. Sounds like a movie title, right? Well, with every great flick, there's usually a sequel. Now it's time to write yours. Will part two be more enjoyable, more adventuresome, more dramatic, more humorous? It can play out however you want it to.

Of course, you may just want to pocket the box office sales — take the $100,000 or $500,000, or however much you've made from your franchise and head off to Cancun — indefinitely. But unless you're retirement age, most people usually get itchy after a while and are ready again to star in a more active role: Life after Being a Franchisee.

Learning from your experience

In order to look ahead, it's best to look back at your past. Rewinding your experience as a franchisee in your head helps you determine whether you want to do this again, do something similar, or do something entirely different.

So hop on the couch for another self-analysis session. Before you bought a franchise, you asked yourself a lot of questions to see whether you were cut out to be a franchisee. (Go to Chapter 3 to refresh your memory.) Now, based on your experience, revisit those questions and see whether your initial answers really held up. This exercise helps you determine what you've learned about yourself.

Before you got started, you had to make sure you weren't very entrepreneurial. Well, did it bother you to always be concerned about rules, standards, and consistency? Did you have to control many urges to do it your way? Were you devastated any time the franchisor flatly rejected one of your suggestions? Or were you thrilled that you had a system to follow — that someone was always there to lead the way?

You also asked yourself whether you're a people person. Were you comfortable dealing with customers? Were you able to coach employees — motivate them, criticize them, teach them, and praise them? Or did you cower under the table when you had to confront someone or were confronted?

Reflect on the responsibility. We warned you going in that the franchisor does not run the business for you. Were you able to keep up the pace — work those long hours? Did it bother you to get called back to the shop for an emergency just when you were settling in to watch a Sunday football game? Did you pitch in and mop the floor with a smile on your face when an employee called in sick?

In addition, we stressed up front the importance of the franchisee/franchisor relationship. How would you rate yours? Were you at loggerheads with the franchisor, or did things run pretty smoothly? Did you milk the system — get involved with other franchisees and tap into the franchisor's resources? Did the franchisor come through? Were you a good franchisee?

Think about your particular franchise. Did it end up matching your interests? Did you have the right skills? Were you happy on the job?

The most telling question of all is one you pose to existing franchisees during your due diligence: Did you have any fun? Would you do it all over again? Well, would you?

Keeping noncompete clauses in mind

If you've learned one thing from your franchise experience, it's to always check the rulebook. Well, it's no different once you've relinquished your title as franchisee. Before you plan your next move, go back to your franchise agreement to see whether you're bound by any restrictions.

Virtually all franchise agreements (other than hotel franchise agreements) have noncompete clauses that are in effect both during and after the contract. Post-term, the contract usually prevents you from owning or operating a competing business in a defined geographic area for a certain number of years. Two years is typical, but it can be longer. The noncompete clause may cite specific businesses, industry segments, or whole industries. It also may cite specific distances from the original franchise, another franchisee, or a company-owned location, or have a blanket restriction.

At Wendy's, franchisees whose agreements are terminated or expire may not be involved in any quick service business that sells chicken sandwiches, hamburgers, or food similar to Wendy's for two years within the designated market area of the restaurant. So someone can open a pizza shop or muffler repair shop down the block (because Wendy's doesn't sell pizza and certainly doesn't sell mufflers). But if they're stuck on hamburgers and chicken, they'll have to move out of town to set up shop right away or wait out the two years to open in the same market.

Making your next move

Football players have hung up their jerseys, lawyers have thrown out their law books, and doctors have put away their stethoscopes — all to become franchisees. No kidding; it's happened. So it follows that if you want to be an ex-franchisee turned football player, lawyer, doctor or anything else, you should go for it. There's nothing wrong with doing something totally different (even if you're not going through a midlife crisis).

But, based on your franchise experience, you may want to begin again in franchising. Here are some options you may have:

✔ **Becoming a franchisee of the same chain.** Maybe you'll relocate to another area (warmer weather, here you come), buy multiple units, or become an area developer this time. Or how about taking the concept to Paris, *oui?*

✔ **Switching to another franchise system.** You could stay in the same industry or try a totally different industry. Perhaps you had a retail store before and now want to try a service business — one that doesn't require as much overhead. Check your noncompete clause before doing anything.

New beginnings could also include the following:

✔ **Trading up to be a franchisor:** A handful of former franchisees have bought the very franchise companies they were a part of or have become franchisors of different systems. The insight they've gained from being on the frontlines is invaluable. Remember that Dave was an early KFC franchisee.

✔ **Working for the franchisor:** You may want to stick with the same franchise, but work on the inside — at regional or corporate headquarters, for example. More commonly, the reverse happens — corporate employees become franchisees.

✔ **Becoming a consultant:** You may want to compete with Michael and become a franchise consultant. (Michael was a franchisee and a franchisor before he became a franchise consultant.) Depending on your years in the industry and your expertise, you may have a lot of insight to offer franchise neophytes. You've come a long way, baby!

Whatever your long-term plans, whether you choose to stay the course and continue with your location, expand the business into different cities, or sell and go to Tahiti, the one underlying thing you need to remember is that if you do your homework on the front end, if you understand the agreement, and if you plan for your future, you will have more options and probably a happier future.

Part V
But I Want to Be a Franchisor!

In this part . . .

Understanding what it takes to become a franchisor and how franchisors operate and grow their businesses is essential if you want to become a franchisor yourself. In this part, we look at the elements necessary for a company to become a franchisor and how great franchisors are set up to provide their franchisees with the support they promised to give them. We also discuss how franchisors expand their systems domestically and internationally.

Chapter 16

From Small Business to Franchisor

In This Chapter

▶ Determing whether your business is a franchisor candidate

▶ Marketing your business to franchisees

▶ Finding people to help you develop your franchise

*B*efore a single franchisee exists, there has to be a franchisor. In the next two chapters, we give you a very brief glimpse of what it takes to make the transition from running your own business to becoming a franchisor. You probably won't be surprised to find out that while you have to have legal agreements and disclosure documents to offer franchises, you first need to assess a host of business issues before you get anywhere near that point.

Feasibility

Being the only one offering your product or service isn't really important. Being the first franchisor offering similar products and services isn't, either. And certainly, although large, established franchisor competitors should make you take notice, being new isn't a real barrier, either — it may even be an advantage. All you have to do for inspiration is take a look at Dave Thomas and John Schnatter.

When Dave started Wendy's, many pundits said that the market for hamburger chains was already saturated. After all, large, established franchised hamburger chains existed back in August 1972 when Wendy's sold its first franchise to L.S. Hartzog. The same thing was said about John Schnatter's chances in the pizza industry when he founded Papa John's Pizza in 1983. Pizza Hut had begun selling franchises in 1959, Domino's in 1967, Pizza Inn in 1963 — and those were only a few of the established franchisors against which John had to compete. Looks like the experts got it wrong.

When I started Wendy's, a lot of people told me I was making a mistake, that the fast-food industry was saturated, and that America didn't need another hamburger restaurant. Every day, I'd see articles in some business publication about new fast-food places. But I knew something that they didn't know. I created Wendy's menu based on my 20 years of experience in the restaurant industry, and I knew what people wanted.

No matter what the pundits say, the market will always accept great products, services, and concepts that provide consumers with what they want — in the way they want it.

Large, established companies often suffer from Incumbent Inertia. That's a phrase we use to describe companies that feel so secure in their market position that they don't innovate their product and services and methods of delivery, don't feel threatened by new small competitors, and ultimately wake up to find out that they're not the big boy on the block anymore. Thank the lord for Incumbent Inertia — it allowed for the creation of Amazon.com, Starbucks, Kinko's, Home Depot, FedEx, CNN, and thousands more.

In this section, we look at the feasibility of taking your small business and growing it into a nationally known franchisor. You may even want to compete with Dave or John. Impossible? Who knows?

Deciding whether your business can be franchised

In the United States, believe it or not, except for the few states that require presale registration of a franchisor's disclosure document, no regulator ever has to see your franchise documents before you give them to a prospect. Becoming a franchisor is that easy. Even Uncle Sam doesn't want to see a copy. Outside of the United States, having a disclosure document may not even be required.

So — whatever business you're in — it probably can be franchised. That's not really the question to ask, though. The question you should be asking is, *should* my business be franchised?

Not everything should be franchised. You have to have a concept that you can teach and that's very simple to execute. There has to be an advantage to franchising for you and your future franchisees, and the concept has to be able to make money.

Meeting the legal requirements

When you franchise your business, you're offering a license to someone to operate under your brand name. In 14 states, before you begin to offer franchises you will have to present your legal document to state regulators whose approval is required before you begin to solicit franchisees. It's important to understand, though, that all the regulators are doing is making certain that your franchise documents meet the minimum legal standards in their states. There is no regulatory requirement that says that your franchise has to be based on a good idea. No requirement even says that it has to be a workable idea, that it's been tested, or that it's ever made a dime. (Those issues, if covered at all, can be disclosed as risk factors in your UFOC, which we cover in Chapter 6.) Your attorney's ability to get you registered is not an indication of the franchisability of your business; it's an indication that your attorney is a good legal draftsman.

Think of franchise registration as an automobile emissions test: If your car passes the test, it probably means that you can legally drive it on the street. It doesn't mean that the car will make it at Indy, or even that the car will make it out of first gear. Truthfully, it doesn't even assure you that you have enough gas to get it off the lot and down to the corner.

All *franchise registration* means is that you can legally drive your franchise off the lot. But before you begin to develop your franchise system, before you invest in the creation of brochures, before you invest in the creation of legal documents and hire franchise sales and support staff, you'd better first find out whether what you have is franchisable.

When my firm looks at determining whether a client is franchisable, we examine a broad spectrum of the client's business during a franchise diagnostic examination. We compare the client's performance against other franchised and nonfranchised businesses *(benchmarking)*, conduct analytical examinations, and perform other tests — all designed to help the client determine whether he should become a franchisor.

But we do follow one set of principles — even before the diagnostic examination begins. If your business is . . .

- ✔ Only a concept
- ✔ Only has a limited operating history
- ✔ Not profitable
- ✔ Not currently achieving a reasonable return on investment

then it is not franchisable.

The bottom line: Franchisability means that the franchisee is not the guinea pig in the relationship. You've operated the business — profitably, and more than once.

Looking at the criteria for a good franchise

What do you look for to determine whether your business can be franchised successfully? That all depends on your business. One size does not fit all. The following are some general criteria you need to look at.

Do you have a unit prototype?

If you don't have an operating business, *stop.* Go develop one. Run your prototype for a long while; make sure it works. Make certain you understand its ebb and flow, its seasonality, its customers, its suppliers, its competition, its positioning, and brand personality. Understand everything about it. After you've developed one location, develop another one, maybe more. Then come back.

You should have ownership of your trademarks and service marks, and they should be federally registered. Remember that franchising is all about licensing a brand. If you can't give the franchisee clean use of your name, what are you licensing?

Is replication feasible?

Okay, so you have an operating business; now you need to ask yourself some hard questions:

- ✔ Can you deliver "the look" to franchisees: the design, decor, signage, site criteria, and plans for construction?

- ✔ Are you able to tell franchisees how much it costs to develop the location — not just the fixed costs but the expenses from the day they meet you until the day they no longer have to fund working capital out of their own pockets? Remember that the franchisee is relying on you to be knowledgeable — especially when it comes to getting the business up and running.

- ✔ Do you have systems for operating your business? Remember — as a franchisor — you want your locations to run consistently so that every customer is delivered the same product, the same way, every time. Are you able to document those procedures in operating manuals, and do those procedures work all the time?

- ✔ Can you teach your system for operating the business to franchisees and their staff? Can you teach them in a reasonable period of time — or do they need to spend the next five years in class before they can open their doors?

I didn't want to be a franchisor, because I'd seen the problems the Colonel (Kentucky Fried Chicken) had run into. He didn't have the programs or the training. He had the concept, he had the chicken, and he had the pots. Well, he didn't really have the pots, 'cause they blew up on you all the time. His objective was to sell the secret spices and make $1,000 per month. There were no menus, there was nothing. Contracts were a handshake or written on a napkin. Today, you can't get away with what the Colonel gave his franchisees years ago. You need to provide not only the methods of preparing and delivering the products or services, but also the methods of operating the business.

Are your products and services any good?

Although having great products and services is no guarantee you'll succeed, it sure can't hurt. You need to find out the answers to the following questions:

- How do your customers view your products and services?
- Are they different from — better yet, are they superior to — your competitors'?
- Will your products and services carry to the next town, the next state, or across the country?

If you see new faces every day but wish some of the old ones would come back, you may have a problem. At some point, you'll run out of new customers. Having a product that someone wants to come back to buy — hopefully, often — is the measure you have to meet.

As a franchisor, your product and services also have to meet the test of distance. Even if you have the best products and services in town, do you know whether anyone outside your neighborhood will want them? To determine whether your concept has franchisability, opening up locations out of town is often necessary.

Will your customers want your products and services tomorrow?

Things change rapidly today. Products and services often have a half-life equivalent to that of a fruit fly in September. What's hot and "essential" today could be a faint memory tomorrow. Here are some things you need to consider:

- Are consumer-purchasing patterns changing, and will they affect the popularity of your product and services?
- Can other companies absorb your product or service? If they do, will that place you at a competitive disadvantage?
- Are alternatives to your products or services being introduced or even discussed?
- Do you have a strategy to adapt to changing market conditions?

You need to be alert that your business isn't simply the latest fad. Franchise systems have to have staying power and need to be built on a consumer demand that is growing and secure.

There's never a guarantee that a "hot" product will stay hot forever; the graveyard is full of once hot products. Remember all those chains that specialized in serving frozen yogurt? The few that have survived did so by *consolidating* (purchasing other yogurt chains or being purchased by other companies), selling their product to other vendors, co-branding with other franchisors, or adding other products to their menus. Many today think that the same fate is in store for some of those chains that specialize in selling vitamin- and mineral-enriched health drinks. How long before others add those products to their menus? Maybe as a part of a menu, sure, but as a singe-product franchise for the long haul? You be the judge.

Will consumers need your products and services tomorrow?

A long list of products and services has vanished either because consumers didn't need them any longer or needed them less often. You need to determine the following:

- How improvements in the products you service will affect the frequency of their use by consumers
- Whether you will be able to adjust your price to offset the lower use
- Whether any environmental regulations are being proposed that would affect your industry

We don't have to go all the way back to buggy whips in the age of automobiles to find examples. We simply need to look at the specialized automotive tune-up franchises in the age of computers.

Remember the days when your car got a tune-up every 15,000 miles? Those were the days when the only options for automobile service were the new car dealer that charged high prices and gave you bad service or the local service station that charged you high prices and gave you bad service. Automotive tune-up franchisors flourished because they met a market need: a convenient and fair-priced service that the customer needed on a frequent basis.

Cars are pushing 100,000 miles today between tune-ups. Engines have become so sophisticated that soon the only place you'll find a timing light will be the Smithsonian. Servicing an engine now requires computers and other expensive, high-tech equipment. New car dealerships are doing a great job of retaining their customers by marketing quality service at fairer pricing and bundling it with other scheduled maintenance, such as oil changes and tire rotations. Specialized tune-up opportunity in the next millennium? Probably not as a stand-alone specialty. Technological improvements in cars took care of that.

Do you know who your competition is?

If you sell pizza, are your only competitors pizza parlors, or do people eat other food? If you become a franchisor of pizza parlors, will your only competitors come from the other pizza parlor franchisors? Guess what? People invest in other types of business opportunities.

As a franchisor, you will have at least two levels of competition:

- ✔ Other businesses that offer products and services similar to yours. Those are the folks who compete head-to-head with your franchisees and company-owned locations.
- ✔ Other investment opportunities and franchise opportunities that compete for your targeted franchisee's dollars.

You need to understand and define what your competitive strengths really are. Are they innovation, quality, speed of delivery, and cost? Will your franchise system have endurance, the ability to upgrade products and services, innovative computer technology, an e-commerce platform or superior real estate site selection capabilities? As a franchisor, you need to be sure that you possess these strengths.

Who are your competitors? Try this definition: If they're targeting your customers — and a purchase from them means fewer purchases from you — then by definition, they are your competitor.

If you're not brutally honest in looking at yourself in comparison with the competition, you'd better find a way to hypnotize the public — because you forgot to send them the rose-colored glasses you're wearing.

Are your growth plans realistic?

If all you want is a couple of locations, company-owned operations are probably a far better way to grow than franchising. But if your plan is to open 50 franchises in the next 12 months, then franchising may be the right way to grow.

Many of the stories in the pop culture media lead you to believe that franchising is a quick growth strategy. It can be, but for most new franchisors, it's not as fast as they expected. Depending on the industry and the investment range, a typical franchisor opens fewer than ten locations in the first year of operation; the average is probably closer to five. Five to ten new locations in a year is still a pretty impressive growth rate for a new company.

You need to ask yourself these questions:

- ✔ Are my expansion goals realistic? Can I support those goals financially?
- ✔ Can I operate my existing business while I'm developing and operating the new franchise system? What happens when I begin to open in more than one market?

✔ Are there sufficient numbers of prospects available to meet my goals?

✔ Will this be the type of franchise people will be proud to own?

✔ Will prospects be able to afford my franchise?

We're not talking about simply affording your franchise fees and royalties but everything, including site development, interior design, equipment, training costs, and working capital — all the costs to get into the business. If your targeted prospect can't afford to get into the business, you have to either rethink and adjust who your prospect is or find a way to reduce the entrance costs.

What skills do your franchisees need to run the show?

To expand your franchise system, you need franchisees who can do the job. Here are some questions you need to ask yourself:

✔ Are the skills that your prospects need so specialized that finding enough prospects will be difficult?

✔ Will your franchisees be able to hire enough help with the necessary skills?

✔ Do you have the ability to train franchisees and their staff in your procedures, policies, and systems?

✔ Can the training be completed satisfactorily in a reasonable period? (See Chapter 7 for a discussion of training.)

For your business to be franchisable, you will need a pool of potential franchisees who are not only willing to buy your franchise but also can operate it to your standards. That also means they have to be able to recruit sufficient staff with the skill level to do the job. Is there a skilled labor pool available to support your franchise system's development and growth?

Will anyone want your franchise?

We know that your Mom keeps telling you that you should start a franchise. Everybody she knows says so. But has anyone *besides* your Mom ever told you that? Eventually, people outside the family have to step up to the plate. Will they?

Before you develop your franchise, you should know something about your potential franchisees.

✔ Do you know what the profile of your typical franchisee is?

✔ Who's going to be attracted to your opportunity?

You can't wait until you're trying to sell franchises to figure out the answers to the preceding questions, because you may find

Doc in a Box

We're making up a new franchise called "Doc in a Box."

Imagine this scenario: In managed health care, hospitals are cutting costs, outsourcing everything they can, reducing their need for nurses and medical technicians, and looking forward to the day when they will run more like high-tech hotels. The doctors and other service providers will rent space in operating rooms and will provide all the other services performed by today's hospital. The hospital ultimately will become a shell where professionals share services and the hospital advertises for patients. Sort of like a medical time-share. Is this health care of the future? Maybe.

You are a well-known arthroscopic surgeon. You agree with our view of the future and think you can capitalize on the trends. You're thinking of franchising either one of these concepts:

✔ Branded arthroscopic surgical practices, where doctors will buy franchises and offer their services under your brand.

✔ A business that maintains and sanitizes arthroscopic surgical suites, surgical tools, and equipment.

Which one could be franchisable?

Joining a surgical franchise probably would have little appeal to surgeons. Surgeons have invested too many years and dollars in becoming surgeons. Besides, many of them have built their practices on their personal reputations and are not likely to want to work under your brand or be good franchisees. What compelling market forces would support a branded surgical practice called "Doc in a Box"? What benefit would it bring to the hospital? Would it attract new patients? Would it improve the doctor's performance? Probably not.

On the other hand, the cleaning and maintenance franchise may be the perfect vehicle. Nurses and technicians are trained and licensed and understand the requirements of operating rooms; as hospitals downsize, there are fewer jobs to go around, and the ones that are available may be lower-paying positions not attractive to nurses and technicians. There may be a market need for such a franchise. Hospitals have to provide the surgeons with a proper operating facility and need to maintain the doctor's tools and equipment, but they need to do it in a less costly way.

Hospitals may be reluctant to sign contracts with local independent providers, but the branded quality and consistency found under a franchise is something they can count on.

That's the difference. Market need. The cleaning and maintenance franchise may be a business that could benefit from branding. A sufficient number of qualified potential franchisees are likely to be looking for a business just like yours. Surgery franchise? No. Surgical suite maintenance? Maybe.

✔ The pool of potential franchisees out there may not be sufficient to meet your expansion goals.

✔ The pool of franchisees may be sufficient, but the pool has little interest in what you have to offer.

✔ The cost of acquiring the franchises may be too high or take too long.

The cost and timing of acquiring franchisees will affect your financial viability and therefore your franchisability.

Do you have the ability to operate a franchise system?

You may be the best mechanic in all of automotive history or the best hamburger cook that ever faced a grill. You may have run a company-operated system for many years, but you've never been a franchisor. Ask yourself these questions:

 ✔ Can you and your existing staff operate and grow the business?

 ✔ Can you afford to hire any additional talent you may need?

Having the right people in place to execute a franchise strategy is important. If all you can afford to hire is you and your spouse, and you are already running your existing business, you're in for some interesting times.

What type of support can you deliver to your franchisees?

Great franchisors try to deliver all the elements their franchisees need for success; others provide very little. For some, fewer services are reflected in lower fees, but for many, there doesn't seem to be much of a link between fees and services.

You need to deliver a *sustainable competitive advantage* to your system. This means continually providing products, services, marketing, and so on that enable your franchise system to operate at the head of the pack for the long term. Ask yourself these questions:

 ✔ What type of support programs do you need to put into place to assist your franchisees and to operate and grow the franchise system? Can you put those systems into place?

 ✔ How will you provide continual training, field and headquarters support, marketing support, research and development, new product introduction, and all the other services required to make yours a great franchise system?

 ✔ What about research and development? Can you develop additional products or improvements to those you currently offer to keep your franchise fresh and your franchisees profitable? Before you say yes, be sure that you know how you'll do it.

How much should you charge for your franchise? Will it be enough?

To be franchisable, you must have a business, not just a concept, and the business has to be profitable. But now you need to look at the business once it becomes a franchise.

You're going to expect your franchisees to pay you a fee to get into the business *(franchise fee),* continuing fees *(royalties),* and maybe other fees, such as for additional training, marketing, and advertising.

Maybe you'll earn income through the sale of products to your franchisees or collect income or rebates from manufacturers on system-wide purchases. Some franchisors lease equipment or property or have other sources of revenue. Once those fees are deducted from the bottom line, you need to know the answers to these questions:

✔ Will the franchisee still be profitable?

✔ Will the franchisee receive an acceptable return on investment?

Even if the answer to both of those questions is yes, you still have to consider other issues:

✔ Are there enough prospective franchisees who can afford your franchise?

✔ What will be each franchisee's total up-front investment?

✔ How much of the initial investment will be needed in cash?

✔ Can a franchisee finance any portion of the initial investment?

If your prospective franchisee is the operator of a single-unit mom-and-pop business, she may be asking herself whether the franchise will give her a better income than the job she's thinking of leaving. However, if the franchisee is a sophisticated or institutional investor, and many franchisees are, she will ask whether the franchise can generate a sufficient return on her investment consistently and predictably. She will want to know how the return on your franchise stacks up against her other investment opportunities, and how long before she can break even. When looking at the total investment required by a franchisee, you also need to factor in some other realities of your business:

✔ Does your type of business have any serious short-term or seasonal cash flow problems? If so, these problems could affect franchisees' total investment, depending on when they buy your franchise.

✔ Will franchisees need to carry a significant level of inventory?

✔ How often will franchisees be able to turn over their inventory?

✔ If food is involved, what's the rate of spoilage?

You need to have a complete grasp of your assumptions and facts in order to determine what initial investment will be required by your franchisees.

And don't forget that the franchisee is not the only one in this relationship. To meet your own needs, you must know the answers to the following questions as they relate to your future franchise company:

- ✔ Do you have any idea how much it will cost to develop a franchise system for your company?
- ✔ Can you afford to develop a quality system?
- ✔ Will you be able to finance any shortfall in your development costs?
- ✔ Will the fees you charge be enough to sustain you?
- ✔ Will you be able to achieve a reasonable return on your investment?

Establishing your fees is a complex process that requires you to balance the needs of the franchisee with those of the franchisor.

Setting your fees

Setting your fees is not as simple as opening up one of the franchise directories and seeing what the competing franchise systems are charging. Basing your fees on what the average franchisor is charging is an even sillier notion. Unless you establish your fees based upon the economic realities of your franchise system, you're heading for potential disaster. Marketability against the competition needs to be a factor, but recruiting franchisees to your franchise system, based upon a fee structure that is too low to cover costs and give you an adequate return, only means you will be a franchisor for a very short period of time.

Your goal is not just to sell franchises. Your goal is to sell them in a way that allows you to meet your commitments, stay in business, and make a return on your investment. Your investors and your future franchisees are counting on it.

Before you can set your fees, you need to consider these issues:

- ✔ How much will it cost for you to deliver the services you intend to deliver to your future franchisees?
- ✔ Are the fees high enough to allow you to pay those costs and still get the financial return you're counting on?
- ✔ When you establish your fees, you need to be careful. If you set the fees at too high a level, your franchise may not be marketable against the competition. If you set your fees at too low a level, it may damage your ability to provide the services you've promised to your franchisees.

A trick used by some of the *franchise packagers* (a less-than-complimentary term to describe legal and consulting firms that develop new franchise systems; as if one size fits all there's more to come on franchise packagers later in this chapter) is to base fees on those of direct competitors. They often simply look up the fees in *Entrepreneur Magazines Annual 500* or some other franchisor listing. Even if your franchisees offer the identical products or services as those of another franchisor, you probably won't be offering identical services to your franchisees; you probably will not have the same cost structure, growth strategy, exit strategy, or a host of other variables.

Setting your fees based solely on what the competition charges is foolish. Doing so may save your legal or consulting packager the time and money required to do the hard work of financial modeling, but it may leave you with fees that hurt your franchise system's viability. Your fees need to be based on the reality of your franchise and your business, not on a shortcut to save the packager time. Franchise packagers — both in the legal and consulting community — that shortchange the strategic process should be avoided. Plenty of franchise professionals in the legal and consulting arena — certainly the majority — do it the right way.

In developing your fee structure, a part of your decision rests on the questions of what markets you intend to enter and how many units you will require a franchisee to develop. On a per-unit basis, supporting one franchisee who owns ten units is cheaper than supporting ten franchisees who each own one unit. Likewise, servicing a market that grows to ten units in two years is cheaper than servicing a market that grows to ten units in ten years. How you grow the business and what markets you will be required to service will affect how realistic your fees and income projections are.

When you establish fees for your franchise system, you need to be satisfied that you have answers to some other basic questions:

- How long before you will be making any money?
- What is your investment hurdle, and will the system generate that return for you?
- Do you plan to use a licensing method, such as master franchising? (See Chapter 2 for a discussion of master franchising.) The franchisor may share with the master franchisee a portion of the initial franchise fee and continuing royalty payments. If you have to share a portion of your income, how will doing so affect your financial performance and your system's ability to deliver the promised services?

Being able to set fees at an appropriate level isn't easy. Many franchisors have long-term difficulties because they don't establish their fees correctly.

So, what do you think? Are you ready to become a franchisor? Feasibility is only the first step. You still have a lot more to do.

Prospective franchisor entrepreneurs often have difficulty in objectively determining whether their businesses are franchisable. For that reason, you may find it useful to work with a professional who can help you through the process. The International Franchise Association's Council of Franchise

Suppliers is a good source for franchise consultants who can assist you. You can find a list of those companies by going to the IFA Web site at www.franchise.org.

What kind of business lends itself to franchising?

Most any business lends itself to franchising, but historically, companies that sell their products or services at retail have had wider appeal. Here's some advice on deciding whether your company can be successfully franchised:

- ✔ Most restaurant concepts can be franchised, but those that need chefs rather than cooks or that have intricate menus and recipes are more difficult.

- ✔ Companies whose products and services have broad consumer acceptance are a natural as long as the market trends support long-term viability and growth.

- ✔ Companies whose operating margins allow for franchise fees to be charged and still leave an adequate return on investment for both the franchisee and franchisor usually are suitable for franchising.

- ✔ Companies in *fragmented industries* (that's an industry where most of the businesses are independent operators) that would benefit from branded consolidation are franchising candidates. A good example of this was the hair care industry 30 years ago — it was mostly barber shops and salons owned by barbers and stylists. Flash ahead, and now you have large franchise chains like Supercuts and Great Clips dominating the market. It's still a fragmented market — even 30 years later — so the opportunity for growth is still good.

- ✔ Companies in a stable or growing industry, unburdened by significant regulation, are franchisable.

- ✔ Companies that have systems that are simple to execute, that can draw from a large pool of qualified candidates, or that can train franchisees to use the technology in a reasonable period of time will work as a franchise.

Franchisee Marketing Objectives and System Support Programs

Let's assume that your concept is franchisable. Congratulations. Do you hurry up and start to develop your legal documents and marketing brochures? Hold off a bit more. You have a host of business issues to focus on and decisions to make before you bring in the legal and marketing troops.

Selecting the right markets

It's not enough to say you want to grow in the top 100 cities; you need to determine where and when, as well as which markets are your primary targets and which are secondary targets.

Franchisors need to have a market penetration strategy in order to determine the timing for entry into new markets and the critical mass requirements in those markets. *Critical mass* refers to the number of units a franchisor should optimally develop in a market.

An unfocused expansion strategy is potentially dangerous to a franchisor, because it costs money to service distant, isolated locations, and the entire system may suffer for lack of attention to quality standards and other aspects of performance. Failure to establish and stick with a rational expansion strategy also wastes marketing resources. "Shotgun" marketing may also not be as effective as targeted development, because it doesn't give you any focus on where you will be growing. An unplanned growth strategy can be very dangerous for new franchisors.

An unfocused market development strategy (one in which the areas for development are selected by where the phone calls from prospective franchisees come from) causes the company to be reactive rather than proactive, at all levels. For example, without a market development plan, the company may miss sales opportunities because of failure to register its franchise in key states, or incur unnecessary expense to register in states where it is not prudent to expand yet.

An unfocused market strategy also doesn't allow you to make business decisions based upon measurable criteria. For example, franchisors need to evaluate the various methods of expansion available to them (including company-owned, individual, and multi-unit strategies) in different markets. To be prudent, a franchisor should include critical mass reviews in selecting markets. Critical mass reviews help a franchisor reduce its field service and distribution costs per unit, and are the most effective way for them to determine local marketing possibilities.

The goal for franchisors is not merely to enter new markets, but to enter them successfully. Therefore, franchisors must distinguish their core market strategy from their tertiary market strategies (*core markets* being major and secondary urban areas, *tertiary* being all others).

Keep in mind that it's expensive to support one franchisee with field support and advertising if it's the only franchisee in the market and market critical mass requires that you have 15 units in the market. Defining your critical mass requirements enables you to plan your growth.

If you already have company-owned locations spread out over a host of markets, evaluate whether it may be appropriate to franchise those stores and put the proceeds from the sale into growing company-owned units elsewhere. Doing so is part of the process we call "repositioning the inventory of locations."

Defining the franchisee profile

Not every person who calls up a franchisor and says he wants to become a franchisee is the right candidate.

Franchise systems that let all candidates in simply because they have the money use a franchisee selection strategy we call in franchising "fogging the mirror." If the prospective franchisee is alive, as indicated by their breath on a mirror, and has enough money in their checkbook, welcome on board. In fact, some franchisors who use brokers to select their franchisees or sell franchises through the mail never meet their franchisee until they attend training. This is similar to selecting a candidate for local office who died a week before election but still had enough votes to get elected. (By the way, that really happened.)

In defining who should be a franchisee, you need to determine many traits of a franchisee, including

- ✔ Who has the ability to successfully operate your locations?
- ✔ What financial resources does a franchisee require?
- ✔ What background does a franchisee need?
- ✔ Are there prospective franchisees living in the markets in which you want to develop franchises?
- ✔ Can you determine whether a franchisee fits well with your concept, organization, and other franchisees?

The franchisee profile that you develop will be based on your criteria and will serve as a set of guidelines that will help you select suitable candidates for operating a successful franchise. In developing the profile of your franchise candidate, you begin to understand who your potential franchisee is and what sources of marketing will be most productive for you to use in recruiting them.

Marketing for franchisees

Shotgun advertising (advertising to the general population, without criteria as to whom the franchisee is or what markets you want to develop in) may generate potential franchise leads, but it won't necessarily generate franchisees you want and need. That's one of the problems some franchisors are having with leads coming from the Internet. After all, getting leads over the Internet is great, but how do you sort out the real candidates from the 12-year-olds with a mouse?

In establishing your marketing plan, you will need to answer at least four questions:

- ✔ What are the appropriate sources for recruiting franchisees that best fit the franchisee profile you have established?

- ✔ What methods will you use for evaluating potential franchisees (financial, personal, and so on)?

- ✔ What procedures are appropriate for approving franchisees?

- ✔ What administrative procedures and negotiating strategies will you need to have in place to close the sale — and do it legally?

To be successful in closing franchise sales, you need to address these basic issues before you start spending money on marketing — not after.

In marketing for franchisees, franchisors use a wide variety of marketing and advertising vehicles. The ones they select are based upon their determination of which vehicle will reach their targeted prospect, and may include

- ✔ Franchise trade shows

- ✔ Local and national newspapers

- ✔ The electronic media — television and radio

- ✔ Franchise directories

- ✔ General business publications

- ✔ Franchise-specific publications

- ✔ Franchisor Web sites

- ✔ Articles in publications developed through public relations

- ✔ Franchise literature exhibited in existing locations

- ✔ Targeted mailings to potential franchisees that meet the franchisor's criteria

- ✔ Trade missions

Supporting your franchisees

In supporting your franchise system, you need to always focus on two basic areas:

- ✔ How do you want your company-owned and franchised locations to operate at the local level?

- ✔ What types of support programs and corporate organization must be in place to meet that requirement?

The keys to establishing a successful support structure are:

- ✔ Determining what needs to be accomplished

- ✔ Selecting the right people to accomplish your goals

- ✔ Providing your support team with the necessary information to do their jobs

- ✔ Giving your support team clear direction

- ✔ Providing them with training and the resources to do their job properly

- ✔ Trusting their judgment and ability to make decisions

Great franchisors develop their support team to be ready, willing, and able to provide leadership and support to the system's local operations.

Field personnel are only one element of the support a franchisor provides to its franchisees. But field personnel are probably one of the most critical elements in the assistance franchisors can provide to their franchisees. Most franchisors provide some level of field support to their franchisees and company-owned locations. Some franchisors use one set of field personnel to work with company-owned operations and another to work with franchised operations, while some combine the field support organization.

The key is that, regardless of whether franchisors use one support team or multiple support teams, the field support in great franchise systems is organized around the following principles:

- ✔ Field visits are for more than just monitoring franchisee compliance.

- ✔ Field visits are based upon established standards, and one of those standards is that field consultants are judged by the measurable impact they make on the performance of the locations they are responsible for.

- ✔ Field visits are set to provide a minimum number of visits to a franchisee during a period of time, but the overall number and frequency of the visits are based on the needs of the local unit.

✔ Field visits provide the franchisors with the ability to measure unit results and, more importantly, field consultants have the ability to rapidly communicate the results throughout the company so that action can be taken to provide support to the franchisee.

✔ Field visits are designed to improve unit and system performance.

To accomplish these goals, the first step great franchisors do is to define the standards for field visits. The franchisor's entire organization has to understand what the field organization is trying to accomplish, and the field consultants are provided with the training, tools, and support required to do their job.

To do their jobs successfully, field consultants must

✔ Understand unit operations, because they have operated units.

✔ Be trained so that they understand how to work with unit operators — both company-owned and franchisee — to improve their operations.

✔ Have tools such as compliance checklists and up-to-date system performance information, including sales, cost of sales, and cost of labor — anything that helps them help franchisees improve their efficiency and grow their businesses.

Determining the frequency of visits is important in providing support to franchisees. Many systems visit every franchisee on a standard cycle: once a week, twice a month, every six weeks . . . you get the idea. But not every location needs the same level of support. Some locations are humming along and are leaders in performance. Others may be close to closing their doors.

All field visits do not need to be done in person. As important as the personal visits to locations are, other methods may be used to keep in regular contact with franchisees and managers, including telephone, e-mail, letters, and so on. These non-personal visits allow the field staff to stay in touch with local operations and market needs.

Successful franchisors capture information about their franchisee's performance and develop methods to analytically measure critical performance indicators, including the following:

✔ Sales

✔ Cost of sales

✔ Labor cost

✔ Shrinkage

✔ New customer percentages

✔ Return customer percentages

> ✔ Customer complaints
> ✔ Other key ratios

Based on the collected information and continual communication between the field staff, headquarters, and the local operations, field consultants define the needs of the franchise locaton, determine what they want to accomplish during their visits to franchisees, and determine the frequency in which they visit a location.

The goals for field visits are different for each location, and these goals may change each time the consultants visit a location. Staff retention may be an issue one month, and the next month, the problem may be poor results from local marketing. Or the concern may be a small elevation in product waste or theft (we call that *shrinkage*), which could be an indication that something is wrong with local unit supervision. Trained and intelligent field consultants can take the information available, analyze it, and customize their visits to have real impact.

The role of the field consultant is to act as the franchisor's first line of support to the system's location. It is one of the most tangible measures of support provided by a franchisor.

Becoming an effective franchisor: Tactical Execution

When Rocky Balboa was training for his fight against Apollo Creed (you didn't think you could learn anything from B action flicks like *Rocky,* but you can learn anywhere), his trainer, Mickey, told him that the only way to win was speed — greased-lightning speed. The same is true of business today.

To be effective today, companies are abandoning old techniques that required all strategies to be made at headquarters by strategic planning teams. (*Strategic planning teams* are usually a group of folks whose primary job is to create four-volume doorstops designed to tell the people who are paid to execute the strategy what they should do).

Companies today are adopting tactical execution processes and are becoming tactical companies. In a tactical company, a multidisciplinary team made up of the people who have to execute the strategy now do the planning. In addition to operations, field support, training, marketing, legal, procurement, and other company personnel, these teams include outsiders whose job is to push the organization outside of its comfort zones and, most importantly, franchisees. Many companies also include younger staff that can challenge the company's sacred cows — and also near-retirement curmudgeons who can honestly assess the company's past activities.

To be effective, a tactical company moves the decision making from being the sole responsibility of headquarters personnel to a process where decisions are made quickly throughout the organization. In those organizations, here's what's happening:

✔ Strategic thinking takes place at all levels. Every member of the organization thinks strategically about customers' needs, competitors, and competitive advantage.

✔ Every member is provided with information on the business, in real time — and the information is not limited just to his or her piece of the rock. To execute effectively, all members of the team have knowledge not only about their own business but also about the competition and the environment they work in.

✔ Organization members understand and believe in the company's mission and vision.

✔ Strategies are crafted rather than calculated.

✔ Planning is an evolutionary process, and initial decisions and external events flow together.

✔ Changes in the company's plan aren't viewed as errors in forecasting. Change is celebrated when it seizes on competitive opportunities and is based on an organization that has the knowledge to react quickly and intelligently.

✔ Learning, experimentation, and adaptation are critical elements:

  • Quick response replaces delays in decisions from headquarters.

  • Execution is based on the reality of the marketplace — measured in real time.

✔ Execution of the plan is flexible.

  • It deals with market disruptions created by technology and other changes.

  • It relies heavily on conceptual abilities.

  • It continuously monitors the company's brand positioning.

  • It uses knowledge in real time.

  • It embraces speculation — the future moves quickly.

  • It measures results as they are happening.

  • It connects information to the decision makers.

  • It expands who those decision makers are.

Tactical execution is not an abandonment or substitution for planning. It's a philosophical shift in how the plan is developed, executed, measured, and adjusted so that you can stay ahead of the competition.

Operating tactically is easy once you understand the basics, but you need to have the right corporate culture, information, and trust in your team.

Your corporate culture

Your corporate culture helps to ensure the consistency and quality of your products and services. This culture conveys to everyone in the system how the business is supposed to operate at all levels (headquarters, field operations, franchise, and company-owned locations). When everyone understands the corporate culture, support for the franchise system is based on the system's needs rather than upon fixed rules set by headquarters.

To ensure consistency and quality, the corporate culture

- Must be the central focus of the franchise system.
- Must be the rallying point for franchisees, unit personnel, field staff, headquarters personnel, and consumers.
- Must be the "fabric" that transcends the manuals, the forms, and the written procedures.
- Must generate the feeling of "ownership" in the brand and, most important, loyalty.

It enables the franchise system to be entrepreneurial in its focus on system support, as well as proactive to change, and allows the system to take advantage of opportunities as they present themselves.

Information management

Franchisors need to be ready to accumulate and disseminate information throughout your system — and that information is not just the numbers but the actual experiences of the system's unit managers, franchisees, field staff, and so on. The key is to share the relevant information so that ideas and solutions can be developed.

To be effective, a tactical company needs to

- Learn what its competition is doing.
- Learn what its consumers are looking for.
- Learn from its unit management — both franchised and company owned.
- Learn from its support personnel in the field and at headquarters.
- Learn from its vendors — they can be early indicators of trends and actions by your competitors.

Franchise Advisory Councils

I was a stakeholder in a franchise with Kentucky Fried Chicken, so I know what it's like from the franchisee side. Franchisees are valuable, and it's right to expect franchisees to work hard for the money they make.

At Wendy's, we think of our franchisees as our customers. It may sound like an odd concept, but it's true. They are paying the royalties for certain services that we provide, and we have an obligation to satisfy their needs.

We also think of our franchisees as partners — not in the legal sense but in the operational sense. We have a Franchise Advisory Council that meets regularly to discuss issues that affect our franchise community. Members of the FAC are a sounding board for changes or improvements we plan for our stores. For Wendy's to be successful, we all must work together toward a common goal: to serve the best-tasting hamburgers in the business and be the restaurant of choice for our customers.

Franchisees are included at all levels of the information-gathering and decision-making process. The information they have is discovered first-hand from working with the system's customers.

Accumulating and sharing the information throughout the network is vital in a tactical company. Information mobilizes the organization, fosters innovations, allows for the sharing of new ideas, and celebrates changes. Doing so allows your system to remain competitive and flexible.

Managing a business today without real-time information is like asking commercial pilots to fly from California to New York using a sextant, the moon, and the stars to guide them. Care to get on board that plane?

Even in a company that uses a tactical approach to decision making, the franchisor is making the decisions concerning how the brand (including products, services, marketing, and so on) is provided to the public. Being tactical requires many time-sensitive decisions to be made outside of headquarters. Becoming tactical is a management and competitive tool. Allowing decisions to be made outside headquarters is not a threat to the control a franchisor has over how the system operates.

Take chances, make some mistakes, and move forward

Look for opportunities and adjust your tactics to capitalize on both short- and long-term openings when they appear. In order to be able to do so,

- Your corporate strategy must be clear and easily understood by those empowered to make changes.

- You have to communicate tactical changes quickly and effectively throughout the system.

✔ You need to solicit feedback and analyze that feedback quickly.

✔ You must be willing to adjust your tactics to meet the needs of the market.

✔ You have to trust your team.

The last point — trust your team — is probably the most important element for a company to be truly tactical in its approach to managing change. Business today requires companies to be flexible, innovative, and market driven. The execution of your strategy must be flexible enough to allow the system to seize upon competitive opportunities without constantly seeking senior management's approval of every change in tactics. Waiting on members of the senior management team to bless every change costs you opportunities that may vanish while their decisions are being made.

This advice is not a call to anarchy. Far from it. It's a call to empowering your organization at every level to do the right thing for your business, simply because the speed of competitive change in the new millennium doesn't give you the luxury of time.

A tactical approach to business requires those in senior management to trust that they have put into place an organization that can execute the mission — without them. It requires them to be able to say the following:

✔ We trust that we hired intelligent personnel at all levels of the company.

✔ We trust that we have not hidden anything from them.

✔ We trust that we have defined the mission and vision of the company clearly.

✔ We trust that we have given them the information to do their job in real time.

✔ We trust that they can see opportunities.

✔ We trust that they can formulate changes to tactics quickly.

✔ We trust that they will execute against the mission.

✔ We are certain that we have the structure in place to facilitate clear communication within the business.

✔ We are certain we have the ability to measure results, in real time, and the confidence to continually make changes when they are necessary.

If you're a new franchisor, use what you learned in the feasibility examination as a jumping-off point to develop into a tactical company. If you're an established franchisor, build on what you know, but don't get locked into what you think you know. Because converting to a tactical company may create some initial stresses in an existing organization's management, it is usually a good idea to go outside of the company and seek assistance from advisors who can work with you in making this change.

How leadership can change a franchise system

Mail Boxes Etc. (MBE), a franchise system based in San Diego, California, began operations in 1980. At that time, it was one of the "lowest-tech" operations you could imagine: It rented mailboxes to the public, sold stamps, and wrapped and shipped packages. It also provided faxing and photocopy services. Its biggest competition was the U.S. Postal Service. Even in a low-tech world, having as your principal competitor one of the historically poorest run operations, the United States Post Office, opens up some interesting advantages.

A few years back, MBE hired Jim Amos as president and chief operating officer, and the world changed at MBE. When Jim joined MBE, the system clearly had its problems. It had a high turnover in franchisees, stagnant unit sales, and franchisee litigation. But it also had 3,000 locations strategically placed throughout the United States and in 20 countries worldwide.

Jim is a former Marine and can easily be described as driven. Those who have worked with him (including coauthor Michael, who served with Jim on the board of directors of the International Franchise Association) consider him one of the smartest and most creative executives in franchising today. Tie those talents in with an unsurpassed moral compass, and you have the new MBE.

If e-commerce has one major hurdle today — and there are several — it's how consumers who are unsatisfied with their purchases can return the merchandise to a cyberstore. With an investment of $10,000,000 in satellite dishes and communications technology, MBE converted its "bricks and mortar" franchise system into a powerhouse "clicks and mortar" operation. One example is its recent deal with eBay, one of the largest e-commerce sites on the Web today.

MBE now offers eBay's sellers and buyers the bricks-and-mortar infrastructure to solve their packing and shipping problems. MBE provides a place where eBay's customers can go for the delivery, inspection, and return of merchandise.

Mix some old bricks-and-mortar locations with new e-commerce technology, combine in some vision and a driven leader, and you have the new MBE — a clicks-and-mortar operation.

Making changes to take advantage of e-commerce

One thing is certain: Business today requires companies to move quickly if they want to succeed. They need to be able to anticipate events, take advantage of opportunities that present themselves quickly, and more importantly, create new opportunities.

A great example of this is the effect e-commerce is having on franchising today. Some franchisors were so focused on their traditional businesses and the belief that their only competitor was other franchise systems that they didn't focus their attention on what the rest of the world was doing — creating e-commerce Web-based businesses. (Remember our discussion about Incumbent Inertia in the beginning of the section on "Feasibility," earlier in this chapter.)

Now these franchisors are in a scramble to solicit support from their franchisees for the changes they'll need to execute on an e-commerce platform. For many, their competitive positions will be severely harmed because of their incumbent inertia.

Franchisors can have a real advantage in e-commerce today. They've established locations — what we call "bricks and mortar." When you successfully tie an e-commerce operation to an established bricks and mortar distribution system, presto chango, you get "clicks and mortar" — the marriage of old and new. While franchisors may have the right to establish e-commerce sites on the Web, having franchisee participation and support is important.

Helping your attorney prepare your legal documents

After you complete all your tactical planning, you still need to have legal agreements developed. The agreements convey the information that legally binds you and your franchisee. In the United States and some other countries, you also have to prepare a disclosure document. (See Chapter 6 for a discussion of the UFOC.)

Tactical planning documents are long and may contain information that your attorneys really don't need. Besides, they are usually so voluminous that your attorney probably doesn't want to see them anyway. But, to be effective, your attorney needs information.

We recommend that you prepare for your counsel a document called a business overlay. A *business overlay* is a simplified version of your tactical plan that explains all the key issues to your attorney so that she can prepare the franchise agreements, franchise offering circular, and other required legal documents.

After you complete the tactical plan, meet with your attorneys and present them your business overlay. Seek their input and advice, because they have experience that will prove beneficial. Certainly respect their advice when it comes to the law. If you're smart, you've involved them in much of the tactical planning process. Most have business experience that will prove extremely helpful in the development of your strategy. However, remember that franchising is primarily a business strategy, not a legal strategy. Your legal agreements need to reflect the decisions you made in your plan. If the language in your agreements doesn't reflect the thinking of management, speak to your attorneys before they are completed. They may be able to provide you with alternatives.

I don't always listen to attorneys. If you did everything that the attorney thought you should do, you wouldn't do anything.

Most attorneys practicing franchise law have forms and checklists to help their clients prepare legal documents. These are usually well-developed forms that deal with many of the business and other issues you may have addressed during your tactical planning. Review these forms and checklists and make sure that you answer all your attorney's questions in the business overlay. Doing so ensures that your attorneys can prepare the required documents for your system in an efficient and reasonably priced manner and that their end product reflects the business realities of your system. This process is not something you should do only when you start your franchise system. Thoroughly reviewing your franchise agreements and making changes, as your tactical plans require, is an ongoing effort.

Getting Help in Developing Your Franchise Program

Developing a franchise program is a complicated procedure. In addition to all the business issues that franchisors need to address is the reality that franchising is a highly regulated business. How you choose to proceed with the development of your franchise program is important to your success as a franchisor. Doing it yourself: success or suicide?

Sometimes prospective franchisors try to save money on professional fees by going it alone. They order self-help kits with fill-in-the-blank forms for franchise agreements and UFOCs (see Chapter 6). Or they get a copy of an established franchisor's UFOC and figure that if it worked once, it should work again. They scan the document into their computer and cut and paste the established franchisor's information with theirs. Is this an option? We don't think so.

The design, development, and implementation of a franchise system is complex. Unless you've spent your professional life as a franchise executive and have established a franchise system before, it's not the playing field for amateurs today.

If your goal is to save money because you're short of capital to pay professional fees, remember that the fees are the least expensive portion of developing and operating a franchise system. If you're short of capital, maybe you should wait until you have the money you need before you begin, or maybe you should seek other sources of funding.

Doing it yourself may not be an immediate suicide, but it may be a slow death for what could have been a promising system, as well as the franchisees who relied on you.

Franchise packaging: One size fits all?

Most professionals serving the franchise industry — the consultants and the attorneys — are highly trained and experienced. Others, though, are referred to as (and this is not a flattering term) "franchise packagers."

Franchise packagers can be both business advisors and legal advisors. They also can be brokers who sometimes put your system together quickly and inexpensively so they can sell your franchises for you.

A franchise packager often takes off-the-shelf legal documents, marketing materials, manuals, and training programs and fits a company into this pre-existing mold. The process has little regard for the realities of the company or whether the company should have been franchised in the first place. Feasibility studies, if conducted at all, are cosmetic and superficial and almost always lead to your concept being proclaimed an exciting franchise possibility.

Lawyers criticize franchise packaging the loudest. They're probably the most vocal because lawyers often see a franchisor client for the first time only after the company has experienced difficulties with regulators or with their franchisees. In many cases, these difficulties result from structural or management problems that should have been addressed at the outset of their franchise program's development.

Every franchisor is different, even from direct competitors. The process that packagers tend to use causes the concern. In replacement for a strategic process, packagers often provide their clients with a lengthy questionnaire about such things as fees, relationship issues, and disclosure issues. Strategic planning, if attempted at all, serves only as a motivational exercise, engineered to cement the client's decision to franchise. Clients are asked to answer questions that will have a long-term impact on the company, and they may not have an adequate understanding of the dynamics of franchise distribution. The advice, if they receive any, is often provided only after a superficial examination of the company and is often simply strategy adopted from other systems that seem comparable.

The legal agreements and other franchise documentation may often miss significant issues because they are presented as part of a cookie-cutter, one-size-fits-all package. Typically, the company is presented with the packager's standard franchise agreement, disclosure document, marketing brochure, and other related documentation and asked to simply fill in the blanks. The emphasis in development is placed on completing the assignment quickly, at a low cost, possibly to maximize revenue to the packaging firm or allow the broker to begin selling franchises.

Unfortunately, franchise packaging is not relegated solely to the consultant and broker. Just as attorneys are rightly critical of the franchise consulting packagers and brokers, franchise consultants are rightly critical of those attorneys who have a similar style of developing legal documentation for new franchisors. Some attorneys who work with start-up franchisors seem to believe that the legal documentation, being necessary to sell franchises, is also sufficient to define the franchise system. In fact, far more business issues than legal issues need to be addressed in developing a franchise system. The business determinations must define the content of the legal documents, not the other way around.

Working with a franchise packager may not be much better than doing it yourself with one of the fill-in-the-blank kits you can get in the back of some magazines. The most significant difference will be that your wallet will be substantially lighter if you use a packager.

Finding professional advisors

Unless you're experienced in franchising, it's important to find professionals who can help you determine the feasibility of your franchise and help you design and develop your franchise system. You may already know of a consultant and attorney who are qualified to give you the help you need. If not, here are some tips for finding the right help:

- ✔ Don't rely on yellow pages listings. Get referrals from people who know you and the type of business you're in, and who have gotten good results from the professionals they're referring.

- ✔ Make an appointment to meet with several candidates before you choose one. If a candidate is vague or speaks only in technical terms, search for someone else who can answer your questions clearly.

- ✔ The candidate should be familiar with businesses of your size; familiarity with your industry is even better. The fact that a candidate has large corporate clients won't benefit you unless you are a large corporation.

- ✔ Be prepared to speak candidly about the candidate's fee structure and what services are included. Make sure that you understand what you'll be getting.

- ✔ Talk to some of the candidate's clients and see whether they're satisfied with the level of service they've been getting.

- ✔ Be comfortable that the professionals you choose are not only qualified but will communicate with you throughout the development process about the future of your business and how they can help you reach your goals.

✔ When you're choosing an attorney, you may want to check out the American Bar Association Franchising Forum at their Web page — www.abanet.org. You can purchase a membership list of attorneys who belong to the ABA Franchise Forum.

✔ One of the best sources for recommendations is the International Franchise Association's Council of Franchise Suppliers. Most of the legal and consulting firms that are knowledgeable about franchising are members of the CFS.

If you've noticed, we never mention the need to select an advisor who is nearby. The right professionals may be right around the corner, but they could also be in a different city, state, or even country. Professionals are used to traveling to work with their clients, and in the age of electronic communication, the distance you are from your advisor is really of little, if any, consequence.

As we have said numerous times throughout *Franchising For Dummies,* we recommend you avoid using the services of a franchise broker. This is even more important when choosing advisors to help you make the determination of whether your business should be franchised and the structure of the franchise system.

It's difficult in one chapter to give you everything about feasibility and the development of franchise systems. But we give you a start. Most of us who work in franchising as franchisors, franchisees, and suppliers learn something new every day from experience and seize every opportunity to attend professional forums where we can exchange ideas with other professionals. That's why it's so important that you seek out qualified professionals.

Our last bit of advice is to take your time and don't get caught by entrepreneurial fever: "I must get it done now." Take the advice we give you, thoroughly review all the chapters in this book, and seek out professionals who can help you through the process. When franchising is done well, there's no better method of business expansion.

Chapter 17

Building the Network: Expanding Wisely

*Y*ou're ready to begin offering franchises — certainly at home as soon as you've established a solid domestic base, maybe soon internationally. If you're at this stage of the process, here's what you already should have done:

✔ Developed your prototype operation

✔ Tested it in more than one location or market

✔ Built an operating history that shows continuing profits and success

✔ Hired a recognized franchise consulting firm that verified with you that your concept is franchisable

✔ Recruited an executive and support team for the franchise company

✔ Developed a tactical strategic plan for the system

✔ Put together all your systems and manuals

✔ Properly funded the system

✔ Prepared your offering circular and agreements

Now all you need are some candidates who want to become your franchisees and an understanding of where and how you should grow.

At this point, it's only natural to be nervous. So far, the only people you've had to convince that your creation would succeed were yourself, your employees, and maybe your banker and family. Getting people to queue up for your franchise is the real test.

In this chapter, we let you know when — and how — to start your expansion.

Heeding the Expansion Rules of the Road

When you enter the franchise arena, you have to be ready — very ready. You have to be committed to becoming a franchisor and operating the system for the benefit of both your shareholders and your future franchisees.

If you're expanding in the United States, your company's Uniform Franchise Offering Circular, or UFOC (see Chapter 6), must be prepared and ready for delivery to prospective franchisees nationwide. It's the law in the United States.

If you're in a state that requires registration or filing, or you plan to offer your franchise in one of those states, you're required to meet that state's registration or filing requirements before you solicit franchisees. The registration states are California, Hawaii, Illinois, Indiana, Maryland, Michigan, Minnesota, New York, North Dakota, Rhode Island, South Dakota, Virginia, Washington, and Wisconsin. Other states, including Florida, Kentucky, Nebraska, Texas, and Utah, require franchisors to file a notice with the state, but don't require franchisors to forward a copy of their UFOC to any state agency. For more on this, check out Chapter 6.

Although you're required to have the UFOC to be a franchisor, having the UFOC alone is not sufficient. You have to be able to fulfill the promises in that document — and then some. Franchisees expect two fundamental things:

- A great concept
- Support service

So, before you begin soliciting franchisees, make sure that you've completed all the ground rules — the key operational components. Use this checklist:

- **Operations manuals:** You don't know the true meaning of *paper* until you start printing out these babies. Manuals on how to operate the franchise are the mainstays of your operation and often can run well over 1,000 pages. In addition to the unit operations manual, you need manuals on site development, field services, local marketing, and multi-unit operations (if you're using an area development or master franchise arrangement as your mode of expansion), and that's just for the basics. Plan on manuals for your franchisee, headquarters staff, and a section of the unit manuals written so that all unit personnel can understand it.

  The manual doesn't have to cause one single tree to fall. This is the age of electronic information. You can put your manual online in a secure site on your Web page, and your franchisees can download not only the manual but also the changes as you make them. You can even verify electronically which franchisees have downloaded the update and which haven't.

✔ **Training programs:** Make sure that training for unit franchisees, managers, crews, field consultants, and headquarters staff are in the bag. This task includes formulating the curriculum, hiring trainers (will you personally play a role?), establishing testing procedures to verify that you've communicated the information, and setting an exit strategy for franchisees who aren't up to snuff. For example, will you return franchise fees to candidates?

A *master franchisee* is a person or entity that you've granted the right to offer franchises to subfranchisees. If you sell master franchises, training for these people is more extensive than for unit franchisees because they, in turn, will sell franchises to third parties and probably provide some support services; therefore, they need to know how to recruit, train, and support subfranchisees. Someone has to teach them; it had better be you.

✔ **Sourcing merchandise:** Franchisees expect you to guide them on where to get merchandise, supplies, equipment, signage, insurance, and financing — consistently and reasonably. Make sure that you pinpoint suppliers, negotiate deals, or set up your own distribution facilities.

✔ **Administrative requirements:** It's easy to know what's going on when you're running one or two locations. Now, however, you have to keep tabs on a large number of people: your headquarters team, your field staff, franchisees, their staff, suppliers, customers, and so on. To do so, you need the following:

- Forms and procedures to monitor franchisee compliance with the franchise agreement and to determine franchisees' financial and operational performance

- Forms for franchisees to provide you with information on their operations, and instructions about how they should send you your royalty fees and other payments

- Clearly defined roles for your field consultants (the folks on your payroll who visit franchisees to check on compliance and to provide them with local support) and the forms or methods they use to communicate with headquarters and franchisees

- Forms and procedures to assess how successful you are with consumers

- Procedures to help your franchisees obtain merchandise from vendors and manage vendor rebates

- Procedures to help you manage the system

Franchisors today get their information by using communication systems that provide them with information as it happens; we call that *real time.* Getting information in real time allows them to better manage the franchise system. Franchisors have introduced smart cash registers (point-of-sales systems) that quickly communicate information to the franchisor's headquarters. Field consultants have e-mail access and can often go online to their computer in the office through intranet connections. Franchisees can visit chat rooms so they can talk with other franchisees. Vendors receive current information so they can make sure that products are shipped when the stores need them. Having access to information at a speed that enables the franchise system to analyze it, share it, and use it in a timely, effective manner separates the underperformers from the leaders.

- **Food safety:** If you're in the food business, make sure that your procedures for safe food handling are in place. Establish a way to enforce your safety standards, and see that your franchisees and their staff understand and follow them.

- **Non-food safety:** Establish procedures that give your franchisees guidance on running their operation safely so that they can limit the chance of injuries to staff and customers. Procedures on how to wash the floor, lift boxes, store merchandise, and so on ensure that your franchisees have the tools to operate safely.

- **Personnel:** Franchisees aren't going to be thrilled if they call headquarters and nobody answers. They also won't be happy if someone does answer but doesn't *have* answers to their questions. Carefully select your management and support team according to your tactical plan. (We discuss tactical planning in Chapter 16.) Certainly you need to train your staff technically in the systems procedures, but, just as important, they need to understand how to deal with franchisees, who, after all, are the system's immediate customers.

Although you need a franchise development team to offer franchises, that's not even the beginning. Remember that a franchisor has to operate and support a franchise system. You need operations, training, financial, marketing, merchandising, research and development, administrative, and a host of other bases covered. The personnel you'll need should already be onboard or scheduled to be hired and trained in time to service the system.

Is your field staff in place? What geographic territories can they reasonably support?

If your field staff is in San Francisco, think twice before selling a franchise in, say, Maine. Regularly servicing only one location in a distant market is unrealistic and not cost effective. In addition to the cost of lost time, the cost of travel could wipe out any royalty payments and then some.

Many start-up franchisors have their staff perform double and even triple duty. The head of operations may also conduct training and visit the franchisee's location. The person in charge of real estate support may also be responsible for product sourcing. You get the idea. For new franchisors, this approach is fairly normal and cost effective. But having a staff so limited that the franchise system is not being served because the franchisor doesn't have sufficient capital to hire staff may indicate that the franchisor wasn't ready to franchise. Having adequate staff and money is one of the baseline requirements to be a franchisor.

✔ **Marketing materials:** You should have whipped up brochures, ad slicks, employment applications, and a Web site. If you plan to use a public relations firm (one of the best early investments you can make), make sure that the company understands both franchising and your specific concept. The PR firm needs to know what gives you that sustainable competitive edge and be ready to pitch your virtues — wherever they need to be pitched, from small-town newspapers to *Good Morning America*.

You can find public relations firms experienced in franchising by looking at the membership of the IFA's Council of Franchise Suppliers (CFS). You can locate the membership of the CFS at the IFA's Web page at `www.franchise.org`. By the way, Michael (the coauthor of this book) is past chairman of the CFS.

✔ **Fee structure:** By this point, you've set your fees: initial franchise fee, royalty structure (an ongoing fee most commonly based on a percentage of sales), your system advertising fund contributions, and so on. Base these fees on the value and marketability of the franchise, the costs of providing services to the franchisees, and the return-on-investment hurdles you established for the franchisor and franchisee.

If the only thing a franchisor has to offer a franchisee, or the only distinction it has from other franchisors, is a lower fee structure, it has little to offer and nothing to make it very distinctive.

✔ **Legal:** In order for franchisees to sign on the dotted line, you must decide the terms and conditions that are included in the franchise agreements. In the United States, you need to develop a Uniform "Franchise Offering Circular (see Chapter 6) and may even need to provide some disclosures internationally (discussed later in this chapter in "Franchise Law Around the World"). In any event, your franchise agreement needs to define all the terms of the relationship; those terms determine the legal relationship between the franchisor and franchisee.

Expanding nationwide during your initial period of franchise development is potentially dangerous. Therefore, completing the registration process in all the states that require registration on your first day as a franchisor may be a waste of legal fees and registration costs. Establish your expansion plans during the strategic process, and if national expansion isn't in your immediate future, register your franchise only in the states where you plan to expand. Save your money for the things you're going to need immediately. It's sort of like buying a car for your son when he's only 14: It may be nice to admire in the garage, but he won't be driving it for a while.

Understanding the markets

Imagine throwing darts at a map and locating franchises wherever they land. Easy, yes. Smart, no. An unfocused expansion strategy is financially dangerous — to you and your franchisees. It wastes marketing resources, makes it difficult to maintain quality standards, makes it cost-prohibitive to support the system, often leaves your franchisees in a poor competitive position in their markets, and ultimately can lead to franchisee unrest — or worse.

There's only one right way to franchise your concept, and that's through planned and controlled growth. You have to select markets from the get-go that strategically make sense. What we're talking about is *market planning:* determining which markets are your primary targets, which are your secondary or tertiary targets, and which aren't targets at all.

Criteria for choosing markets typically include the type of products/services your locations will be selling, demographics in the markets, competition, and the location of your headquarters and regional support staff. The criteria also have to include *critical mass* (the number of locations you need to have up and running in a market for your franchisees to be competitive and for you to effectively support the market). Having one unit in a market that does not have the resources to market effectively or that can't obtain supplies in a cost-effective manner makes little sense for the franchisee. Spending all your annual royalty dollars on making one or two field visits to a market makes no sense either. Focusing your growth into markets that you can support is the proper way to go.

Say that your franchise sells pool supplies. You don't need us to tell you to begin franchising in areas flooded with swimming pools. In a simplistic model, you'll likely find great markets all over the South.

But what if choice of location isn't quite so obvious? Say that your franchise supplies practice management services to doctors and hospitals. Sure, these medical facilities are everywhere. But for your franchise to succeed, it may need a minimum number of doctors and hospitals per capita, maybe even a certain percentage of doctors in group practice. That requirement significantly reduces the number of markets — and takes some market research to narrow down.

During the strategic planning process, you have to understand who your customers are. You'll want to know some basics, such as their age, race, income, household size, and age of their children. This data gathering is called *profiling.* Understanding your customers enables you to not only select which markets to expand into but to zero in on specific neighborhoods and even street corners in those neighborhoods that have the best chance of success.

Demographics are so important that some franchisors base franchise sales on specific populations rather than a blanket territory. For example, Computertots offers computer-based education and fun to children ages 3 to 12. When selecting a market, the company looks for a territory with 40,000 to 60,000 children between the ages of 3 and 12. It has no interest whatever in how many seniors or teens there are; those folks may buy golf clubs or CDs but are not the population that uses kids-only training.

Don't rely on intuition or general rules in making decisions about markets. Assumptions that seem right are often wrong. It may make absolute sense to you that cold weather is death for frozen dessert sales. Surprise: Boston is one of the top ice-cream consuming markets in the United States — even in frozen February.

Also consider the competition. If a market is already saturated with a similar product or service, are you offering a revolutionary twist, or is your brand name so recognizable that you'll declare war on other players? Conversely, will your franchise sit idle because customers are already well served?

Establishing a network

Now that you're eyeing specific markets, it's time to get franchisees to fill the spots. Historically, and most commonly, franchisors establish networks by selling units one-by-one. Some, however, sell multiple units — two-by-two, ten-by-ten, and so on. Other franchisors sell area development rights or master franchising rights. (You can read more about these expansion methods in Chapter 2.) Your approach depends on how fast you want to expand and how much control you want.

So how do you lure candidates to your team? Advertising is the name of the game. The trick is to tap media that produce leads in your target market and with your profile franchisee. A national business publication may not be the best choice if you're searching for Farmer Joe in a rural community or a specific market, but it may hit the spot if you're looking for well-heeled investors to develop larger territories.

Advertising nationally may get you leads in markets you're not interested in entering or may get you leads in states in which your franchise is not registered. A franchise sales compliance program, established by your attorney or consultant, can teach you how to deal with those prospects correctly.

Many franchisors successfully use the Internet to generate leads. PostNet — a major player in the franchising of postal and business service centers — has substantially reduced its cost of recruiting franchisees and has increased the quality and number of franchisee leads through its system's Web site and sales procedures.

However, because every 10-year-old knows how to use the Internet, many franchisors are finding that, while the number of leads coming from the Internet is impressive, sifting out qualified leads is a big problem. Processing leads costs money — a lot of money. Working out the issues on how to effectively process Internet leads is one of the challenges that franchisors face today. Plan on developing an Internet screening process to work through this issue.

Franchise and business opportunity trade shows have been a staple for recruiting franchisees, but many franchisors are becoming lukewarm on franchise shows in general as a recruitment vehicle. The smaller shows, especially the ones that blend business opportunities with franchises, aren't as effective as they once were. However, some of the larger shows still draw considerable crowds interested in acquiring a franchise. The International Franchise Association sponsors several franchisor trade shows in the United States and overseas. You can check the date of the next show in your market by contacting the IFA at 202-628-8000 or its Web site at www.franchise.org.

Several companies hold franchise trade shows around the world:

- ✔ MFV Exposition: 888-872-2677; www.franchiseexpo.com
- ✔ The ASM Group: 408-295-4500; www.franchise.com
- ✔ E.J. Krause & Associates, Inc.: 301-493-5500; www.ejkrause.com

The U.S. Department of Commerce also regularly holds trade missions internationally where franchisors recruit franchisees for their overseas opportunities. You can reach the USDOC at 202-482-4756.

In addition, most of the franchise associations around the world regularly schedule trade shows regionally or in their home countries.

We have to depend on our people to select the right franchisees for Wendy's. That's why out of 7,000 to 10,000 inquiries a year for a Wendy's franchise, we award only 25 to 40. We have to be sure that franchisees have both the money and the ability to adhere to our type of operations. They have to be dedicated. We want them to be owner-operators. We don't want absentee owners. That requirement kicks out the investors — the people who want to have a franchise but don't want to work it. Now, more than in the past, franchisees have to be willing to start with one restaurant, and the choice of location sometimes kicks out a lot. They may want Manhattan, and we may already have sufficient franchisees there. Financing, unfortunately, kicks out a bunch of prospects. And others just leave after they go through the training process because they realize that franchising involves a lot of work — that this business isn't just a matter of opening a restaurant and letting it run itself.

If you're going to succeed as a franchisor, never merely sell a franchise. Offer it to candidates you think can do a good job. Then select and approve only those candidates who meet your standards. Anybody can make a sale. Great franchisors know the difference between selling and selecting.

Taking Your Franchise International

Okay, 'fess up: Ever since you memorized the poem about Columbus sailing the ocean blue in 1492, you've dreamed of traveling internationally like Christopher Columbus, Amerigo Vespucci, Leif Eriksson, and Marco Polo. Now you think that franchising can land you a place in history — as an explorer who transports products and services to new worlds.

We're sorry to burst your bubble, but if that's your mind-set, don't set sail just yet. International franchising is not child's play. No question, international expansion can add prestige to your brand and pride to your domestic franchisees — suddenly, they're part of a worldwide organization. But to be successful, you have to go for the right reasons, at the right time, and with the right partners.

Facing the complexities and frustration

Success at home doesn't guarantee success abroad. Unfortunately, war stories abound about franchisors who have gotten wounded on the international front. Dozens of chains have pulled out entirely or ended up reselling the franchise rights to a second or even third partner in certain markets. They wasted both time and money. Worse, they ruined their image, which forced them to have to try even harder the next time around. They took their licks because they didn't dedicate resources or personnel, misjudged the market, or picked the wrong partner. Are we scaring you? Good. You need to get soaked with ice-cold water.

Kay Ainsley, managing director of Michael H. Seid & Associates and former director of international development for Domino's Pizza and Ziebart, warns that, "Going global takes longer, costs more, and is more frustrating than you'll anticipate. Franchising is not a fix for other problems in a franchise system. You need to have a stable and profitable domestic operation and an organization that has the ability to leverage its resources to support an international presence. Selecting the appropriate franchisee takes time, and supporting them requires you to internationalize your products and services to meet the demands of the new markets. Failure to prepare properly for international expansion is foolish and unnecessary." Going global simply because you received a call from an exciting and intriguing overseas destination can be a serious mistake — and one that could damage your domestic operation.

Dave's issues to look at when going global

When Wendy's looks at international operations, here are some of the elements that the staff examines:

- ✔ Local economic issues
- ✔ Government stability (unrest)
- ✔ Supply issues
- ✔ Local partners
- ✔ Cultures
- ✔ Corruption
- ✔ Local laws

Here's the biggest reality check: money. International streets aren't paved with gold; it takes time before royalties start flowing your way. And revenue projections have to factor in different parameters — perhaps stiffer wages, benefits for employees, or rental costs. According to Ainsley, "In some markets, you are not just hiring an employee — you're almost adopting them." Can your products or services command a higher price to make up the difference in costs?

And while jetting to Venice may sound glamorous — and a romantic ride on a gondola is very appealing — be prepared to cough up lots of lire. What often sounds like a huge up-front fee — anywhere from $50,000 to $500,000 — for the right to develop a foreign territory gets used up quickly to support overseas operations. Marcel R. Portmann, director of international development and global marketing at the International Franchise Association, issues this warning: "Don't think of the fee as money in your pocket. At least 80 percent of the master franchise or development fee goes to expenses."

Franchisors can expect to visit potential foreign markets many times. You have to conduct demographic studies, including population size, education, per capita income, standard of living, and religious and cultural issues, and determine whether the local population will buy your product or service in the way those at home do. You must eyeball the local and foreign competitors who are in the market. They will impact your potential market share, site selection, marketing, and labor and supply issues.

Also expect to meet with potential candidates on their turf — a lot. Wining and dining a foreign partner once won't do it; international deals usually happen after relationship building. Educate yourself to be culture-sensitive. Foreign deals are often years in the making.

Get a good attorney

Legal fees can also add up — for registering trademarks, preparing franchise agreements, and meeting other government regulations. Contrary to popular belief, the United States isn't the only country heavy with franchise laws;

other countries also require disclosure documents for prospective franchisees. Even if such documents aren't required in the country you're entering, smart prospects are going to ask for them, so be prepared.

The most avoidable mistake when franchising internationally is the failure to meet that country's legal requirements. Besides understanding the local requirements, attorneys experienced in international franchise law understand the nuance of how the laws are applied in each jurisdiction and the traps you can inadvertently fall into — even when you think you understand that country's law. When a deal is ready to be cut, you want the ability to move quickly. Experienced attorneys working with business consultants knowledgeable about international commerce can save you time and money in getting the deal done correctly.

"Don't assume that any good lawyer can handle an international transaction," warns Philip F. Zeidman, Partner, Piper Marbury Rudnick & Wolfe, Washington, D.C., and General Counsel, International Franchise Association. "Don't even assume it about your domestic franchise lawyer. Don't be embarrassed to ask hard questions when selecting your international advisor: How many international cases have you and your firm handled? In how many countries? In the country I'm considering now?"

"One service an experienced international franchise counsel should be able to provide an international-bound franchisor is a checklist of the key legal issues it will face in an another country, such as the applicable withholding tax on royalties; the enforceability of covenants not to compete; currency exchange restrictions; the impact of any required government approvals; and the costs associated with closing a deal such as translation and recordation costs," says Joyce Mazero, Partner, Jenkins & Gilchrist, Dallas, Texas.

The International Franchise Association's Council of Franchise Suppliers (www.franchise.org) and the American Bar Association's Franchise Forum (www.abanet.org) can provide you with information on attorneys who specialize in franchise law. In addition, the International Bar Association's Section on Business Law International Franchise Committee has over 600 members from 78 countries who regularly work in international franchising. Located in London, the IBA can be reached at 011 44 171 629 1206 or through their Web site at www.ibanet.org. Another source for qualified international franchise counsel is the Law Business Research Ltd's *International Who's Who of Franchise Lawyers.* Published in 1997, the listing is currently being updated. Law Business Research is based in London and can be reached at 011 44 171 486 2611.

If you're a franchisor in the United States or another country that requires presale disclosure, you're probably used to giving prospects a copy of your disclosure documents. Ask your attorney whether this step is required as you enter international markets. For example, if you're a U.S. franchisor, you may not need or even want to provide your domestic UFOC to an international prospect. A recent case in the United States, Nieman versus Dry Clean

U.S.A., Inc., concluded that the FTC Rule doesn't apply to international transactions where the franchisor was selling franchises outside of the United States. In addition, in a recent proposed change by the Federal Trade Commission to the FTC Franchise Rule, the commission explicitly disclaimed jurisdiction over international transactions. Local national laws may vary. Most professionals in franchising feel it doesn't make any sense to give international prospects information about a deal that may not even resemble what you're offering them in their market. Instead of giving a prospect your domestic UFOC, consider putting together an international UFOC conformed for any country's laws. Just as with domestic prospects, it's important that your overseas prospects know as much as they can about your company, the background of your team, and what the deal is so they can make an educated decision. Making the sale is relatively easy — the long-term relationship takes the hard work.

Once you strike a deal, it's not "take the money and run." You have to translate documents, marketing materials, and signage; train partners; and schedule more on-site visits (maybe then you can sneak in a gondola jaunt, or if you're entering the United States, the wine country in Northern California is lovely in the spring).

Consider the implications of language and culture

Many U.S. franchisors naturally make English-speaking countries their first stop. After all, they speak English, so it should be a cinch, right? Don't let the common tongue fool you. Even English-speaking countries have different mentalities, consumer attitudes, and ways of doing business. And pity the Spanish-speaking franchisor who thinks that the markets in Madrid and Mexico City are the same just because the language is similar.

Lease negotiations may vary, and labor laws or hours of operations may be more restrictive. Consider this: A chain that delivers food by car in the United States could only navigate the United Kingdom by moped, raising new issues about security and handling hot food. Language, although English, still has its quirks. For Decorating Den, the word *color* is vital to its business. Years ago, when it swept into the UK, it had to change the spelling to *colour* in all its literature.

So, no matter the language spoken, expect to modify your system and, most likely, your product or service. What at first glance can appear to be minor changes can be major changes for systems that thrive on consistency. For example, limited real estate may require you to downsize your units. A restriction on meat in foreign countries may alter your menu. Are your domestic marketing materials suitable? Don't take things for granted. At home, your franchisees may automatically send in their sales reports and royalty checks. Abroad, some countries require invoices before franchisees can send money out of the country. And you have to adjust reporting requirements based on a Monday through Friday week for countries whose weekend is Thursday and Friday.

Also, keep in mind that there is not one international market. Paris and Bonn are as different as Cincinnati and Carmel, which are as different as Hong Kong and Shanghai. So, despite due diligence and support in one market, you may have to start from ground zero in the next.

And don't forget about laws and taxes

We're not done shaking you up, yet. Depending on the country, you may face tariffs, monetary exchange restrictions that prevent the *repatriation* (transfer back to your home country) of profits or limit royalties, taxes, restrictive labor laws, and prohibitive import rules. For example, what's the point of setting up a frozen yogurt franchise if you can't import your proprietary product, and revenues don't justify setting up a local dairy?

Concerning product sourcing, not every country has what you need, when you need it, at a price you can afford. If you do source locally, you'll save import tariffs and transport costs. A word to the wise: Thoroughly check out local distributors to ensure that your secret sauce remains a secret. Your local embassy can provide you with sources for raw materials and products. You can also contact the local branch of your accounting and law firm in the country to provide you with assistance. Once you find suppliers, check often that what they produce is indeed your secret sauce and not their local variation.

Trademarks and trade names are other big issues you must consider. Watch out for countries with loose trademark protection laws. Check the cost and time involved with registration. Just because you own a name at home doesn't mean you can count on it abroad. Trademark pirates may have registered your very name right under your nose, hoping that you'll sniff them out and hand over big bucks to get it back. Otherwise, it's a waiting game. The bottom line again: time and money. Deal with trademark issues at least a year or more before you begin to seek franchisees in an international market.

Depending on what country you're entering, you may need to be concerned with other laws as well. Remember that every country has laws that, while perhaps not aimed explicitly at franchising, affect franchising as well (for example, the local equivalent of our own antitrust laws). In addition, if you will be marketing in Europe, you will be governed by the European Union's laws, which are applicable in each of those countries. Philip Zeidman, of the Washington office of Piper Marbury Rudnick & Wolfe, explains: "For the last decade, franchisors have enjoyed the benefits of a 'block exemption,' carefully drawn so that, if its requirements are followed precisely, a franchisor can avoid what would otherwise be the prohibition against traditional U.S.-style franchising created by the European Union's anti-competition laws. In 2000, a revised version of that exemption becomes effective." With the benefit of expert advice, franchisors should be able to continue franchising in that market much as they do at home.

Franchise laws around the world

Many countries have laws that deal with the offer of franchises in their countries. An understanding of the requirements to offer franchises before you begin to solicit franchisees in a country is critical. The following is an overview of some of the franchise laws around the world.

Australia: Australia adopted a mandatory Franchise Code of Conduct on July 1, 1998. It has the force of law under the Australian Trade Practices Act. The government or private parties may enforce the code. The code mandates a disclosure prior to a franchise sale, renewal, or extension. Overseas franchisors must comply with the code unless it grants only one franchise or master franchise to be operated in Australia. (The Australian Code is currently under review.)

Brazil: Brazil formalized its regulations in 1995 by requiring franchisors to provide a disclosure document prior to the execution of a franchise agreement.

Canada (Province of Alberta): The Province of Alberta is the only region to adopt and implement franchising regulations. The newest form of the law was enacted in 1995. It abolished the previously required registration provisions but set forth new regulations for presale disclosure, civil remedies, and the self-governance of the franchise community. (Ontario has introduced franchise legislation — the *Franchise Disclosure Act,* 1999 — in its provincial parliament. Ontario does not currently have franchise legislation.)

China: China began to regulate franchising on November 14, 1997. The Chinese Ministry of Internal Trade issued Trial Implementation Measures for the Administration of Franchise Operations. The regulation generally requires a written disclosure document and imposes general good faith provisions on both franchisors and franchisees. The disclosure document must be registered with the China Chain Enterprises Association.

France: The French law went into effect on December 31, 1989. It requires the disclosure of specific information prior to the execution of the franchise agreement. Failure to deliver a disclosure document according to procedures is a quasi-criminal offense punishable by fines and/or imprisonment and is enforceable by the government and through private action.

Indonesia: Indonesia adopted regulations in June 1997 to require disclosure to prospective franchisees. It also requires the franchisors to register the franchise agreement and disclosure document with its government agency. The agreements must be written in Indonesian and be governed by Indonesian law. It further stipulates that any master franchisee must own and operate its own unit, priority must be given to the use of local goods or raw materials, and the franchisor must provide guidance and training to the new franchisee. The minimum length of a franchise agreement is five years. There are other special stipulations for overseas franchisors.

Italy: Although there are no formal regulations in place, the Italian Franchise Association adheres to a strict code of self-regulation. It requires all members to provide presale disclosure, to file the franchise agreement with the association, and to follow correct procedures for terminating a franchise. The code came into place on January 1, 1995. The agreement must be for a minimum of three years, specify the assistance given by the franchisor, and describe the territory exclusivity granted. Further, for terminations, there must be an *opportunity to cure* (a period of time to fix the problem). Automatic terminations are not permitted except for a breach of an extremely important requirement.

Japan: In the absence of a franchise-specific law, many laws combine to regulate franchising. Applicable are the general contract laws under the Civil Code, the Antimonopoly laws of the Fair Trade Commission, the Japanese Franchise Association Guidelines, and the

Medium and Small Retail Business Promotion Law that provides for disclosure even though franchising is not specifically mentioned.

Malaysia: In December 1998, Malaysia enacted a disclosure, registration, and relationship law. It covers any franchise that is to be operated in Malaysia, whether the offer to the franchisee is made in Malaysia and accepted by the franchisee within or outside of Malaysia, or is made to the franchisee outside Malaysia and accepted within Malaysia. The franchisor must submit, prior to sale, a complete disclosure document, a sample franchise agreement, the operations manual, the training manual, the latest audited financial statements, and other documents required by the Registrar of Franchises. The registrar may approve or reject the submission. Annual updates to the submission are required. Terms must be for a minimum of five years. Violations are punishable by fines and other administrative measures. Foreign franchisors are also required to submit an application to the registrar to be able to sell in Malaysia or to a Malaysian citizen.

Mexico: Mexico has federal legislation regulating franchising that generally requires presale disclosure and the filing of information about the franchisor. The regulations have been in effect since June 28, 1991.

Romania: Romania enacted legislation that defines the franchise relationship, requires presale disclosure, and mandates the inclusion of specific terms in the franchise agreement.

Russia: Part Two of the Civil Code of the Russian Federation, enacted in 1996, contains a registration requirement that imposes the obligation on franchisors to register each signed franchise agreement. It also contains other substantive provisions.

South Africa: In the absence of specified franchise legislation, the Franchise Association of Southern Africa (FASA) members follow a stringent "Code of Ethics," published in 1994, which includes the obligation to provide prospective franchisees with a full disclosure document and

a seven-day cooling-off period before commitment. There is no statutory obligation to disclose. However, some experts believe that as a consequence of consumer protection and other laws in South Africa, failure to do so could create a private right of action.

South Korea: South Korea has addressed franchising through administrative rules that were enacted on April 7, 1997, by the "Criteria of Unfair Trade Acts in the Franchise Business" promulgated by the Fair Trade Commission. Franchisors are required to provide necessary information in a disclosure document. Franchisors are not permitted to unreasonably require franchisees to purchase equipment or commodities, services or business activities; unilaterally amend franchise agreements; or impose post-termination noncompetition agreements without rightful cause.

Spain: Spain requires a franchisor intending to sell within the country to register with the government and to provide written presale disclosure about the franchise system. The law has been in effect since January 15, 1996.

United States: The Federal Trade Commission (FTC) requires, since 1979, disclosure to prospective franchisees through the Uniform Franchise Offering Circular (UFOC). Certain states additionally require registration with state authorities and contain provisions prohibiting specified unfair practices by franchisors. The FTC Rule applies also to the territories of Puerto Rico and U.S. Virgin Islands. The FTC has recently proposed changes to the Franchise Rule.

There have been recent proposals to develop regulations in several additional countries, including Argentina, Taiwan, Canada (Ontario), Albania, Belgium, Bermuda (Prohibited Restaurant Act), Kazakhstan, Kyrgyzstan, New Zealand, and Ukraine.

Source: Piper Marbury Rudnick & Wolfe, Washington, D.C., www.piperrudnick.com, *December 1999.*

Deciding when to go international

To go or not to go? That is the question. The answer to whether to expand internationally really boils down to timing.

Most franchisors head overseas after an unsolicited query gets their adrenaline pumping. Others pursue international markets out of ego. They figure that being the head of an international company will make interesting cocktail party chatter or that globalization will attract more domestic franchisees. Others are lured by the idea that going international is a quick fix for domestic cash flow problems. (As we say throughout the book, the opposite is true.) Still others simply like the appeal of international travel; hey, it's a great excuse to buy new luggage. Sorry, these are all the wrong reasons.

Smart franchisors head overseas only after intensively planning for international expansion. If you're crossing the border because the timing is right, give yourself a healthy pat on the back. That's strategic development.

Before entertaining international proposals, franchisors should have a strong and profitable base at home. To do otherwise is like serving dessert before the main course. We can't pinpoint an exact number of units you need at home, but your domestic operation should have a significant number of franchises in various regions and be supporting itself from royalties before going international. A saturated domestic market is a clear green light.

Other things also need to be in place. Internally, executive management must be committed to being in the game for the long haul. Too many international programs are severely damaged or killed when franchisors pull back resources because early results fall short of expectations.

Long-term commitment to international franchising includes shifting or adding staff who solely focuses on foreign turf. It is not unusual to have field staff, marketing support, product sourcing, operations, and training staff all focused on international expansion and being supported by the rest of the organization. As your international operations get even larger, you may need to establish whole divisions that mirror the domestic organization. Franchisors need to have surplus capital resources for providing support services, modifying operations, and making on-site visits.

In addition, no training is universal. You need to weave adaptations for international operations into your standard training. If you offer franchises to master franchisees who will select franchisees in their markets and also provide franchisees with support, you need to be prepared to train them on how to be "franchisors" at home. After all, they will be performing many of the same tasks you do as a franchisor: franchisee selection, training, and support. They need training in the following areas:

 ✔ Recruiting and selecting franchisees

 ✔ Administrative functions

 ✔ Site selection

 ✔ Marketing and advertising

 ✔ Training for personnel who will be trained locally

 ✔ Standards enforcement and discipline procedures

 ✔ All those other services they will provide in the market

If you don't train them, who will?

Keep one eye on international operations and one eye on domestic. Don't forget about the here and now in your excitement of looking to the future. So many times franchisors let their focus stray from their domestic business — the thing that got them where they are in the first place — and get caught up in the excitement, sometimes fantasy, of going global. Make sure that you have the organization to manage both areas adequately — or wait until you do.

Externally, you have to have a product or service that meets the needs of consumers in that market. Despite a shrinking world, not everyone needs or wants everything just the way you have it at home. Make sure that your product or service — and your operating system — can fly within the framework of local laws and cultural differences, and that you can make any necessary adaptations while maintaining the integrity of your concept. Food franchises, for example, must weigh religious and dietary issues. Although it's no big deal when a residential cleaning franchise had to retool its mops to accommodate the smaller hands in some markets, a convenience store chain built on 24-hour service loses something in the translation if local laws greatly restrict trading hours.

We've clearly tried to adapt at Wendy's. We've gone in and changed the menu to meet the local customs, but we haven't had great success when we've done so. For example, in some countries, we offered beer or wine. Doing so was such a departure from our core business that it met with lukewarm results. We've tried variations of foods as experiments, and we're leaning toward staying with our limited menu and focusing on the products we're internationally known for. So we're essentially saying, "We're a Western restaurant chain serving Western food." We believe that's probably the best way of remaining true to our image. Part of that approach has to do with international travel. The areas we're going into are high-tourist areas with a lot of traffic and English-speaking folks. In a tourist area, customers want and expect to find the same Wendy's they ate at in the United States. In fact, at times, internationally, we're singled out because people want to have a taste of the food back home.

In addition, registering a franchisor's trademark as early as possible is a critical ingredient in border hopping. As soon as you select the countries you plan on entering, you should begin the process. No joking around here: You have to work with your local and international attorneys. And make sure that the political and economic climate is ripe for building a business. No one wants to risk employee safety or the economic viability of a start-up if unrest fills the air.

Look at the flip side for a moment. Don't leave home if

- ✔ You're looking for a quick fix to cash flow problems.
- ✔ Executive management is not committed to long-term development.
- ✔ You're not prepared to invest time, effort, and resources.
- ✔ Your product or service doesn't meet local needs.
- ✔ You're unwilling to or can't modify your product or service to the local market.
- ✔ You can't secure trademark protection.
- ✔ Your operating procedures are so rigid that you can't or don't want to accommodate cultural or legal differences or requirements.
- ✔ There's political or economic instability.

Finding the right partner

So you've got your passport in hand? Not so fast. A big chunk of international expansion hinges on teaming up with the right partner. If you're a U.S.-based franchisor, the exceptions may be Canada and Mexico; many franchisors sell directly to franchisees because proximity is not much different than, say, an East Coast company servicing franchisees on the West Coast.

Once you leave North America, it's a different story. Except in the hotel and some casual dining restaurant concepts, partnering is pretty much the way to go to speed the learning curve because of a franchisor's distance and unfamiliarity with local customs. As much as you may think you know a foreign culture, you don't. (Your post-college trek around the globe won't cut it.)

Franchisors typically expand in these ways:

- ✔ **Master franchising:** A master franchisee follows a development schedule that calls for X number of units over X number of years. The master franchisee opens its own outlets or subfranchises them, or both. As a mirror image of the franchisor, it provides support on the local level in exchange for a percentage of franchise fees and royalties.

✔ **Area development:** A franchisee develops an area and relies more on the franchisor for support services than in master franchising.

✔ **Joint ventures:** The franchisor and a local partner share expertise and cash. This option gives the franchisor more control. And a franchisor's equity participation may make a deal more credible.

Our primary goal at Wendy's is to grow internationally through franchising. We don't have an overwhelming desire to have a lot of company restaurants overseas. We're looking for strong entrepreneurs who have the ability to open multiple locations. Once you're established in an area, it's easier to open new restaurants. Going into a brand-new country and opening a restaurant is hard.

Not just any warm body will do when you're looking for a franchisee. The biggest reason international franchise attempts fail is poor matchmaking — someone who is undercapitalized, is inattentive, didn't adhere to a development schedule, or wanted to do it his or her own way. Distance makes this a double-whammy; it's harder and more costly to nip a problem in the bud when you're thousands of miles away and in a different country. By the time you find out about it, it may be too late. It could take years to straighten — or litigate — it out.

In scouting a franchisee, trust should top your list of qualities in a candidate. You're entrusting this person to build a network, protect and grow your brand name, and uphold your standards. You'll want some assurance that this person will put her heart and soul into the deal. What you may not want is a large company swimming in so many directions that your franchise drops to the bottom of the ocean. Your brand deserves capital and staff to support a development schedule, and your brand deserves focus. If a foreign franchisee has access to real estate and local suppliers, it's a real plus. And they should be knowledgeable about local customs, laws, and business methods. If they're up on franchising, all the better.

Internationally, your franchise prospect may differ from the candidate you typically look for in your home market. The prospect may be bigger and better financed and have more resources and more bargaining power. This has its minuses as well as its pluses. It may also mean that you'll consider (or even target) the type of franchisee you'd probably shun at home: the company that already owns other franchises.

Entering a foreign market

Let's cut to the chase and round up some international partners. Just like domestically, everyone wants to attract the best-suited franchisees — efficiently and without a lot of problems.

The first in line isn't always the best in line. Check out all prospective franchisees very, very carefully. Rely on national franchise associations, local franchise attorneys, the local office of your accounting firm, knowledgeable consultants, potential suppliers, officers at foreign branches of your country's embassy, Interpol, and the international credit and reference services. If you're a U.S. franchisor, check out the International Trade Administration's Trade Information Center at 800-USA-TRADE.

Begin your search here:

- ✔ **Trade missions:** The U.S. Department of Commerce and the International Franchise Association (IFA) usually cosponsor three trade missions a year. Each mission lasts 10 to 12 days and spans three to four countries. It includes meetings at U.S. Embassies and one-on-one appointments with potential investors, prescreened to meet your requirements for a franchisee. Hurry, space is limited to about 15 companies each trip. The Commerce Department also sponsors other Certified Trade Missions; contact its International Trade Administration at www.ita.doc.gov.

- ✔ **Trade shows:** The annual International Franchise Exposition held in the United States typically draws thousands of foreign visitors in search of franchise opportunities. Contact the exposition's producer, MFV Expositions, at 201-226-1130 or at its Web site: www.franchiseexpo.com.

  You can also check out franchise trade shows sponsored by many of the National Franchise Associations held all over the world. You can obtain a list of National Franchise Associations from the IFA's web site at www.franchise.org.

- ✔ **Embassies:** These government offices in foreign countries can help you network and qualify locals. You can also try joint chambers of commerce and industry associations.

- ✔ **Referrals:** Contact franchise consultants and attorneys with affiliate offices in foreign countries. Franchisors of noncompeting concepts may also be willing to share leads. Give them a call.

- ✔ **National Franchise Associations:** As testament to the growth of franchising, many countries have established National Franchise Associations. These organizations can help you understand franchising in their countries, provide you with help in locating potential franchisees and suppliers, and provide guidance on local regulations.

- ✔ **World Franchise Council:** The World Franchise Council is made up of approximately 30 National Franchise Associations. Its purpose is to encourage international understanding and cooperation in the protection and promotion of franchising worldwide. For information on the World Franchise Council and its member associations, you can contact them through the Franchise Council of Australia at www.fca.com.au.

You won't find an American Franchise Association or a United States Franchise Association — so you can stop looking. Back in 1960, Bill Rosenberg, the founder of Dunkin' Donuts, together with several of the leading franchisors in the United States at the time, decided they needed an organization that would be "The Voice of Franchising," and they formed the International Franchise Association. Many of the other national associations might feel that the IFA should change its name to the American or the United States Franchise Association, but the IFA is not going to change its nomenclature any time soon. It's not that the members of the IFA are showing their global ego; it's simply the name chosen by the founders, and it's pretty descriptive of the IFA's global reach, purpose, and function. The IFA is the leading association in the world representing franchisors, franchisees, and suppliers. As franchisors in the United States have expanded internationally, the IFA has led the way in working with governments around the world and with other national associations to develop franchising internationally. For information about the IFA, check out its Web site at www.franchise.org.

✔ **Advertising:** You can advertise for foreign franchisees in publications that cover franchising, international business, or trade industries in specific markets. In choosing a publication, keep your audience in mind.

If you're thinking about using a broker to handle your international expansion, think again. Making a mistake in selecting your franchisee overseas is likely to be more devastating to your expansion plans than making a similar mistake domestically. Dave and I warn you in chapters 4 and 16 about not relying on brokers at home. The same advice applies if you're expanding abroad. Always use internal personnel in your international expansion program. If you use a broker, limit the broker's role to making introductions.

Negotiating the deal

If you think you can saunter in and crank out a franchise agreement like you do in your home market, forget it. If you're used to saying "take it or leave it" at home, don't expect this approach to get you far on the international scene. Internationally, negotiation is definitely the name of the game. Because you're usually dealing with larger territories and big front-end fees, much more is at stake — for you and your prospective franchisee. So get ready to negotiate.

The key to negotiating is building a trusting relationship. Make sure that your foreign prospect understands their obligations — and that you understand yours. Because there's often a language barrier, review everything — and then review it again — to avoid miscommunication.

Keep cultural differences in mind when you're negotiating. It's not uncommon for people to want to establish friendships before getting down to business.

Your flexibility should depend on your thirst for the deal and that particular partner. If a prospect is thinly capitalized and lacks experience, you don't have much reason to bargain. When in doubt, walk. However, if your prospect is well capitalized, has sources for products, owns real estate perfect for your concept, has a great reputation as an ethical businessperson, and wants to open up a bunch of locations, this prospect is worth negotiating with.

Strike a balance, though. The key is not to give away the store; too much flexibility doesn't bode well for your system.

Don't be surprised if fees are a bone of contention. Your asking price should reflect your size and trademark, and your expenses. But to prospects, international price tags often sound like they're for the rich and famous. It may be bad precedent for future relations to reduce the fee. Rather, smart franchisors throw the following items on the table to make the front-end fee more palatable:

- ✔ Extra training
- ✔ More on-site support
- ✔ Translation of materials
- ✔ Additional advertising
- ✔ Discounts on the initial inventory

Kay Marie Ainsley, managing director of Michel H. Seid & Associates, warns, "But keep in mind that if you are sharing resources with your domestic operation, you can't borrow long term from Peter to pay Paul if the results are that Peter then gets into trouble. The transaction has to make sense economically on its own and risking your core domestic operation is never a wise move."

Building in growth incentives also works as a bargaining chip. You could reduce royalties based on exceeding sales targets, or lower per-unit fees for surpassing development schedules.

Talking about development, specify a certain number of units that a master franchisee must build themselves before sub-franchising so they work out any bugs in the translation. Other contract issues include noncompetition covenants, termination rights and obligations, supplier restrictions, and local insurance requirements.

Dispute resolution is a big topic everywhere. Although many of the same methods available for resolving problems in your home country are likely available in foreign markets (arbitration and mediation), let your attorney — in conjunction with your in-country lawyers — guide you down this path.

Striking a deal is just a small first step. The giant step is making the deal work.

Bringing Foreign Franchises to the United States

Although many Americans may not believe it, the United States isn't the only mother of invention. Companies worldwide are giving birth to their own franchised concepts — with increasing frequency — and are crossing borders and offering franchises all over the world.

Because of its size, the U.S. market is extremely attractive to many foreign franchisors. Americans have a deep-rooted familiarity with franchising, have high disposable income, and enthusiastically embrace new products. We're also the consummate consumers — just check out our credit card debt.

The biggest problem for foreign franchisors is that playing the game in the United States costs a lot of money because of the regulatory environment and the size and diversity of the market.

Foreign-based franchisors are patterning after the the U.S. chains that land on their soil — typically selling master franchises or setting up joint ventures. Sound enticing?

Just as with any U.S. franchisor, companies entering the United States need to understand the market and answer some key questions for themselves:

- ✔ Do you have a successful track record at home suitable to support the system in the international system until it's profitable?

- ✔ Where else have you planted roots?

- ✔ Have you grown successfully on foreign soil before?

- ✔ How well do you know the market? It's not enough to have visited once — or often.

- ✔ Do you truly understand that the United States is really a conglomerate of smaller markets, that New York City and Des Moines are as different as night and day in cost structure and consumer lifestyles? How do you plan to deal with this?

- ✔ Where will you start to franchise in the United States, and what does your expansion strategy look like? How many cities do you plan to enter and in how many years?

- ✔ Do you have the financial and human resources to support franchising in the market?

  ✔ Will you have field offices?

  ✔ What local support will you provide?

  ✔ How and where will you train your franchisees?

  ✔ In what language will you conduct training?

  ✔ Are your materials available in English? If you're heading to markets where the predominant language is Spanish, are you prepared?

  ✔ Is there demand for your product or service in all your target markets?

Even if you're convinced that the concept will work, you could drain your financial resources if you miss the mark.

Working far from home presents challenges that you have to be ready for:

  ✔ Will you adapt the concept to the local market? Who will control the adaptations?

  ✔ Are inventory and equipment available locally? If they must be imported, what are the duties, shipping costs, and time constraints?

  ✔ Will you store inventory locally to make up for potentially longer delivery times to your franchisees of the products and supplies they will need?

  ✔ Does your brand have enough name recognition to demand a higher price — especially compared to local competition — to cover any increased costs?

  ✔ What happens if things don't work out?

  ✔ What are your termination provisions and dispute resolution procedures?

  ✔ What's your corporate culture like? Is there open communication? How will you communicate to franchisees that speak a different language than the rest of the system?

Just because a franchisor is from overseas doesn't mean that it doesn't have to meet all the requirements of a domestic franchisor. If a franchisor is offering franchises in the United States, it must provide a UFOC (see Chapter 6). If a franchisor is offering franchisees in other countries, he may have to meet those countries' disclosure rules. Just as with U.S. franchisors going overseas, franchisors entering the United States should work with U.S. consultants and legal counsel. The United States is a tough and unforgiving market. Historically, few foreign franchisors, including those from nearby Canada, have prospered in the United States. The size, costs, diversity of markets, and the different culture of the American franchisee and consumer often overwhelm them.

Dave's tips for selecting franchisees

Dave has a few simple tips for selecting franchisees.

✔ Do they have adequate capital? How much of their assets are easily turned into cash? (Liquidity is very important.)

✔ What are their business skills? People skills? Coaching skills?

✔ Do they pay attention to details? How are their organizational skills?

✔ Are they team players, or do they work better alone? (They have to be both a leader of their people and a follower of the franchise system.)

✔ Will they stay committed? What is their track record in business? (If they keep switching jobs or careers, you need to question their ability to be a long-term franchisee.)

Part VI
The Part of Tens

"I've had trouble keeping help."

In this part . . .

In this part, we give you some insight into the ten keys
to franchise success. We also list the ten questions to
ask before you buy a franchise.

Chapter 18

Ten Keys to Franchise Success

In This Chapter

▶ Having enough money, discipline, and personal support

▶ Recruiting, retaining, and training your employees

▶ Serving your customers, community, and franchise

*M*aking any business reach its full potential takes talent, and ensuring that your customers are always satisfied isn't that easy. If you've selected your franchise well, your franchisor will be able to help you avoid many of the mistakes new independent start-up businesses make. However, they can't guarantee your success — that's up to you.

In this chapter, we offer you our list of considerations that may make your franchise experience a success and hopefully help you stay in front of the pack.

Make Sure That You Have Enough Money

Before you make your decision to invest in a franchise, make a personal financial plan.

First make a determination of how much you have to invest, how much you're willing to risk, and how much you will need to live on for at least 12 months. Remember that you and your family will still have to live, and fun is something you need to budget for also. Unfortunately, so are emergencies. Carefully go over your personal finances with your accountant or some other investment advisor.

Next, from the information you obtained during your examination of the franchise system, including the disclosure document, conversations with franchisees, and other research, make sure you understand the initial investment required, and make certain you include those funds you'll keep in reserve. Discuss with the franchisor how much of the initial investment can be financed, but remember you will have to factor in your payments to the lender out of your cash flow or reserves.

Finally, make a careful and rational decision. Seek the opinion of someone your trust and respect: your accountant, financial advisor, or banker. And don't let the franchise salesperson pressure you into a deal until you know it's right.

Follow the System

Follow the system sounds like obvious advice. Who wouldn't follow the franchisor's system after going through all the effort and expenses required to join the franchise? You'd be surprised. Franchisees, on more than the rare occasion, will get the business up and running, and then they begin to tinker: changing or adding products, modifying the advertising, customizing the services, the hours, and even the quality and consistency of the products and services they are licensed to deliver. They want to be entrepreneurial.

In addition to violating your franchise agreement and possibly putting your whole investment in jeopardy should the franchisor have grounds to terminate your franchise, when you independently change the system you alter its consistency, and consistency is what the public expects in a branded franchise system.

By following the system, you preserve the brand and protect your investment and those of your fellow franchisees — because you're giving consumers what they expect. Hopefully, they will reward you by spending their money at your location. However, if you have what you think is a good idea, don't sit on it. Inform your franchisor so that they can give it consideration, possibly test it, and maybe even approve it. You have a role in evolving your system, and most franchise systems have clear procedures to help you do so.

Don't Neglect Your Loved Ones

Starting any business is hard work. When you couple starting a business with franchisor-provided training and the requirement to follow procedures, starting a franchise can take even more work. There's pressure — some self-imposed, some imposed by the franchisor — to get the job of opening the business done on time. And there can be fear — primarily of failure. Hard work and pressure and fear can have an impact on your personal life. Be prepared.

You may be prepared to work the long hours necessary to get your franchise off on the right foot, but make sure you budget time for your family and friends, too. All work and no play makes one burned-out franchisee!

You'll need the support and understanding of your loved ones during the launch of your new business — especially when the pressure places you in a mood that even your mother couldn't love. Don't forget to acknowledge their sacrifices. Set aside time for just you and the important people in your life. If the only time you have for your kids, for example, is when you grab a quick bite with them at night, be sure to spend that time focused on them, not on the business.

Your friends are important allies right now. They may be less demanding than family members, and they can offer you a much needed balance by lending a sympathetic ear, offering an extra set of hands, or just dropping in to say hello. Allow them to participate in this new chapter of your life and bring their special blend of understanding, support, and humor.

Be an Enthusiastic Operator

It's a safe bet that the success of any business is linked to the level of enthusiasm the unit management bring to the job. In franchising, the most enthusiastic operator is usually the one who has the most to lose if it fails: the franchisee.

Enthusiasm is contagious:

- ✔ It brings a level of excitement and energy to the operation that everyone can feel — including your customers.
- ✔ It motivates your staff by making your location a better place to work.

Your mood translates immediately into the mood of your entire operation. No matter how your feel, no matter what the problem is, no matter who you're mad at, when you come to work, be enthusiastic and upbeat. You may only be trying to fool your staff and your customers, but if you keep it up long enough, you might even fool yourself.

Let your staff in on the fun. If many of the jobs are routine, your staff will tend to get bored. One way to break the monotony is to cross-train your staff; that is, train them to do more than one job. Then you can rotate their work assignments. Couple that with acknowledgment of good work and some other recognition, including the occasional raise, and their enthusiasm may start to equal yours.

Recruit the Best Talent and Treat Them with Respect

Good help is hard to find; great help is essential. Even when you are faced with a tight labor market, there are ways to attract the best people into your business. Your job is also to keep them there.

How do you find qualified, reliable people?

Some sources include

- High school placement offices
- Other employees
- Newspaper advertisements
- Religious advisors
- Word of mouth
- Other competing businesses
- State and local government employment agencies
- Current applications on file
- Former employees who left in good standing
- Employment agencies
- Walk-ins

Don't overlook this valuable resource — the senior citizen. Many seniors like working and have a wonderful work ethic that makes them terrific additions to your team.

Senior citizens generally make outstanding employees. Senior citizens are the fastest growing segment of the population, and with the recent change in the rules affecting their social security earnings cap, the pool of potential workers is likely to grow even more. You might have to make adjustments to their schedules or workloads due to physical limitations or their other interests, but you make those kinds of adjustments for just about every type of employee. But boy, can they give you a talent pool to draw from. Set up a senior citizen recruitment program that lets you target this growing source of talent.

Another sizable pool that is only now being tapped is the physically and mentally challenged. We're not suggesting that you set up a program that makes you feel good because you are hiring the "handicapped." We're recommending it strongly because it will show that you are a smart businessperson who doesn't allow perceived problems to get in the way of the reality of improving the performance of your business.

Before you hire your staff, make sure they understand their job, their pay, the hours they will be required to work, their benefits, their days off, and their vacations. When you find the right people, train them before you put them to work. There is nothing more frustrating to employees than being thrown into a job they don't know how to do. To retain good staff, you must respect individuals, recognize where they are happiest, put them there, and keep them there as much as possible (see Chapter 12).

Here are some other tips on keeping good employees:

✔ Rotate boring and routine jobs. This will keep the staff fresh.

✔ Be fair. Don't show favoritism. There is nothing worse for morale than a boss who isn't fair.

✔ Work with your staff to develop the schedule.

✔ If employees attend school, see if a split shift is better for them. (A *split shift* is when an employee comes to work for a few hours, leaves, and then comes back later to finish the day.)

✔ If employees informed you of hours they couldn't work when they were hired, make sure you don't pressure them to work those hours after they're on the job.

✔ If you have more hours available, and employees want them, give them more hours.

✔ Post the schedule at least two weeks in advance. Let employees plan their personal lives.

✔ Treat your employees with respect. Don't allow any employee to be disrespectful to any other employee.

✔ Keep employees informed of new marketing and other promotions.

✔ Remove the hassles of the day. Ask employees which procedures are working for them and which aren't. If possible, change the conditions that are making them miserable.

✔ Make their workdays challenging — but also make the work fun.

✔ Provide timely performance reviews and wage or salary increases

Teach Your Employees

There's no point in recruiting the best employees in town if you don't plan to properly teach them how to do their jobs. We believe that the happiest employees are the ones who are provided training so that they can do a good job.

In franchising, training should be continuous (see Chapter 12). Employees are your front line. They're the ones who meet and greet your customers and the ones you rely on to help grow your business. Poorly trained staff can break you because they're the ones likely to create dissatisfied customers.

Training classes are a good way to show your employees that they matter to you — and to the success of the business. A good manager praises employees — after making sure they have the knowledge they need to do their jobs.

When putting together your in-house training program:

✔ Get all the training you can from your franchisor — including any training they provide on helping you become a better trainer.

✔ Regularly train and retrain all your employees.

✔ Hold refresher and advanced classes on a regular basis.

✔ Alert your franchisor when you need additional training. Your field consultant can help you, but only if you tell him or her that you need help.

✔ Take advantage of every training opportunity, whether it's offered by your franchisor or by local schools, trade associations, and other sources.

Give Customers Great Service

One of the reasons you invested in your franchise was because it had a system to provide consistent products and services. Following your franchisor's procedures is a good place to start. When it comes to the products and the services, they should be the same from franchisee to franchisee to company-owned location. This is what customers expect and why they may have come into your store or called you for your service in the first place. But consistency does not answer the question of why some franchisees do better than others.

The most important thing you can do — believe it or not — is simply to get everyone to smile. Let the customer know you're happy they chose your business.

Get Involved with the Community

As a local businessperson, you should be as interested in your community as any baby-kissing political candidate. You need to be seen as part of the fabric of your community. Customers like to shop in places that support them. We're not talking about advertising — we're talking about real marketing to your community.

The following activities help build a recogntion in your community that you care about them and want to support what is important to them:

✔ Sponsor a Little League team.

✔ Participate in civic groups.

✔ Start a nursing home visitation program.

✔ Conduct tours of your business for school groups.

✔ Set up a kiosk at community events — if your franchisor allows.

✔ Get together with other franchisees in the market and sponsor an event together.

✔ Set aside a day to give a portion of your proceeds to charity.

✔ Provide students with good grades a discount or free products when they bring in their report card

✔ Celebrate good citizenship by supporting a youth group

Stay in Touch with Your Franchisor and Fellow Franchisees

Most franchisors will invest heavily in communications about new product development, troubleshooting tips, employee relations, upcoming meetings and conventions, franchisee achievements, and other important news. Some of the methods may be old-fashioned: letters, newsletters, phone calls, and faxes. Some may be high-tech: e-mails, intranet sites (that's a closed-system version of the Internet, and it's accessible only to the company's employees), and Internet sites. Many will be face-to-face: training programs, field visits, conferences, and conventions. You should take advantage of every method of receiving information from your franchisor and also take advantage of every chance to provide them with information.

One of the biggest advantages of joining a franchise is the network of other franchisees in your system. Franchisees, after all, are in the same boat as you are and are ready, willing, and able to give you advice and share ideas. In some systems, this is accomplished by having meetings of local franchisees. If your system does not have such a mentoring program, start one with your fellow franchisees. Other systems have Franchisee Owners Associations where franchisees organize among themselves to communicate ideas, set up beneficial programs such as buying cooperatives, or work together to solve disputes with the franchisor.

Contact the International Franchise Association at 202-628-8000 or at their Web site at www.franchise.org and find out if they have a grassroots meeting in your community. These meetings are attended by franchisors and 20 franchisees from many franchise systems, as well as suppliers to the industry. It's a great networking opportunity to learn from other people in different franchise programs.

Watch the Details

Success is in the pennies. To run a successful business, you must minimize costs and maximize sales. Minimizing costs goes beyond cutting the best deal for your raw materials or inventory. Minimizing costs means you have to be diligent and observant of how your business operates day-to-day.

Watch out for your shrinkage. *Shrinkage* is merchandise that is missing and unaccounted for due to employee theft, customer theft, vendor theft, or maybe simple bad management, inventory, and ordering procedures.

We all have family and friends we invite to our houses for dinner. Often, they think that coming to your business is the same as coming to your home — it's free. Remember, you're in business at your business. Establish a friends and family policy — and that includes the friends and family of your employees.

Every time products disappear, are damaged, or are prepared but not sold, that's money out of your pocket. Store operation costs take into account some shortages (your franchisor probably has the percentages), but it's up to you to keep a sharp eye on shipment deliveries, storage, product handling, and store theft.

When you see a vendor improperly handling your delivery, bring it up immediately. The same thing goes for employees who are not handling products correctly.

Plan your labor. Look at any business: Some days are busier than others, and some hours during the day are busier than others. Learn how to schedule to meet your need.

Finally, you have to work hard every day. Some days you may want to kick back just a little and coast and put the business out of your mind for a while. We're not recommending that you deprive yourself of breaks from the business, just that you choose your time away from the franchise wisely.

Chapter 19

Ten Questions to Ask Yourself Before You Buy a Franchise

*T*his is an exciting time in your life. You're looking at your future and weighing your options. Maybe you're a recent escapee from the corporate ranks, or perhaps you've owned your own business before and want a little more support, training, and backup than when you were going it alone. Whatever your reason, we're glad you're considering franchise ownership. This chapter offers ten questions we think are a good jumping-off point when you consider buying a franchise.

Do You Know the Franchisor?

You need to know a potential franchisor on a deeper level than just as a nice person with a winning smile and a great golf swing. In addition, you need to know if the opportunity is as solid as the glossy brochure represents.

We want you to know the person behind the handshake — to know the beliefs, convictions, and ethics of your franchisor. To get that information, you need to conduct an investigation of the opportunity, including talking to as many existing and former franchisees as possible. Don't be shy about asking questions. Your future could depend on the information you are able to gather.

Most franchisors want to make a good impression on you. Their brochures are glossy and slick, and their selling process is well developed and executed. However, although a franchisor may appear solid, you will know the truth only when you ask around. Rely on your research. When in doubt, walk away from the opportunity. There are plenty more to choose from.

Can Your Hobby Turn Into Your Business?

Turning a hobby into a business is possible, but where do you begin? First look inside yourself and determine what makes the hobby so enjoyable. Is it the solitude of doing something for yourself? Is it the fact that you are under no pressure to share the results of your efforts with anyone else? Do you like to work at a slow pace and make sure that every detail is perfect? Do you enjoy the fact that you have developed a new way of doing things?

Next, take a look at the industry that involves your hobby and see if others will pay you to do the thing you enjoy doing. A hobby for yourself is one thing — now you have to make some money for your efforts.

Do a lot of research. Go online to the World Wide Web or to the library and start reading up on your chosen industry. Get brochures and other literature about companies in the industry — whether or not they are franchise systems. Understand the trends and the real world. Select a franchise in the industry that appeals to you, and if you're still inclined to make that hobby into a vocation, the best way to see if the transition will work for you is to work in a franchisee's store for awhile. Get a part-time job with a local franchisee, or ask the franchisor to let you work in one of their company-owned locations.

Perhaps you were right in the first place. What could be more pleasant and rewarding than doing for a living what you love to do for free.

Personal Inventory — Are You Ready to Be on Your Own?

If your calling card is self-reliance, congratulations. Having that quality means you're used to taking care of yourself and doing what needs to be done. Some of the most successful franchisees we know have an enthusiasm and a commitment to making their businesses the best in the system.

Maybe, however, you're independent and are used to doing things your own way. That might become a problem when you have to play by the franchisor's rules. You have to consider many issues before you decide you're ready to join the ranks of franchisees. So ask yourself a few questions:

✔ Can you follow somebody else's road map, or do you have to be in control all the time?

✔ Are you the type who will resent the franchisor two or three years from now when you don't need as much active support?

✔ Do your family and friends support your becoming a franchisee?

✔ How much do you need to live on? Can you live on the anticipated money you will earn from the business?

✔ Do you like to work with people? Do you like to make decisions and have people report to you? Do you trust that you have what it takes to be a success?

✔ Are you healthy and able to work long hours?

The health question is one that doesn't get asked enough. Owning and running a franchise can be demanding and may require a great deal of physical work. You'll have to put in long hours every day and often work up to seven days a week for the first year or so. So ask yourself whether your physical and mental well being can weather the onslaught.

Can You Afford a Franchise?

Buying a franchise is an investment, often the largest investment you will ever make.

While some opportunities can be financed on your credit card for a few thousand dollars, others will require you to come up with ready cash or loans of over $1 million. So don't cut corners when you do your financial homework. Take your time and run the numbers:

✔ How much do you have to invest? How much can you risk losing? How much do you need to live on?

✔ What is the total investment required for getting into the franchise? What portion of the investment can be financed? Can you find anyone who is willing to invest in you and your future?

✔ How much can you earn as a franchisee? How long will it take to break even? What return can you get on your investment? Can you get a better return from another investment? Are the risks equal?

✔ Make certain your research is thorough, and do the research yourself instead of using franchise brokers. Research the industry and the company on the Web, review the company's disclosure document, talk to current franchisees, and talk to former franchisees.

✔ Get the assistance of professional advisors — your banker, accountant, attorney, or someone whose business judgment you trust.

✔ Make a slow and detailed evaluation of the opportunity and whether the opportunity will allow you to meet your financial goals.

Reviewing your financial situation isn't the most exciting part of investing in a franchise — but it must be the cornerstone of the process.

Do You Have the Support of Your Loved Ones?

Keep the lines of communication open with the important people in your life; talk with them freely about the pressures of running your own business and the demands it will likely have on your time. Let them in on the pressure you may be feeling by discussing the risk with them — after all, investing in a franchise is not a 100 percent guarantee of success.

Let loved ones understand that things may need to change as you invest your heart and soul in the business and that you may not be as available as you once were. Let them know why you want to make the investment and what your hopes and dreams are for the future. Tell them of any sacrifices you may ask them to make — including delaying any new purchases until the business is up and running or the hours you need them to invest in helping you run the operations. Help them buy into your beliefs and give their support.

Make sure they're comfortable with your decision before you move forward. You're going to need their support along the way. You will also need to keep your focus trained on your business, not deflected by pressures from home.

In a very real sense, it's not just you who is investing in a franchise; it's you and everyone who is close to you.

Do You Understand the Terms of the Contract?

Franchising is a relationship between a franchisor and franchisee that is governed by a written agreement — the contract. In the process of investigating a franchisor, you meet franchise executives and franchise salespeople who will make you promises. Remember, though, the franchisor's obligations and promises to you, and your obligations and promises to the franchisor — the obligations that are legally binding — will be found in the written agreement you sign. Keep a written log of promises the franchisor makes that you are relying on. You want to make sure that those promises are in the franchise agreement.

Understand what you are signing. Unless you are an experienced franchise attorney, consultant, or someone who has been actively involved in franchising, you need to have an attorney to help you understand the contract. Even if you are experienced, having a qualified franchise attorney work with you is always a smart idea.

Franchising is a complex business and legal relationship. The attorney you hire needs to be qualified and experienced in franchise law. The business advisors you consult need to understand the franchise relationship and, ideally, the industry your franchisor operates in.

Read the agreement yourself first and make a list of questions and concerns. Look at the promises made during your discussions with the franchisor and make sure they are covered in the agreement you're being asked to sign. Discuss your concerns with the franchisor.

If you are satisfied that all your concerns have been answered, work with your attorney in finalizing the agreement.

Are the Other Franchisees Happy with Their Investments?

If you are investing in a franchise in the United States, and in some other countries as well (see Chapter 17), the franchisor will provide you with a disclosure document called the *Uniform Franchise Offering Circular*. In that document, you will find a list of franchisees in the system and a list of those who recently left the system. If you are investing in a franchise outside of the United States, the franchisor may or may not automatically provide you with information about franchisees — if not, ask for it. Getting to know the franchisees is the single most important part of your research.

Get on the phone and start calling. Sound like a lot of work? Maybe, but if you take a second mortgage on your house to buy this franchise, shouldn't you try extra hard to make sure you choose wisely and that your family won't end up sleeping in a pup tent?

If you can, visit the franchisees at their locations. If they'll let you, hang out in their stores. See how well they are managed, if they're clean, and if the staff is happy and productive. Maybe you could even work at a few.

If the franchise system has an association of franchisees — a Franchise Advisory Council or franchisee association — get the president's number and give her or him a call. The president can be a great help in educating you about the franchise system.

Does the Franchisor Have a History of Litigation?

How would you feel about buying into a company that has a history of lawsuits with its franchisees? While having lawsuits is not always an indication of a bad franchisor, it's something that should concern you and something you need to investigate.

As a rule, you should be very concerned if you find a franchisor whose franchisees seem to be constantly bringing lawsuits against it. It's a warning bell of the loudest kind. While it certainly is an indication of problems with some franchisees, it could also be an indication of a poorly managed franchise system or a franchise system that is not meeting its commitments. Rather than seeking solutions through active discussions, some franchisors and franchisees manage problems through their lawyers.

However, if a company has an isolated lawsuit, this may not be an indication of any serious problems. Check out the specifics of the lawsuit. What were the circumstances and the outcome? Did the lawsuit have to do with a breach of the agreement by the franchisee, such as nonpayment of fees or quality concerns?

Also look at settled cases and when cases took place. Franchise-system management changes, and that can drastically impact the relationship between the franchisor and franchisee. Often, the lawsuits were products of the former management's style of doing business. Ask the existing franchisees if the issues involved in those older suits still exist with the new management team of the franchisor. Equally, though, look at lawsuits that were dismissed because of legal technicalities. If the basis of the dispute was not sufficient for the courts to deal with it, or the suit was dismissed because of a legal technicality, that doesn't mean the underlying issues were not valid. Discuss your concerns with the franchisor's management and the leadership of the franchisee association or Franchisee Advisory Council.

Can You Make Money with This Franchise?

Guess what? Profit isn't a dirty word. That's why we're in business. You want to know whether you can make enough to live on and put some aside for a rainy day. You want to make certain that the money you invest in the franchise can make a return as good as other opportunities you may have — including simply putting the money in the bank.

Your goal is to make a return on your investment. Even if the franchisor provides projected earnings for a location, the best indicator of how well you can actually do comes from franchisees already in the system.

When you speak with established franchisees, get as much information as they are willing to give. Here are some suggested questions for you to ask:

- Are you making money with this franchise investment?
- How long did it take you to break even? How long before you started to make money?
- Was the investment estimate the franchisor gave you accurate? If not, how much more money did you need?
- Was the estimated working capital accurate? How much did you need to have and how long before you could take money out of the business to live on?
- Are there any mistakes you made in starting up the franchise that cost you money? How can I avoid the same problem?

Take a look at Appendix A for suggestions of additional questions to ask.

While it's not likely the franchisees will share their profit and loss statements with you, it doesn't hurt to ask them about their profitability. If they are willing, they can give you information that will help you develop your own projected financial information for your location.

The type of information to look for is

- Size of location.
- Number of staff hours required per week.
- Type of labor required — you want to determine how much it will cost you to get the same quality labor in your market.
- Amount and types of local advertising required.

You get the idea. The dollar amounts may not be as useful as other information that you can build your financial model on. What good is knowing that the franchisee is paying $50,000 a year for labor, for example, when qualified labor in his market is available at minimum wage and you will need to pay $10 an hour? What you need to know is the number of staff necessary and their qualifications. Work with your accountant to determine what information will help you develop your own financial projections.

Is the Franchisor Making Money, and Where Is the Money Coming from?

You will be relying on the franchisor to provide the promised services and to keep the concept fresh. You want a franchisor that is financially solid — not just today, but for the long term. A franchisor that has financial problems is not a franchise system you want to get involved in — unless you like added risk.

New franchisors may receive the majority of their income from the initial fees they charge the franchisees. That's normal.

Franchisors that have been around a while, however, should be supporting their systems from continuing revenue — such as the royalties paid by the franchisees. (*Royalties* are the continuing fees paid by the franchisee to the franchisor for the use of the trademarks and the system.) If royalty income is not able to pay for the support services, what will happen to the franchise network if expansion slows down or stops?

Building a franchise organization by relying on up-front fees paid by the franchisees is building a house of cards. Occasionally, franchisors that have underlying financial problems will try to cover them by selling territories to countries internationally. The large up-front payments they receive from international franchisees can make the franchisor appear profitable. However, the fee is received only one time — the cost of providing services to the franchisee may eat up most of the fee — and the underlying problems, while camouflaged, are still there.

Be sure that your franchisor is on firm financial ground and able to provide support over the long term. Have your accountant review the franchisor's financial statements.

Does the Franchisor Understand Franchising?

It's not enough for a franchisor to be able to work the grill or change a muffler. That's your job, the job of the other franchisees, and the job of the managers of the company-owned operations.

Operating and expanding a franchise system, as well as providing support to franchisees, requires different skills than simply running a single or multiple location. To make sure your franchisor has the necessary skills, you need to answer the following questions:

✔ Does your franchisor have adequate staff, resources, and trained personnel to meet its commitments to you?

✔ From your meetings with the franchisor, review of its disclosure document, and speaking with the existing franchisees, do you feel the franchisor has the appropriate temperament to operate a franchise system?

✔ Does the franchisor staff attend seminars on franchising and management? Do they know about the latest changes in their industry? Are they active in the trade associations for their specific industry and are they active in the International Franchise Association, the industry trade association for franchising?

✔ Has the chain been growing? Are new locations being added on a regular basis? How many locations closed in the past few years? You need to find out why.

✔ Are the sales within individual stores on the increase? This is different from whether sales for the entire chain have increased. They could have added new stores to the system, and even if unit sales went down, the system sales might still go up. You want to determine if individual store sales are increasing.

✔ Does the company have an active research and development department that introduces new products and services?

✔ Do the field staff act as consultants and advisors, or do they act as police personnel (inspecting franchises and writing up violations, but not offering help and guidance)?

We promised you 10 questions and gave you 11. A good franchisor goes beyond what is promised in the contract, and it was time for us to put our money where our mouths are. The last question was a bonus.

Appendix A

Making the Franchise Decision

•••

*T*his appendix contains a list of sample questions for you to consider in reviewing a franchise opportunity.

Section 1: The Franchisor

1. Name of franchise: _____
2. Address: _____
3. Contact person: _____
4. Title: _____
5. Telephone: (___) _____
6. Fax: (___) _____
7. E-mail: _____
8. Web site: _____
9. Date of first contact: _____
10. Type of first contact: _____
11. Date of first meeting: _____
12. Description of franchise: _____
13. Date founded: _____
14. Date franchising began: _____
15. Number of company-owned locations:

    Current _____   Last year _____
16. Number of franchised locations:

    Current _____   Last year _____
17. Number of units closed during the past 24 months: _____

    Where and why? _____

    _____

18. Number of units reacquired during the past 24 months: _____

    Where and why? _____

    _____

19. Names, addresses, and telephone numbers of franchisees who have left the system in the past 24 months:

    _____

    _____

20. Number of units in the United States: _____

    (Obtain a list of franchisees and location of units.)

21. Number of units internationally: _____

22. Projected number of franchises to be established during the next 24 months, domestically and internationally: _____

23. Number of full-time personnel on staff: _____

    Name _____ Title _____

    Duties_____

24. Is there a separate organization for domestic and international franchise systems?

25. Does the franchisor seem focused more on system expansion or more on franchisee performance?

26. Is the organizational structure weighted toward franchisee performance or franchise sales?

27. What service departments does the franchisor have?

28. Is the company using the services of a franchise broker?

29. What is the background of senior management, field staff, trainers, and support personnel? Much of this information is included in the UFOC (Uniform Franchise Offering Circular), but probing for answers in this area is a good idea.

30. In what threatened, pending, or current litigation is the company involved?

31. In addition to that disclosed in the UFOC, is there any additional litigation that was not deemed to be material?

32. What is the bankruptcy history of the company, affiliates management, staff, and franchisees?

33. Who owns the trademarks, service marks, and so on?

34. Are the marks federally registered?

35. Are any disputes pending or threatened against the trademarks?

36. If the trademarks are licensed to the franchisor, what are the terms of the license?

37. Does the company have any current, pending, or threatened regulatory actions from the Federal Trade Commission (FTC), state regulator, or other governmental agency?

38. Is the company considering the sale or assignment of the franchise?

39. Are any senior management or key personnel considering exiting the system?

40. Broadly, what initial and ongoing services does the franchisor provide?

41. Broadly, what are the franchisee's obligations?

42. Does the franchisor have a method to protect its franchisees from poorly performing franchisees?

43. How has the franchisor used these methods in the recent past?

44. Is there a franchisee association? If yes, what is the president's name and telephone number?

45. Is there a franchise advisory council? If yes, what is the president's name and telephone number?

46. Is the franchisor a public or privately owned company?

    (If it's a public company, obtain a copy of its annual report and 10-K.)

47. Is the franchisor a subsidiary of another company?

48. Does this company compete with the franchisees in the marketplace?

49. What is the financial condition of the franchisor? Review the financial statements contained in the UFOC.

50. Is the franchisor profitable? If the sources of revenue are not broken out (franchise fee, royalty, and so on), ask for this information. It's important to understand if the company is making money on continuing royalty or system income, or if the company is profitable only if it continues to sell franchises.

51. Will the franchisor finance any of the costs?

52. Is the franchisor willing to negotiate the terms of the franchise?

Section II: Franchise Costs

1. What is the total investment required to own a franchise?

   Franchise fee   _____

   Furniture, fixtures, and equipment   _____

   Leasehold improvements   _____

   Lease deposits   _____

   Other deposits   _____

   Franchise training   _____

   Travel expense   _____

   Supplies   _____

   Advertising and brochures   _____

   Grand-opening advertising   _____

   Initial national fund contribution   _____

   Inventory   _____

   Pre-opening staff costs   _____

   Working capital until breakeven   _____

   Working capital; living expenses   _____

   Other   _____

   Total $_____

2. What are the franchisee's continual financial obligations to the franchisor, the base used for calculation, method of payment, and frequency of payment?

   Ongoing royalty rate: _____

   Ongoing advertising rate: _____

   Base for calculation: _____

   Other ongoing fees: _____

3. What reports are required from the franchisee? Does the franchisor require any of the reports to be audited?

4. Is there an advertising/buying co-op?

5. What are the franchisee's obligations regarding advertising and buying co-ops?

6. Must the franchisee purchase any products or services from the franchisor? If yes, will the franchisor earn income on purchases? How much does the franchisor earn? How are the products distributed, and how long does it take for orders to be filled?

7. Does the franchisor provide income projections for existing operations? Obtain a written copy of any earning claims made. What is the basis for the earnings claims?

8. Is financial assistance available? How much? From whom?

9. Do you lease or buy the location?

10. Can you buy or lease equipment and fixtures from someone other than the franchisor?

11. Can you use used equipment?

12. Are any existing franchises available for sale?

13. Does the franchisor specify the layout of the location? Are architectural drawings provided? Can you change the layout?

Section III: Franchisor Services

Site Development

1. Does the franchisor assist in site selection?

2. What type of assistance does the franchisor provide?

3. Does the franchisor assist in lease negotiations? What type of assistance does the franchisor provide?

4. Does the franchisor sign the lease and sublet the location to the franchisee?

5. Does the franchisor assist in site development/construction? What type of assistance does the franchisor provide?

Consumer Research and Marketing

1. What type of consumer research has the company conducted?

2. What were the results?

3. What type of consumer advertising does the company recommend?

4. What types of cooperative advertising programs are being used?

5. What percentage of sales is recommended or required for advertising and marketing?

6. Are there any advertising co-ops? How are they structured and what are the costs?

7. Is the franchisor investigating the use of the World Wide Web for e-commerce?

Training and Operations Manuals

1. What are the location, duration, and additional costs of initial training?

2. Who must attend training? What is the cost of additional staff attending training?

3. What is the training curriculum?

4. Who conducts the training, and what are their backgrounds and other responsibilities?

5. Who pays for transportation, room, and living expenses?

6. What topics does the initial training program cover?

7. How is the staff that does not go through franchisee initial training trained?

8. Does the franchisor provide training materials for training new staff in addition to the operations manual?

9. Does the franchisor staff provide hands-on assistance during the pre-opening, grand opening, and initial period? Of what type, duration, and cost?

10. Are there any regularly scheduled, continual training programs? What types of additional training are provided? Who can attend? What is the cost of training?

11. What does the operations manual cover?

12. How often is the operations manual updated?

Continual Services

1. What other initial and continuing services does the franchisor provide?

2. Are they firm obligations or are they on request or at the franchisor's option?

3. Are there additional costs for continuing services?

4. What methods does the franchisor use to communicate with the franchisees?

Financial and Local Operational Issues

Note: Unless the franchisor has included an earnings claim in its UFOC, it may be unable to answer all your questions on unit performance. The failure to include an earnings claim is not atypical in franchising. You can address economic questions that the franchisor cannot answer to franchisees when you call them, or you can obtain the answers from other sources.

1. How many employees and management staff are recommended to staff locations properly? Part-time? Full-time? What is the cost?

2. Is absentee ownership allowed?

3. Does the projected cost of staff include the franchisee as manager?

4. What is the breakdown of cost of sales?

5. Is the business seasonal?

6. What are typical break-even sales?

7. What are typical or average unit sales in the early years?

8. What should employee costs average as a percentage of sales?

9. How much debt service can the franchise afford?

10. What is the return on investment?

11. What size location do you require?

12. What is an acceptable range of real estate costs?

13. How long will it take before the franchise can support you?

14. Do you need to be concerned with any licenses or zoning requirements?

15. What are the insurance requirements and costs?

16. What is the average time from the purchase of a franchise to the location's opening?

Territory

1. Is there an exclusive territory? Describe it. Is it well defined?

2. Is the franchisor able to open company-owned units in protected territory? Describe.

3. Are there any locations within protected territory that are excluded (malls, stadiums, arenas, and so on)?

4. Does the franchisor or any affiliates or other licensees distribute the product or service into the territory in an alternative distribution method, under the same or different name?

5. Can you choose the location or the territory?

6. Does the franchisor conduct any market studies on the territory to ensure that it can support a franchise?

7. What population is required to support a franchised location?

8. If there is no protected territory, what has been the company's policy on opening new locations? How far apart?

9. What are the demographics required to support a franchise?

10. What are the traffic counts required to support a franchise?

11. What is the company's policy regarding e-commerce and Internet sales?

12. Do the franchisees share in the sales made by the franchisor through e-commerce, in their market area?

Marketing and Advertising

1. How do the franchisees obtain their sales leads or customers?

2. Who are the prospects for the franchisee's products or services?

3. What is the franchisor's national/regional advertising program?

4. What is the national/regional advertising budget?

5. What portion of the national/regional contributions is spent in the contributing market?

6. What percentage of the national/regional advertising contribution is used for administrative/corporate/agency expenses and fees?

7. What are the primary advertising/marketing vehicles? Circle all that apply:

   Television, Radio, Outdoor, Newspaper, Magazine, Direct Mail, Couponing, Public Relations, Internet, Other _____

8. What is the grand opening advertising program and cost?

Field Support

1. What are the roles and responsibilities of the field staff?

2. With how many locations does each franchise consultant work?

3. What is the background of the franchise consultant who will be working with you? Can you meet that person before purchasing the franchise?

4. What are the names and telephone numbers of franchisees the field consultants have worked with?

5. How often does the field staff visit a franchisee's location?

6. What is the additional cost of field services if the franchisee requires it?

Market

1. Has a franchise even been awarded in the area(s) you are considering?

2. If so, is it still in operation?

3. Name and telephone number of existing franchisees in the area.

4. What are the names and telephone numbers of former franchisees from the area you are interested in?

5. What is the reason they sold, transferred, or closed?

6. Are any existing franchises available for sale in the area you are interested in?

7. How many inquires for franchises have they had in your area of interest in the past 24 months?

8. Why were franchises not awarded, if there was interest?

9. Has the franchisor performed a competitive analysis for the area of interest?

10. If not, who will perform the analysis?

11. If yes, is it available for your review?

12. What is the present population of the market? What is the anticipated growth over the next five years?

13. Are there any new highways or construction planned that will affect your franchise?

Products and Services

1. What products or services are under consideration for addition to the franchise?

2. When are they likely to be introduced?

3. What is the estimated additional cost for adding the new products or services?

4. What is the demand for the product or service? Is it a fad, staple, or trend?

5. Are there any restrictions on the distribution or sale of the product?

6. Is there a guarantee or warranty program? How is it administered, and what is the cost?

7. What is the company's pricing policy?

8. Is the price competitive?

9. Are suppliers specified, or can you buy from other than designated suppliers?

10. How is the product packaged?

11. Does the product packaging meet legal guidelines?

12. Is there any celebrity associated with the franchise? What would the effect be if the celebrity withdrew his or her support?

Franchise Ownership

1. Are all the locations owned by franchisees?

2. If some of the locations are company owned or owned by management or related parties, did they start out that way or were they repurchased from franchisees? How many have been acquired during the past 24 months? List the date and location of the most recent acquisition. What is the name and telephone number of the former franchisee?

Other

1. Is the franchisor a member of the International Franchise Association?

2. Does the franchisor ascribe to the International Franchise Association's Code of Principles and Standards of Conduct?

3. Do you have the right to assign the franchise?

4. What restrictions do you have on transfer to new ownership, including heirs, in case of death?

5. How can you terminate the franchise?

6. How can you be terminated by the franchisor?

7. How are disputes settled? Arbitration or mediation? Where are disputes adjudicated?

8. What are the restrictions on other businesses or investments during your ownership of the franchise?

9. What are the franchisee's post-termination restrictions and obligations?

Appendix B

Common Franchise Terms

• •

*D*on't look for the following definitions in any legal journal. We want to give you a sense of what people in the industry mean when they say something — not turn you into a franchise attorney. Here are some of the more common terms used in franchising:

Advertising fee: Franchise systems advertise to consumers — a lot — and most of the cost of developing the consumer marketing material is paid for out of a fund. Depending on the system, the fund may also pay for the cost of placing the ads you see on TV and hear on radio or elsewhere. The money to produce and place the ads gets there when the franchisee makes a contribution to the fund. That's what we call the advertising fee.

Area franchisee: If you want to open and operate many locations and are willing to make the commitment to a franchisor that you will develop an agreed-upon number of locations during a defined period — and in a defined territory — you're an area franchisee. You usually pay an area fee for the rights granted by the franchisor.

Broker: An outside salesperson or firm. For a fee — usually a commission — brokers sell franchises for a franchisor.

Business format franchising (BFF): Wendy's, Midas, and Mail Boxes Etc. are business format franchisors. In a business format franchise, the most important thing you get from the franchisor is the method to conduct the business. See the definition of *Product and tradename franchising* to understand how BFF differs.

Churning: Sometimes franchises fail, and the franchisor becomes the owner of the failed location. In the hands of a non-franchisor, who does not have the ability to franchise the location to another person, the location may be a candidate for closure, if the non-franchisor did not think the location could be turned around. In the hands of some franchisors, though, that location, even with the prospect of continuing failure, is resold, sometimes again and again to new franchisees, who also eventually fail. It's not a common practice in franchising — but it does happen. Beware of franchisors that churn.

Company-owned location: The locations owned and operated by a franchisor. They should be identical in appearance and operations to those locations operated by the franchisees.

Continuous training: In most franchise systems, you and your managers and staff receive initial training when you join the system. In a good franchise system, the training is continuous, meaning that the franchisor offers you training throughout the term of the franchise relationship.

Conversion franchisee: An independent businessperson who owns a business and joins the franchise system. He or she changes the business name, adopts the franchise system's methods of operation, and agrees to pay fees.

Copyright: The franchisor's ownership rights over the manuals and other published materials that you use in the system.

Design: Includes everything that makes a location look like all the other franchise locations: the layout, colors, signage, logo, and so on.

Disclosure document: Also known in the United States as the UFOC, or the Uniform Franchise Offering Circular. In the United States, all franchisees must receive a UFOC at least ten business days before they sign an agreement with the franchisor or write the franchisor a check. Disclosure documents are not required everywhere around the world. In the disclosure document, you find information about the franchisor, including the obligations of the franchisor and the franchise, fees, start-up costs, and other required information about the franchise system.

Distributorships: The right granted by manufacturers or wholesalers to individuals or businesses to sell their products.

Exclusive (protected) territory: If a franchisor agrees to give you an area around your location where it will not put another franchise or company-owned location, you have an exclusive or protected territory. The area can be quite small — the four walls of your store — or it can be quite large — cities, counties, states, or countries. Most often, it's somewhere in the middle.

Feasibility study: A study of a company that is thinking about becoming a franchisor. The company usually hires a franchise-consulting firm that looks at the company and gives management its opinion of whether the company can become a successful franchisor.

Federal Trade Commission (FTC): The agency of the U.S. government that regulates franchising.

Field consultant: Field consultants usually work for a franchisor. Their job is to make sure that the franchisees are following the franchisor's rules. In good systems, field consultants are also responsible for giving the franchisees advice and assistance in running their businesses.

Franchise: Every franchise is a license — but not every license is a franchise. Confused? A lot of people are. A franchise is a special type of license that usually has three elements: (1) the franchisor lets the franchisee use the franchisor's name and marks; (2) the franchisor provides the franchisee with assistance or has some control over how the franchisee operates the business; and (3) the franchisee pays the franchisor some money. In the United States, the fee is $500 or more during a six-month period.

Franchise agreement: The written contract between the franchisor and franchisee. The franchise agreement tells each party what it is supposed to do and what it is not supposed to do.

Franchise attorney: A franchise attorney is a lawyer who specializes in franchise law.

Franchise consultant: A franchise consultant is a business advisor with significant knowledge of the design, development, and operation of franchising and the underlying franchise relationship.

Franchise fee: When a franchisee signs a franchise agreement, he or she usually writes a check to the franchisor — that's the franchise fee. The fee is the cost of joining the system. The fee is typically a flat fee, as opposed to a percentage of sales like the royalty.

Franchisee: The person or company that gets the right from the franchisor to do business under the franchisor's trademark and trade name.

Franchising: A method of distribution; in other words, a method of growing a business.

Franchisor: The person or company that grants the franchisee the right to do business under their trade or service marks.

Initial investment: The initial costs of getting into business, which usually include the franchise fee, the cost of the fixed assets, leasehold improvements, inventory, deposits, other fees and costs, and the working capital required during the start-up period.

International Franchise Association: The industry trade association that represents franchising.

Location: The site of the franchised or company-owned operation.

Manuals: The bible of a franchise system. The manuals are the place to look for instructions on how the franchisor wants the locations to operate and for other policies concerning the system.

Master franchisee: Take a look at the definition of *area franchisee*. Now, in addition to operating its own locations, the master franchisee also gets the right to sell franchises to sub-franchisees within the master franchisee's specified territory. The master franchisee may provide to the sub-franchisee some of the services provided by the franchisor and will typically split with the franchisor the franchise fee and royalties paid by the sub-franchisee.

Product and trade name franchising: Pepsi and Ford are product and trade name franchisors. In a business franchise, the franchisee sells or distributes a specific product using the franchisor's trademark, trade name, and logo (automobile dealerships, truck dealerships, farm equipment, mobile homes, gasoline service stations, automobile accessories, soda, beer, bottling). The most important thing you get from the franchisor is the product the franchisor manufacturers, not the system of running the business, as in business format franchising.

Retrofranchising or refranchising: Retrofranchising and refranchising are not the same as churning. These are existing locations that may or may not have ever been franchised before but are currently operated by the franchisor. The franchisor that is retrofranchising or refranchising locations is selling the operating business to a franchisee. In these situations the franchisor has an expectation that the business will be successful. See *churning*.

Quality standards: Some systems have high quality standards. Some don't. If franchisors want to control quality, however, they tell the franchisees what those standards are in their training programs, manuals, and other communications. Quality franchise systems tightly control these standards for the benefit of the franchise system and its franchisees.

Registration: Some states in the United States require the franchisor to send the state its disclosure document for approval prior to offering franchises. No registration is required at the federal level.

Royalty fee: The franchisee sends the franchisor a check on a regular basis to stay part of the franchise system. Usually, the payment is based on a percentage of the franchisee's gross sales, but it can be a fixed fee or calculated on some other basis. That continuing fee is the royalty fee.

Success: How do you define success: profit, growth, or return on investment? In some franchise systems, success often simply describes the absence of failure or the closing of a location. It may have nothing at all to do with unit sales or profitability.

Trademark: The marks, brand name, and logo that identify a franchisor. It's the name that the franchisor licenses to the franchisee.

Turnkey: A location that a franchisor builds and then sells to a franchisee fully equipped and ready to operate.

UFOC: Uniform Franchise Offering Circular. See *disclosure document*.

Index

• *G* •

• *H* •

• *I* •

Notes

Notes

Notes

Notes